The Archaeology of the Iberians

The Iberians inhabited the southern and eastern Iberian Peninsula between the Phoenician and Greek colonisation, beginning in the eighth century BC, and the Roman conquest. This was a period of significant change in native Spanish societies, and the emergence of urbanism and the adoption from the colonists of ideological symbols and technological innovations created an important and unique Iron Age culture. The archaeology of the Iberians has consequently much to contribute towards the archaeology of culture contact and culture change in Iron Age Europe, and the integration of native societies into the early Roman Empire. Yet information about them is relatively sparse. In this first scholarly synthesis of the period for more than thirty years, two leading Spanish archaeologists, Arturo Ruiz and Manuel Molinos, combine a sophisticated synthesis of Iberian culture, which includes important work not available to English-speaking audience, with a fascinating case study of change within a specific complex society.

Arturo Ruiz is Professor of Prehistory at the University of Jaén, Spain and Manuel Molinos is Professor of Archaeology at the University of Jaén.

The Archaeology of
the Iberians

Arturo Ruiz and Manuel Molinos

*Translated from the Spanish
by Mary Turton*

CAMBRIDGE
UNIVERSITY PRESS

PUBLISHED BY THE PRESS SYNDICATE OF THE UNIVERSITY OF CAMBRIDGE
The Pitt Building, Trumpington Street, Cambridge CB2 1RP, United Kingdom

CAMBRIDGE UNIVERSITY PRESS
The Edinburgh Building, Cambridge, CB2 2RU, United Kingdom
http://www.cup.cam.ac.uk
40 West 20th Street, New York, NY 10011-4211, USA
http://www.cup.org
10 Stamford Road, Oakleigh, Melbourne 3166, Australia

Originally published in Spanish as *Los Iberos*
by Crítica, Barcelona 1993
and © Arturo Ruiz Rodriguez and Manuel Molinos Molinos
First published in English by Cambridge University Press 1998 as
The Archaeology of the Iberians
English translation © Cambridge University Press 1998

Typeset in Garamond 10.5/12.5 pt [VN]

A catalogue record for this book is available from the British Library

Library of Congress Cataloguing in Publication data applied for

ISBN 0521 56402 6 hardback

Contents

Contents

Illustrations

Acknowledgements

We should like to express our appreciation in these pages to all the authors quoted in the text, both for their contribution to the archaeology of the Iberians and for the use we have made in many cases of the pictures and figures that are included in the work.

We should particularly like to thank the following for contributing texts, sometimes unpublished, and giving their opinions, in the framework either of wide-ranging debate or simply of discussions arising on a particular topic: Pedro Aguayo, Martín Almagro Gorbea, Oswaldo Arteaga, Maria Eugenia Aubet, Francisco Burillo, Marcelo Castro, Francisco Contreras, Teresa Chapa, Concepción Choclán, Cristobal González, Francisca Hornos, Consuelo Mata, Fernando Molina, Gerard Nicolini, Francisco Nocete, Juan Pereira, Fernando Quesada, Carmen Rísquez, Alonso Rodríguez, Gonzalo Ruiz Zapatero, Vicente Salvatierra, Alberto Sánchez, Juan Antonio Santos, José Luis Serrano, Marcelo Tagliente, Mario Torelli, José Uroz, Narciso Zafra, etc.

We whould also like to acknowledge permission granted for the reproduction of plates and figures by the following persons:

A. García y Bellido and J. Pereira, figure 4; E. Barba, figure 5; F. Chaves and M. L. Bandera, figure 6; N. Schubart, figure 7; J. Fernández Jurado, figures 8, 31 and 46; E. Cuadrado and F. Cuadrado, figure 9; M. Fernández Rodríguez, figure 10; G. Trías de Arribas, figure 25; F. Nocete, figure 28 (1); F. Murillo, F. Quesada, D. Vaquerizo, J. R. Carrillo and J. A. Morena, figure 30 (1); F. de Amores and I. R. Temiño, figure 30 (2); J. Santos, figure 32; A. J. Domínguez, figure 33; J. Bernabeu, H. Bonet and A. Mata, figure 34; A. Oliver, M. Blasco, A. Freixa and P. Rodríguez, figure 35; E. Sanmartí, figure 36; J. A. Benavente, figure 37; M. Miret, J. Sanmartí and J. Santacana, figure 38; J. Barberá and X. Dupré, figure 39; J. A. Martín, figure 40 (1); J. Ruiz de Arbulo, figure 40 (2); G. Rancoule, figure 41; A. Rodríguez Díaz, figure 42; S. Broncano and J. Blánquez, figure 47; J. Bernabeu, H. Bonet, P. Guerin and C. Mata, figure 48; E. A. Llobregat, figure 49; F. Gusi and C. Olaria, figure 50; J.

Sanmartí and J. Santacana, figure 51; E. Junyent and V. Baldellou, figure 52; J. M. Llorens, figure 53; J. M. Luzón, figure 56 (1); J. Coll, figure 56 (2); A. García y Bellido, figures 56 (3) and 62; A. Madroñero and M. N. I. Agreda, figure 57; M. Fernández Miranda and R. Olmos, figure 58; Curel, figure 59; F. Andouce and O. Buchsenschutz, figure 60 (2); R. Pallarés, F. Gracia and G. Munilla, figure 61 (1); E. A. Llobregat, figures 61 (2) and 67; P. Gross and M. Torelli, figure 63; A. Arribas, figures 64 and 97; L. Abad, figure 70; J. M. Blázquez, figures 73 and 95; F. Presado, figure 74; F. Quesada, figures 78 and 80; A. González Prats and J. A. Piña, figure 83; G. Nicolini, figure 87; D. Fletcher, figure 88; J. Untermann, figure 89; I. Negueruela, figure 91.

The translator wishes to thank the following for advice on language and terminology: María Eugenia Aubet, Paloma Bevir, Henry Blyth, Richard Harrison, Arturo Morales Muñoz, Andrew and Sue Sherratt and the Light Armour and Early Metallurgy Group of the Department of Engineering, University of Reading.

The translation of this work has been made possible by a grant from the Dirección General de Libro y Bibliotecas del Ministerio de Cultura de España.

Glossary

adytum innermost part of a temple

atalaya observation post, incorporating a small settlement

barrio quarter or district of a town, e.g. *barrio judío*, Jewish quarter

basileus petty king or lord

campiña large, usually flat, area of cultivated land

caserío small settlement or hamlet

foedus contract or covenant

garrigue scrubland with Mediterranean-type vegetation

garum Roman sauce made from fermented fish

meseta tableland, plateau, particularly the high central plateau of the Iberian Peninsula

oppidum (pl. *oppida*) a settlement that shows signs of an urban layout

pagus rural area

pilum heavy javelin

piedmont plain at the foot of a range of mountains or hills

rambla watercourse or torrent, often dry

regulus petty king or chieftain

sierra mountain range with a serrated skyline, typically Spanish

soliferrum javelin made of iron

spicatum spiked

vega extensive, fertile tract of land, flat and often grass-covered

vicus village

Introduction

Iberian culture, Iberian peoples, Iberian states: different conceptual terms have, historiographically speaking, covered the long period between the sixth century BC and the first century, when Romanisation came fully and definitively into effect; in short, almost the whole of the Iron Age in the Mediterranean area of the Iberian Peninsula.

Depicted by some as 'almost savages' in contrast to the powerful 'civilising stage' that followed, and by others as a 'high culture', the Iberians have given rise to an image both of a child-like culture, in a biologicist scheme of archaeology, and of a mature culture that can take its place among the great Mediterranean centres. Portrayed by some, because of their strong autochthonous tradition, as a model of 'the Hispanic', or by others as the fountainhead of the various peoples in Spain, the Iberians have ranged through the history of Spain in the past century as contemporary parties to the historical debate that led to the civil war in 1936. The work by Fletcher (1949) at the end of the 1940s should not be forgotten; he felt obliged to entitle it 'In Defence of Iberianism'.

There can be no doubt that the inventory of Iberian sculpture, from the first finds at the end of the nineteenth century (the Lady of Elche, the Cerro de los Santos assemblage) to the most recent at Cerrillo Blanco de Porcuna, demonstrates the complexity and refined technique of Iberian art. However, with the exception of Antonio Arribas' book in 1965, there have been few synthesising studies that have attempted a general survey of what was known about the Iberian peoples. But if that book was produced at a time when descriptive archaeology was dominant, the developments in archaeological work and especially the changes that have been taking place since the end of the 1960s in the way it is handled, on both a theoretical and a methodological plane, mean that the time is now ripe for a review of the direction research into the Iberians has been taking these past two decades.

However, for the reasons already given, it is impossible to broach the

1

Figure 1 The Lady of Elche
(drawing by P. Ibarra Ruiz from a photograph by A. Ramos)

subject without knowing something of the theoretico-methodological mould that has been broken, or of how the new contextual paradigm has modified knowledge of a basic historical period, in order, in the last resort, to define the consolidation of aristocratic power, that is to say, the end of prehistoric society.

The phrase with which Daniel (1967) ends the first chapter of his *Origins and Growth of Archaeology* carries a heavy ideological charge that is worth recalling here; he writes: 'Through archaeology, we own the pleasures of past time as well as its historical witness.' It is impossible at the end of the twentieth century to relinquish the fun aspect undoubtedly offered by archaeology; but we must stress here the twofold danger that this implies: either separation from history, which encourages the practice of collecting and thereby the intrusion of market forces into the guardianship of our heritage, or else interaction with history in an elitist framework which, in line with Daniel's comment, would only generate pleasure for scholars – academic pleasure – with the consequent isolation and ultimate death of archaeology.

We may allow ourselves a simile reminiscent of Holmes' remark to Watson, expressed with that academic cynicism that was typical of the drawing-room detective story: 'There are no crimes and no criminals in these days . . . at most some bungling villainy with a motive so transparent that even a Scotland Yard official can see through it' (Conan Doyle, *A Study in Scarlet*). We should remind archaeologists, who are generally fans of such detective novels, of the words of Raymond Chandler in his analysis of Hammet's work, when he said of the latter that he was someone who 'took murder out of the Venetian vase and dropped it into the alley' (Chandler, *The Simple Art of Murder*), a clear allusion to the world of Holmes and Poirot, and he ended by emphasising that 'he gave murder back to the kind of people who commit it for reasons – not just to provide a corpse'. Perhaps the well-known exhaustion suffered by archaeology in the 1960s, and enshrined in the attitudes voiced by Daniel, achieved with Binford, Bianchi Bandinelli, Clarke, etc., what Hammet had done for murder.

This book was born when the process of an encounter between society and archaeology had already started and was even demanding new inputs of imagination and critical attitudes in some of the theoretical approaches, which, in a kind of circular argument, were moving towards a collision with the old, exhausted positivist position. In its approach, this book prefers to move forward, with an attempt to bring archaeological theory face to face with its practice in the case of the Iberians. But, despite this assertion, we think it right to make two suggestions as food for thought.

In the first place the book has been structured with the aim of providing material for a historical analysis. We should like to point out in this connexion that, despite the possibility of error to which, as historians, we are exposed, our approach obliges us to enter into analysis of the underlying structure resulting from the naiveté of the positivist tradition, and to adopt theoretico-methodological positions; the critical terms used in no way diminish the respect due to the work of many researchers through whom we arrive at the Iberian problem after a century of research, and we are aware that it is to them we are indebted for the fact that we can write these pages.

Secondly, the attitude referred to, which at times even leads us to indulge aloud in a game of exposition, reflexion and analysis, does not claim to impose the conclusions reached as the last word in a unique learning process. In any case, we have sought to achieve an approximation and a first attempt at a representation of what was the history of the Iberians. To summarise, we agree with the response of Bianchi Bandinelli in 1950:

> At the end of the class, the American girl came to my desk, wagging a reproving finger and said that she was not satisfied with the lesson because I had set out three mutually exclusive hypotheses while telling the students 'what they should think'. I detained her longer than normal in order to explain that I ought instead, despite the specific problem treated, to have taught the method by which she could come to form her own idea and that this was the most important thing that European culture could teach.
>
> (Bianchi Bandinelli, 1982, p. 181)

The Iberians: a national question

But we must look at the history of the subject if we are to assess where the proposed paradigmatic change lies. In 1903, the *Essai sur l'art et l'industrie de l'Espagne primitive* was published. This wide-ranging work by Pierre Paris (1903–4) was arranged in accordance with the classic scheme for art history – architecture–sculpture–lesser arts (pottery) – and gathered together the series of finds, which was large even then, evaluating it, with extensive descriptions, according to the influences undergone and the chronology ascribed; but the review undoubtedly aroused maximum interest when it came to what the investigator declared to be the main point of the work: an exquisitely beautiful bust of a woman which he insisted on seeing from that moment as the material symbol of the newborn culture: the Lady of Elche.

In the French author's approach to his analysis we can see clearly the dual component of the diffusionist matrix that would prevail throughout the

Figure 2 Sketch of the position of the bust at Elche at the time of its discovery
(from M. Campello)

twentieth century, since, if on one side a civilising component finds expression
in those Greeks who transformed barbarian depictors of wild boars into
creators of exceedingly stylish works, on the other a component to be civilised
is defined, consisting of a relationship of dependency on the former. Thus the
old diffusionist mould is broken, the one that was defined by a single element,
the civilising invader, who with his position supplanted the previous invader
or subjugated him by force. On the contrary, in the new matrix set out by
Paris, the second component takes on a special interest, since in it are
enshrined, in their customary form, the racial characteristics of the land in
which it thrives and of the nation where it is studied.

The diffusionist matrix, which has been so beloved of archaeologists, has its
origin in a reaction to the effects that could be inferred from what Fontana
called 'Kantian universalism as well as from the Hegelian interpretation of
history, not only for what it contained of philosophic history in the tradition
illustrated, but for what it contained of transmutation into a revolutionary
interpretation' (Fontana, 1982, p. 126). In archaeology the model illustrated
had been fashioned into a one-track, teleological and universal evolutionism;

faced with that, diffusionism opposed immutability, particularism and contact, which usually found expression in the method of parallels and comparison, with a philosophic background based on a revision of Kant from the standpoint of neo-Kantianism, of idealist historicism and a rigid and theoretically aseptic positivism.

In reality, there are no great differences between one-track evolutionism and diffusionism; the two tendencies, in opposition, have built up just one 'domestic argument', which in neither case questions the existence of a subject-present-from-all-time, a protagonist of history. So their presences and ascendancies are a response to two very different sets of circumstances: while universal evolutionism arose in circumstances immersed in the framework of bourgeois revolutions, when increasing optimism that they had triumphed over the *ancien régime* was in the air and progressive responses were accepted as necessary, diffusionism, by contrast, was born after 1848 and its origins lie far off in the historical positivist approaches of Ranke in his *History of the Roman and Germanic peoples,* published in 1824. In other words, it rested on the reactionary Prussian ruling classes and the timid French bourgeoisie of the middle of the nineteenth century, who, when their alliance with the proletariat had been broken, constructed an edifice so planned that nothing should change once its historical role had been legitimised.

Diffusionist archaeology and a triumphant bourgeoisie were most fully in agreement at the end of the nineteenth century as a result of imperialist expansionism, because it is on that historical fact that the encounter between civilised Europe and the Third World took place. From that project a cultural programme was generated that would disguise the actual reality implied by the new distribution of the world market, and a paternalist relationship was built up between the coloniser and the colonised, which has its archaeological expression in the new diffusionist matrix that we read in Paris and will be following in other authors. Thus the concept of the civilising invader (the myth of the Greek or Phoenician coloniser teaching the natives to use the potter's wheel, to grow olives or to domesticate fowls) would grow up within the framework of an integrating and never conflictual matrix – except when the sources rendered it impossible – at a time when different degrees of native reaction were taking shape: the Baeticans accepted Roman civilisation before the Cantabrians because they were not so barbaric, and so recognised the benevolence of the coloniser.

We turn now to the second component of the diffusionist matrix, the natives, so as to analyse their evolution in detail, since that is where the theoretical basis linking idealist historicism with the diffusionist matrix is most sharply delineated. In order to analyse it we shall move on to 1917, when

Cabré published his 1916 season of excavations in the Iberian sanctuary of Collado de los Jardines de Despeñaperros; there, yet again, we come up against the diffusionist matrix enunciated by Paris, but, unlike him, the Spanish researcher identified with the indigenous component.

> We do not think there is anyone who would venture to claim . . . that these Iberians were of such obtuse understanding that not only had they forgotten the art they would inherit from Altamira but that they were incapable of learning what they saw foreigners doing; that although those Iberians had relations with civilised peoples and were capable of a kind of culture, they were nevertheless so idle that it was necessary for people to come from outside and issue rules for their social life and make works of art for them to put in their houses and temples.
>
> (Calvo and Cabré, 1917, p. 27)

In his writings of 1917–19, Cabré reflects a nationalist position with xenophobic overtones, very typical of the image of the intellectual of his day, in the Krausist tradition. The effects of this tradition can be appreciated in his seventh rule for systematic archaeological excavation in which he proposes that the workers be instructed in the 'historical and archaeological merit' of the finds, in keeping with the proposition summarised by Ortega years later in his *España invertebrada:* 'A nation is a human mass organised, structured by a minority of elite individuals' (Ortega, 1921). Similarly, this tradition made itself felt in his preoccupation with Spain, a theme already being taken up by Picavia's regenerationism, the arguments of Costa, the men of '98 and, years later, the 1914 generation (Tuñón de Lara, 1970), and which was an unfailing topic of conversation among the liberal bourgeoisie of the beginning of the century (Villacorta, 1980).

However, as would frequently be the case among the intellectuals of the time, this approach of seeking solutions in the face of the most reactionary despotism would eventually have them drinking at the philosophical springs most opposed to those processes of change, thereby generating a latent contradiction, which is very present in authors like Maeztu, who would ultimately be converted into a theorist of the most reactionary right wing by renouncing liberal humanism in favour of the transpersonalism of values (Tuñón de Lara, 1970), paving the way for the most classic approaches of fascism. In a less effective form, but still on the critical topic of nationalism, this weakness came to light as early as 1919 in some of Cabré's thoughts, which, significantly, are connected with the Iberians.

> The pre-Roman Iberian peoples were powerful, strong, hardworking and disciplined; their lives were inspired by two great ideals which may perhaps not

have entirely died out in our race, namely: enthusiasm for their independence and a yearning for an intense religious life.

(Calvo and Cabré, 1919, p. 14)

This concept of the national must, of course, be linked with the diffusionist matrix, with the development of German historicism and its antecedents (Niebuhr, Humboldt, Ranke, etc.). Indeed, a critical assessment of the specific position of Ranke is necessary (Fontana, 1982, p. 130), stressing the conceptual identification of nation and state in his work. This would lead inevitably to transcending the internal conflicts of society, so as to delight, in line with the most reactionary tastes, in a history of peoples, in other words, of interclass units bonded together in a common sentiment of nationality.

It is interesting to note how the effects of idealist historicism gave rise to continuous controversy in Spanish life at the beginning of the twentieth century. In 1915, Bosch Gimpera, in his first systematic classification of Iberian pottery, defended the existence of three linked areas – Andalusia, the Catalan–Valencian–Murcian area and the central Ebro valley – based on a compromise between the historical sources and the archaeological information. Thus three large fields of work were foreshadowed, which, *grosso modo,* outlined the Tartessian area, the Iberian area itself and the Celtiberian area. The scheme was, of course, a response to a programme of systematic classification which, moreover, would be fundamental in the years that followed – Tarradell and Sanmartí approved it as setting up the third phase of Iberian investigation between its publication and the civil war (Tarradell and Sanmartí, 1980) – but alongside this it implied an alternative approach from the peripheral nationalities to the problem of national unity.

After his stay in Berlin, where he was in touch with Wilamowitz, whose master–disciple relationship with Schulten is well-known, Bosch Gimpera set out with that work along a path which, in parallel with his growing political awareness as defender and propagator of Catalanism, led him, scientifically and in line with the earlier attitude, to a common project that claimed to promote study and research into the Catalan national past. This found clear expression in his work, even in zones outside the Catalan national territory (the Matarraña zone), within a classic expansionist model that enabled him to distinguish and contrast cultures as peoples-nation and disseminate a culture: that of Catalonia.

Bosch's plan, which became more radical, particularly from 1923 on, that is to say, when, politically, the autonomous model was suffering the political repression of Primo de Rivera's dictatorship, was only put forward as an alternative insofar as it identified a historic nation that was not Spain but

Catalonia; indeed, his ideological position moved, politically, towards the Lliga de Cambó and during the civil war his position was that of Acció Catalana. However, his political tendencies at the time he was writing the archaeological work we are studying here (i.e. the period before 1922), with reference to the First World War were, not surprisingly, Germanophile (curiously, they coincide with those of a by no means liberal personage like the Marquess of Cerralbo). We stress these aspects so as to link the origin of this plurinational current with archaeological historicism, with the same theoretical models that defined the other line: nationalist centralism. We know that motives similar to those that inspired Cabré to write the texts that we picked up in 1917, in other words, the *Institución Libre de Enseñanza* and Krausism, were present in a Bosch Gimpera who went to Germany in 1912 because it was made easy for him by Giner de los Ríos himself.

Without severing the ideological links underlying both positions, that is, without abandoning the historicist component, from 1923 on, history, its political practices and its results ended up confronting both positions. Bosch Gimpera wrote in 1932: 'The Iberian civilisation of the third to second centuries, despite its known common features, which apparently seem to establish a great cultural unity in the Peninsula, is, in reality, a mosaic of survivals and local phenomena' (Bosch Gimpera, 1932, p. 14).

Some years earlier, in 1925, on the occasion of the publication of the chambered tomb at Toya, Cabré returned to Gómez Moreno's proposal to include Iberian culture in a 'Hispanic period'. This clearly had political overtones and occurred after Gómez Moreno's work on the pre-Roman languages and the appearance of two distinct linguistic areas (Tartessian and Iberian), which could have subdivided the already 'divided Spain' still further and legitimised such a division historically (Cabré, 1925).

Cabré, who seemed to take the opposite line to Bosch, abandoned his more liberal positions during the excavations of the Iberian sanctuaries at Jaén, perhaps because of his marked links with someone as conservative as the Marquess of Cerralbo, but primarily because he was already unveiling a political position.

The death of the Iberians

The first stage of this conflict culminated in the special circumstances of the fall of the republic.

Iberian culture is none other than the reaction of the Spanish spirit, personalism under the classical influence, the re-working of classicism which of course, while giving them an archaic flavour, includes the oriental elements inseparable from our racial and mental being.

(Martínez Santaolalla, 1946, p. 98)

Well-known historical motives in the end strengthened the centralised national view, as we see, throwing into relief those aspects that were best suited to the monolithic language of fascism. The Iberians, defined as part of our 'racial and mental being' and framed in the pan-Germanism peculiar to those states sympathetic to Nazism, were going to be forced to abandon their very outworn African origins and, in the midst of this turmoil, discover their links with – how could it be otherwise? – the Aryan race, and so their unitary Hispanic character, which was already foreshadowed in Gómez Moreno's proposition.

What, historically, we call Iberians, and, archaeologically, Iberian culture is neither a race nor a culture since it is a matter of that very Hispanic ethnicity in which, at most, a greater proportion of pre-Aryan elements must be recognised, with the frail inputs of Mediterranean logic.

(Martínez Santaolalla, 1946, p. 97)

The propositions of Cabré and Gómez Moreno had in their time been a response, according to a concept of 'the national', to an ever-more excessive division of the Iberian areas and had defined their inevitably conservative position on Spain, but they assumed a different character here, which ultimately strained the actual scientific fact; it started from a series of considerations corresponding exactly to a political programme that took an extremist view of history, seeing the Neolithic as 'utterly wretched', the Roman Empire as 'magnificent', Celtic culture as 'robust', etc.

The long autocratic period that Spain would live through after the civil war would, in the early days when the struggle was still close, foster a rejection of the Iberian idea. The effect of this political reaction implied, on the scientific plane, a rapid change of attitude concerning the chronologies of the most significant Iberian works, bringing them forward to the third century BC; this meant they would eventually be subsumed in the provincial sphere of Rome as provincial products of the influence of the classical civilisation on the Iberian world.

In 1952–4 Menéndez Pidal's *Historia de España* was published. The time that had elapsed since the end of the civil war had toned down significantly the militant positions reflected in Martínez Santaolalla, but had not shaken the theoretical foundations nor the problems created by historicism, which would become more acute with the triumph of fascism. The work directed by Menéndez Pidal, which gave entry to the most outstanding archaeologists of the day, may be seen as the final culmination of the historicist debate in the terms in which it had been presented. We nevertheless see here a continuation of Martínez Santoalalla's approach, apparently depoliticised, without the overweening rhetoric of the fascist texts of the 1940s, and with a pronounced interest in being incorporated into that Europe from which the Spanish political system was movng further and further away.

In the general context of the work, an interesting debate developed, which can be appreciated in the position of García y Bellido and Almagro Basch. This is reflected in a sentence from the first of these authors:

> A Celtophile current, which a short time ago led to startling consequences, has sought to deny even the physical existence of the Iberian people and an Iberian culture – racially speaking – maintaining the latter to have been merely a consequence of the impact or influence of the august Mediterranean cultures on a single people, the Celts, who were thought to occupy almost the whole of the Peninsula in the final centuries before Christ. For those centuries, the Iberian culture of the coast would have been just a Celtic culture modified by the impact of the Greek and Punic colonies and hence the people of Iberian stock a mere shadow and an ethnically arbitrary designation.
>
> (García y Bellido, 1952, p. 304)

The controversy occupied a good part of the decade of the 1950s. It should be remembered, as already stated, that the pan-Celtic approach of the 1940s had found a fertile field due to a certain change of position concerning the chronological assessment of Iberian art on the part of García y Bellido, who was, as we can see, a firm opponent of that concept in the 1950s. Teresa Chapa, who has studied the problem from this angle, concludes that García y Bellido's stylistic revision is no more than a means of justifying a dating system that attributed to Rome what archaeological tradition had accepted as the outcome of Greek influence. In 1943, García y Bellido defended some stereotypical analyses of the diffusionist matrix and, for lack of sustainable chronological datings, applied an ideological project that implied a return on the most serious levels to that incompetence of the native that Paris drew attention to for psychological and moral reasons. This position on the one hand destroyed the possibility of any Iberian art and, on the other, made it possible to incorporate a biological scheme of culture, which necessitated the existence, prior to a classical period, of another that was archaising and formative (Chapa, 1986, p. 49).

11

We must suppose that the change from Greece to Rome proposed by García y Bellido was justified by the absence of any reliable stratigraphic document and by the belief in political rather than cultural diffusionism, together, of course, with the charm that the mythical relationship of Mussolini's fascism with the great achievements of Rome would have had for the Spain of the 1940s. The fact is that, Iberian culture up until the Second Punic War remaining unacknowledged, it was easy for pan-Celtism to appropriate the technical and cultural terms that at other times belonged to the Mediterranean world.

As was observed some years later in Arribas' new compilation (1965), the more systematic excavation techniques that arose at the end of the 1950s from the definitive acceptance of stratigraphy as an instrument and aim (and here we place one of the new problems research into Iberian culture was to experience), would quickly make that controversy appear old-fashioned, so that today, years later, it seems remote, the outcome of a certain political and markedly ideological situation and of a lack of theoretical and documentary support. But if the ultranationalist and historicist component in the diffusionist matrix became old-fashioned, the same cannot be said of positivism, which, already present from the start of research and gradually developing during the decade of the 1930s, found in the stratigraphic revision of the late 1950s the breeding ground from which to capture and ultimately dominate the research model.

On the grounds that all that was needed was to bring together enough well-documented facts for the science of history to arise spontaneously, workers in Iberian archaeology, whether consciously or not, deployed this assumption from the last years of the 1950s, so as to deny the validity of theory in history and create the concept of a blank and naive history that would shun the fiasco of classic historicism and the strongly ideological attitude characteristic of the 1940s.

Relying on the Spanish technocrats of the 1950s, positivism finally consolidated its position and denied any possibility of making historical judgements, on the grounds that there were no data adequate for drawing conclusions.

Having analysed the situation, two basic questions of archaeological positivism in the investigation of Iberian culture remain to be evaluated. In the first place, it must be understood that at no time was this presented as an alternative to the historicist current, but it is a fundamental component of the diffusionist matrix that we have been considering ever since Paris. It did not originate in the decade of the 1950s, but was very much present in the way archaeologists have been working throughout the twentieth century and from the end of the nineteenth, although it became the dominant factor once the other component reached crisis point. Tarradell and Sanmartí (1980) describe the decade from 1960 to 1970 as a period of crisis and renewal of ideas. In our opinion, it is simply a matter of readjusting the diffusionist matrix, which now preferred to conceal its theoretical foundations, from an alleged ingenuousness and a marked scepticism. In the second place, the flight from any involvement with historical conclusions led directly to a revision of excavation technique. This meant making the obtaining of a parallel or a date the aim and object of excavation work. In general, the positivist scheme can be followed in the establishment of a model of publication that is repeated from author to author: description of the site of the excavation, area within the site where stratigraphic sections will be made and a description of them, description of each one of the objects obtained (always in strata), parallels for these objects in other stratigraphies and chronological conclusion. The problem posed by this second question concerning archaeological positivism is that it produces no theorisation of method to replace historicism, except that, having established the stratigraphic outline, this not only becomes the aim and object of the work but is accepted uncritically by the researcher as if it were a matter of scientific law. This fact shaped other fields of investigation such as surveying, whose sole purpose would be to find sites with good stratigraphies or to give rise to a rigid plan of excavation, which finds its mentor in Wheeler's 1954 book, *Field Archaeology*, first published in Spain in 1961. With its famous chequerboard model, it established the only norm for good excavation. The definitive result of this whole approach was that excavation technique underwent a process of mythification, with a dual component, stratigraphic and typological, in a scenario where the method is none other than description.

— 1 —

From type objects to type products

Difficulty of achieving a typology for Iberian pottery

From the 1960s onwards, typological projects have proliferated. We can recognise three distinct levels of typological work. On the first, research into Iberian pottery has laid down two different lines of work: one synchronic, the other diachronic. The former is linked to the cataloguing of material assemblages, in many cases without assigning a stratigraphy. What might be termed synchronic models have been used, which merely claim to arrange a mass of material into groups or types and later, in each case, to add the chronological factor if possible. The second model, the diachronic, tries to assess the evolution of certain types. In the first case, that of synchronic work, Pla and Aranegui's typology of Iberian pottery (1981) deserves attention, as does that of Pereira for the material from Toya (1979), or analyses of very specific types such as the stamped ware or the lugged urns from museum assemblages. Within the diachronic model, which is found mostly in analyses of specific sites where the time variable is not in doubt, we can cite those carried out by Ruiz Mata on Torre de Doña Blanca (Ruiz Mata, 1987), by Pellicer on Cerro Macareno (Pellicer, 1982), by the same author together with Amores on Carmona (Pellicer and Amores, 1985), or by Ruiz Rodríguez and others on Cerro de la Coronilla de Cazalilla (Ruiz et al., 1983).

On the second level of typological investigation, the scope of the sample has to be evaluated, that is to say, whether the sequence comes exclusively from one site – Pellicer at Cerro Macareno, Ruiz Mata at Torre de Doña Blanca, Cuadrado at El Cigarralejo (1972 and 1987a) –, from a strictly defined region or zone – Aranegui studied the Valencian zone using the material from La Bastida, Nordström studied Alicante (Nordström, 1969), Pereira did the same on the Guadalquivir (1988 and 1989a) –, or whether, on the contrary, it is a question of a typology generalised throughout the Iberian world; no examples of the latter are available because of the complications that can arise.

14

The third level of typological work consists in sorting the pottery into groups associated either with broad assemblages or with a more restricted scale, such as Pereira's studies (1988 and 1989a) or Pellicer's (1969) on painted wares, Aranegui's (1975) or Roos' (1982) on grey ware, or Cuadrado's on red-glazed ware. Lastly, we should mention those who work with types and wares of a very special character, as in the case of Ruiz Rodríguez and Nocete (1981), Cura Morera (1971) on stamped ware, Belén and Pereira (1985) or Fletcher on the specific case of the lugged urns (1964), or Ribera (1982) on amphorae.

We should also point out that, if the space variable tends frequently to be defined when settling on the methodology to be used, the latter is worked out from a geographic perspective but never from a functional one – different site models (for example, settlements or necropolises) or, on a more reduced plane, departments of a different or similar functional character.

Staying with the third of the levels cited, since the first two will be dealt with later on, one of the few global assessments of the Iberian pottery assemblage was made by Tarradell and Sanmartí (1980); they arranged it in seven groups of wares:

1 Kiln-made wares, well fired, with an oxidising technique, often painted, extending over the whole Iberian area.
2 Polychrome ware, restricted to the south of Valencia in Alicante province.
3 Grey ware, with fine walls and well fired, developed chiefly in Catalonia. It is fairly widespread, although limited towards the south.
4 Stamped grey ware, different in form and fabric from the above.
5 So-called 'red-glazed' ware, located in the south and with a boundary between Murcia and Alicante.
6 So-called 'Ilergetan red-glazed' ware, located in the eastern part of Catalonia.
7 Pottery for domestic use and cooking; it is called Liria archaising ware by Ballester, Fletcher and others, and is largely a legacy from the pre-Iberian substrate.

It would be interesting to compare this overall assessment with the one being made on certain of the Andalusian sites. Take the case of Pellicer (1982) at Cerro Macareno:

1 Red-glazed ware.
2 Decorated wares (monochrome and polychrome painted).
3 Grey wares, called western grey. This group includes common kitchen wares.

4 Pottery from the Greek world.
5 Amphorae.
6 Bowls, etc.

If we eliminate from Pellicer's classification groups 5 and 6, which refer to actual forms, and group 4, which is clearly imported and foreign, the remaining groups fit in to groups 1, 2, 3, 5 and 7 of the preceding classification, leaving only 4 and 6, which belong by definition only to Catalonia.

We could make a similar assessment of examples from other sites already included in Tarradell and Sanmartí's Iberian area; which, it must be assumed, excludes the former Tartessian area, later Turdetania.

It can be inferred from all this that, eliminating the local component and the decorative and formal elements (which also vary by area within the typical light-coloured or oxidised Iberian ware of Tarradell and Sanmartí's first group), the basic groups of Iberian ware would be:

1 Oxidised or light-coloured wares, painted or not, monochrome or polychrome with geometric or other types of decoration.
2 Grey or reduced ware with a much wider area than the authors state. It occurs frequently throughout the Iberian area, including Turdetania, although the forms, as these authors point out, are different from area to area.
3 Coarse or domestic grey ware, very different (both in fabric and technique and certainly in use) from the fine grey table ware.
4 Red-glazed ware, including Ilergetan products.

Of these four groups, the last is deserving of special attention, since the ware called red-glazed, or red slip by other authors, fits the classic typological model set up by Cuadrado. In it the two basic assemblages, the eastern Tartessian or western Phoenician and the Ibero-Tartessian, are grouped together. The first is much in evidence in the coastal trading posts in the south of the Iberian peninsula and the second, with its clear indigenous filiation, developed over a wide area in the south east, the upper Guadalquivir, the *meseta* of La Mancha, Estremadura and the Ilergetan area. In reality, if the final stage of the first group is set, like much else, in the middle of the sixth century BC, way outside the scope of Iberian pottery, the second poses serious problems for lack of chemical analyses that might indicate the extent to which surface treatments do not correspond to painting, which has been treated later as a spatula technique or even burnishing, or a red slip as some authors describe it (Negueruela, Schubart). From our point of view, given the differentiating technical character of this product, similar in every respect to oxidised or light-coloured ware and only distinguishable by the forms and decorative technique, which are ill defined anyway, it would merit inclusion in the first group until a more thorough analysis has been made. Nevertheless, seeing that it might be a question of a distinct technical process, we shall keep to the differentiation.

First group: light-coloured wares

This first group has been the subject of the largest number of studies in specific terms, that is, studies that tackle its problems alone. In the Valencia–Alicante area, mention should be made of the typological projects of Nordström in 1969 and of Pla and Aranegui in 1981 and, more recently, of Mata Parreño in 1987. In the French zone, Solier's work (1976–8) is outstanding. In Andalusia, we should mention the wide-ranging analyses of Pereira and Escacena on the Guadalquivir valley, plus those of Pellicer on Cerro Macareno and Carmona – in the latter case with Amores – those of Ruiz Mata at Doña Blanca, of Campos, Vera and Moreno (1988) on San Isidoro, of Ruiz Rodríguez et al. (1983) on Cazalilla, and of Molinos in connection with the pottery assemblage of Puente Tablas (1986).

Fundamentally, the authors agree in establishing three basic fields:

1 *Field of attributes of a technical nature.* So far, and with the exception implied in the work of Anton Bertet (1973), González Prats and Pina (1983), and Rísquez (1992), use has not been made of chemical and experimental analyses in this field of attributes, which has confined itself to empirical statements such as types of degreasers, compactness, fragmentation shapes of the fabric, decoration techniques and surface treatments.

2 *Field of attributes of a decorative nature.* Usually, especially in more recent times, the tendency has been to make tables of motifs and their associations, adding, in each case, the colour variable to indicate polychrome or monochrome work.

3 *Field of formal/functional attributes.* This is the field that, in more recent years and especially since the establishment of stratigraphy in archaeology, has put the other two in the shade. The form/function association has involved a complex framework of analysis because, if there were problems with the first in establishing the hierarchy of variables or relating one with another, the second confined itself to transposing ethnographic parallels in some cases, or parallels peculiar to classical societies in others; all this as a consequence of a theoretical vacuum that prevented a critical examination of the methodology used. Thus, identifying such a well-known item as the 'plate' involved projecting a model, a present-day norm, into the past and

	Pereira	Pla y Aranegui	Mata	Cuadrado	González	Solier		Pereira	Pla y Aranegui	Mata	Cuadrado	González	Solier
	1A1	–	–	–	B1	III		5·A	24	II·4·1	18	B·25	–
	1A1	25	I·21	1 2A 2D 6	–	I2 I3		5·B 5·C	1·A	II·2·2	2B 2C 36 26 4	–	I·1
	1·A2	23	I·22	3A 5 7	–	I·3 I·2		–	2	I·3 II·3	–	–	–
	1·B	1D	II·2·2	–	B2 B7	I2		1·D 6A 7	1B	II·2·2	8 9 48 49	–	–
	1·D	18	–	–	–	–		6B	6	II·2·1	2C	B·12	–
	1·E	1·C 5	III·1·2 III·1·3	53 33 42	B4	IV·2		–	9	II·7 III·2	27 28 29 30	–	–
	2	8C	–	23·A	B·9 B·10	–		8A	16A	–	12	–	–
	2 12	8·A 8·B	III·2	11 22 23 56	–	–		8B 8C	16·C	II·12	54 57	–	–
	3·A	–	II·2·3	–	B·11 B·21	II		8D	17	II 6	13	–	–
	3·B	22·A	–	–	–	–		11 10	21	I·2·1 II·2·1	–	–	–
	4	–	–	–	–	IV·1							
	5·A	4	II·4·2	10 14	B·20 B·26	–							

	Pereira	Pla y Aranegui	Mata	Cuadrado	González	Solier		Pereira	Pla y Aranegui	Mata	Cuadrado	González	Solier
(vessel)	–	20	–	58 / 15	–	–	(vessel)	–	11A / 11B	–	40	–	–
(vessel)	–	–	II 9	–	–	–	(vessels)	–	7·D / 7·C	V3	–	–	–
(vessel)	–	–	II 8	39	–	–	(vessels)	13A / 13B	7	V·1 / V·2 / V 4 / V 5	19 / 46	–	–
(vessel)	–	26	–	–	–	–	(vessel)	–	–	24 / 25 / 36 / 37 / 38	–	–	–
(vessel)	–	–	–	35	–	–	(vessel)	15	10G	III·5	50 / 51 / 52	B·32	VI·2
(vessel)	–	–	–	43	–	–	(vessel)	16	10A / 10D / 10H	III·9	P5 / P10 / P13 / P15	B7	–
(vessel)	9A	12 B	–	16 / 17	–	–	(vessel)	16	10 B	III·8	P·7 / P·8 / P·14	–	–
(vessel)	9B	–	–	55	–	–	(vessel)	17	10C / 10F	III·7·1 / III·7·2	P·1 / P·2 / P·4	B·5 / B·6 / B40	VI·1
							(vessel)	17	10E	III·7·2	P·6	–	–
							(vessel)	14	15	VI·1	16	–	–

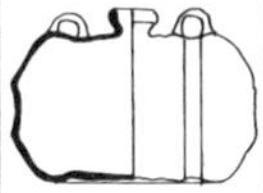

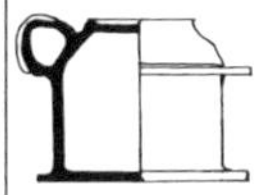

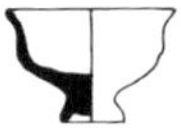

Figure 3 Comparison of some typologies of light-coloured wares
(by the authors on the basis of the authors indicated)

thereby establishing an ahistoric cultural value for that form. No thought was given here to the impossibility that the 'plate' could have functioned culturally in the same way as it does today, but there was a lack of analyses based on archaeological methodology by which it could be checked.

Moreover, the topic presents certain discrepancies that should be assessed with reference to some other example. At Cerro Macareno in 1982, Pellicer identified a group of vessels with the term 'strangulated bowls'; a year later, with Amores, the same author presented this functional form under two different names: either plates with a profile broken by carenation (the more open ones) or carenated vessels. As a matter of fact, this change is understandable in view of the actual investigation process used, but the discrepancy is clear to see. If we follow this form in Pla and Aranegui's typology (1981) we can identify it as their 'wide low pots'. In other authors it would be cooking pots; in others platters, etc.

Although the sketch accompanying the description obviously leaves no room for doubt about the identity of these pieces and their similarity, in spite of the different nomenclature used, it is immediately apparent that the dysfunction is not exclusively terminological, because that could be resolved in a meeting that would lead to agreement between the different specialists as to the appropriate or consensual term to use. The question goes beyond the descriptive level and lies at the heart of a methodological approach and a particular theoretical conception, which, in epistemological terms, belongs in the normative model by which the archaeologist goes beyond the form to the 'very essence of the object'; that is to say, to an ideal and ahistoric (transhistoric) pattern, which, in accordance with Krieger or Ford's criticism (cf. Contreras, 1984), claims only to encounter in the very essence of the object the idea that the researcher her- or himself shares with the artisan, in this case an Iberian. For want of a prior critique on the part of the typologist, this neo-Platonic approach is assumed unconsciously, as the result of a heavy subjective load that leads to identifications with cultural and historical types existing in the culture the researcher has known in his or her own environment.

This normative tendency has led to the establishment of the 'type fossil', that is to say, types significant on a fundamentally chronological level, and to the stipulation of parallels as a methodological model for fitting the different stipulated phases into space, without taking account of the actual cultural discrepancies that may frequently occur. A significant example is the use by Pellicer of the term 'thistle' vase to define a type that Pla and Aranegui call chalice shaped. If we observe the distribution Belén and Pereira give for this type (type II2Ba1 in their typology), we confirm that the model they set up is only documented in Lower Andalusia during the seventh century BC, while it appears with a post-sixth-century chronology and never in the fourth century BC in Upper Andalusia and Valencia. And yet Pellicer's 'thistle' type, very different if assessed on measurements, from the classic type studied by Belén and Pereira, has a chronology of the middle of the third century BC. In this case, a type fossil, that none the less continues to be useful, would reveal an appalling discrepancy if an attempt were made to tie its presence to just one phase.

Moving on to analysis of more specific cases, Nordström, in 1969, set up a typological classification project. His model fitted in with an earlier approach that involved:

1 Technical class.
2 Functional form (FF).
3 Geometric form (GF).
4 Accessory elements (rims, handles, bases).
5 Decorative themes.

Despite a somewhat complicated presentation, Nordström's project set out to create types on the basis of the association of a technical class, an FF, a GF, a type of accessory element (which might or might not be present, like handles) and a decorative theme involving the component, composition, position and subject.

Clearly, this example sets up an analytical model that does not hierarchise the different variables and that fits very neatly into a positivist position:

> I shall treat Iberian decoration on pots from an objective point of view, that is to say, what the eye sees, what the spirit can accept psychologically. I shall not try to investigate, least of all in this work, the possible intentions of the painter on Iberian ceramics nor the possible symbolic meanings.
>
> (Nordström, 1969, vol. II, p. 117)

However, when, in the conclusion, Nordström elaborates a typology for studying frequencies and chronologies, he clearly establishes a hierarchy, defined in the first place by the variable of technical class and in the second by functional form, while other variables, more capable of objective treatment, since there are no technical or functional studies of the first two parameters, such as geometric form and the variables of the accessory elements, practically disappear.

The author is undoubtedly faced with a serious problem in elaborating the variable of geometric form, since in defining it he has taken account only of the simple forms of the vessels, and in carrying out his research, he observes how closed and open vessels are associated in a single form. Consequently, it is the second and weaker factor, functional form, that in the end fine tunes the geometric form and creates the type. Nordström himself takes that for granted, saying:

> The functional aspect demands the employment of terms that give an idea of the vessels' use (craters, goblets, etc.) or that are traditionally reserved for vessels in common use. These terminologies (nomenclatures) give no idea of geometric forms but they evoke the aspect of the vessels in a general way.
>
> (1969, p. 105)

Now, it happens in his specific case that the functional form is elaborated, as he clearly states, from the traditional types of the eastern Mediterranean, and this reinforces the diffusionist position underlying this example.

On the other hand, in the absence of chemical analyses, and being restricted to describing fabric and surface colourations, the use of degreasers and surface treatments, that is to say, being less capable of objective treatment, reliance on the technical class variable in the long run supports the weakest aspects of the project, where the likelihood of subjectivity is greatest. In short, the analytical project ends up being devoured by its own least objective variables, in other words, it is nothing but the triumph of the subjective view that the author had in all probability foreseen before embarking on the work.

All in all, Nordström's work represents a great step forward in the typological analysis of Iberian ceramics. Firstly, with reference to the Alicante region (Llobregat [1972] would rely on this work for his *Contestania ibérica*), where he relies not only on cataloguing but on working out where the individualised piece is subsumed in the whole. Secondly, because, for the first time, the analytical project claims to study the piece of pottery by separating it into its components, that is to say, producing tables of rims, handles, bases and decorative motifs, all of which (except the last mentioned) imply a conception very different from the treatment the material had received previously.

Following on from Nordström's work, we have to look at that of Cuadrado in 1972 on the Iberian pottery from Cigarralejo, that of González Prats in 1983 on Crevillente, and, on broader lines, although starting from one settlement (La Bastida), that of Pla and Aranegui in 1981. In the following pages we shall analyse Cuadrado's project and the last two to have been carried out, both in 1987, on two very different areas: that of Pereira (1988 and 1989a) on the Guadalquivir valley and that of Mata Parreño (1987), based on the site of Los Villares de Caudete in Valencia.

In 1972, in opposition to Nordström's functional model, Cuadrado proposed a typology, which, with its timely publication and orderly systematisation, deserves to be treated separately. With his characteristic ability to systematise, Cuadrado laid down from the outset the inductive bases of his project: 'We firmly believe that the study of Iberian ceramics, and of a general typology for it, requires in advance particulars of each typical site' (Cuadrado, 1972, p. 123), and his positivist working objective: 'The aspiration to classify this pottery into types is not a grandiose scheme but has a strictly practical aim which is to simplify the description of the pottery' (p. 123).

In this work, he started from a division into plates and vases as an alternative to that of closed–open receptacles and created a total of fifty-eight types of vase and sixteen of plates. Although these forms treated each assemblage in too individualised a manner – hence his large numbers, and one of the problems presented by the work – his typology introduced a series of indices that undoubtedly opened up the field of morphometry to Iberian ceramics.

Once he had got his tables, the author consciously laid down the points from which the forms would move on. From these the types were defined in detail, using qualitative variables regarding certain components, while the variables were defined in successive subdivisions of the indices.

Actually, Cuadrado's model did not break with the normative tradition: his first project defined the form and then matched it to the indices, but he undoubtedly gained in objectivity by explaining those indices. Furthermore, once the form, with its types and variants, had been defined, the author embarked on the question of its 'usefulness' and by so doing he prevented the form being defined by its functionality. In short, despite the difficulty implied by the creation of so many forms, the model is a step forward in the creation of a set of rules for the production of Iberian pottery of the first group.

An important step in the field of Iberian painted pottery is provided by Pereira's typology (1988 and 1989a) for the Guadalquivir valley between the sixth and third centuries BC. His approach, as he says himself, is formal.

> In this classification, we have followed broad descriptive morphological criteria from a general point of view, according to the open or closed tendency of the different pottery profiles in order, on a more concrete plane, to delineate the bulk of those profiles in simple geometric forms by outlining a series of sectors like rim, neck, body, foot, elements for lifting and/or carrying.
>
> (Pereira, 1988, p. 87)

Unlike Nordström, Pereira consciously took for granted the hierarchical arrangement of the variables on three levels: form groups, types and variants. Altogether he established four groups of open and twelve of closed forms, and in fact, as he says, this variable was fundamental to his typological elaboration of the groups. We would point out that, at this first level, another variable for presence/absence was already included, as in the case of the handles, or the feet or, with regard to its development, the neck. Lastly, Pereira added, in exceptional cases only, specific details concerning the rim or the forms of the body and the neck.

In fact, the typological project he established was not far removed from a normative form model. That is to say, the form groups he drew up corresponded to forms on which a consensus had been reached in the process of the research carried out over the last two decades, with the difference that they were now rationalised from a more thorough analytical position than Nordström's first approaches. The two authors differ moreover, not only because Pereira rejects the functional terminology drawn from the eastern Mediterranean, which in this author is confined to his form group 9 (Pereira presents it as the one that reproduces 'more or less faithfully forms, proportions and elements of ceramic vessels of Attic provenance', 1988, p. 962), but because he tries to avoid the functional factor being the one that defines each form group.

On a second level, the elaboration of types and variants conforms to fine distinctions within each form group. For example, in form group 3, defined by its closed tendency, the use of a lid, the absence of a neck and the globular body with an uneven rim, the difference in the second scale is marked by the presence of breasts pierced on the rim (3a) or the dentate form of the rim (3b) (see Figure 3). At other times, it is the development of the neck, the distinguishing feature, because of its bell shape, in form 4 (classic 'thistle' vessels), that distinguishes a first from a second type, depending on how the latter has evolved. Lastly, on occasions it is a presence/absence concept, transferred from the form group to the type, as can be seen in the distinction between types 1B and 1C or between types 1D and 1F. Among the variables, although not emphatically so, it is usually differentiation by the type of rim or whether the piece is stylised or not that is much in evidence. On this level, the weakness of his typology becomes very obvious, because it repeats variables from the previous level, so breaking the established hierarchy.

Pereira's typological work has the merit of having systematised an assemblage of forms, recognised and used by the archaeologists of the Iberians, which at no time had been evaluated over such a broad area as the Guadalquivir valley. Hence his greatest successes lie in distributing the types on a cartographic plane, that is to say, incorporating the time–space variable.

From the other side, that is, from a position defending the functional factor, Mata Parreño (1987) worked out a typology for material from Los Villares de Caudete.

Mata Parreño places questions of a functional character on a first and second hierarchical level. The first level, in which she works out the range of groups, is defined by the function, in the broad sense, performed by the group in the cultural and economic context: storage, domestic, table ware, kitchen ware, small jars and pottery other than vessels. On the second level, she resorts to traditional functional typology, already used elsewhere by Fletcher, Pla or Aranegui. Ot this level, she introduces a parallel morphometric factor in a very wide sense (such as size). Lastly, for subtypes and variables, a system of morphological tables is drawn up for the lip or rim, neck, base, body, handles and decoration, which at times she extrapolates to the type when it is common to subtypes and variables, that is to say, to lower scales.

The model is interesting because its author has clearly defined the hier-archical process of the variables that she had followed in establishing the groups, despite a few problems arising in some of the groups she identified (small vessels). The second level seems to us less useful; here again, the norm governs the model on grounds that have very little archaeological verification. All in all, this model, together with Pereira's exclusively morphological one, must be evaluated not only as a very recent contribution (1987), but because both are conscious of going as far as the morphological and functional approaches of normativism allow. Moreover, as heirs to a long tradition of over thirty years, they are logically planned and capable of presenting the current position of research in the materials we are analysing, the ceramics, in a systematised form, not to mention the fact that they open up possibilities for a new analysis of the pottery that may overcome the discrepancies and restraints created by traditional methodology.

In Figure 3, without wishing to construct a general typology of forms for this ceramic group, and indeed with the aim of facilitating the reading of subsequent pages in which reference will be made to forms and special types and, of course, to avoid repetition in the description, we have drawn up a table of the principal forms and types with the nomenclature used in the typologies of Cuadrado, Solier, Pla and Aranegui, Pereira, and Mata Parreño, simplifying all the typology cited, since it is not the purpose of this book to deal with pottery in detail.

If working out a typology for the forms of the vessels is complicated, the complex painted decoration that generally accompanies them is even more so. Firstly, of course, because it is difficult to apply a morphometric model to decorative elements, but even when this could be managed, as in the case of the geometric or stamped decoration (Ruiz Rodríguez and Nocete, 1981), the process would undoubtedly be further complcated when that is coupled with figurative motifs.

For the moment, and even when we embark subsequently on chronologi-cal details about each decorative model, we are assemblng here in a simplifi-

25

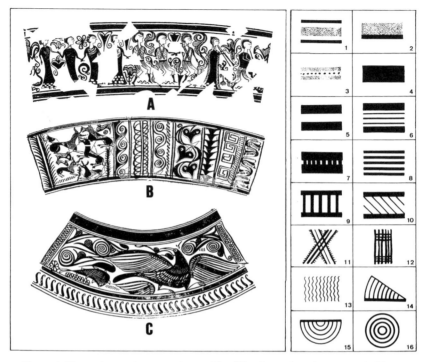

Figure 4 Figurative and geometric motifs of Iberian painted pottery. A. Dance scene on a vase from Liria. B. Scene on a vase from Azaila. C. Metope composition from an Elche-Archena vase (detail) (from García y Bellido, 1952), 1–16 Decorative geometric elements at *El Pajar de Artillo* (from Pereira, 1988)

ed form the ordering of the different styles worked out by Cuadrado (1984):

Floral decoration: realist style
             stylised style
             Fontscaldes style
Figured decoration: silhouette style
             classical line style
             baroque style
Floral and figured decoration: mixed.

A second classification gathers together the two great schools that have traditionally been studied: one represented by Elche–Archena, also known as the symbolic style and the other, in the Oliva–Liria group, called narrative style. While the first group is characterised by very careful drawing in very dense compositions, in the centre of which some figured subject stands out

26

(wolves, birds, figures like the *Potnia Theron*, or simply a winged deity), the Oliva–Liria style, as far as themes are concerned, offers hunting or war scenes or scenes from everyday life, less carefully drawn than those of the previous group but none the less expressive for that.

According to Cuadrado, within the floral-realist style a very simple decoration mingling plant elements with some that are geometric should be singled out. This style, together with the stylised floral, which may or may not be accompanied by figures of birds, wolves, small animals and winged female figures, constitutes the basis of the Elche–Archena assemblage, although for Cuadrado, these figures might be found in some of the scenes on vessels from Oliva and Ampurias.

The Fontscaldes type, with ivy-leaf decoration, would have been located in Catalonia (Tarragona, Puig Castellar or Tivissa).

The figured decoration of the style with silhouettes infilled with colour can be appreciated in a few examples from Liria, such as that of the ritual dance, and from Allora, as well as, occasionally, from Verdolai. The classic lineal style with lines running round the vessel, bands crammed with painting, and details shown 'in reserve' (that is, directly on the clay, without paint) is present throughout the coastal region; good examples are the warrior vase from Archena, the vase with the horsemen from La Serreta and many of the finds from Liria. Lastly, the baroque decoration is rather similar, but with spaces crammed with plant motifs and a host of legends (an example is the warrior vase from Liria). Finally, we would draw attention to the floral and figured decoration, also known as the Azaila type, based on garlands of ivy, solar circles, birds, animals and men in silhouette.

If the painted figured decoration has been the subject of a number of studies – the well-known work on the ceramics from San Miguel de Liria, in which a table of motifs is drawn up, or, for the Elche region, the animalistic study made by Nordström, to name but a few, to which we should add the more recent work of Elvira Barba (1979) on the Liria motifs – by contrast, the geometric decoration has not been the subject of any detailed work. Nevertheless, a twofold division can be made on the basis of two parameters defined by Llobregat (1972):

Simple geometric style: with monochrome decoration
                        with polychrome decoration
Complex geometric style: with monochrome decoration
                        with polychrome decoration
Standardised complex geometric style
Degenerate geometric style.

To conclude this brief review of the decorative styles, we have excluded the orientalising figured style, characterised by lotus flowers, animals and even human figures, which is documented in the Tartessian zone as far as Obulco in Jaén, because it has some very old chronologies (seventh century BC), which link it to a world in which the Iberian culture was still in a formative phase.

Second group: grey ware

The grey-ware group has so far stimulated a similar debate to that centring on the light-coloured wares, painted or not, although the points at issue in this case lie somewhat later in time, having had to await the work of Almagro Basch in 1949 and 1953 and that of Lamboglia in 1953. Until then it had been mentioned in work by Cazurro or Bosch as 'greys of the Catalan coast' without receiving any thorough treatment. Almagro Basch made a typological assessment of the pitchers with handles as early as 1953 and settled on the name of 'Phocean grey ware' but, in every instance, the grey ware located up to 548 BC in Ampurias seems to be, at least in part, of Greco-oriental provenance. Parallel with this and starting with the establishment of stratigraphic sequences in the south, a grey ware began to be identified, which is found from Cerro del Real in eastern Andalusia to Carmona in the west, taking in Phoenician trading posts like Toscanos. The fact is that from these first indications, to which other sequences were added later (Cerro Macareno, Colina de los Quemados, Cazalilla, Saladares, to cite instances scattered across a wide territory) it is possible today to infer with certainty the existence of a second centre located in the south, whose more northerly sequence would be linked with the one in Saladares and Penya Negra de Crevillente, with the name 'western Phoenician grey ware' (Pellicer, 1982; Roos, 1982), which had already been studied by other researchers like Aranegui (1969).

Recently, these productions have been studied at different times and and in different areas in other works.

In the Valencia and Alicante zone, in 1975, Carmen Aranegui studied the Valencian production and its articulation with that from the hinterland of Ampurias and the productions from the south. González Prats (1983) proceeded along the same lines with productions obtained from Crevillente. In Andalucia, outstanding studies have been made by Belén (1976) on the grey ware from Huelva, and by Roos (1982), centred fundamentally on Andalusia, on productions from before the middle of the sixth century BC. We would also add the studies by Arcelin (1978) and Nickels (1978) on the French zone.

Focusing on this example, all the researchers agree in establishing two clearly differentiated groups: one located around Catalonia and the other in

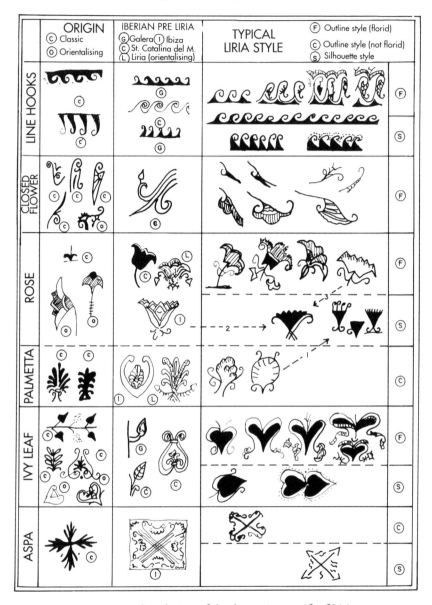

Figure 5 Origins and evolution of the decorative motifs of Liria ware
(from Barba, 1979)

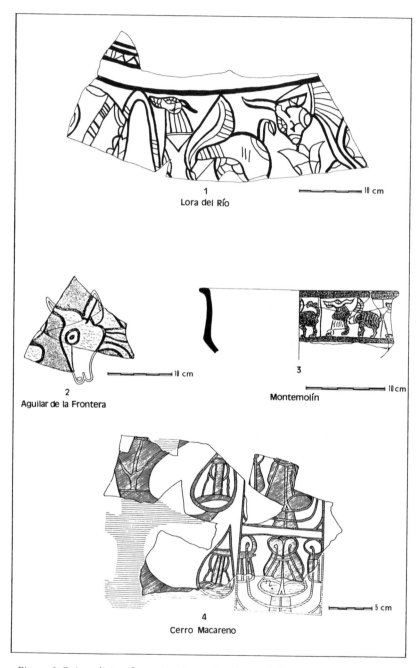

Figure 6 Orientalising figurative decoration (1, 2, 4, from Remesal Rodríguez, 1975; 3 from Chaves and de la Bandera, 1984)

Andalusia, with techniques and forms that may seem to be similar but, of course, correspond to very different assemblages. They appear to be of foreign origin, but, at the same time and once the technique has been taken on board by the indigenous world, not only were the imported forms limited but forms originating in the indigenous tradition would be transferred to this production.

> They are considered to be of indigenous manufacture and are not always wheel-made, that is to say that, typologically, this is a form known before the effects of colonising contacts were felt, but when the use of the wheel was adopted, it came to form part of the skilfully produced grey wares.
>
> (Aranegui, 1969, p. 351)

Roos also stresses this:

> Excepting those examples that can be considered to be imported, it seems clear that the majority of the wheel-made grey ware present in complexes at the beginning of the early Iron Age in the Peninsula turn out to be a continuation of other similar wares that were being made by hand during the Final Bronze Age and were therefore traditional within the various indigenous cultural spheres.
>
> (Roos, 1982, p. 43)

Despite the great leap forward that has occurred in the past few years in clarifying the origin of this pottery, little has been done concerning its evolution in specifically Iberian times; so the two typologies for Andalusia refer to early types.

Belén organised his typology on the basis of articulating rims and feet, since the vessels concerned are open (plates), and he varies the subtypes by a group of secondary variables. His plan is formal and analytical, logically constructed so as to determine types in the abstract based on the different combinations and to establish six, one of which is not documented although the rest are, with their variables.

Roos' typology establishes eighteen shapes in all, for plates, bowls and vessels, without determining a hierarchy of variables and with just descriptive readings of each form. Of these, only one, form 2, shows two variants concerning thickening of the rim. It should be emphasised that, from this assemblage, the author documents only four forms in the sixth century BC that could have formed part of the Iberian world (all open vessels), although we must add that her form 12 is also documented on the upper Guadalquivir, in horizons that are already Iberian (Cazalilla) (Ruiz Rodríguez et al., 1983).

Starting with Pellicer's work, a series of sites in Seville have been analysed on the basis of their grey-ware production. In Cerro Macareno it was Pellicer himself who evaluated five groups of ceramics ('species'). The first of these, characterised by its excellent and refined clay with small inclusions of mica, high firing temperatures, very uniform light-grey colouration and polished, almost burnished, on the wheel, would, according to the author, correspond to Almagro Basch's group of Phocean grey ware (1949), dated from the beginning of the seventh century BC (bottom of the site) to the early years of the sixth century, when it was abundant, and from then until the second quarter of the fifth century in insignificant proportions. The forms, all open, correspond basically to the ones studied by Belén and Roos.

The rest of the species, four in all, are ascribed to local production, although two of them (D and E) belong to the coarse or common ware, while, for Pellicer, B is a degenerate form of A, with less purified clay, inclusions of quartz, a dark grey colour and the surface treated by brushing on the wheel and a whitish-grey slip. Finally, C is catalogued as fine textured, with a barely perceptible presence of mica and a very dark colour. For the rest, chronologically, until the middle of the sixth century BC, bowl forms with a thickened rim are reported as dominant, while during the fifth century it was carenated forms.

In her 1975 publication, Aranegui showed a greater interest in the Catalan than in the Andalusian productions, since she found a more direct connection between the former and the few productions from Valencia. She grouped the productions into three assemblages: the first a survival of indigenous forms; the second an imitation of classic forms; and lastly a late production of small bitroncoconic jars with a handle and, generally, ribs in relief on the carenation. No typological programme was applied within these assemblages.

Third group: red-glazed ware–red-slip ware

Repeating word for word the opinion of Jodin (1966), Siena concludes from a few chemical analyses that the so-called 'red-glazed ware' is the result of a bath of slip very rich in haematites, applied to the piece after a first firing, at a temperature similar to the first (1,000–1,100 °C). It was thanks to the work of Cuadrado, who started studying this pottery which he called 'red ware', in 1953 and to his agreeing with other researchers, such as Tarradell, who already defined it as 'red slip' in 1952, that we find this group standing alone in studies of Iberian pottery today.

In 1969, Cuadrado defined the following characteristics:

1 'The colour of the red-glaze varies from vermillion to dark red, brownish red and violet, by way of light colours like yellowish red or orange' and the

surface has a brilliant effect as if polished, burnished or smoothed with a spatula, according to some authors and, according to others, owing to the glaze itself.

2 The characteristics of the 'glaze' have still to be determined. There is talk of glaze, slip, burnished paint, etc. In any case, recent work being done on chemical analysis has yet to be assessed.

3 The part of the vessel treated is always the most visible (inside in open vessels, outside in closed ones, the upper rather than the lower part), although there is always a tendency to cover the whole piece.

It was Cuadrado, too, who would distinguish two large groups, primarily as a function of their chronology, but also from their regional distribution and above all by their forms. The first, which he called 'Tartessio-oriental', would be described later as 'Phoenician red glaze' or 'Phoenician red slip'. From this group, and especially from the open forms, Schubart elaborated his typology of plates that has been so much used as a method of relative dating. A great many investigators, such as Cuadrado himself, Schubart, Niemeyer, Pellicer and Negueruela, have worked on this group; we are more interested in the forms of the second group that Cuadrado called 'Ibero-Tartessian'. Its space–time range was at first situated at the end of the fifth century BC and above all at the start of the fourth century BC; geographically, it stretches from Huelva to Alicante, including the *meseta*. Later, the work of Junyent in Lérida established the existence of a small, late nucleus (end of the third century BC) located in the Ilergetan world (Junyent, 1974).

In spite of all this, although it is true that particular forms appear at first sight to be well defined, especially when the decoration covers the whole surface, it proves difficult to distinguish others that reproduce painted themes with a magnificent surface treatment. We are of the opinion that effective differentiation of this group of pottery – we are referring to the Iberian and not the Phoenician, obviously – may be possible when chemical analyses that allow paint to be distinguished from glaze or slip have been studied more deeply. Meanwhile, and since tradition has assumed the existence of this pottery to be separate from painted wares, we are gathering together here the types elaborated by Cuadrado with a few new forms, established later.

The typology produced in sucessive years (1953, 1962 and 1969) is, of course, a summary of forms, the fruit of the personal experience of the investigator who first started work on El Cigarralejo, initially with eight forms, which he extended later in successive campaigns to sixteen in 1962 and to twenty-two in 1969.

Each summary of forms follows the same plan, starting with the open ones

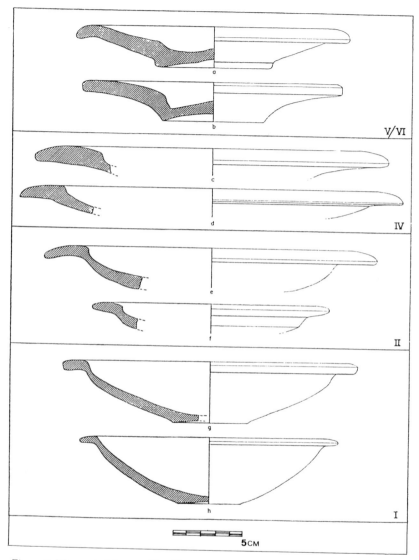

Figure 7 Morro de Mezquetilla: Phoenician dishes from section 7/8, indicating the strata (from Schubart, 1979)

and continuing with the closed, with certain exceptions, like form 10, and this makes it difficult to get an overall view of the assemblage. Moreover, the author describes them only from some basic element, which leaves each form or type ill defined. But it is surprising that, while the Phoenician group has been the subject of later systematisations, the Iberian, by contrast, has seen neither alternatives nor additions since 1969. We should just cite, and these are not global typologies, the work of Junyent (1974) in Lérida, and of Fernández Rodríguez (1987) on Alarcos; in her Tables 3, 4, and 7, according to the author, forms appear that were not described by Cuadrado. However, the forms of the first two groups could be identified with Cuadrado's form 9, which, as in the earlier examples and given the lack of rigour in the description, could have variants that might extend its range. Similarly, some elements are reminiscent of Cuadrado's form 16. In short, a new system needs to be worked out for the pottery group as a whole.

Cuadrado interprets this production as the result of three factors: on one side, continuity of the Phoenician tradition, which seems to be present in form 1; on another, the introduction of a Greek influence, which shows up in elements like forms 3, 9, 11, 13 and 14; and lastly, the appearance of a production of traditional indigenous forms, which are seen in many elements of the typologies (as in types 7 and 8, for example). In this way the author establishes a reflux theory, similar to the one that was much in vogue for the bell beakers, by which, after the expansion of the first Phoenician productions from Lower Andalusia and the coast towards the south-east, a relaunch occurred with new and evolved forms, which advanced towards the Guadalquivir and the *meseta* and succeeded in reaching Liria and Sidamunt along the coast. The theory cannot be verified until advances have been made in analysing the classification of production techniques and in elaborating sequences that accurately assess each of the forms in its chronological contexts, since form 1, for example, was present only for a short time along the whole of the Guadalquivir owing to the evolution of the early 'plates of Phoenician red slip ware' themselves. Another instance might be that of the 'bowls with the inturned rim' of form 11, which are found less frequently on the lower Guadalquivir and which could be of later date on the upper course of the river than in Murcia, for example.

One very interesting case is the Ilergetan area, which Junyent situates in a short period of time around the third century BC and which is linked through certain written historical sources, to the capture of Indíbil in Cartago Nova. Because of its historical nature, we shall return to the subject in the appropriate place.

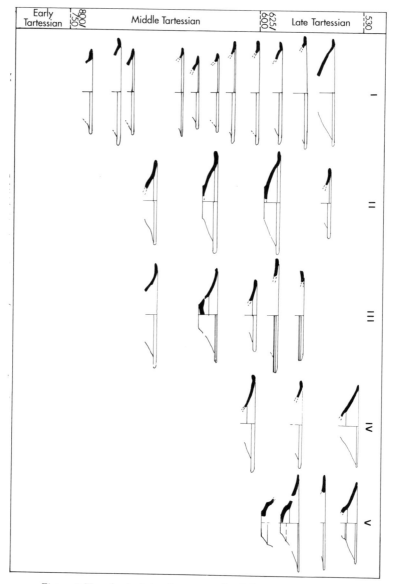

Figure 8 Typological development of red-slip dishes at Huelva
(from Fernández Jurado, 1986)

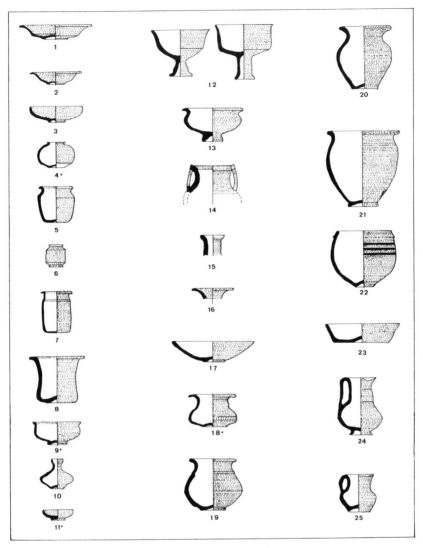

Figure 9 Typology of red-glazed pottery
(from E. Cuadrado, 1969, and F. Cuadrado Insasa, 1968).

Figure 10 Distribution of red-glazed pottery (by the authors, based on
Fernández Rodríguez, 1987)

Fourth group: coarse-ware production

González Prats defines this fourth group in general terms as a wheel-made production, crude looking, with reddish, greyish or drab-coloured rough surfaces, and with degreasing material in its fabric, in amounts customary in handmade prehistoric pottery (González Prats, 1981).

As González Prats states, this production, because of its aesthetic character and its crude technical treatment, has not received much attention from the classic researchers. But the secondary interest it aroused in people like Ballester is noteworthy; he described it in 1947 as 'archaising pottery'. A first typological project, arising from the study of La Bastida by Ballester *et al.* (1954), has

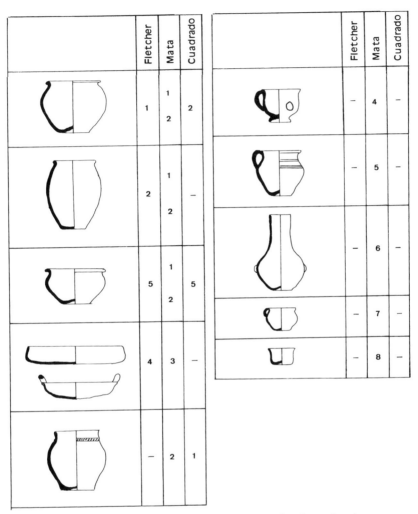

Figure 11 Forms of coarse or 'kitchen' ware (by the authors)

proved over the years to be the only one made, if we discount the recent contributions in the 1980s by González Prats on Crevillente, by Cuadrado on El Cigarralejo, and by Mata Parreño on Los Villares.

Significantly, this pottery, which, with its brushed surface treatment and its rough fabric, is sometimes very difficult to define technically, proved extremely useful in its day – the 1970s – as material to justify certain Mesetan incursions into the Andalusian area; once the years of the Celtophile boom were over, these were defined as being by 'people from the north' (Blanco, Luzón and Ruiz Mata, 1969). In this case, only the kind of pottery that was clearly handmade, with incised geometric decoration, pinched lines or finger decoration was asssessed and outstanding among these forms were the globular urn and the vessel with the flared neck, as well as the bowls, basins and vase supports, datable to between the eighth and sixth centuries BC.

Cuadrado acknowledged this years later, saying: 'The first time we looked at this pottery we said it was in the Celtic tradition because, in fact, this type of vessel reached the Iberian world, possibly handmade, with the "urnfields", but later it was made on the wheel' (Cuadrado, 1987a).

What is certain is that these productions appear to be linked more to specific functions in the economy of the settlement than to external influences. Indeed, when they find their way into the Iberian culture, they are already fashioned on the wheel, like a small group of preferably closed forms, which undoubtedly, from their shape, technical manufacture and function within spatial limits, could be explained in terms of their belated development, that is to say, their conservatism (in any case, all we can say is that in this specific type of form, the neck is reduced to a small rim above a strangulation of the body). Note too that some authors, like Pellicer, prefer to include them in their grey-ware species D and E (Pellicer, 1982).

Suggestions for an alternative typology for research into the material culture of the Iberians

Typology, like excavaton, is an empirical practice, a technique capable of facilitating interpretation in archaeology, but isolated and lacking any theoretical approach to underpin it; it is an endless and accumulative practice, and is ultimately inimical to the archaeological patrimony itself, owing to its all-consuming character. This character is what must be challenged first of all by researchers so as to avoid being consumed by their own operational practice. So far so good. We would add a second point by way of solution to the first: to prevent the practice from transforming itself into the aim of archaeology, the researcher can rely on only one weapon – the conceptual framework, that is, theory as the arbiter of practice.

We shall start with these two notions, in the form of question and answer, in order to emphasise that it is fundamental when launching any project that claims to be scientific, to make quite clear what place each phase (not in a temporal-lineal sense) and each practice or concept occupies in the development of that project.

So far, we have seen how in the best work on elaborating typologies for

Iberian ceramics, the weakness of the models has in the end produced results so subjective as to make their verification and comparison impossible. Consequently, it became necessary to revise those results in order to improve the practice itself by incorporating new techniques borrowed from other sciences, also concerned with the material that is the subject of the typology; alongside this, there is a need for a theoretical approach that may lead to the elaboration of a methodology that would establish the when and how, and above all, the wherefore of its own typological practice.

In recent years, archaeologists have discovered information science and statistics; sadly, these discoveries have been applied with considerable delay to the Iberian culture, and those who have used them, immersed in new currents within Iberian research, have devoted their work to analysing assemblages of tombs or closed spaces in the houses of a settlement but not to typologies.

So, what of significance was implied by the articulation of these two practices in the attempt to become more objective? We agree with Lull and Esteve (1986) in setting two different levels in this encounter. On the one hand, on the descriptive side, statistics are valid because of their capacity for marshalling the 'appearance of the pieces of evidence observed'; on the other, from the inferential side, in reality, they do no more than check the description of an apparent phenomenon against a model of probabililstic functioning. In short, they enable us to verify but without confirmation, thanks to the ability to discover more objectively. Nor should we forget that this statistics-information science project constitutes only one of the new possibilities for articulating practices in the interests of objectivity; that is to say, the new articulation allows formal morphology to be replaced by morphometry, but, equally, the practices of chemical and physical analysis open up a new road to technical variables that had previously only been assessed subjectively.

As far as the inferential side is concerned, typology has played a dual role in the field of research into things Iberian: on the one hand, it facilitates the cataloguing of the objects and, on the other, starting from the model of the parallel and in the frame of stratigraphic sequence, it becomes a source of chronological information; but it has contributed very little more to the general business of historical research or to what might be an objective analysis of Iberian societies. We should remember at this point various critical contributions that arise from the neofunctionalist models arrived at by 'systems theory' (Clarke, 1968) or from Chang's interpretation (1967), when, in evaluating the settlement as a structural unit, he established that the meaning of the object only begins to make sense in the spatial context.

If structuralism or neofunctionalism fosters a new approach to the conception of the object and hence of its variables in the new hierarchical framework implied by the classic history–space–time articulation, it also impinges directly on the concept of the stratigraphic section as a provider of typological material, since it must logically be allowed that a sequential cut passes indiscriminately through a variety of spaces with different functions and, as structuralism would have it, different meanings. Thus the possibilities for checking the evolution or tendency of the types are considerably diminished from an objective point of view.

It is essential, therefore, for sequential or even macrospatial monitoring (different sequences in separate settlements), to insist at the very least on structural equality, from the functional-spatial point of view (a street, a room for purposes of consumption, etc.) in every case. Similarly, this outlook, because of the spatial factor, conditions the actual stratigraphic sequence in its turn, since monitoring studies of occupation floors is not the same as monitoring cumulative post-depositional processes, or, to be more specific, occupation strata, with the same function in the framework of the settlement structure but which may attract, through the action of man, materials from very different areas (sweepings from a house, spillage in the street). This means that for the typology to operate within a framework superior to or different from what is merely a matter of arrangement, that is to say, to make its chronological, not to say historical, function really objective, the methodological process leading to the selection of a particular excavation technique should be evaluated (how difficult it would be to operate in this way within the methodological framework of stratigraphic excavation as proposed in Wheeler's method!).

In 1983, we published (Ruiz Rodríguez et al., 1983) the results of an excavation carried out with limited resources between 1980 and 1982 at Cerro de la Coronilla de Cazalilla (Jaén), following a traditional stratigraphic model – preferably small, and always sequential sections – although with a systematic recording of the two major phases detected: the first in the Copper Age and the second in the Iberian period. In order to construct a typology, the Iberian material was organised on the basis of two factors: the first techno-functional, which, for lack of physico-chemical analyses, was organised in three groups (common or coarse ware, grey and light-coloured wares); the second factor, morphometrico-functional, was established on two levels: on the one hand, on complete vessels and, on the other, on rims (thereby experimenting with what comes up most frequently in the excavation finds). On the first level, sectors, planes and components (handles, feet, etc.) were recorded, which would act as variables whose presence or absence would add up to a total of two forms: open and closed. Working on simple statistical formulae (diagrams for one variable or two variables, Pearson's correlation coefficient, Student's T-test) and adding the time and space variable, we were able to establish five types for the open forms and eight for the closed. At a later stage, the lip was isolated and on it more metrical variables (in angles and distances) were established, blocks constructed by articulating variables (thickening-horizontality factor on the outside to assess the tendency to be open or closed) and a last block or factor to analyse the thickening-horizontality tendency on the inside.

As in the previous instance, four forms of lips/rims were established from the association (presence/absence) of these blocks and the same statistical analysis was performed, taking account of the forms types of the complete vessels and the time and space variables. The aim was to assess whether clear types existed within this level and how the relationship with the complete forms and types occurred; lastly, the decorative factor was added in, so as to observe how this affected the forms and types obtained.

The project gave us a more than satisfactory result in spite of the limited sample. Later, in other studies with a larger sample, some corrections were made to the rim variables and the method of analysing them, breaking the angles down into distances so as to work on homogenised measurements and using multivariable statistics through a computer program that articulates a cluster with an analysis of principal components (Esquivel and Contreras, 1984). The method was found to work quite well, in particular, when the time variable was assessed through the appearance/disappearance of types and the modification of a few tendencies, but when we introduced the space factor, we were barely able to obtain anything more than a mere description, not always interesting.

Something was missing! Probably, we were failing to spot the possibility that a more interdisciplinary analysis of the techno-functional factor must have offered; moreover, the method, as we had assessed it, had to be adjusted to the choice of variables and the statistical technique to be studied, but, above all, to the method of excavation. Failure to assess the whole space in which the pieces were located prevented us from understanding the wherefore of their use in that place and whether that bore a relationship to the types obtained. Certainly, lacking knowledge of the space variable, still with a normative after-taste, the effects of our typology were simply stated within their own limits. In any case, we had succeeded in one of our objectives: a descriptive and morphometric typology with certain rational values, produced by the use of statistical techniques. But that was all.

Some time later we had an opportunity to analyse a case at Puente Tablas working on a more extensive area of excavation. The subject was a complete structure where we were able to apply to the places of activity and the defined structures certain techniques frequently used in spatial archaeology (measurements of central tendency, typical deviation of distances, Thiessen polygons, Clark and Evans index and MRPP [multiple regression] analysis). Immediately, the different types began to take shape and were now associated or dissociated with a sphere of activity, enabling us to understand how they came to be vessels of production, consumption, etc. The change had occurred because the method of excavation in this case had made it possible, but above all because, by articulating the types in a dual space–time variable, the type object had been transformed into a type product (Ruiz Rodríguez and Molinos, 1989).

Within the framework of the artefact–context matrix, the relationship that overrides the strictly formal element in the classification, even in the positivist typology, is in fact specified. We are referring to the dual level of technology–economy, two horizons that are not necessarily comparable, although they may appear to be interrelated at particular levels of knowledge. Godelier says that one is different from the other because the economy 'is not devoted to studying the techniques as such but analyses the relationships that arise at the time when a particular technique appears and spreads' (Godelier, 1981).

The technological version of the artefact (technology in itself) is first and foremost, and as Clarke would say, the articulation that classifies and defines the artefact (Clarke, 1968); it allows the technological level of each site to be both inventoried and quantified, thereby laying the foundations for an assessment of the degree of development of the productive forces at a level where we know what is and is not possible. The economic version of the artefact (technology in the framework of the economy) can be appreciated in the words of Marx (1967): 'It is not what has been done, but how it has been done, with what means of work, that distinguishes economic periods.' The disposition/deposition of the artefact implies the possibility of analysing the technical fact of the work process, but at the same time it offers an opportunity to know what is implied by the actual reconstructed process. The context makes the individualised or collective operation of the person or group discernable, ultimately allowing the technical relationships of production to be analysed and opening up the process of understanding the social relationships coupled with it. By taking its place in the framework of the economic structure, technology converts the artefact into the outcome of a process and so into a product whose use value has to be detected: the artefact is determined historically.

Methodologically and technically, the proposition has recently had its effect (Rísquez et al., 1991) on the basis of a first methodological phase that established the types by articulating a cluster analysis and a factorial analysis, the first to establish the types from the similarity of their variables and the second to see their distribution in a graph. The sample itself was constructed from a single settlement (Puente Tablas) and with sherds.

Once the types had been established, their distribution set out in graphs and the typological dispersion checked by discriminant analysis, the stage was set for the second phase; for that, two different scales of work were defined, the first relating to the house as a unit and the second to the rooms (units) in a house. The contextual analysis model consisted in splitting up the factorial analysis graph into as many units as there were houses studied. The same process was followed for the rooms in each house. If, on one side, the number of elements is dangerously reduced, on the other, the comparison of the graphs one against the other allows significant differences to be distinguished between the spaces compared, and this, in association with other types of information (pollen, carpological, faunal, chemical analyses, etc.) helps to reconstruct areas of activity and to delineate the functional aspects of the types defined in the cluster analysis.

— 2 —

For now, just time

Over the years archaeological excavations have reached a level in the field of chronology that can be described as mature and allows us, through certain selected sequences, to assess the evolution of pottery production, looked at from the angle of what it tells us about chronology, so as to suggest a temporal model for the development of Iberian culture and attempt to extrapolate from it a historical pattern coupled with the rest of the archaeological and written documentation.

In order to develop this section we have divided the Iberian territory into different areas: Andalusia, Valencia–Murcia and Catalonia–Languedoc. This division into areas in no way corresponds to any historical or cultural criteria; they are based in principle on present-day administration, political development and, in the last resort, on academic debate in the universities. We make these comments at this point in the work because our purpose in the next chapter will be to assess the existence of cultural and political areas among the Iberians from a spatial factor; at that stage it will be possible to take a critical look at an Andalusian, Levantine or Franco-Catalan area in the strictly archaeological sense, so as to accept or reject it from a scientific standpoint.

Andalusia

The appearance of the first rectangular houses with stone foundations and mud brick walls is recorded in Torre de Doña Blanca (Puerto de Santa María, Cadiz) from the first half of the eighth century BC, coinciding with the existence of walls plastered with lime and floors or paving of red clay. It is to the same century that the appearance in Acinipo of what the investigator still calls prehistoric huts can be pinpointed and they show clear signs of the transition to forms of partitioned houses (Aguayo *et al.*, 1985; Aguayo *et al.*, 1986). If the process went ahead more rapidly in the Gaditanian area in a

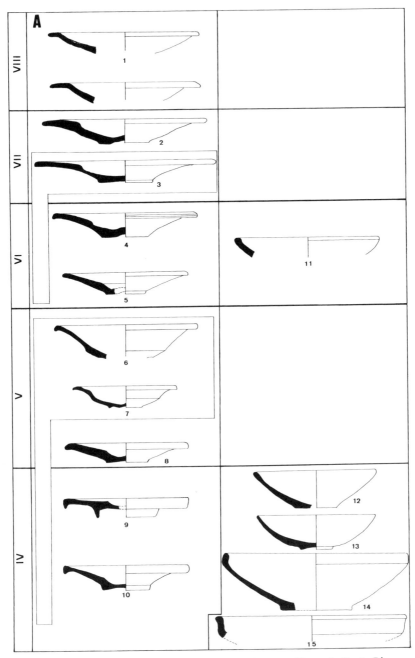

Figure 12 Typological development of pottery forms at Torre de Doña Blanca and at Puerto de Santa Maria. A. Open forms (dishes and bowls); B. Pithoi and urns; C. Dishes, mortars and pots (by the authors, based on Ruiz Mata, 1987)

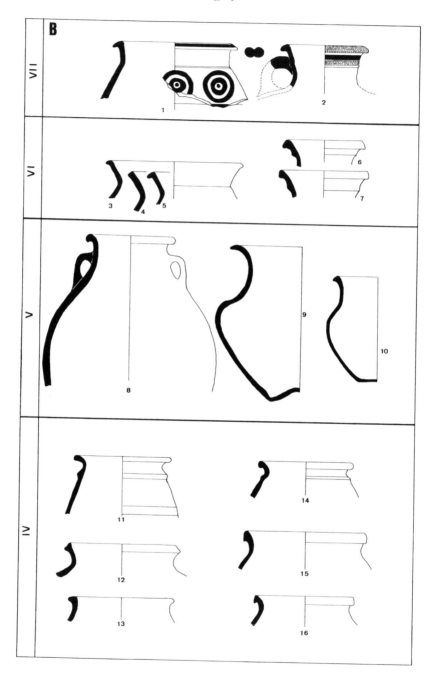

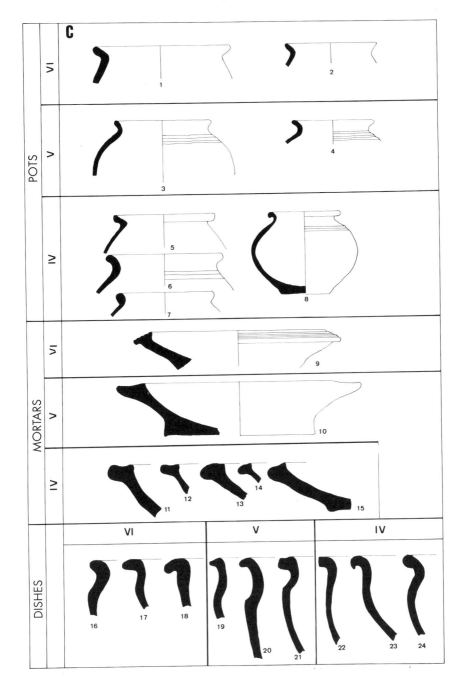

settlement so close to Gades, it may possibly be because this feature stemmed from that colonial world, while Acinipo might represent the indigenous scenario, constituting the other term of the new controversy.

If we look again at this model of the square or rectangular and partitioned house, we shall see how in the first half of the seventh or the end of the eighth century BC, it became generalised in sites such as Acinipo itself in Malaga, Cerro Macareno or Carmona in Seville, Colina de los Quemados in Cordoba, Alcores in Porcuna and Puente Tablas in Jaén, and Pinos Puente and Cerro de la Mora in Granada.

But it is not the only factor to imply a distancing of stratified archaeological materials from the prehistoric world of the Final Bronze Age; iron and wheel-made pottery come to join the new economic and social changes. The consolidation of wheel-made pottery does not involve just the presence of this type of production and the resulting cultural change, but represents a greater control of the family group by the community, or part of it, through the use of high-temperature kilns and the potter's wheel, exclusive to a professionalised sector with clearly defined technical skills.

In some of the sites mentioned, the presence of products with a Phoenician filiation occurs very early. In Torre de Doña Blanca (Ruiz Mata, 1986), whose location facing Cadiz and possible definition as Phoenician have been pointed out, Phoenician materials similar to other older ones documented in Morro de Mezquetilla and Chorreras are recorded; in one case (section 4) red-glazed plates with a 2cm rim, similar to those from Morro de Mezquetilla A/B1 from the first half of the eighth century BC have been identified; the same chronology crops up in Acinipo at a phase, as we have already stated, that is clearly prehistoric from all the material context studied, in which plates with narrow rims (1.7cm), characteristic of the level at Morro, are present and bag amphorae of an ancient typology. Again, Acinipo's situation with regard to the Phoenician trading posts must be looked at because of its ease of communication with the Bay of Cadiz across the river Guadalete or with the mouth of the river Guadarranque across that river itself. The third settlement that can be dated to this first phase from the material collected is Cerro de la Mora, where the researchers, from a plate with a 2.2cm rim, an *oenoche* and a chandelier with just one sconce, fix its inhabitants' first contacts to a time around the second quarter of the eighth century BC (Carrasco *et al.*, 1981), thanks to its good position with regard to the Malaga coastline and specifically to Morro de Mezquetilla itself. The same dates (775–750 BC) are given for the imports of red-glazed ware (plates with 1.3 to 1.5cm rims) and bag-type amphorae with a definite shoulder recorded in Pinos Puente, which is already in the *vega* of Granada (Molina González et al., 1981).

The case of Huelva must be included in these first native–colonist relations; there, thanks to the discovery of the San Pedro wall, in a technique known in Tyre, there is talk of a chronology around 800 BC; to this should be added a controversial Attic crater of the MG-II type (Rouillard, 1975; Shefton, 1982), which entirely lacks context and whose presence in that place is commonly attributed to the Phoenicians; also the recent finds of red-slip ware plates with rims of less than 3cm, like those already mentioned, with parallels in Morro de Mezquetilla and located in successive campaigns in the town centre (Fernández Jurado, 1984 and 1986). Taken together, all this helps to gain acceptance for the idea that these first imports, which all the researchers agree in dating between 800 and 750 BC, are articulated with a more or less sophisticated indigenous world, characteristic of the Final Bronze Age and which, in a case like that of Acinipo, comes to be mingled with Cogotas-type pottery.

A second level of contacts would occur during the second half of the eighth century BC, spread over a wider area. It can be followed well in the settlement below Carambolo, where the plate rims do not excede 3.5cm and red-slip bowls are found. As a whole, the group has its place at the end of the eighth century and, like much else, the beginning of the seventh century BC, coinciding with the Carmona assemblage, dated between 750 and 700, which contains the same elements as the previous settlement. These facts seem to open up the route of the river Guadalquivir towards its source, coinciding theoretically with the introduction of these products to the upper Guadalquivir from the *vega* of Granada. However, if the phase starting at the end of the eighth century BC shows very clearly the spread of these imports in the areas mentioned, they seem much more difficult to define in settlements like Colina de los Quemados or in Puente Tablas, near Jaén, where the red-glazed productions documented could be said to have spread from the indigenous area to other peripheral areas that were also indigenous.

The clear fact is that, at a date between the end of the eighth and the beginning of the seventh centuries BC, a complete change took place in the indigenous material culture. This is the time when, in Huelva, occupation of Cabezos de la Esperanza and the Cementerio Viejo came to an end; at the same time the generalisation of the partitioned square house is confirmed, reaching now as far as the upper Guadalquivir – Colina de los Quemados (Luzón and Ruiz Mata, 1973), Alcores (Arteaga and Blech, 1988) or Puente Tablas (Ruiz Rodríguez and Molinos, 1989); and, parallel with that, the creation of powerful fortifications would be recorded, such as those at Tejada in Huelva or Puente Tablas in Jaén, built on a slope using a dry-stone technique and resting on a very thick, upright facing-wall, the whole, as at Puente Tablas, with rectangular bulwarks-buttresses at intervals, using the same technique, and a complicated internal system of passages, marking a strong contrast with the previous prehistoric phase (Ruiz Rodríguez and Molinos, 1986; Fernández Jurado, 1987b).

If this can be deduced on the construction level, it becomes even clearer when the process of pottery production is followed, and specifically the gradual disappearance of handmade wares over the course of the seventh century BC.

In the system of periods elaborated by Fernando Molina for the south east (850–750) (cf. Molina González, 1978), he classified the indigenous wares of Final Bronze II into three groups: pottery with metal incrustations; pottery with burnished reticular decoration; and the Real-type pottery. The three indigenous productions were present before 750 in the south-east, being attested above all in the hut bottom at Cerro del Real in Galera and confirmed in Monachil. The non-existence of these products from the date when the Phoenicians reached the zone more frequently induced Molina to state that these productions did not last in the south-east beyond the middle of the eighth century BC. Against this, the finding of painted wares in strata 21 and 22 at Cerro Macareno caused Pellicer et al. (1988) to set up an opposing theory linking these productions to the very end of the seventh century BC on the grounds that these are late wares that were unable to compete with the new manufacturing techniques. So, if it is certain that this pottery was present in contexts of the wheel typical of the seventh century BC (Puente Tablas, Cástulo, Cerro Macareno), it is also certain that the finds at Granada occurred in contexts that were clearly eighth century with a material culture that is prehistoric; so the latest positions of Almagro Gorbea or Molina need to be evaluated; they claim a long period of two centuries for these productions, although with differences in form and decoration that still have to be determined in detail. The same might be said for analysis of the wares with burnished decoration.

If this is the pottery production that was beginning to decline, wheel-made wares increased considerably throughout the century. At Torre de Doña Blanca they amounted to 90 per cent of pottery production in the second half of the century; three groups can be distinguished, which became generalised in all the indigenous settlements (Ruiz Mata, 1986 and 1987).

Red-glazed ware

Plates with a rim of 4 to 5cm, pateras and chandeliers with two sconces make up the basic types of this group; in Acinipo, the same types are noted, with the addition of a greater variety of forms (bowls or carenated vases). At Pinos

Puente, too, we know that these productions were present and they have parallels in the horizon of the storehouse at Toscanos, with the wider-rimmed plates already mentioned, which, with rim measurements of 4.8 and 5.6cm, are documented at Cerro de la Mora. Fewer of these products are reported further into the interior, at Puente Tablas, for example, where, in phase III, only two very narrow-rimmed forms are recorded; these could be seen as parallels to the indigenous imitations already present in areas like Huelva.

Grey ware

There can be no doubt that its presence in Toscanos and appearance in a few settlements at the end of the eighth century BC, accompanied by red-slip ware, means we can speak of a clear horizon in which these productions were imported; this is the case in Acinipo, where the production reproduced the same open forms as the red-glazed ware. However, during the seventh century BC this pottery was developing its own forms, as occurred at Cerro Macareno with bowls with the rim thickened on the inside and even plates with an almond-shaped rim and marked carenation on the outside that were recognised from the sixth century BC in Cazalilla (Jaén). So the problem is to establish when these products came to be made locally on the wheel; in this we disagree with the opinion of Pellicer, who places them some time in the sixth century (Pellicer, 1982), and of Roos, who situates them at the beginning of the seventh or end of the eighth century in sites such as Alcores, Colina de los Quemados, or Pinos Puente, among others, including Cerro Macareno itself (Roos, 1982). One thing is certain, in sites such as Pinos Puente, Acinipo or the Campiña de Marmolejo (Jaén), local kilns have been found which suggest that these productions were being made locally before the sixth century BC.

Polychrome wares

If to begin with this production is of no more significance than the red-glazed or the grey wares, gradually, with its classic patterns in red and black, preferably in association with bands or fillets, or in other instances concentric circles or spirals intersected by a narrow band, or chequerboards, it would come to define the start of what would, in its time, be the great tradition of Iberian production. Unlike the previous groups, the polychrome types have already established their most classic forms, outstanding among them the Cruz del Negro urn and the *pithoi*, with the forked handles starting from the neck and running to the shoulder.

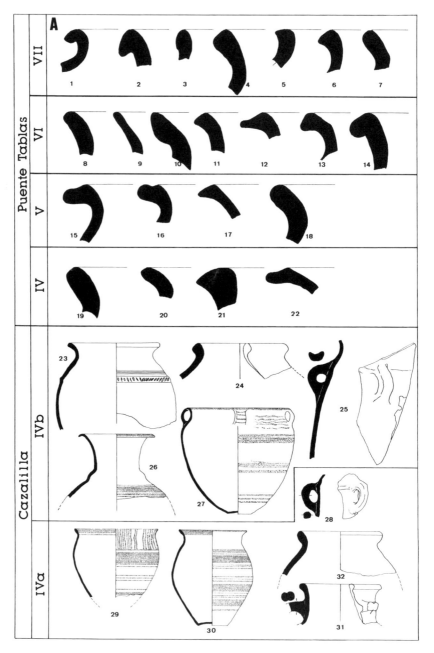

Figure 13 Typological development of pottery forms at the Plaza de Armas de Puente Tablas and Cerro de la Coronilla, at Cazalilla (Jaén).
A. Closed forms; B. Open forms (by the authors)

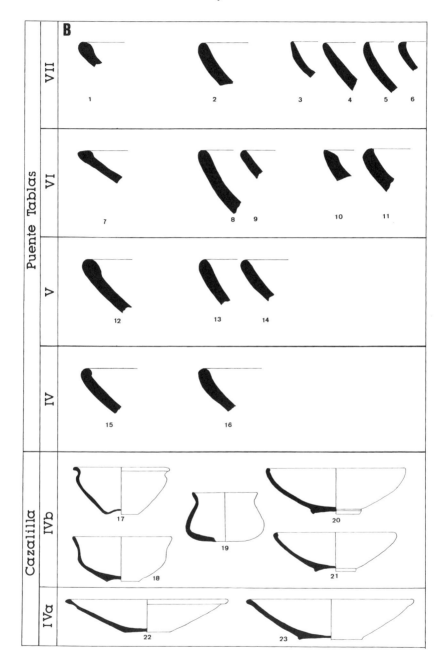

Within this context of wheel-made productions, the phytomorphic and zoomorphic decorations are especially significant; they are well documented in the area of the lower Guadalquivir, at sites such as Setefilla (Aubet et al., 1983), Montemolín (Chaves and Bandera, 1984) and in relatively remote areas such as Acinipo (Aguayo et al., 1985) or Aguilar de Cordoba (Remesal Rodríguez, 1975). Although in these cases a chronology has been given that places these productions firmly in the sixth century BC, it seems more appropriate nowadays to place their development during the phase under discussion (the seventh century BC).

Around 600 BC and up until 450 BC, according to Almagro Gorbea, who calls it late orientalising (1977), and Molina González, who defines it as early Iberian (1978), and between 575 and 450 BC, proto-Iberian or late Tartessian according to Pellicer (1980), lies a stage that undoubtedly, and despite discrepancies, implies a chronological unity, broken only because a few researchers prefer to set the end of the period somewhat earlier, between 550 and 500 BC for the Huelva region and, it must be assumed, for the lower Guadalquivir generally, in the light of a historical fact like the fall of Tartessos, and of archaeological information: the sudden cessation of imports of Phocean Greek wares into the Huelva region (Fernández Jurado, 1986).

Puente Tablas IV–V and Cazalilla IV–V enable us to assess significant restructurings that took place on the upper Guadalquivir. The clearest of these is the actual duration of the settlement of Cazalilla; its early phases correspond to a different period (Copper Age) and its end coincides with the start of a massive influx of red-figured Attic Greek products.

At Puente Tablas, the fortification of the settlement, although keeping the same structure and building technique, now underwent a restructuring: the system of internal passages of the earlier phase was eliminated, while the urban layout of the settlement was completely restructured internally, and the structure of a few streets that would develop from then until the end of the life of the settlement was established. Cazalilla is, by contrast, an example of a settlement that was small in size and clearly strategic in character; this can be seen from its position on high ground and its fortifications reinforced at the weakest point by a bastion-buttress. The settlement shows three different phases: the first two well stratified and the third largely eroded. In the pottery assemblage, no remnants of red-glazed ware are documented, whereas the other two groups of ceramics are well established and the handmade vessels disappear, leaving a type of coarse rough ware with incised corded decoration on the upper part of the body. Of the two groups mentioned, the grey ware reproduces open forms, sometimes taken from the Final Bronze Age tradition, like the plates, and at others develops forms already known, like the bowl with the lip thickened on the inside. The second group, with the polychrome ware, continues the motifs of the seventh century and the red and black polychrome. A degree of evolution is observable from the first phase, with large red bands outlined by black fillets, to the second with narrow bands and the same range of colours. Also to be seen are the circumferences crossed by a line and the very roughly sketched wavy lines of the earlier period. As for forms, in the group of closed vessels we find the Cruz del Negro form, the *pithoi* with double handles from the mouth, as well as strangulated cooking pots or ovoid vessels with a marked rim. Lastly, among the open shapes, bowls stand out as a characteristic feature, always with a thickened lip.

The final phase, which reveals a few basic new types like the lugged urn, coincides with other necropolis phases, like I–II at Puente del Obispo, where the 'thistle' vase appears, or the 'Toya'-type urn, the distribution of which was studied by Belén and Pereira (1985), defining an area that coincides with the eastern region of Andalusia. Levels IV–V at Cerro de la Mora also demonstrate this, with the Cruz del Negro type again, as does stratum VII at Llanete de los Moros in Cordoba (Martín de la Cruz, 1987). So much for settlements, while among the necropolises, Toya, Castellones de Ceal or La Guardia show this same phase.

In western Andalusia, still on the basis of Torre de Doña Blanca, where the difference from the indigenous model of settlement and material culture was becoming more and more diluted, Ruiz Mata stresses the continuity of earlier forms until the definitive creation of what the author calls 'Turdetanian types'. In this phase and in the middle of the sixth century BC, the author sets the appearance of the plates with a small central hollow, which are interpreted as having evolved from the early red-glazed wares and this is when, among the closed forms, necks develop or become flared; they are documented with the same shape in Cerro Macareno and Montoro. Lastly, we must stress the development of bowls with strangulated necks and cooking pots in this phase, coinciding in this respect with the sequence in San Isidoro and, generally, as to forms, with the types characteristic of the upper Guadalquivir. At this point Pellicer's amphorae forms B and C were beginning to appear frequently; according to the author, they were not imports but were already produced locally.

It is interesting to point out in the assemblage of this production that the broad lines observed in the earlier phase continue during this stage and also how, from the middle of the sixth century BC, and especially at the end of it, two large differentiated areas are beginning to emerge, which, *grosso modo*, have been defined as late Tartessian and Turdetanian, corresponding to Lower Andalusia up to a line marked by the rivers Guadajoz and Salado de Porcuna

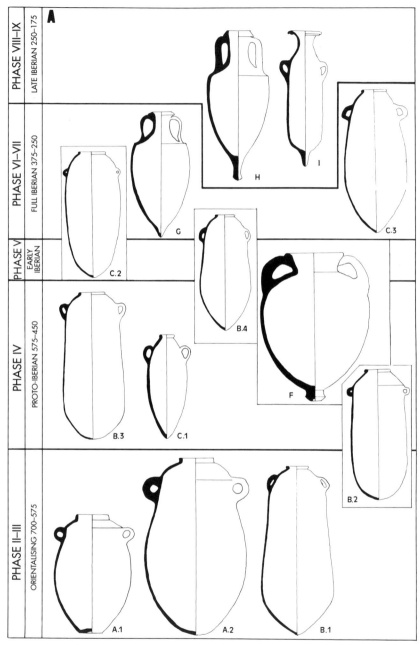

Figure 14 Typological development of pottery forms at Cerro Macareno (Seville). A. Amphorae; B. Vessels; C. Bowls (by the authors from Pellicer, 1982, and Pellicer *et al.*, 1988)

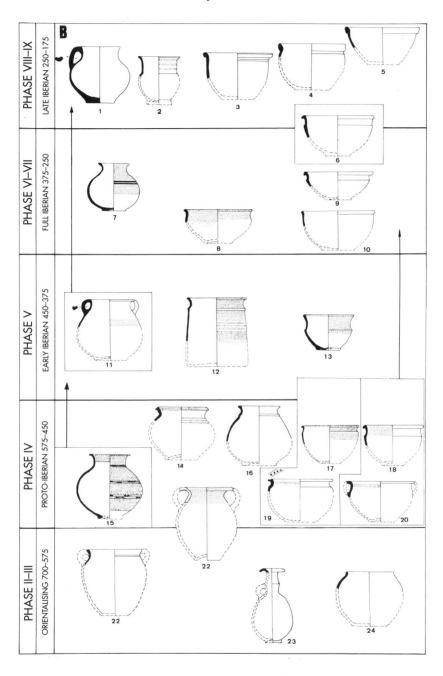

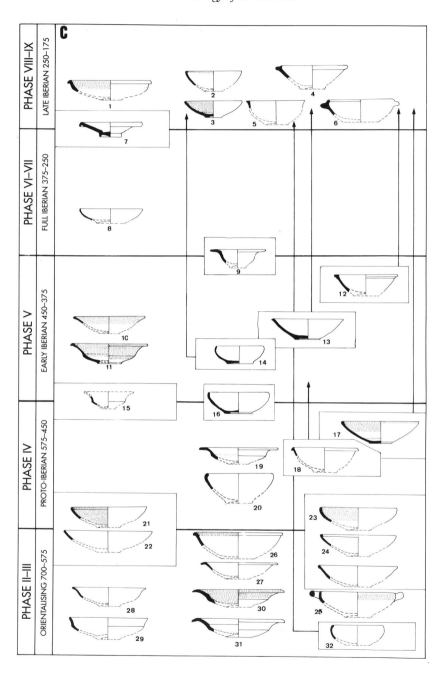

and, further east as early Iberian. This is still further accentuated by the distribution of the necropolises and their most significant types.

Elsewhere, the period began with big changes such as the disappearance of Pinos Puentes and the development of small settlements of the Cazalilla type, and it faded with the abandonment of other centres such as Setefilla, Montemolín (if we follow Escacena's [1987a] reading of the stratigraphy), Carambolo, Alhonoz, Ategua and Montoro, the last three with a big gap. These breaks in the sequence would have to be interpreted as the direct effect of a politico-economic change, in line with the Tartessian crisis already mentioned, but it is interesting to point out that, although this period shows for the first time marked effects of the Greek contacts, in the material culture these manifest themselves in a very different way; for if, in the eastern region, they seem assured in the style of the sculptural assemblage at Porcuna, the presence of other more common Greek elements is almost unknown and yet they are widespread in the Huelva zone. There, from the end of the seventh century BC, prestige objects like the rhodium bronze vases, the griffins adorning Samnian bronze cauldrons or the columned craters are recorded, especially as, from the year 580 and up until 540–530 BC, Phocean elements reveal, in addition to luxury pieces, more common pots like the first Attic imports, 'comasley' cups and *skiphos* or amphorae from Clitias. In Cerro Macareno it would be the Ionian B-2 cup and the Greco-Italic amphora, that marked the end of the period, but in this case the assemblage had nothing to do with the products from the Huelva region, which disappeared immediately before it. In strong contrast, the Huelvan products were frequent, as we shall see, in the Levantine area, where they marked the start of a new phase, which would unfold through the following period, and this may be the one that marks the first testings.

In general, all these elements constitute for the moment a very valuable assemblage for determining the chronological adjustments of this period. We shall return to them later on.

It would be the Greek products too (columned and bell-shaped craters, *skiphos*, etc.), but especially three items – the Cástulo cup, the San Valentín vase and the Pintor de Viena II 6 *kylix* – that would define the period between 450 and 350 BC, a period that in a few sequences could last until the end of the fourth century BC, as at Puente Tablas. According to Almagro Gorbea's proposition (1977), this phase must be deemed to last till 200, although in our opinion, and for reasons that will be analysed, that would prove too long and should be subdivided into two parts. Pellicer (1980) sees it that way, although with different specific dates, distinguishing a first phase, up to 375 and another from then until 250 BC.

The period we are analysing covers the three groups already mentioned with a few transformations, to which of course must be added the group of coarse or kitchen wares. But while the red-slip group now has nothing whatever to do, in treatment and type of slip, with the old Phoenician traditions, in the third of the three groups we can begin to distinguish two large areas: one bounded by the valley of the Guadalquivir and the other linked to the zone nearest the coast, that is to say, the provinces of Malaga, Granada and Almería. The first abandoned the polychrome type, although exceptionally it used white paint with the red, and in many cases blended particular shades of red to dark brown by way of violet, while the second kept to the decoration of black fillets mentioned in earlier phases. As to decorative themes, the pottery from the Guadalquivir valley would tend to confirm a process of enrichment of the motifs, which would eventually become standardised with a more geometric line, finer drawing and a more refined technique; in this way concentric circles, quadrants of circles or combs, and tresses or waves, very standardised, combined with the broad and narrow bands and fillets, constitute the dominant models.

To continue with the forms in this group, the disparities previously described between the two stretches of the Guadalquivir become more accentuated now and a series of types peculiar to the eastern area is defined, such as the imitations of columned or bell-shaped craters or, at a late stage around the third century BC, the big, heavily decorated barrel-shaped vessels, or the mass of *kalathos*, strangulated at first and later with the classic form of an inverted top hat; these are set against others in the western area, such as Pereira's type IB with handles starting from the rim on globular vessels or the small vessels with horizontal handles at the side, not to mention the huge flood of other items, such as plates with a small central hollow and a drooping lip. However, in general terms, we are aware of processes in common, such as the bevelling of the rims of open vessels and, in a few areas such as the eastern part of Jaén province, the considerable 'trill' in the rim of the closed vessels, hanging down and giving rise to a panel in which there was often stamped decoration, at a period that can be placed as early as the middle of the fourth century BC.

As for the grey ware, this period reveals the same tradition of light-coloured, open vessels, especially in the bowls, with a tendency to sharpen the rim.

More significant is the case of what Cuadrado defined as Iberian red-glazed ware; spread equally over both zones, at least as far as the plates are concerned, it had evolved from the ones known as Phoenician red-glazed ware, documented in places as far apart as Torre de Doña Blanca and Puente Tablas, but absent from Cerro Macareno, where the closed forms are most frequent.

The process followed by the bowls used as lamps, which appear at much the same time, is different; although the form is documented throughout the Andalusian sphere, the red-slip version seems to be centred mainly in the north-eastern territory of Andalusia and coincides with a great profusion of this type in La Mancha and Murcia.

In general, the Andalusian sequences reveal a conflict in the final stage of this period; so in Puente Tablas the sequence seems to break off at the end of the fourth century BC and this seems to happen in other settlements in the Campiña. When the place was occupied again throughout the third century BC, the concept of settlement and even the construction model of the fortifications would have varied. As happens in other areas of the Iberian world, and always with the Bell Beaker A-type fossil, the sequences reveal a period that can be followed only on a few sites with long sequences but, as we have seen, after an earlier gap, at Alhonoz or Puente Tablas, or possibly after a transfer of the population, as at Alcores de Porcuna, Itálica in Seville, Castellar in Jaén. The general picture is of continuity from the earlier groups, although appreciably modified; in fact, the slip tends to lose its traditional indigenous forms, while in the grey ware, at the same time as the open forms continue to develop, the first big closed vessels appear.

The process followed by the painted wares is undoubtedly significant, at least in the Guadalquivir valley, with the red monochrome, although the decoration becomes even more profuse and in one case begins to appear on the inside of the plates. This is also the time when the *kalathos* and big, decorated, barrel shapes develop. For this period we would single out Alhonoz II, which – we agree with Pereira – must be dated to well into the third century BC, Puente Tablas VIII, Cerro Macareno VIII or the Castellar sanctuary. From the comparison we get an overall view of how the plates with a small central hollow developed in Alhonoz and Cerro Macareno, as well as of the break in red-slip products, while towards the eastern part and especially around Cástulo we note the development of the decorated barrel shapes and the move towards 'trilled' rims with a drooping panel.

A second period is defined in Alcores de Porcuna, dated by Arteaga and Blech (1988) between the middle of the second and the first half of the first century BC, with late A and B Bell Beaker as well as Dressel 4 amphorae; or in Itálica, where we know the successive studies in Pajar de Artillo or the Casa de Venus (Pellicer *et al.*, 1982). The first sequence shows the continuity of the forms already mentioned, especially the appearance of the closed grey forms, while at the same time the tendency to sharpen the rim of the bowls is confirmed, lengthening it and generating a fine carenation on the outside, which ultimately forms a flange.

Itálica is undoubtedly the settlement that best defines this phase in the evolution of the Iberian material culture at present, despite the controversy concerning its origin and matching it to the historical sources, since it was founded by Scipio. The sequences from Pajar de Artillo, Casa de Venus and Cerro de los Palacios (Bendala, 1982) allow an evaluation of two different periods to be made: the first coinciding with the one we have established in Alhonoz and Puente Tablas VIII with Bell Beaker A wares, Ibero–Punic amphorae with the rim continued to the outside and thickened on the inside, and the characteristic bowls and chandeliers mentioned above; the second period (strata 4 and 5 at Cerro de los Palacios and stratum IV at Casa de Venus) is characterised by Bell Beaker wares A and B and Dressel amphorae IA and IC, and by the evolution of bowls that show thickening on both sides of the rim or, and to a lesser extent, the paterae that evolve towards flanged rims, while in the closed vessels the tendency develops for the rim to droop and turn inwards, although with less irregular edges than on the upper Guadalquivir.

The final stage that, in cultural terms, defines an Iberian pottery production, begins about 40–50 BC and includes all the first century AD. It is precisely from the end of this final phase that we know the evolution of the pottery forms, thanks to Choclán's study (1984) of the late-Iberian forms from the Horno de los Villares de Andújar. At the same time we can see how these are documented in those villa-type settlements that developed from the Flavian period on, recognisable in the Cástulo excavation (Blázquez *et al.*, 1985). Iberian production was undoubtedly entering a phase of decline in competition with fine wares such as Samian which was already being made in local kilns (Spanish Samian) (Sotomayor *et al.*, 1979; Sotomayor *et al.*, 1981), and both the surface treatment and the decoration become much cruder, despite an attempt to compensate with a return to the polychrome, chiefly by resorting to white mixed with red.

Valencia, Murcia and La Mancha

Research into stratigraphic phases has promoted the appearance of two opposing positions in the interpretation of the origins of the Iberians in the zone, in relation to the different substrate underlying the settlements.

In the first place, the selection, at an early stage in the research, of castellated settlements such as La Bastida de Mogente in Valencia or Puig d'Alcoi in Alicante provided a sequence that unrolled a stratum characteristic of the Valencian Bronze Age. This gave way to another, typical of the classic periods of the nascent Iberian material culture, in the opinion of the group of investigators at the SIP (Servicio de Investigaciones Prehistóricas) and the University of Valencia, who defend this position. This is how they expressed it in 1978: 'The Iberian civilisation did not involve a radical change in relation to the Bronze Age, either in the topographic situation of the settlements or in their structure' (Fletcher et al., 1976–8, p. 86).

The second position took shape from the excavation at Los Saladares by Arteaga and Serna (1975), but it was reinforced thanks especially to the successive digs and interpretations at Vinarraguell (Mesado and Arteaga, 1979), Penya Negra en Crevillente (González Prats, 1982) and the revision of Los Villares de Caudete (Mata Parreño, 1987). The approach of these authors rejected the first position by documenting sequences that paralleled the results obtained with the stratigraphies in Andalusia; besides, the settlements had a special topographic structure and were, of course, very different from the well-known castellated *oppida*.

Saladares started from an indigenous settlement documented between 850 and 750/725 BC. This same model is recorded at Penya Negra with differences in size, although, according to the author, with a chronology that would stay fixed between 850 and 700/625 BC. This Final Bronze Age that Arteaga linked with the Final Bronze Age in the south-east, but from which Urnfield influences, stronger in Vinarraguell and weaker in Penya Negra de Crevillente, are not ruled out (González Prats, 1985), would give place in phase IA3 at Saladares and from Penya Negra II, to the first wheel-made products, which would start as amphorae with a marked shoulder (Saladares IA3) and evolve in phases IB1 and IB2 (675–625/600 BC) to include *pithoi* with a double handle starting from the mouth (a typical piece of the polychrome group), grey wares, red-slip wares, tripod bowls and small flasks, as well as double-spring fibulae. González Prats and Pina have taken a very interesting step in determining the provenance of these pieces by carrying out an analysis of the fabrics, so as to determine the presence of the geological components and thus the provenance. In this way they have confirmed the existence of two groups, one imported and the other local; the first with great similarities to the Guadalhorce products, which suggests to the researchers that they came from Phoenician trading posts in the Malaga area; the second group, right from the first documentation of imports into Penya Negra, shows the presence of a pottery production similar in typology to the previous group, but local, which suggests to the researchers that from the very beginning, a group of Semitic craftsmen had settled on the site (González Prats and Pina, 1983).

Alongside this process, González Prats documents the existence in Penya Negra, during the Penya Negra I phase, of three structural models: hut bases, round houses and angular dwellings (González Prats,1985) underlying the appearance of the exclusively angular house models of the following phase. The process may have occurred somewhat earlier at Saladares, since we

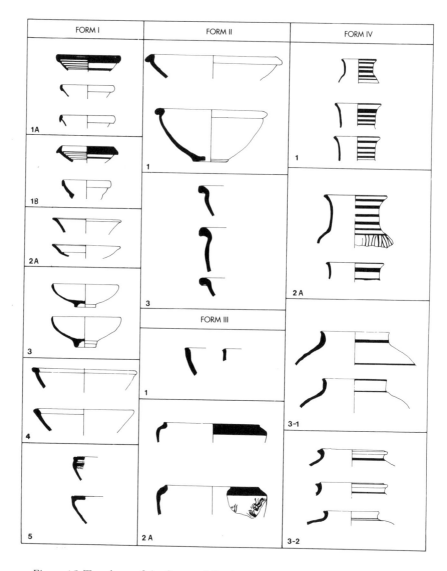

Figure 15 Typology of the forms of Iberian pottery at Los Villares de Andújar (Jaén) (by the authors, based on Choclán, 1984)

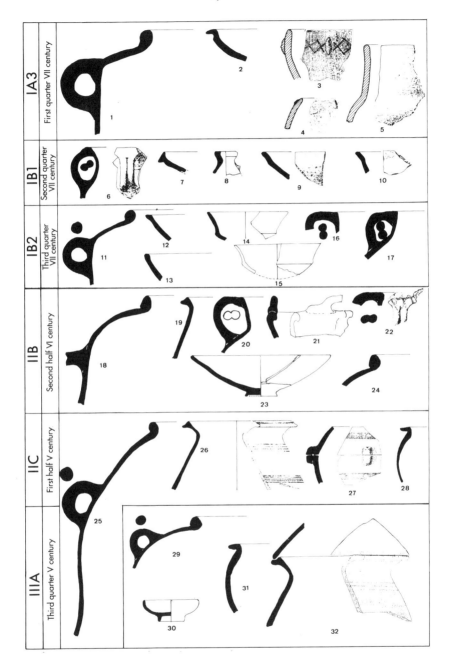

confirm that in phase IA3 buildings on a rectangular plan are documented, with mud brick walls on stone footings. Coincident with these changes, which we have observed in the same set of circumstances in the great Andalusian sequences, the settlement grew larger, spilling over on to terraces.

A bit to the north-east, the settlement of Los Villares de Caudete, which would be excavated from 1956 on by Pla (1962), reveals a first occupation level, which has been studied recently by Mata Parreño (1987), who defined it as Hallstattising in its material context, combining the angular house with mud brick walls on stone footings with an assemblage of products consisting of amphorae, *pithoi* and dishes within the group with polychrome decoration, grey ware, etc., dated to the first half of the seventh century BC.

This process is known in the sequences that have been excavated in the north of the zone – Puig de la Misericòrdia de Vinarós between units 219 and 216, Puig de Bencarló in its phase V (Gusi and Oliver, 1987), and Vinarraguell in phase III – since these settlements previously revealed a Hallstattian level, although much stronger than that documented in Penya Negra. At Vinarraguell, Mesado and Arteaga (1979) produced still further details on the subject, reporting the existence of a local Final Bronze Age with added Urnfield influences. In Puig de la Misericòrdia, too, these researchers noted the existence of a series of forms that could be attributed to a local Final Bronze Age. The subject is of great interest in that it reinforces the second position *vis-à-vis* the evolution of the full Bronze Age forms. Besides, it is from this substrate that the old castellated settlements have changed into settlements on hillsides with oval huts and, significantly, pottery, which, early in the eighth century BC, was subject to the Urnfield influence, at least in the sherds found, an influence that would also be noted in the angular structure of the houses and the adoption of cremation. It is this local later Bronze Age horizon, plus the Hallstattising factor of the Urnfields, that would, at a given moment, receive the first wheel-made productions, as documented at Los Villares de Caudete.

It is really difficult to accommodate the dual position proposed, given the different character attributed to the period opening with the Final Bronze Age, and which would develop well into the sixth century BC, starting from the intrusion of the wheel-made products. But, in fact, the indisputable presence of this sequence has forced a revision of the old hypothesis in two senses:

1 Aranegui minimises the role of these settlements, which she considers marginal, inasmuch as their sequences never achieve the splendour of the Iberian era, which, according to the author, would develop in the castellated settlements after the fifth century BC. Consequently, in her opinion,

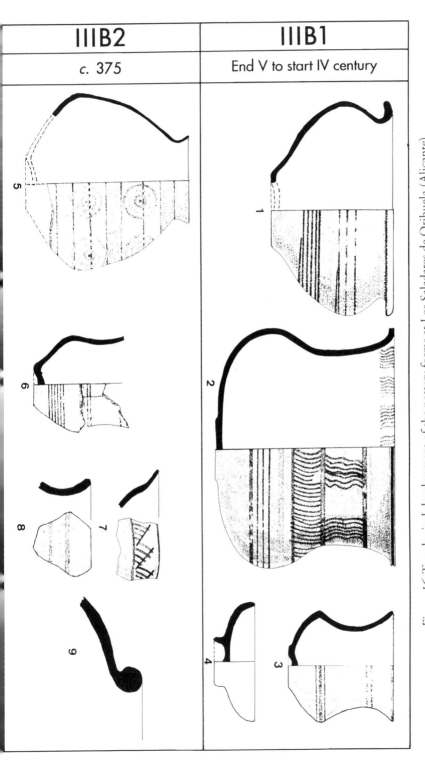

IIIB2	IIIB1
c. 375	End V to start IV century

Figure 16 Typological development of the pottery forms at Los Saladares de Orihuela (Alicante) (by the authors from Arteaga and Serna, 1975)

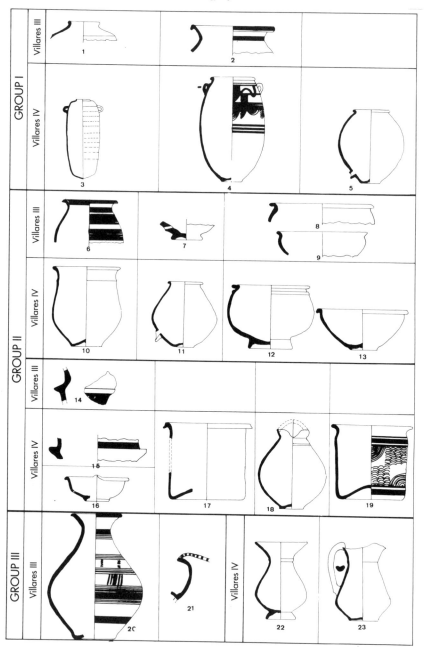

Figure 17 Typological development of the pottery forms at Los Villares de Caudete de la Fuente (Valencia). Phase III: 580–550/480–450; phase IV: 480–450/210–200 (by the authors from Mata Parreño, 1987)

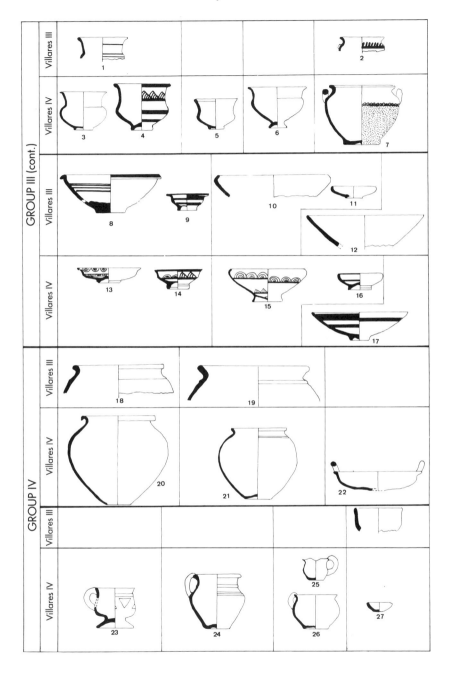

the Iberian horizon had to start from the moment when the Greek commercial factor began to impinge on the zone and a withdrawal occurred, not of the Phoenicians but of Tartessos, the nerve centre that fostered this development by creating settlements of the Saladares or Penya Negra type. For Aranegui, the revision of the old sequences in the upland settlements would in time give rise to the existence of a Valencian Final Bronze Age, leading directly to the Iberian culture without the existence of an orientalising period (Aranegui, 1985).

2 For her part, Gil Mascarell suggests that the problem lies in evaluating the nature of the process. For that, she first defines the Final Bronze I villages, located in upland settlements that would carry on the development of the Valencian Bronze Age, although with certain influences from the Urnfields and, in a few cases, from the Andalusian Final Bronze Age. These villages would eventually be abandoned, producng a break in occupation, which would be filled later by Iberian settlements of the classic period. Secondly, the Final Bronze II villages were characterised by their new topographic conception and they were inhabited from the outset by Final Bronze Age peoples strongly influenced by the culture in Andalusia at that time; this does not rule out the Urnfield influence at a later date. Both village units would coexist for a brief spell but it would be the second that would persist until Iberianisation (Gil Mascarell, 1985). For this author, the role of the Urnfields, with its uneven impact in different cases, is one of the basic factors of the process.

The issues raised, as González Prats rightly points out, leave unresolved methodological questions concerning the analysis of the stratigraphic discontinuities, which render the antiquity of the Urnfield materials open to question, and the continuity of the sequences in the upland villages through to Iberianisation, which cannot be demonstrated for lack of a factor like the actual archaeological context investigated. But there are still more questions: the minimalisation of the presence of elements from the Andalusian Final Bronze Age and of the subsequent connection with the Phoenician trading area, when defining the Iberian in that zone, implies an ideological problem that has traditionally had Valencia constantly on the defensive: the identification of the Iberian with the historical territory of Valencia, a problem that could degenerate into an ideological debate – which empirically, to quote the lowest theoretical level, is beginning to be demonstrated.

Another problem refers to the appearance of iron in the sequences studied, and two positions are starting to emerge. The first has it starting to be exploited at a point in the seventh century BC when contacts with Phoenician trade were in force; there can be no doubt about this, since one of the aims of those relations was this particular trade – witness the upgrading of the Angares route, which started by coupling the settlements of Vinarraguell and La Torrassa, and even the shift of population between the latter settlement and the one at La Punta (Oliver et al., 1984). The second position, on the other hand, couples the appearance of iron with the first angular houses, a result of the first contacts with the Urnfield culture, based on items like a fragment of iron from Vinarraguell II, which might have pre-dated the Phoenician contacts; but this is a problem we shall deal with in the case of Catalonia, where the Urnfields had a greater impact.

The horizon traditionally defined as early Iberian can be studied most directly and completely in two of the settlements mentioned. In Saladares throughout phase II, which has been subdivided into three periods – the first (IIa) between 625–600 and 575–550, the second (IIb) between that date and 525–500 and lastly IIc up until 450 BC – the sequence is reminiscent, with a few minor differences, of the one documented at Cazalilla (IVa, IVb and V). As the authors point out, from phase IIa onwards, there is a tendency in the decoration to develop narrow bands outlined with black fillets, which would gradually be imposed on the monochrome; as to the forms, after a first period, when there was continuity with the forms of the preceding stage, from phase IIb on, and especially in IIc, the classic early Iberian forms prevail, such as the biconical urn with the duck-head profile, the urn with perforated lugs and the big, wide-mouthed pots. In Los Villares in phase III, dated from the middle of the sixth century to a moment that might correspond to the second quarter of the fifth century BC, a similar tendency to the one described is observed with the predominance of wheel-thrown over handmade products, and the appearance of one of the defining elements of the new change that would take place in the zone: the Ionian B2 cup, a harbinger of the growing Greek influence.

In fact, as Aranegui states, the limits of the first Greek imports in the zone lie in the necropolises of Orleyl and Sagunto, which record materials from the sixth century BC. But it is at the end of the century that the importation of the Ionian B2 cup, the amphorae and the Attic cups type C becomes generalised (Aranegui, 1985), indicating a widening of the area of Greek influence, and this is reflected in the known sequences. So Penya Negra closed its phase II and, at the same time, the life of the village, some time between 550 and 530 BC. The new village barricaded itself in the settlement of Forat and in the lookout posts of Castellar and Cantal de la Campana, after an apparently violent end. In el Puig de la Misericórdia this period is hardly documented at all – by contrast, El Oral appears to spring up at this point (Abad, 1986 and 1987), yielding in its sequence an Attic cup with a low, black-glazed foot dated to the end of the sixth century and an archaic Greek *olpe* – although there is something of a revival starting at stratum 215, involving the development of the lugged urn and dated between the end of the sixth and the beginning of the fifth century BC. In Vinarraguell a break is recorded, which, as in the previous case, would be remedied in its phase V with the characteristics recorded at El Puig.

This change, which, in the case of pottery, went on reproducing the same forms as had been documented in Upper Andalusia, also opened up ways into the interior of the Peninsula. Thus we begin to document the first Iberian sequences in La Mancha.

This area, about which little is known so far, has been examined by Ruiz Zapatero (1978) in his study of the Urnfields and their influence in that zone. According to this author, around the eighth to seventh centuries BC, a disintegrating Cogotas I horizon received a few isolated Urnfield items, like the grooved ware, and he does not rule out the possibility that small infiltrations may have occurred, as in the case of Negralejo or Ecce Homo. Possibly the first effects of an already advanced phase of Iberianisation were being felt on this level; this is demonstrated by the earliest dating of Pozo Moro, proposed by Almagro Gorbea (1983b), to the end of the sixth or beginning of the fifth century, at all events before 480 BC; or the recent dates from Pedro Muñoz in Ciudad Real, established by a southern Italic *skiphos* from the middle of the fourth century, underneath, and the two-spring fibula on top, and an assemblage of material with duck-head vases, or bowls with the rim thickened on the inside, which the author dates from Saladares IIC (Fernández, 1988).

From the middle of the fifth century, coinciding with the establishment of monochrome decoration and the confirmed evolution of the population in the upland settlements, a new stage began, which Arteaga as well as Mata and Oliver identify as the start of the full Iberian, while others, like Abad, delay the start until 425. This stage is defined in Saladares by phase III, which was prolonged in three subphases until 300 BC. This is the period of the classic decorations, already recorded in Andalusia, in which the full Iberian forms are defined, or imitations of Greek products like *kylix, skiphos*, goblet or crater shapes, *pyxis*, etc. We see the same in Los Villares IV or the phase that developed from stratum 214 at Puig de la Misericòrdia, established by the Cástulo cup, where lugged wares or vessels with duck-head rims still persisted.

Another interesting item from the point of view of pottery production is the spread, from this phase on, of red-slip productions in Iberian forms, which, as they spread through the area, according to different studies (Cuadrado and Fernández Rodríguez), covered up to a northern limit along the river Júcar; on the other side of the river they are recorded only in San Miguel de

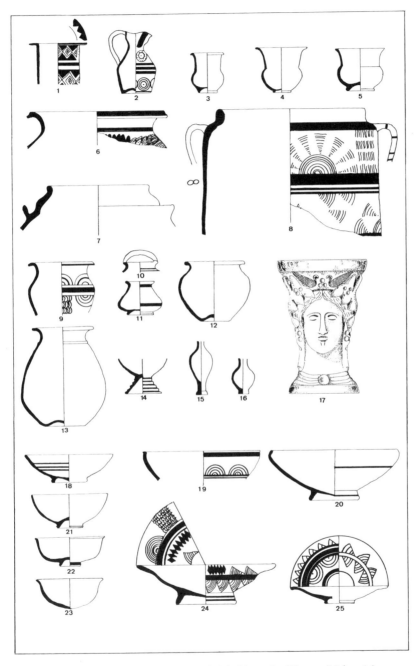

Figure 18 Pottery forms at el Puntal dels Llops, in Olocau (Valencia) (by the authors, from Bonet and Mata, 1981)

Liria and in the Ilergetan nucleus, a matter we shall return to later. It is interesting to point out that the Júcar, as has occasionally been suspected, seems to constitute a cultural boundary delineating what, in earlier phases, may have been the area of greatest Tartessico–Phoenician influence. It must be understood that this pottery group extended throughout the La Mancha area, as has been studied in Alarcos and verified at other points in the zone.

From archaeological evidence, Tarradell (1961) assigned the effects of the treaty of 348 BC between Rome and Carthage, delineating zones of influence and marking the destruction of a series of townships, such as La Bastida, El Puig, Covalta, or Lloma de Galvis, among others, to the end of the fourth century, or at least to its second half. Apart from the need to verify these facts, which have yet to be confirmed in other settlements and perhaps should be revised in some of those mentioned, what is certain is that the end of the fourth century reflects signs of crisis in Upper Andalusia as well, which are manifested in sites like Puente Tablas or Colina de los Quemados. All this coincides with a significant change in the evolution of pottery production as well as with the confirmation of new settlements that make their appearance in this phase; or at least, as the stratigraphy shows, reflect a major restructuring, since in cases like El Amarejo (Broncano and Blánquez, 1985), or el Puntal dels Llops (Bonet and Mata, 1981), the first in Albacete and the second in Olocau (Valencia), the level recorded is from the end of the third century with Bell Beaker A (Lamboglia's shapes 23, 27c, 28, 36a; Morel's 68 and 60c and Ricci's chandelier type D and E in Puntal dels Llops; Lamboglia's shapes 27b and c, 38a and b and 34 in El Amarejo). In both cases, however, Attic red figures of the fourth century are documented and, in the case of Albacete, small seals as well.

The appearance of these settlements with a late third-century level stimulates two lines of thought:

1 The presence of Bell Beaker wares at the bottom of the structures places them at the earliest point documented stratigraphically. This does not imply that the foundation of the structure containing them must necessarily date from the same time; it might be of an earlier date than that attributable to the productions of the small seals, so infrequent in the region. This means that, from the crisis of the late fourth century, a period dawned with an absence of Greek productions, which in many cases makes it very difficult to determine the date of the start of the settlements; not so the final stage, which, as already stated, is clearly delimited chronologically by the Bell Beaker A products from the end of that century and beginning of the next.

2 The same conclusion could be drawn from the presence of Attic red figured ware, which initiated the life of these structures from the middle of the fourth century. In this case the crisis that occurred fairly generally at the end of the fourth century should not be forgotten; it even meant abandonment in the odd case like Puente Tablas VII–VIII. Consequently, there are only two possibilities on a stratigraphic level: either the earlier strata have been swept away by the building system, in what might have been a restructuring process to level the ground – since a foundation would have left plenty of evidence – or else the material, reassessed in view of the absence of any Greek products, degenerated in two or three generations to the level of the third century BC, so giving rise to stratigraphic confusion.

Aside from these lines of thought, the cultural complexes of El Amarejo and Puntal dels Llops reveal significant changes from the earlier period, and although in their turn differences exist between them, such as the presence (El Amarejo) or absence (Puntal dels Llops) of red-slip ware, or the appearance of the Oliva-Liria style of decoration in Puntal or of white paint in El Amarejo, the enrichment of the decorative elements is common to both. Now wavy stems or T motifs (El Amarejo) are added to the semi-circles or bands, and a wider complex of pottery forms, like the barrel-shaped vessels, vases with double rims, with dentations or sinuous profiles, incense burners with a female head or ornithomorphous vases, to mention just a few extra items.

The presence of the Oliva-Liria style in Puntal justifies Bonet and Mata (1981) in revising the chronology of this group, based on analysis of the productions found at San Miguel; they conclude that these did not evolve during the second and first centuries BC only, as reported, but must have been produced between the third and early second centuries. All the same, recently, Pla himself again announced a chronology of the last two centuries BC for the development of this decorative style.

Another production of great interest is the grey ware; if in the previous phase it had shown a preference for developing open forms, as well as bottles and bitruncoconical vessels, in the phase that was unfolding from the third century on, chalice-shaped vessels were particularly striking, and especially the small carenated pitchers with a handle, which reach their full flowering from this point on. These little pitchers, absent from Andalusia, indicate the crossing of influences that becomes frequent in this area, though it should not be exaggerated, as can be seen from their absence from Puntal dels Llops and their presence in a few rare sites both in the Valencian (San Miguel de Liria) and Alicanten areas (Tossal de Manisses or La Caleta and La Serreta). The stage that starts with the abandonment of settlements such as Puntal

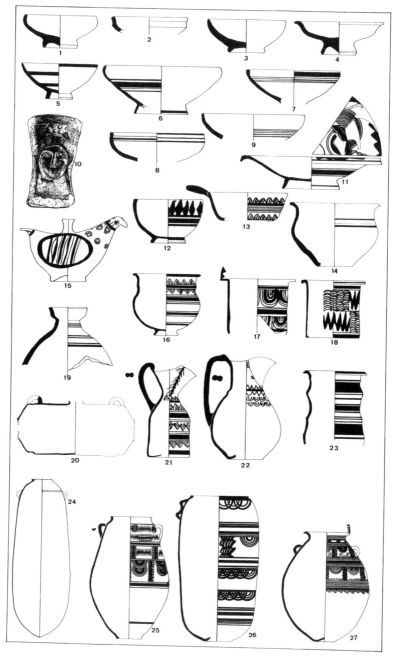

Figure 19 Pottery forms at El Amarejo, in Bonete (Albacete)
(by the authors from Broncano and Blánquez, 1985)

dels Llops, El Amarejo and La Escuera or, if we follow Mata and Bonet's revision, of San Miguel de Liria, that is to say, at a period early in the second century BC, as in other areas, is of little use at present for determining what went on archaeologically. The old excavations like Tossal de Manisses have hardly clarified what is distinctive about this phase, which gets lost in the development imposed by Rome; moreover, it is still early to assess the work of Ribera (1982) in Valencia or Aranegui in Sagunto (1988). Nevertheless, and to bring the sequential process in the region to a close, we shall consider some of the information provided by Ramos from the big site at La Alcudia de Elche, where in phases II (Ibero-Punic, late third to middle of the first century BC), III (Ibero-Roman, middle of the first century BC to middle of the first century AD) and IV (fully Roman), certain details of the process of evolution that occurred become clear (Ramos Fernández, 1984). Thus Ramos Fernández fixes the production of the Elche-Archena style in the first of these phases, noting how in phase III these motifs were lost, while others like the bands of esses, which previously were secondary, come to be basic, and there is a tendency to use stems and leaves schematically at the same time as modifications are observed in the treatment of the drawing, which is set off by lines scraped to reveal an undercoat of a different colour.

Some thoughts on Estremadura

In the west, in Estremadura, a long way away from the region we have just been considering, results of sequence analyses for the later phases are not impressive, but we should like to highlight the work of Rodríguez Díaz (1989) on Lower Estremadura, because he takes up the Medellín sequence again (Almagro Gorbea, 1977), which, from 450 on, presents difficulties in the clarification of the Iberian phases. This sequence would continue in Cancho Roano, dated by Maluquer de Motes from the late sixth century BC and ending around 370 BC (Maluquer de Motes, 1981 and 1983). Cancho Roano, because of its special functions, will not be treated here, but Medellín provides the first imports at a time that must coincide with the start of the seventh century (Medellín I), which produced the gradual replacement of the most characteristic Final Bronze Age items by genuinely orientalising ones and wheel-thrown pottery (Medellín II). Medellín III started around 600 with the development of a local orientalising culture, with the wheel fully dominant, grey ware becoming firmly established and imports of red-glazed ware. From the point of view of ceramics specifically, Almagro Gorbea has divided the wheel-made production into three groups, the first being Phoenician-type amphorae with an angled shoulder, manufactured locally and also imported;

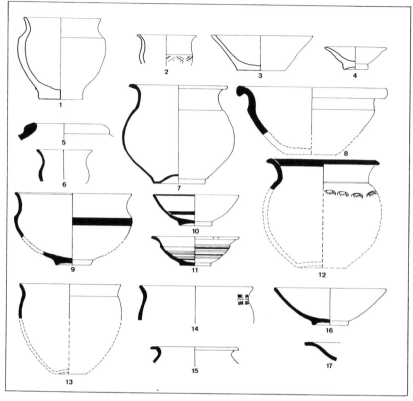

Figure 20 Pottery forms in Martela II, at Segura de León (Badajoz),
second half of the fourth century to the second century BC
(by the authors from Rodríguez Díaz, 1989)

the second, grey-ware productions that increase steadily from the lowest to the most recent phases, notably urns, which tend to increase, but without reaching high percentages. More significant is the production of open forms, with carenated forms predominating at first and being replaced from 600 on by bowls with a marked small rim on the inside. The final group, oxidised ware, shows the same tendency as the grey wares in the urns, and yet the opposite is true of the open products, compared with the grey ware.

Martela phase II has to some extent merged with Medellín IV or Iberian inasmuch as it has been dated (Rodríguez Díaz, 1989) from the second half of the fourth century to the second century BC. The researcher has divided the production into three groups: a first group of hand-thrown wares, which, with incised and impressed decorative motifs (seals), maintains a broad connection with the world of the *meseta*; oxidised wares follow with stamped and the classic geometric decoration found on the Guadalquivir and in La Mancha; lastly, grey wares, mingling open and closed vessels with stamped decorative motifs.

Catalonia, Aragon and Languedoc

In the past few years the importance of the Phoenician factor in the Iberianisation of Catalonia has been defined (Sanmartí *et al.*, 1978). Thus three cultural groups have been established, which impinged on the indigenous population throughout the seventh and sixth centuries BC. However, if the matter is beyond doubt in these three factors (Urnfield, Phoenician and Greek), today a controversy has been generated that is difficult to resolve outside the indigenous context, which must be the one that, in the final analysis, defines the historical process once the existence of colonising groups has been established. Pons sums up the positions in three trends, by making a link with the appearance of iron and determining who brought it (Pons, 1986).

The first trend she defines stresses the lack of stratigraphic continuity between the first iron products and the first productions of wheel-thrown pottery; this can be seen in the case of Lérida, where the Hallstatt typology is accompanied over a long period of two centuries by the presence of slag, meteorites and iron oxides. Since these are not manufactured products that would be particularly attractive to this society, it seems likely that it has followed the logical process of discovering and working iron. In fact, analysis of this topic has not, in our view, reached a very sophisticated level; we are referring to the historical contextualisation of the appearance of iron, which, being a process linked to the evolution of the seventh century, must undoubtedly have had a clear impact on the spatial structure of the society that obtained and worked it.

The second trend is represented by linking the appearance of iron with the first wheel-thrown products (and, logically, their contents, as in the case of the amphorae, that is to say, wine and oil). It is firmly established on the basis of the influence on research of the work at Saladares, Vinarraguell and Penya Negra. Little by little, the work of Sanmartí, Padró and Arteaga has documented the presence of these products in at least two centres, from the middle of the seventh century. They are located in the area of the mouth of the Ebro and the coast of Ampurias and Languedoc, where so far, and sadly devoid of context, at least one horizon of pottery container products has been determined, located in a first centre (the mouth of the Ebro) in the villages of

Coll Alt de Tivissa, Coll del Moro de Gandesa, Piuro del Barranc Fondo and Tossal Redó, among others, the important settlement of Aldovesta being outstanding; and a second centre in the Illa d'en Reixac and the Palaiapolis of Ampurias. There is also a second horizon of fine table-ware products that should be mentioned. Examples are the grey-ware flask from the necropolis of Mas Mussols, the globular vessels with bands of red glaze from Coll del Moro de Gandesa, or the tripod bowls like the one from Piuro del Barranc Fondo, as well as the four vases imitating Phoenician forms from Agullana or the five handmade ones, also Phoenician imitations, from the necropolis of Gran Bassin I (Mailhac). To these products the authors add the double-spring fibula or the Egyptian scarabs, also from the Phoenician trading centres. Altogether, there is a tendency for the pro-Phoenician argument to assert itself in recent years, although it must be acknowledged that the objectives that explain the contacts with the two centres never in any instance included setting up colonies nor even the transfer of a specialised artisan population, such as can be seen at Saladares or Crevillente. On the contrary, this system of contacts merely opened an access route for finished products or others of value, such as wine and olive oil, which appear to have reached only prominent sectors of the community; but in no case does it open up the process noted in other areas, leading to urban development and a swift modification of the productive structures of the settlements. Even in spite of this lack of impact at an early period, it seems clear that the pottery models, to cite one instance, would ultimately impose themselves and would be visible in the development of this production some time later.

The third route was proposed by Maluquer de Motes on the basis of recognition of the Phoenician products on the one hand and their supposed coupling with the historiographic sources on the other. Consequently, it was Samnians and Phoceans who were operating in the uncolonised zone of the Levant and in the areas of the Phoenician trading posts at a time immediately preceding the consolidation of their position in the zone with the founding of Massalia in 600 BC (Maluquer de Motes, 1986b).

The last two positions give a clear glimpse of the old Greco-Punic argument, based on the same recorded empirical elements, in a difficult dialectical game of identifying the bringers of the item being diffused, as in the case of the first position. Once again, an adequate historical contextualisation would bring us close to the historical fact but, of course, and this seems sufficient for the moment, evidence of the real Phoenician presence in the Levantine zone amply explains the impact those people had on the area, at least from the mouth of the Ebro (Mascort *et al.*, 1988) and possibly from the gulf of Rosas, in their quest for alternative routes to avoid what was already, at the end of the seventh century BC, a conflict between Tartessians and Phoenicians, making it difficult for the latter to control and monopolise the tin trade. On the other hand, and the question arises immediately, it is surprising that in the whole period, which covers almost half a century if we consider the date provided by the few stratigraphies obtained, no products have been recorded linked with traditional Phocean trade, like those confirmed in recent years in the Huelva area. Lastly, if it had been the Phoceans who had opened up these routes, that would not explain the hiatus corroborated in the Castellón area and in some settlements, such as Vinarraguell, from 550 on, the date when Massalian operations became more effective in the zone.

Around 550 BC consolidation of these first contacts with the indigenous world took place after a brief period in which the Phoenician withdrawal and the reported Massalian impact appear to have occurred. On the basis of three sequences at two different points we can substantiate these facts:

1 Pech Maho, in the valley of the river Aude, not far from the coast, has its beginnings confirmed (Pech Maho IA) at a little before 550/540 by the presence of a 'buccero negro' pitcher and an Ionian B-2 cup, but still mixed with Phoenician products. But from that date (Pech Maho IB) and up until the end of the sixth century or beginning of the fifth (around 480), this phase shows the development of Phoenician prototypes (painted wares) and exclusively Greek imports like the Cassel cup. The whole phase reproduces a prehistoric habitat system with round huts (Solier, 1976–8).

2 In its phase Ia, between 600 and 575, Illa d'en Reixach reveals Phoenician amphorae; in phase Ib, between 575 and 550–540, the Ionian B2 cup and imported grey ware appear and, not far off, el Puig de Sant Andreu, which forms part of the same settlement unit, yields Etruscan and Ionian imports. The phase is characterised by round houses but, at the start of the following stage (IIIa, II), dated between 550–540 and 500 BC came the change to the rectangular house with stone footings and mud brick, and the use of the potter's wheel; and now black-figured Attic ceramics, datable to between 540 and 535, must be added to the earlier imports, as well as a Massaliot amphora and western grey and pseudo-Ionian wares (Martín, 1987).

3 La Penya de Moro de Sant Just Desvern is located in an area that has not so far shown the first effects of a Phoenician presence. Its siting is critical for access to the interior of Catalonia and the coastal depression and it is situated on an exceptional coastal enclave. Around 550, in a phase stretching to 500, a rapid concentration of population took place through a

development that must certainly have culminated in the colonial system we noted in earlier sequences. The phase is dated by black-figured *kylix* from the workshop of the minor masters, an Ionian B-3 cup and an Etrusco-Corinthian cup (Barberà and Sanmartí, 1982).

As far as pottery production is concerned, the overall assessments of Sant Just Desvern are interesting inasmuch as the predominant group is the unpainted Iberian ware, always coming after the handmade productions, while painted and grey wares are clearly documented; underneath lay the group of amphorae, the provenance of most of which is difficult to determine, with the exception of one Phoenician fragment, another that is Greco-Punic and a third Massaliot. In addition, amongst the wheel-thrown painted ware, duck-head borders and lugs are documented and in the decoration, narrow bands predominate and bichrome work is recorded. In the group of grey wares, closed vessels and cooking pots with an external lip are reported.

In Illa d'en Reixac too, hand-produced wares predominate, repeating the elements found in Sant Just Desvern. But it is interesting to note the existence of red-black bichrome wares with chequerboard and dog tooth being the most significant motifs. The grey-ware group has the same forms as the light-painted wares, once they begin to be manufactured locally. Lastly, Pech Maho shows the same groups again but the Indiketan bichrome items of Ullastret are missing.

Towards the interior, around Lérida – in what would become the Ilergetan area – the site at Vilars de Arbeca (Garcés and Junyent, 1988) reveals a broad sequence, in the first phase of which, dated between the second half of the seventh and the start of the sixth century BC, attention must be drawn to a stratigraphic context of Urnfield pottery. By contrast, in Vilars II, with a chronology betweem 550/525 and 425/400 BC, we find, alongside the development of the handmade production, a wheel-thrown assemblage with a painted group and another grey group, which, because of the length of this phase, is linked to the development of Ampuritanian production, Ampurias having now, since the economic decline of Massalia around 500 BC and for the first time since its foundation, seized the economic reins in the area, as an 'independent polis'. From now on the consequences begin to be seen, not only in the revitalisation of a few remote centres, which from this time on receive Greek products, but also in the hinterland itself, in the dearth of our information concerning the zone, in the disappearance after a while of Illa d'en Reixac and in the modification of Pech Maho (IIa), which moves towards a more definitely urban model with houses with Hellenic foundations, and a re-modelling of the defensive system.

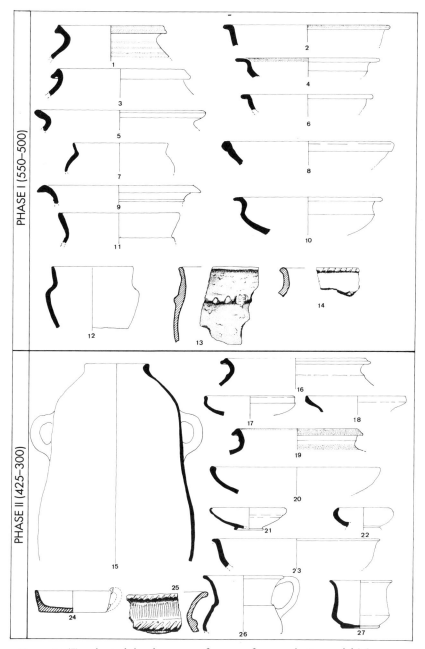

Figure 21 Typological development of pottery forms at la Penya del Moro,
in Sant Just Desvern (Barcelona)
(by the authors from Barberà and Sanmartí, 1982)

It is within this dynamic of promoting the economy of the Ampurias area that the following stage (450–300) must be evaluated; it covers a good part of the full Iberian period, with the definitive development of Puig de Sant Andreu and the recovery of Sant Just Desvern, now accurately dated by red-figured and black-glazed Greek productions. In both settlements important transformations can be observed, such as the building of the second rampart at Ullastret (Puig de Sant Andreu) in 375 or in the field of ceramics, from the middle of the fifth and especially in the fourth century, the establishment of local pottery production with white paint and the appearance of geometric and plant motifs imitating Attic themes. In the second of the sites mentioned, appreciable changes occur in the structure of the settlement, and in the pottery, painting diminishes and a vigorous handmade production still develops.

However, this strand can be followed in the demographic evolution of all the areas, not just on the coast but in the interior as well, as Tornabous shows (Maluquer, 1986a), and on the Greek side, where it involves the strengthening of the second Rhode colony, which yields its first archaeological data in the middle of the fifth century, but attains its maximum development a century later, perhaps as a result of interest in the region on the part of Massalia. It must be evaluated on the archaeological plane by checking the dual circuit created in the Indiketan area, on the one hand by Ampuritanian and Iberian white-painted products and on the other by the productions of Greek imitations from Rhode (Martín, 1987). The end of this stage is marked by the culmination of a crisis in Pech Maho with a destruction equal to what happened in Mailhac in Languedoc or in Sant Just Desvern.

Around 250, as happened in other areas, a new phase is observed with the appearance of new settlements. From north to south Puig Castellet, located near Lloret de Mar to the south of Emporion and Ullastret, must be cited as the type case (Pons, Toledo and Llorens, 1981); it was founded around 250–240 and ended between 220 and 210 BC, judging by the presence of black-glazed pottery from the western workshop of the 'pátera of three palmettas'. Its researchers have subdivided the pottery production into four groups: the first made up of amphorae (Maña C1, D and E and the 'Catalan coastal' type); Iberian ware with mortars, tankards and *kalathos*; Ampuritanian pottery with the classic handled mugs and paterae with inturned rims; and, lastly, a mighty handmade production with forms following the indigenous tradition or imitating light-coloured forms. This is the dominant group, while the Iberian outnumbers the Ampuritanian grey.

A little more to the south, in the estuary of the Llobregat, the Mas Boscà site in its level III shows a context of abandonment with the characteristics we

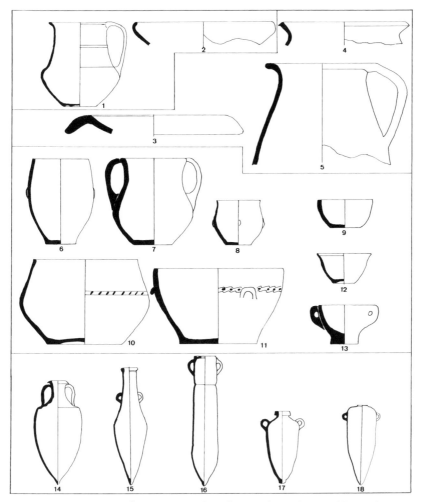

Figure 22 Pottery forms at Puig Castellet, in Lloret de Mar (Gerona) (by the authors from Pons *et al.*, 1981)

reported for Puig Castellet; it is dated between 222 and 187 by Bell Beaker A (Lamboglia's shapes 21, 24, 27 and 28) a Hellenic chandelier, etc. The only feature not present on the previous site is the minimal presence of white paint of the Ullastret type (Junyent and Baldellou, 1972).

Towards the interior, the site at Margalef (Junyent, 1972), in the commune of Les Garrigues, brings together some of the elements mentioned in the earlier sequences, since, although we note the great importance of handmade

87

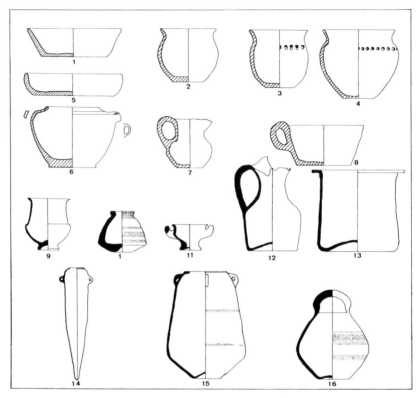

Figure 23 Pottery forms at Margalef in Torregrossa (Lérida)
(by the authors from Junyent, 1972)

production and the classic types of Ampuritanian grey production are present, the weight of the Iberian painted production is greater than at other sites, with an assemblage of richer motifs (twisting stems, ivy leaves, fan-shaped pal-mettas, circles crossed with a red infill, etc.) all this associated with the *kalathos*. Similarly, the Ilergetan red-glazed production and grey ware with seals appear, connecting this area with the lower Ebro and the northern part of Valencia (Junyent, 1974).

This assemblage of sequences was suddenly interrupted by the dominating presence of Rome, which, as was frequently the case, caused an abrupt decrease in information. As a final example, the case of Arguilera de Castelldefels will suffice; although it yields imports from the fourth century BC, a horizon has been isolated during investigation, dated to the last third of the second and beginning of the first century BC by Bell Beaker B, late A, a Dressel-Lamboglia

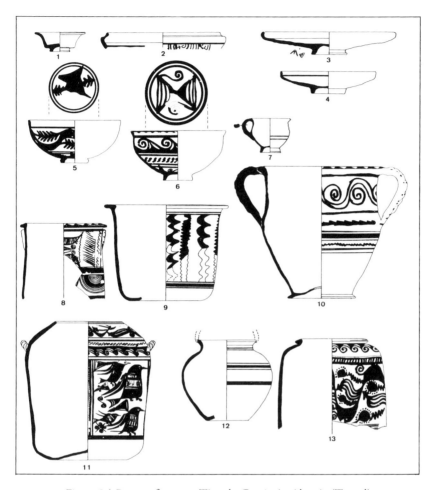

Figure 24 Pottery forms at Tiro de Cañón in Alcañiz (Teruel)
(by the authors from Perales *et al.*, 1983)

1B amphora and fine-walled wares of Mayet's forms II and IIA among other items. We can see here the drastic reduction in handmade pottery and the increase in Iberian productions, in which the *kalathos* and the patera with inturned lip are dominant; for the rest, we would merely point out that grey-ware production was maintained in significant proportions of 5 per cent with paterae and small bitruncoconical beakers (Sanmartí *et al.*, 1984).

Towards the interior, in Aragon, the analysis of Tiro de Cañón (Perales *et al.*, 1983), located on a flat-topped hill in the Alcañiz district in the region of

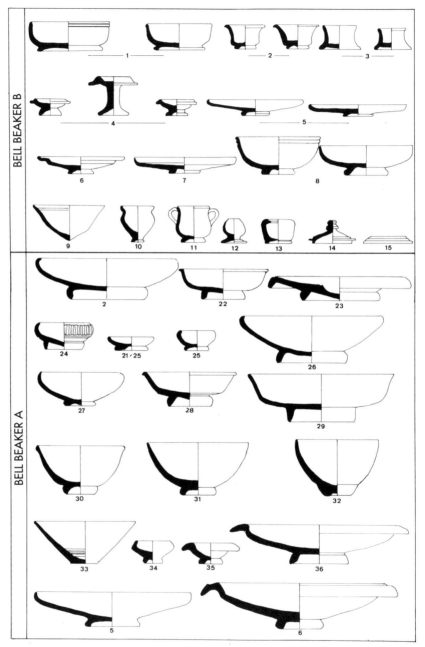

Figure 25 Typology of Bell beaker pottery forms (from Trías de Arribas, 1967)

90

Guadalope, is very useful for an understanding of this phase. The phase documented there dates a level with Bell Beaker A and B, fine-walled wares (Mayet's form III) and Dressel amphora I, which gives a chronology from the second to the first century BC. The indigenous production fits in well with that recognised and studied at Azaila (Beltrán, 1976), with imitations of Bell Beaker forms, pitchers, cylindrical beakers and the inevitable *kalathos*, all associated with geometric, plant and bird decoration that has parallels in Azaila and Alcorisa, that is to say, in the region of the lower Ebro.

Pottery time

Through stratigraphic investigation we have followed the process that leads ceramics from the first wheel-thrown productions up to their surrender to the classic Roman productions of Hispanic *sigillata*. Throughout this analytical process we have been made aware that other processes were being generated in parallel with the typological development of these productions (building systems such as the appearance of the square or rectangular partitioned house with mud brick walls, the appearance of iron or the change in population due to the development or disappearance of some of the settlements). But we shall have been aware all through the description of how a 'long time' has been gradually being broken down into different stages.

Traditionally, in attributing these phases, use has been made of the magic number three, the classic system in prehistory ever since Thompsen's classification using the model of the three ages. Thus the Iberian culture has been incorporated into the old biological scheme whereby a culture has a formative stage (early), a time of maximum development (full) and a stage of decadence and degeneration (late). So it will not have seemed strange if, following this tradition, we have spoken of early, full and late Iberian. On the other hand, stratigraphic results have been incorporated into this scheme; furthermore, as it was done on the basis of diffusionism, the scheme has been constructed on the presence of imported material, creating a state of affairs in which the horizon that would corner the largest quantity of red-figured Greek products had become the 'full' horizon, while decadence set in from the third century BC, coinciding with the sharp fall in imports, in an inevitable process of cultural degeneration. The presence of these foreign products is undoubtedly of fundamental value in establishing the periods, firstly because of their great chronological value, and then because it locks them into a framework of Mediterranean interrelationships, which undoubtedly plays an important role in the history of the Iberians. But the analysis requires a preliminary methodological stocktaking.

1 As Pierre Vilar would conclude from a re-reading of Braudel, historical time has ceased to be conceived of as a single line, still less is it a biological or cyclical concept, as beloved of Spencer or Toynbee (Vilar, 1974). Any analysis must be able to articulate different and occasionally conflicting times into the study of a historical process, not in the limited sense of 'long time' or 'short time', as Braudel would say, but in the framework of the object–subject it claims to evaluate.

Thus there is a global time that must be borne in mind when analysing Iberian society and culture, which overrides their chronological limits and pertains to the historical process defining a social and economic model. This transitional process contains a time that unites the different histories of Egypt, Greece and other societies, even some that come later in lineal time, such as the Aztecs. On the other hand, on a more limited level, we must conceive of a time for each social formation, from a socio-political point of view. In this way the history of Ancient Rome has its time, but because in a previous step its specific character as a social formation had been defined.

In our case, the need to couple together these two different times for a single process is obvious: on the one hand, the time that produced the disappearance of the kinship models and gave rise to the formation and consolidation of aristocracies; and on the other, the specific time when Iberian society was being formed, a time that in turn requires prior definition of the ethnic or political character of the temporal space we are defining as Iberian. But, furthermore, since it is not always possible to make a historical distinction between ethnic and social formations, one may speak on this level of two different times: one cultural and the other historico-political.

2 Archaeological information, as we have seen, is presented to us without this prior critique, because, at a particular moment, and for lack of other data, an empirically attested fact like pottery production may ultimately constitute the only time valid in the instance studied. It might be alleged that the addition of other material elements further enriches the established period system, but, though it is true that it may delineate more clearly certain points in time that are difficult to allocate, that still does not imply a qualitative leap in the theoretical framework produced by this way of working.

On the other hand, the poor definition of Iberian culture, demonstrated all through this process, contributes still further to the difficulty of establishing a historico-cultural time and, in the long run, makes it impossible to lead to an evaluation of the historico-political time that would enable us to follow the specific nature of the different social formations of which the sources tell us.

For all these reasons, the necessary introduction of space, or rather of different spaces, is the essential prior basis for defining the system of times we claim to elaborate; only thus is that global time explained that can produce processes tending towards the same end in Greece, Egypt, China or the Aztec world, and only thus do the times and information provided by the Iberian ceramics and fibulae make sense, so as to succeed in generating a system of cultural periods that can avoid certain subjective weightings that are inevitable at times, owing to the very dynamic generated by positivism.

That is why the archaeological object contains a lineal and descriptive time, but the products that go on to form part of the level of development of the productive forces of a social formation rely on a historical time. We have a clear example of these latter models of analysis in Junyent's study (1974) of Ilergetan red-glazed ware productions, in which he couples them with the written historical sources reporting the presence of Indíbil in Cartago Nova and his liberation by Scipio. Another model, which this time does not count on written historical sources, is that of González Prats and Pina (1983) on the analysis of clays of the orientalising wares at Penya Negra and their theory that artisans coming from the south of the Peninsula brought these first wheel-thrown pottery types to those lands. In both cases, the temporal, formal and descriptive pattern has been transcended by coupling the models with factors that surpass the actual archaeological object.

Notwithstanding these problems, and since pottery was the key incentive of the stratigraphic phase, we shall look at the particular process of its development and classification into periods. We note firstly the general tendency for the common launch of the first wheel-thrown types to start from Phoenician prototypes. Secondly, we have to evaluate how, from the start of the Phoenician withdrawal and especially from the moment when the scope of Ampuritanian activity took off, a tendency arose towards diversification of types by areas; this is particularly evident in the evolution of certain groups like the Ampuritanian grey ware. We must also consider how, in the same phase, the red-glazed group became firmly established in a different area (the south and south-east), without reaching the zone where the Ampuritanian influence was greatest. This tendency increased considerably from the fourth century BC on and particularly in the third century BC, when, within the two large areas created, decorative styles and particular forms were produced, which created new zones. Thirdly, we must be aware that, during the whole period, a series of type forms, such as the lugged urn, the 'thistle' vessel, the vessels with a duck-head rim or in the later stages the bowls used as lamps and the *kalathos*, were present throughout the area, generating an expansion range that coincides in general terms with the whole of the area designated as Iberian.

Consequently, in order to establish a structured system in stages of pottery time, we shall have to speak of:

Iberian I (600/580–540/530 BC)

Characterised by typological uniformity throughout the area (tripod vessels, vessels with triple handles running from the mouth to the shoulder, red-glazed forms and Phoenician amphorae), clearly linking the period with the tradition of the Phoenician world.

Naturally, the indigenous substrate was present in the continuity of the handmade productions, and the greater incidence of these types in one area or another shows clearly that fine distinctions existed between areas, witness the difference of the Andalusian Final Bronze/Urnfield substrate or the greater proximity to Phoenician nuclei.

This first stage, with a host of fine distinctions, might comprise a period ending around 540/530, which would have started, depending on the consolidation of wheel-made production in each area, around 600/580 in Andalusia, 575/550 in the region to the south of Valencia or, even though not well documented, in the interior of Catalonia. These are the times called proto-Iberian or early Iberian (Pellicer), late orientalising (Almagro and González Prats) late Tartessian (Fernández Jurado) or early Iberian (Arteaga, Ruiz, etc.).

Iberian II (540/530–450/425 BC)

This phase is characterised by the establishment of new Iberian prototypes, at times clearly linked to the previous stage (lugged urns, 'thistle' vessels, evolved Cruz del Negro urns, bowls with rims thickened on the inside, vessels with duck-head rims and, of course, polychrome wares). As to imports, defining fossils for the period are the Ionian B-2 cup and the Attic cup, type C, implying a time of Greek pressure, exercised first from Massalia and then later from Emporion, although the latter is coupled with the old roots of the Phoenician protoypes already mentioned. Its beginnings coincide with the end of Tartessos and the increase in the economic importance of Emporion, while the end is marked by the red-figured Attic wares; hence the chronological variations depending on the finds: 450–425 BC in general and even for some authors 475, which implies the end of the Ionian B-2 cup (Mata).

Iberian III (450/425–350/300 BC)

This period implies the first well-defined diversification of the pottery groups, which are no longer present in every area; so we find white paint in the Indiketan area, Ampuritanian grey in the Catalan–Valencian area or Iberian red-glazed ware in Andalusia, Murcia, south of Valencia and in La Mancha. The polychrome generally disappears, although in certain areas such as the coast of Andalusia and the Serranía de Ronda it is preserved; the same thing seems to happen with the commoner types of the earlier phase, of which some, like the lugged urns, while disappearing completely from the upper Guadalquivir, would still persist among the groups in the north.

The phase coincides with the climax of the Attic red-figured wares; hence the complications when it comes to deciding when it began; for some authors, this occurred around 450, while others place it around 425 with the horizon of the Cástulo cups at first and of the Pintor de Viena 116 *kylix* later.

The end of the stage poses still more problems, since the sudden break, around 350–325 in imports of Greek wares leaves open a period until the end of the third century, for which very little is known about the pottery typography, although the break cited in many stratigraphies at the end of the fourth century would incline us to end the stage around 300. The period corresponds to that known as early Iberian (Aranegui) or full Iberian (Pellicer).

Iberian IV (350/300–175/150 BC)

Very little is known in general about the way pottery evolved in this period, except in the final years of the third century, its start having been fixed by Greek productions from the western colonies and its end by Bell Beaker A.

Pottery diversification now attains its maximum extent with the appearance of the Liria styles and the phytomorphic decorations of Elche and Ullastret; there is a spurt in production of red-glazed ware in the Ilergetan area and of the group of stamped wares. This is also the period when the development of the *kalathos* began, or the ornithomorphic vessels in the Albacete–Valencia area, or the closed shapes in Andalusian grey wares.

The period has a clear end before the appearance of Bell Beaker B and is connected historically with the Roman administrative restructurings at the end of the Second Punic War.

Traditionally for some authors it is linked to the full horizon (Arteaga, Pellicer, Ruiz Mata), while for others it is already late Iberian.

Iberian V (175/150 –60 AD)

This new stage is, of course, clearly linked to the Roman productions that reached the zone (Bell Beaker late A and B, fine-walled wares, Aretine, Italic or sudGallic *sigillata*, etc.), although there is a general dearth of sequences.

The phase is defined by the continuation and evolution of the productions of the preceding phase (the Azaila style comes to the fore now and the differentiation in Elche–Archena becomes more clear-cut, etc.), while various tendencies towards unification occur with the appearance of new forms imitating Roman productions. Nevertheless, the bulk of production continues to correspond to Iberian pottery as documented in the stratigraphic assemblage.

On the other hand, there is talk of extending the end of the period in view of the continuity of the types during the era of Caesar and Augustus, understandable because till then it does not seem as though the craft had planned any change in the table ware in favour of Hispanic *sigillata*.

The stage corresponds to late Iberian.

Iberian VI (60 AD to the second or third century AD)
This is already a marginal production and is characterised by the virtual disappearance of the diversified styles.

This classification project does not correspond to a cultural model; consequently, it does not claim to be a system of periods for Iberian culture but only for the pottery. Nevertheless, it will be of great interest when coupled with the new horizons of knowledge which have been emerging during the 1980s.

— 3 —

Economy and territory of the Iberians

Basic elements of the Iberian landscape

In the *oppidum* of the Plaza de Armas de Puente Tablas there are two pollen columns, which have been studied by Yll. In order to verify the results adequately, the first was set up inside the inhabited area but, to ensure that the sequence could not correspond to functionalities that differed according to the period reflected in the stratigraphy, a street was selected which had existed as such since the beginning of the sixth century BC. The second column was bored on the outside of the fortification.

The contrast between the two sequences allowed a first reading to be made of the countryside surrounding the settlement. In the first place, the valley of the river Guadalbullón stands out as an important natural refuge for holm oak – totally absent today – at a time when the mixed holm oak wood appears to have been in retreat. The interpretation deduced from this first assessment is that the high percentages of holm oak would have indicated, given the character of its pollen taxons, that it was found not very far from that place, whereas pine and other Mediterranean species would almost certainly have covered the lower slopes of the *sierras* around the present-day city of Jaén. Secondly, and around the *vega* of the Guadalbullón, a kind of gallery wood-land must have been in place with the characteristic river-course vegetation (tamarisk, willow, black poplar and bramble); the additional presence of ash and alder defined a period of greater humidity, since, with the exception of these last two species, the rest are still there today. Lastly, a third area of a steppe type was defined (with sagebrush, esparto grass, thyme, etc.) and a few spots of very open *garrigue*.

In general, the areas delineated coincide with those existing in the present day, since to the east of the settlement today the landscape that opens out is defined by its triassic formation, with soils full of gypsum and salts and a plant cover of a very degraded type of thyme scrub; towards the west, by contrast, first the river, with its characteristic vegetation, and then some deeper soils, with silts and miocene clays, give rise to what today is an area of olive groves. The scene is shut off to the south-east by the Sierra de Jaén. Over this landscape, with the exception of the *sierra*, a long way from the settlement, and the eastern area, of little value for agriculture, lie the quaternary terrain of the river and the miocene soils of the western bank, which offer greater possibilities for agrarian production; this latter area must, in its day, have constituted an open landscape with scattered holm oaks, witnesses to an ancient woodland, such as it is still possible to find in other parts of the valley.

Alongside this, the important role of cereals must be stressed, with two points of maximum development in the sequence judging by the percentages that can be assigned to the middle of the fifth and the end of the third century BC. The percentages of this family overtop those of legumes (peas, lentils, chickpeas, broad beans and vetch), olives (for the moment it is difficult to distinguish between wild and cultivated olives) and vines (documented in a later carpological study by Buxó and González, so far unpublished).

From the overall analysis we can deduce the enormous importance of cereals in the zone (17 per cent in the street column, 6 per cent in the external one) and this was later pinpointed in the carpological study (although it refers to earlier phases), according to which spelt (*Triticum dicoccum*) was the most abundant, followed by hard wheat and barley, with smaller proportions of millet and *Triticum monococcum*.

The territory these crops must have occupied undoubtedly spread over the area of holm oak wood and over the gallery woodland, the only areas offering suitable conditions for their development; proof of this may be found in the confirmation of how the proportion of tree species along the river tended to decline from the beginning of the sixth century with a sharp fall from the end of the fifth and beginning of the fourth century BC. We shall refer to this fact later, when attempting to relate it to other economic sectors.

The second case we selected for assessing the landscape structure of the Iberian settlement was Castellones de Ceal, also in the province of Jaén, but in its south-eastern corner. This is the poorest and most arid region of the zone, since the soils today are very eroded. The dryness of the climate and overgrazing have led to a classic 'badlands' landscape with thyme-scrub vegetation and an abundance of steppe species. Only the river Guadiana Menor, with a small valley, provides a contrast to the impoverished landscape.

The pollen sequence at Castellones de Ceal (López, 1984) shows a gap, owing to lack of information, although certain common features can be seen giving a general idea of the landscape that surrounded the settlement.

In contrast to Puente Tablas, Castellones de Ceal shows a predominance of pine, which, even at the lower levels, amounts to 40 per cent of the total (80 per cent at times). Its presence there seems to be connected with the proximity of the Sierra de Cazorla in the east and the long distances the taxons of this species can travel. The rest of the tree species show us a river population which must have been linked with the course of the Guadiana Menor (savins, poplars and olives) and we cannot rule out the manufacture of oil, when we see the great leap made by this tree (4 per cent) at the end of the sequence and note the discovery of an oil press during the excavations of the 1950s (Blanco, 1962a).

The contrast with the previous sequence can be seen in the low percentage of cereals (1.7 per cent); these would undoubtedly have had to be grown in the *vega*, which must have provided the minimum basis for a typically grazing or stock-raising economy (a great tradition in the zone).

The third case selected lies in the region of Valencia, in the settlement of Puntal dels Llops, in Olocau. The sequences studied there arouse great interest, consisting of two external ones and one taken from inside a receptacle (Dupré and Renault-Miskovsky, 1981). The settlement lies on the edge of a mountainous zone, which has kept to this day the plant cover of pine (*Pinus halepensis*); to the west stretches the great quaternary plain of Liria. The soils which open out from the site towards the mountainous zone are acid and red, and overlie a triassic substrate, while the plain, consisting of dark limey materials (sands and silts), is much better suited to the practice of agriculture. Overall, and this information is enough to give an idea of the position, only 28 per cent of the soils in Olocau can be cultivated.

As in the previous cases, the analysis carried out leads us to think that the plant cover of the zone has not undergone any great modifications with the passage of time, although the strong impact of humankind on the landscape has undoubtedly degraded the tree cover and so may have fostered a tendency to make the environment somewhat drier, leading to the drying out of the water courses in the gullies that lie round the settlement today.

The treescape must have been largely dominated by pines, high percentages of which are recorded, while the rest of the taxons either did not reach the settlement because of their structure and characteristics, as may be the case for the holm oak, which is very poorly represented, or were sparsely represented in its environs. As in the previous cases, an assemblage of humid species like ash, alder, walnut or hazel is identified, implying a second group supported by the previous species or, in some cases, constituting a *rambla* vegetation, as might be the case of the brackens, also documented. In this way, a woody area is defined to the east and an area opening towards the quaternary plain, where the small percentages of cereals (0.1 per cent and 2.1 per cent inside the receptacle) and the legumes must have been located.

Outstanding in the herbaceous assemblage is the frequent presence of chicory, which is also documented at Castellones; given its usefulness as fodder, it points to the development of livestock; this is not to underrate arable production, which, in this case, in contrast to Castellones, is coupled more with dry farming.

We have selected these settlements because, while the landscape is marked by no great differences and they are characterised by a mixed Mediterranean economy, they show three different vegetation models, the first more suited to vigorous arable production, the other two to a predominantly stock-raising economy, although one had to rely on irrigation and the other favoured dry farming (more so, perhaps, in other inland sites). Despite these differences, the following common features can be observed:

1 The presence of Mediterranean woodland, which still shows extensive clusters around the settlements with high values for pine, contrasting with areas of holm oak, as seen at Puente Tablas.
2 The references to climate definition, although still uncertain, seem to point in all three cases to a situation not very different from what we know today, although with a landscape less degraded by human activity and, tied in with that, a certain tendency to humidity, evidenced by the presence of a few species which no longer exist in the areas studied, such as ash and alder. The same situation emerges from the sedimentary analysis at Crevillente, where the torrents that form the stratum are evaluated, pointing out their lower flow rate, possibly the effect of more regular rainfall, although still within the framework of a climate similar to today's (Box and Bru, 1983).
3 As regards arable production, the role of cereals seems to be maintained and their association with legumes (the beneficial effect of the latter on the land, in restoring the nitrogen lost by growing cereals, is well known); alongside these, other species, like vines and olives (at least in later stages), were being developed, nor should it be forgotten that this was a mixed economy requiring the presence of pastures.

Even allowing for the relative nature of the pollen and carpological information, if we marry these results with the faunal studies (also limited), they enable us to establish different economic models for the Iberian world and its transformations throughout the historical process that marks the first millennium BC. We must bear in mind that serious problems exist with some of the samples, in some cases by the very nature of the methodology of the stratigraphic sections on which they are based, which may have leapfrogged functional spaces that differed from one phase to another, and in others because of the paucity of the remains recovered.

Notwithstanding these problems, a rapid reading of different samples leads us to consider as a hypothesis the existence of two different models within the Iberian area, the first built on the predominance of cattle raising and the second on ovicaprids, even from the very earliest phases. Let us compare, to take two examples, Muela de Cástulo at the end of the seventh century (Morales and Cabrera, 1981) and Los Villares de Caudete I. If in the first one the ratio is 63.4 per cent to 7 per cent, in the second, by contrast, it is 7.5 per cent to 78.6 per cent. This inverse ratio is constant, with very few anomalies, between north and south, at least during the sixth to fifth centuries BC. Thus, Carambolo Bajo, San Isidoro de Sevilla, Puente Tablas (up to phase VII, see Figure 26), Medellín, Penya Negra and Saladares are in line with the first group, while ovicaprids predominate in Los Villares de Caudete, Puntal dels Llops, Sant Just Desvern and Turó del Vent, where, moreover, the percentages of bovines are decidely low, with the exception, perhaps, of Los Villares, which reached as much as 10.8 per cent in some of its phases.

This north–south contrast, with a boundary along the rivers Vinalopó and Júcar, has a few significant exceptions, as in the case of Castellones de Ceal, where the provinces of Jaén and Granada meet; here there is a clear predominance of ovicaprids, explained no doubt by the restraints imposed by the surrounding countryside; and in the north, the site at Vinarreguell, where the early phases show a strong element of oxen. Puente Tablas offers an interesting case; the third-century phase shows an important change from a predominance of oxen to that of ovicaprids (in the heart of the Campiña de Guadalquivir), in a ratio of 53 per cent ovicaprids to 11 per cent bovines, with signs of transformations in the evolution of the settlement and in its change of economic model, as analysed by Paz and Watson.

Pigs too, occupy significant levels among the species documented. In Los Villares de Caudete they can be seen to grow in importance right through from the beginning to the end of the sequence until, in phase IV they outnumbered cattle (13.7 per cent as against 4.7 per cent). In Puente Tablas their biggest rise occurred at the time of the change from cattle to ovicaprids, generating a percentage model similar to that of Los Villares de Caudete in its final phase. In some ways, this indicates a trend towards the rise that is patently obvious at Puntal dels Llops which will be remembered as a monophase centre, where they amounted to 20 per cent (higher than bovines and lower than ovicaprids), just as in the Catalan sites of Sant Just Desvern and Turó del Vent.

The preceding remarks suggest two lines of thought:

1 The high values for cattle in the south of the Peninsula are not new, since they had already been occurring in the Final Bronze Age, at places like

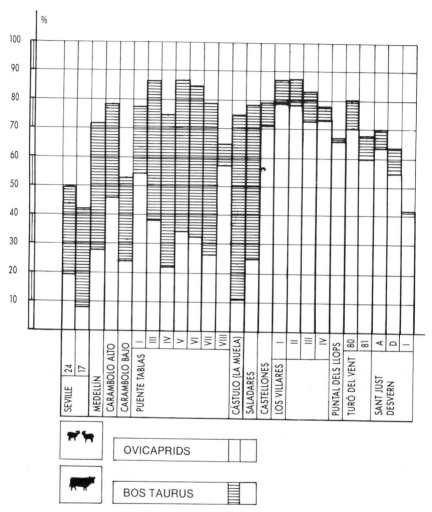

Figure 26 Percentage distribution of faunal remains in some
Iberian settlements (by the authors)

Monachil or Cerro del Real in Granada. Although this species takes second
place in the percentages, after the ovicaprids, in the business of providing
meat, both sites give pride of place to the ox. In spite of this, the Late and
Final Bronze Age settlements still show a predominance of ovicaprids in the
percentages, just as happened in the initial phases of the sequences in Lower
Andalusia, like Setefilla (Esteve, 1983) or Puente Tablas I, dated from the
end of the ninth century BC. This suggests that the rise in cattle may have

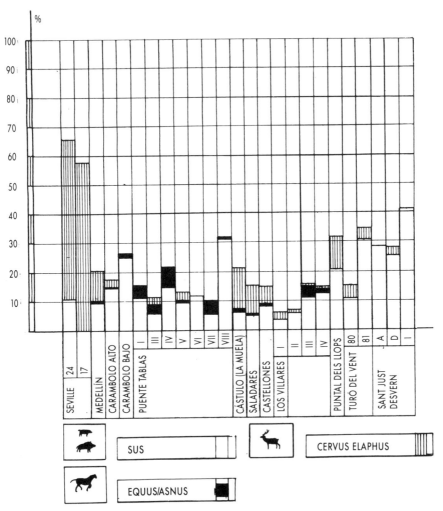

been an effect comparable with other cultural elements present from the end of the eighth century, like the introduction of wheel-turned products or the development of the rectangular, partitioned house and the new Andalusian fortifications. Now, if the case is also documented in Toscanos and is apparently something that developed throughout the seventh century in direct association with the Phoenician world, the initial reference demonstrates that it is an economic process already heralded in indigenous settlements of earlier stages. Add to that the quotations from historical sources concerning Gerion, a cowherd, and we have a direct reference to a tradition that was consolidated with the passage of historical time in Tartessos.

2 Reference must inevitably be made to the dual role that cattle would play as beasts of burden and traction and as producers of basic raw materials like milk and meat. That being so, it is worth reflecting that the consolidation of cattle as the basic species of the stock-raising model brings subtle counter-considerations in its wake, such as the amount of grass needed to make keeping stock worthwhile in economic terms. From that angle, the cow competes with cereals in terms of land as far as the need for vast spaces for grazing and abundance of water is concerned, without in exchange its excrement being of value as top-quality fertilizer, given the whole seeds that it releases as it decomposes, which are prejudicial to cereal production through the rapid spread of weeds. So an economy revolving around cereals and cattle raising can be acceptable as long as the demographic balance is not disturbed, precipitating the need for increased numbers of head of cattle or amounts of land either for grass or for growing cereals. However, as soon as that balance is disturbed it opens up the possibility of crisis for the cattle; in other words, the need for land leads to an inevitable slackening in the volume of meat production, whereas the demand for meat compels livestock to be increased and puts a strain on the rhythm of grass consumption, so that, if insufficient land is available, animal weight falls rapidly and so does the volume of meat, in a process which, through a parallel increase in cereals, will lead to a reduction in the topsoil and accordingly in the agricultural potential of the land.

This theoretical approach leads inevitably to consideration of the change reported in Puente Tablas VIII, which took place after a time in which the percentage of remains of cattle bones reached one of its highest levels, the percentage of cereal pollen reached its lowest levels, and inroads were apparently being made into the galleried woodlands to gain land. The response of Puente Tablas VIII looks to us in practice like a change in agrarian economic strategy, because raising sheep, but not goats, makes it possible to fit cereal production and livestock into the same space, since sheep can obtain nourishment in the cereal field itself and, moreover, their excrement, strong in nitrogen, compensates for the loss of that element to the cereals.

At the same time, the increase observed in pig numbers looks like compensation for the reduction in the volume of the meat required for the people's diet, following the change from cattle to sheep. These changes are interlinked, since going over to pigs requires no increased land if, as we shall see, the holm oak is present in the cereal fields.

Pigs, sheep and cereals could constitute a third strategy capable of replacing the economy based on cattle raising. But the example, which is thought-provoking as an explanation for a theoretical crisis, poses a dual problem: on the one hand, because the Puente Tablas case is unique in a scenario where lack of information is the most characteristic factor; on the other, because it becomes necessary to refer to hunting, traditionally disparaged since the move to the Neolithic, as it is thought to have become more a sport for the privileged than an economic cornerstone of the diet. We know that in Puente Tablas the presence of venison in the diet is minimal throughout the sequence (reaching a high of 3 per cent during the seventh century BC and afterwards in the middle of the fifth century BC), but at the same time cases such as Cástulo, Setefilla, or San Isidoro de Sevilla, Medellín and even Saladares show high percentages, which could offset the case of Puente Tablas. Nor should we forget that roe deer and Pyrenean goat are likewise documented at Muela de Cástulo and that rabbit and hare were present in the majority of the samples and even in carvings like the one at Obulco, showing the huntsman with his dog, catching a hare in his right hand. This means we should reflect on how far hunting might have been an emergency strategy for the crisis we record at other places in Andalusia. To balance this we should remember the quotation from Strabo (III,2,6): 'Formerly much cloth came from Turdetania. Now, very good wool . . . their lambs for crossbreeding fetch a high price.'

Lastly, we shall make a theoretical point. We have set out a thought-provoking hypothesis, confirmation of which will have to await developments in research. But this approach has been made exclusively in terms of ecological balance and economic effectiveness and, as the sole explanation of a crisis which even led to depopulation in areas like the upper Guadalquivir, this could be dangerous because it could lure us into economic determinism if it is not associated with questions as closely linked with the matter in hand as the technology that fostered the formation of the model or the social relationships that would explain it and take it to the ulimate extreme. From that point of view, a population increase that at a particular time explained the disturbance of that balance is not the cause of the model breaking down but is another effect of a more complex socio-economic structure, which may actually lead us to reflect on whether the individuals who would re-establish the economic model of Puente Tablas VIII were the same as the ones who lived through the crisis of Puente Tablas VII.

A model similar to the alternative one in Puente Tablas VIII may have been characteristic of the Iberian area in Valencia and Catalonia. In the former, the case of Los Villares de Caudete reveals an increase in pigs from 3.7 per cent to 13.7 per cent in the final stage, while ovicaprids are a dominant presence in all the phases. We see the same thing at Puntal dels Llops, although there the dominance of goats over sheep is quite clear, leading to a model of a more markedly pastoral character, since this animal needs to be raised in an area devoid of cereals; it is also less selective than sheep in what it eats, which is another factor in the degradation of the countryside, of much greater import than with other species (except humans). The same model seems to operate in Catalonia and in Castellones de Ceal, although in both of them the difficulty of isolating goats from sheep prevents us from clarifying whether one or other species was dominant. What is significant in this case is that the model chosen in these areas, with the exception of the odd case like Vinarraguell and, of course, the settlements to the south of Vinalopó (Saladares, Penya Negra), shows hardly any changes in the economic system, if we except what has already been said about pigs in Los Villares de Caudete; the same would also hold good in the opposite sense for cows, and the fine tuning which may be possible in the future in the assessment of sheep versus goats.

As to cereals, Cubero's carpological study at Moleta del Remei, with dominant elements very similar to those mentioned at Puente Tablas – *Triticum dicocum* (spelt), *Avena*, sp., *Lens*, sp. (lentil) and *Prunus amigdaleus* (almond) – identifies spelt and oats in the area, together with *Triticum aestivum durum*, documented at Ullastret, as the most frequent, thus revealing in general terms a similar cerealist economy throughout the whole Iberian area, based on these three cereals alternating with legumes; to these must be added crops of millet and maize, which are bread grains and have an important protein and vitamin content, or other crops like vines (Puente Tablas, Illa d'en Reixac), almonds (Moleta), figs, blackberries, acorns (Illa d'en Reixac) and certain medicinal plants like mallow (Buxó, 1987).

The establishment of these basic models does not exclude other economic strategies which must surely have occurred over time as a response to economic imbalances, external demands and also specific political problems. We know from historical sources that Saitabi or Emporion specialised in flax (Domínguez, 1986) or the Cartagena region in esparto, but the case of the settlements situated close to the sea is very interesting; their economic development revolved around exploitation of the fishing grounds. In this connection, an abundance of fish hooks, harpoons and pottery products, like amphorae or the so-called 'fish dishes' for consumption of *garum* is documented. Still more specific is the fact picked up by Llobregat (1972) concerning remains of a net found in the Albufereta de Benidorm, recognised from a series of small perforated pieces of lead, which could have been the counterweights of a circular net. In line with this model of a dominant fishing sector, and no doubt with a strong involvement in the system of Mediterranean trade relations, are the references in Ruiz Mata (1987) to Torre de Doña Blanca, when he points out that at the end of the fourth century and during the first half of the third, the settlement was abandoned and the population moved to the coast at Puerto de Santa María, a zone more suited to fishing, and no doubt with potential, in the setting of the Bay of Cadiz from the start of the fifth century, for the development of a salting industry. This can be seen in more than twenty family-type centres designed for its commercialisation, to compensate for the metal crisis in the Huelva zone at the end of the sixth century. The same response appears to have occurred in Huelva itself, when faced with the fall in mineral production, given the appearance of points along the coast, like La Tiñosa, which was undoubtedly linked with fishing; or with stock raising, like El Castañuelo in the Sierra (Fernández Jurado, 1987b).

The existence of these fishing tasks can be seen not only along the Cadiz coast but even at San Isidoro de Sevilla, where molluscs such as clams, cockles, scallops, oysters and dog cockles are documented. But Seville suffered frequent floods with surges in the river originating from the estuary, as is shown by the unconsumed gilthead documented to around the middle of the fifth century BC (Bernáldez, 1988). Further inland (Setefilla), although these products of gathering are documented, the erosion suffered by shells that were empty before being harvested indicates that their function was ornamental and not for the table (Esteve, 1983). However, the collecting of wedge shells is clearly established and documented in huge proportions in Arguilera, with other minority species like cockles, dog cockles and mussels, among others. A case with similar features is Sant Just Desvern, with 81 per cent of glycimens, followed by cockles and wedge shells; although there is a series of shells worn away by sand here, the existence of a fishing sector seems justified, combined with a dominance of ovicaprids and an expansion of cereal growing, as demonstrated by the storage pits at Arguilera and in the Indiketen territory near Emporion.

So, we can summarise the different primary economic models in broad outline:

1 An agrarian model characterised by the dominance of cereals and coupled with cattle raising, which, at certain points, is reinforced by a considerable input from hunting (San Isidoro de Sevilla, Setefilla, Carambolo Bajo, Puente Tablas III–VII, Saladares and Penya Negra). This model has its beginnings in the seventh century in an area corresponding basically to what we might define as southern Iberian. In the odd case, a crisis is observed in this model at the end of the fourth century (Puente Tablas VII,

with reference to Puente Tablas VIII) (Ruiz Rodríguez and Molinos, 1985).

2 A second agrarian model, also basically cerealist, is the one marked by the increase in sheep, with a lesser input from hunting. It is documented in cases like Los Villares de Caudete and provides a norm which apparently tends to prevail over the previous one as the Iberian population develops economically. When this model is situated near the sea, it expands into fishing and mollusc collecting as well (as in Arguilera or Sant Just Desvern, although, in the first case, the researchers are now beginning to argue for specialisation towards fishing exclusively).

3 A model of a more pastoral character (predominance of ovicaprids, and among them goats), coupled with a basic production that does not exclude cereals, seems to become established in zones where agriculture is difficult, as is pinpointed in Castellones de Ceal or Puntal dels Llops.

4 Lastly, a series of apparently specialised cases is reported, like the one that appears to be documented from the third century on in Torre de Doña Blanca, with a strong expansion of fishing, salting or other specialisations such as those that, judging from the sources, can be deduced from cultivation of flax in Saitabi or esparto in Cartagena. These last two appear to be late models.

The configuration of these four models within the general framework of the Iberian economy defines just two main tendencies in practice, spread across areas that correspond in general terms to the two great tracts already described; the third is apparently an adaptation to a hostile environment offering no other opportunities; this one and the fourth may have a place in a larger macroeconomic framework, or one that goes beyond the level of the settlement, owing, possibly, to the way the latter functioned (Puntal dels Llops was an observation post, while Arguilera seems to be identified as a small trading post for fish). A very different case is that of Torre de Doña Blanca, which certainly continued to operate a more complex agrarian system, but where the fishing and industrial sectors were undoubtedly dominant in the phase indicated, deriving directly from its links with the Phoenician area.

The settlement in the territory

A first reflection

The basic structure from which analyses of spatial archaeology have usually started placed archaeological complexes, defined as settlements, and on a second level, the distribution of their artefacts, in a relationship with the physical concept of space in terms of an articulated system that could be read from the narrow limits of a habitation to the widest ones of a geographical region. Now, after making the qualitative leap implied by this approach, the methodology of a project that claims to be scientific demands adequate examination of the concepts underlying the techniques employed, because if they are just taken for granted without critical appraisal, they imply the acceptance of approaches of a neopositivist style in its neofunctionalist version.

This first observation, of a general nature, has to be interpreted on a different plane, epistemologically speaking, from the other that has more often provoked the criticism of traditional positivism. We are referring to the result of deficiencies in the gathering of information, sometimes the result of insufficient checking of records, in the majority of cases due to the absence of appropriate equipment. The practice of archaeological investigation demonstrates that it is becoming daily more feasible to solve this level of error with an appropriate recording technique, the creation of genuinely multidisciplinary teams and an open dialogue between excavation and prospection.

The problem we are addressing here does not question the field generated by spatial archaeology as a horizon of investigation, because the society–nature dialectic is fundamental in historical analysis. We shall offer an introduction of a historiographic character in order to locate exactly where the problem lies.

The horizon of territorial archaeology appeared as early as the 1970s, when Hodder and Orton (1976) articulated archaeological information using the methods of locational geography, analysing the relationship between settlements. Somewhat earlier, the Cambridge group had defined a methodological project on the relationship of settlements to their surroundings in the conceptualisation of *Site catchment analysis* (Vitta Finzi and Higgs, 1970). Following this process, we are indebted to Clarke (1968) for the first systematisation of the subject, and with it the laying of the theoretical foundation of the horizon with its well-known macro- semi-micro- and microspatial models. Until then, the project implied a rejection of the old positivist schemes and, methodologically, prospection of the site reclaimed the role traditionally assigned to it as the exclusive source of information, prior to excavation. Secondly, it is important to assess the framework in which this programme unfolded, which has its place in the last glorious period of neopositivism, before it embarked on the debate that has characterised it in the last decade. It thus takes its place in a gnomological-deductive model, which, in practice, attempts to establish a system of laws for the cultural horizon and, in this particular case, for the siting of and relationship between settlements.

From this point of view, spatial archaeology has taken its methods and techniques directly from locational geography, thereby producing a methodological horizon with a distinctly mechanistic and reductionist outlook, and has consequently produced a welter of schematics and generalisations, has institutionalised the theory of optimisation of resources and has forgotten non-economic factors in the most unadulteratedly economicist style.

Of course, with the use of this system of laws it was claimed to provide a response to positivism, but, in applying it, its adherents forgot that locational geography produced these models in order to study a society structured on the basis of a market economy. Consequently, its direct transposal to pre-capitalist systems simplified the social group's relationship to nature to such an extent that it transformed it into a mechanical, but at the same time natural, action, owing to the transhistoricity of the approach. In this way, economicism and transhistoricity have led to the analysis of the specific being merely that of the place where corroboration of the law should occur, without allowing a dialectical project to be generated in constructing the historical fact; more seriously, this theoretical framework has made it possible for relationships of the market economy to be transformed into the basic principles of any society, so endorsing an approach that explains the system of capitalist laws and relationships not, indeed, as a rational and logical process, but as a structure inherent in history.

In response to these models and within the theorisation we are proposing for territorial archaeology, it must be borne in mind that in pre-capitalist societies the role of nature is the first objective condition of work, but also that the land is the great laboratory that provides the means and materials for work, just as Marx would define it (Marx, 1964).

Of course, spatial archaeology, with its neopositivist approach, has made this awareness possible by articulating the relationship of the social group to nature. But, when faced with the business of corroborating its results, it has discovered that the responses do not always occur on equal terms and has thought it would find in technology the restrictive factor capable of imposing specific limits on similar responses. So technology has been presented, not as a historical factor but as the variable capable of generating models. As opposed to that conception, our interpretation is that nature, the social group and technology form a triangle, articulated not by mechanical laws such as optimisation of resources or degree of effectiveness, but by a system of social relationships of production that can bring different economic and extra-economic factors into play.

Having put forward this view, we shall return to the agrarian models detected in the Iberian area and move on with a twofold question concerning, on the one hand, the character of the settlement in its environment and, on the other, particular aspects of the work process in relation to the new technologies and the spaces for production and/or consumption.

Andalusia: towards consolidation of a nuclear model

The area of the cerealist models has been studied in the upper reaches of the Guadalquivir valley in a succession of works (Ruiz Rodríguez and Molinos, 1984; Ruiz Mata, 1987; Ruiz Rodríguez and Molinos, 1990). Analysis was carried out over the area corresponding geographically to the middle and upper reaches of the river valley, in a zone occupied by the present-day province of Jaén. Within that area, a start was made with those lands situated less than 800 metres above sea level; they delineate the valley area and so have excluded the three mountain ranges around it: the Cazorla and Segura ranges in the east, the Sierra Morena to the north and the Subbaetic ranges to the south. The valley has a different structure in its uppermost reaches from the one it presents on the western side. The course of the river narrows, reducing the *vega* to the Guadalquivir itself and its tributaries, and allowing the southern mountains to advance towards the east–west axis of the watercourse, cut only by tributaries like the Guadiana Menor, the Jandulilla or the river Torres. Towards the north, the river Guadalimar flows in on a north-east–south-west line, leaving a series of high lands, known today as the Loma de Ubeda, between it and the Guadalquivir.

To the west, in the middle to upper reaches of the river, the *vega* opens out appreciably. The Sierra Morena approaches from the north and a triangular space (the Campiña) opens to the south of the river, cut by a series of rivers of a lesser flow than the ones in the area described above, rivers such as the Guadalbullón, the Salado de Los Villares or the Salado de Porcuna. The Campiña, opening towards Cordoba, fluctuates between 300 and 600 metres, with a lower, less hilly zone (300–400 metres), cut only by low hills of about 400 metres or maybe more; the southern area reaches 600 metres with a landscape of more fissured ridges and steeper slopes; lastly, somewhat more to the south, we see a piedmont region up to 800 metres, giving way to the sierra with very steep slopes but also eroded glacis forming broad plains at its foot.

The distribution of the settlements in this region shows them placed preferentially close to the big rivers; they are of three sizes: one of less than a hectare, like Castellones de Ceal, another between 3 and 6 hectares, like Puente del Obispo, and lastly a very big one of over 16 hectares, like Giribaile.

During the sixth century BC, the large/medium-sized settlements were distributed in a more or less alternate pattern with the small ones. Later, with

111

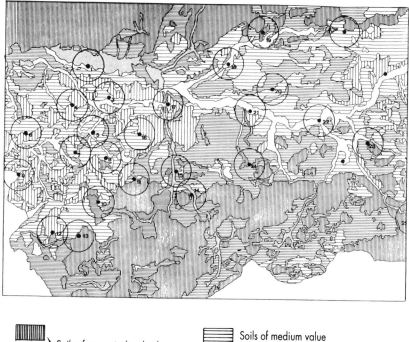

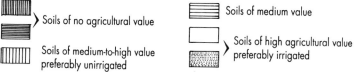

> Soils of no agricultural value

Soils of medium value

Soils of medium-to-high value preferably unirrigated

> Soils of high agricultural value preferably irrigated

Figure 27 Distribution of *oppida* in the fourth century BC in relation to different types of soil on the upper Guadalquivir (by the authors)

the transition to Iberian III, we see, with a few exceptions, the disappearance of these small nuclei and a consequent increase in the average distance between settlements and an appreciable characteristic of longitudinal concentration.

In the Campiña, by contrast, this triple scale is distributed in a reticulated structure with a bigger dispersion index (1.74 on Clark and Evans' scale). Lastly, this stretch of the fertile river plain reflects a model characterised by large settlements, like Los Villares de Andújar, or small enclaves in the plain, of the agrarian trading-post type (less than 0.25 hectares), in a habitat system very different from the preceding ones. However, the transition to the fifth century involves the total transformation of the model with the small enclaves being abandoned and settlements of the type known in the eastern area as 'La Aragonesa' appearing. In the fourth century BC, the model is in total crisis with the second type of settlement disappearing, including Los Villares de

112

Andújar, from where at present no materials from this phase are known.

Application of a dendrogram to the assemblage of settlements, starting from variables relating to visibility, distance to the three nearest neighbours (so as to avoid the errors of the Clark and Evans index), settlement structure and soil in the immediate vicinity, has, for the time being, defined four types for the fourth century (a phase in which the small settlements are not documented, whether they be of the agrarian trading post or the strategic type):

1 Settlement on a plateau, well fortified, with all-round visibility and very little distance to the nearest neighbours, preferably dominating land with medium and medium-to-high agricultural potential.
2 Settlement on a plateau, well fortified, with visibility in one direction (usually backing on to a rather larger hillock), similar distance to its nearest neighbours and lands of medium, medium-to-high or high agricultural potential on one side, while on the other the productivity of the land is low or nil.
3 Fortified settlement on a plateau with little or no visibility and a greater distance to the nearest neighbours; it combines land of high and low productivity but tends to exclude the medium or medium-to-high.
4 Fortified settlement on a terrace with scant visibility and a long way from its nearest neighbours; it disposes of a few lands of high productivity while the rest is absolutely useless for agriculture.

Outside the area mentioned, it is difficult at present to assess the model of association with the territory, since the studies that have been done have either been centred on other periods like the Final Bronze Age/orientalising period, as at Los Alcores in Seville (Amores, 1982; Amores and Temiño, 1984) or else they show the overall population distribution, that is to say, for the Iberian period, without for the moment defining the characteristics of each stage, as at Granada (Aguayo and Salvatierra, 1987) or on the Middle Genil (López Palomo, 1983); in neither case is there any question of systematic prospections that would define the differences of settlements in the plain or small ones, if such existed. The process is more advanced in the eastern Cordoba region, where there is a strong tradition of prospecting from the first work of Fortea and Bernier (1970). Recently maps have been drawn with the distribution by periods (Murillo et al., 1989); these hint at a possible continuity of population or at least of the reticular model documented in the Campiña of Jaén. This is suggested too by the distribution of the great *oppida* of the Torreparedones, Ategua type, at a time when the types already reported for Los Villares de Andújar and the middle to upper reaches of the Guadalquivir can be seen on

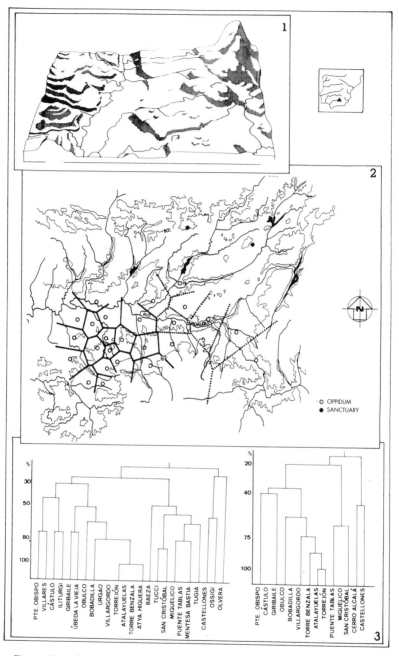

Figure 28 1. Reconstruction of the Campiña de Jaén (from Nocete, 1989).
2. Distribution of the *oppidum* type settlements in the Campiña de Jaén in the
fourth century BC, based on Thiessen polygons. 3. Diagram of association of
the *oppida* in the Campiña de Jaén with and without the size variable
(by the authors)

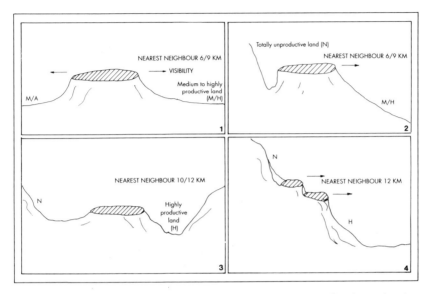

Figure 29 Typology of the *oppida* on the upper Guadalquivir (by the authors)

the *vega* of that river. It is in fact very interesting to note that, during a period that dates broadly to the seventh–sixth centuries BC, the system of agrarian trading posts can be seen, not only in the *vega* but in the lower Campiña, opening towards the settlement of Ipolca (Porcuna) itself. In the same way, fortified settlements on high ground are dated to this phase in the area of Torreparedones. In the following phase, that is in the fourth–third centuries and presumably starting in the fifth, various Iberian stages, the models of which are appreciably different in other regions, are brought together in a series of maps. This makes it difficult to know whether the process between Iberian II and III had the same characteristics as in the Campiña of Jaén, as far as consolidation of the *oppidum* was concerned, since around the third century, in both Cordoba and Jaén, the reappearance of certain small strategic settlements is documented, which Fortea and Bernier would define as fortified enclosures and which on other occasions have been called towers or *atalayas* (watchtowers).

In any case, the occupation of the Guadalquivir valley reveals a type of settlement away from the banks of the river, as the work in the area of Los Alcores shows, with the siting of settlements like Carmona or Mesas de Gandul in prominent positions between the Guadalquivir terraces and the *vegas* of the rivers Corbones and Guadaira, favouring a model of extensive

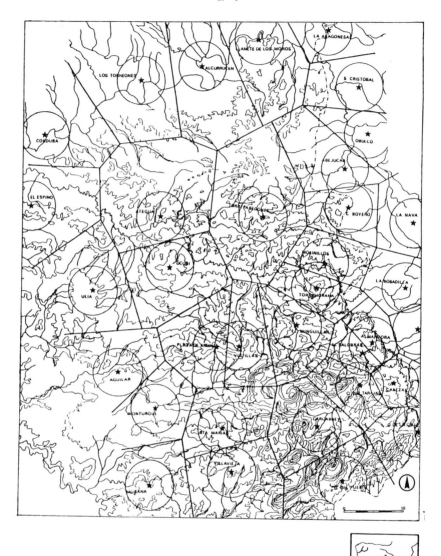

Figure 30 1. Iberian population in Cordoba (from Murillo *et al.*, 1989).
2. Introduction of the orientalising period in Los Alcores, in Carmona
(from de Amores and Temiño, 1984)

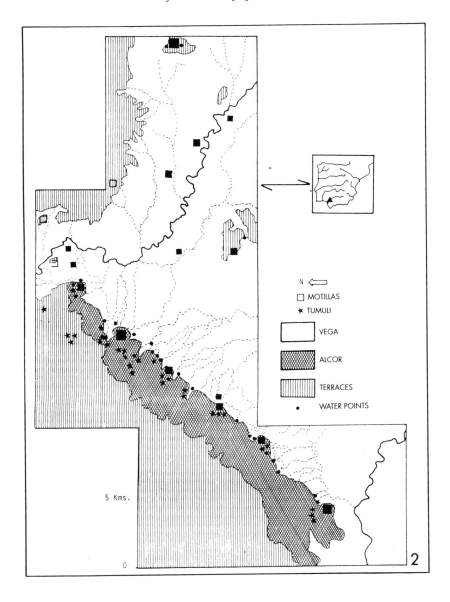

N ⇐
☐ MOTILLAS
★ TUMULI
VEGA
ALCOR
TERRACES
• WATER POINTS

5 Kms.

0

2

occupation of certain lands like those on the *vegas* extending to the east of Los Alcores; because of their quaternary formation, they offer great potential for agriculture. This situation is very different from that attributed to the present-day province of Granada, where what is striking is the occupation of the valleys, with settlements like Cerro de Cantarero de Benalua de las Villas or Los Ayosos in Montejícar, covering the courses of the rivers Cubillas and Guadahortuna in a minimal open space between Sierra Harana in the south and the Subbaetic of Jaén in the north. This model, reminiscent of the one documented in the eastern Jaén region, is found in a similar form on the great high plateaux of the Granada region, as can be seen on the Guadix–Baza–Huéscar plateau with large settlements like Tutugi, on the Granada plateau with the siting of Ilurco (Pinos Puente) in the upper reaches of the Genil, and a series of lesser settlements like Cerro de la Mora or Iliberis, the latter inside the modern city of Granada. In this case we also see the contrast of the abandonment of many small settlements in the transition from Iberian II to III, as demonstrated at Cerro del Centinela in Pedro Muñoz (Jabaloy et al., 1983) or Cuesta de los Chinos on the *vega* of Granada, in Gabia, where, in line with the consolidation of the *oppidum*, we find a process similar to the one already mentioned. However, this is a question we are still far from being in a position to corroborate as a definitive characteristic of the whole zone.

The world of Huelva is particularly interesting; there the impact of the mining centres apparently generated a linear population model, which, before 500 BC, can be seen in the western region across the course of the Tinto and the Odiel in the siting of the two ends of the Huelva–Cerro Salomón axis in Rio Tinto. To the east a second zone is formed connecting the mines of Aznalcollar with a big centre that is fortified and set on a plateau, as is Tejada la Vieja. From there, the village of San Bartolomé de Almonte could be reached along a route leading to Torre de Doña Blanca and Cadiz. In recent work on this area (García Rincón, 1987), surrounded in the west by the river Tinto, in the east by the Guadiamar and in the north by the first foothills of the Sierra Morena, an assessment has been made, on the one hand, of the way the mines are linked to the settlements, confirming that the concentration of mines decreases with increasing distance from the inhabited villages; and, on the other hand, of the existence of two types of settlement: those in the north clearly specialising in mining, as is the case with Tejada la Vieja, and others predominantly agricultural like Huerta Tujena, which in turn seems to offer the highest index of population potential, although at this point it cannot be specified whether it is peopled with farmsteads, that remain constant or are only there at certain cultural phases.

Economy and territory of the Iberians

The spatial transition to a mixed model

Towards the north-east, on the other side of Andalusia and still within a zone of a similar tradition, that is to say, in Murcia and Alicante, archaeological research offers some interesting studies. In Murcia, recently, Santos Velasco (1988) has established three types of settlement: a habitat on the plain or in small enclosures of less than a hectare; villages of around 2.5–3 hectares, often with no fortification but generally with natural defences, and a third level characterised by the big castellated settlements, which look like places of refuge. However, the problem is posed on a chronological level, since the association between the different types is not known. Nevertheless, taken as a whole and when the network of Thiessen polygons is drawn, including the third level, it is worth observing that the boundaries in general terms follow the natural ones: Cocubre shuts off the basin of the river Jumilla, Los Albares the centre of the middle Segura and El Cigarralejo the *vega* of the river Mula, while in the eastern zone, Monteagudo covers the basin of the Fortuna, and Verdolai the eastern part of the valley of the Guadalentín. It is difficult to isolate the analysis of this southern zone of the province of Alicante, where places like La Escuera or Ilici itself (La Alcudia) would have given unity to a fertile territory of which it is difficult today to give an overall assessment because of changes in the population pattern such as the transition from Oral to La Escuera (Abad, 1985). Nevertheless, there can be no doubt that, around its middle and lower reaches, the Segura generated a population system linked to the course of the main river and its tributaries and, even if the complexity of the model still eludes us, it points to a population pattern in the phase of the fifth–fourth century BC with fortified settlements on high ground or small centres with no defensive structure, very different from what we know on the upper Guadalquivir, perhaps because the process of dismantling the undefended nuclei did not occur here – cases in point are Saladares in the Alicante zone or Ascoy and Bolbax in the Murcian (Lillo, 1981).

To the north of Vinalopó the countryside changes considerably and we no longer find the open landscape of the Segura basin. Now the valleys run up into the mountains and give rise to small internal hollows like the one that opens out around Alcoy, where the role of Puig together with other small places like La Serreta (Abad, 1987) stands out, or around Mogente, the role of La Bastida (already in Valencia province), always controlling the quaternary deposits of the inland *vegas*. On the coast a peopling with settlements either larger (Tossal de Manisses) or smaller in size, like Altos de Venimeguia or Campello, is documented, but always close to good harbour situations, like Campello itself or el Peñón de Ifach, and seeking a minimal space for arable

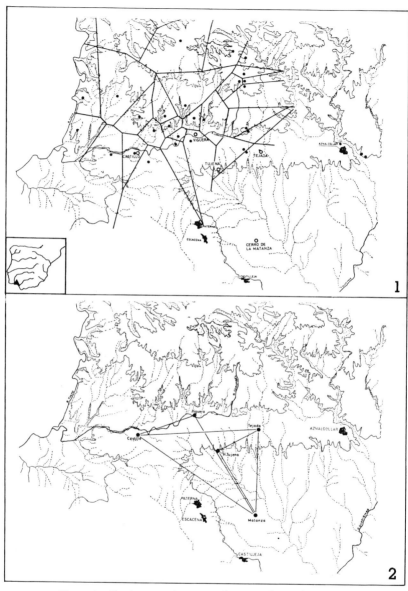

Figure 31 Iberian population in the area of Tejada la Vieja.
1. Distribution by Thiessen polygons. 2. Visual relations. 3. Routes
(from Fernández Jurado, 1987b)

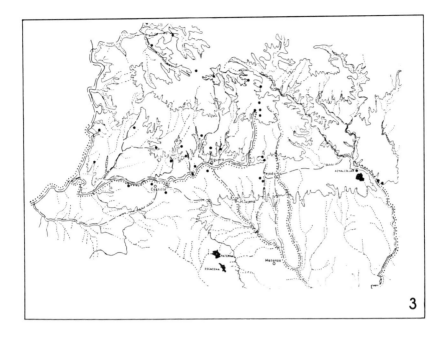

production. Some years ago, the pioneering work of Llobregat (1972) gave us some idea of this north–south dualism, which, with certain natural differences, is reminiscent of that existing among the small valleys to the north of the depressions in Granada province and the ones that developed into units like Baza or Granada. Perhaps of all these zones, the most interesting for comparison with the models of the Segura basin is the south of the Júcar, where we know of a large centre (Saitabi) and a series of small nuclei in the plain, like Vintivuiteca or Els Évols, for which we have proof of abandonment before Iberian III (Serrano Várez, 1987).

In this panoramic view it is difficult to accept the systematisation proposed by Domínguez (1984), on the basis of the scattering of sculpture finds. Once he has established the big centre of La Alcudia de Elche and drawn the network of Thiessen polygons, the author transplants the results from the zone south of Alicante to the north, without taking the peculiarities of the landscape into account. By this method, a secondary settlement like Lloma de Galvis comes to be placed on a level with La Alcudia. The mechanical extrapolation from south to north takes no account of the unit apparently generated around the *vega* of the Segura and its rich lands, nor of other aspects of a political nature, which will be dealt with later.

121

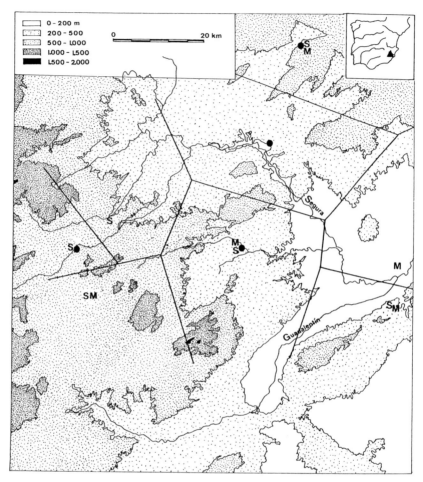

Figure 32 Iberian population in the middle basin of the river Segura. Distribution of the larger settlements. M = funerary monument. S = sanctuary (from Santos Velasco, 1987)

*The case of Liria: a mixed model ('*oppida*'–atalayas–hamlets)*

This population system with undefended settlements situated in the plain coupled with other castellated ones, which is hinted at in the Levantine area, is documented towards the north, along the Mediterranean shore. One of the best thought out models for studying it is the one for the Edeta–Liria territory (Bernabeu *et al.*, 1987). The study was focused in the north of the valley of the

122

river Turia, in an area corresponding to the Thiessen polygon of Edeta–Liria as far as its nearest neighbours are concerned (large settlements): Carenica in the south (on the river Magro), Los Villares de Caudete in the south-east, Sagunto in the north-east and Segorbe to the north. It corresponds in general terms to the point on the coast of Valencia where the Iberian System allows the big coastal plain to extend further towards the interior, following the course of the river Turia, which, together with the Júcar, formed a delta, the most significant evidence for which today is La Albufera. Liria thus defines a piedmont area broken only by the course of the river, which creates a low-lying zone that is flat and well watered.

The authors have defined a scale, as regards size, consisting of cities (more than 8 hectares), large (3–5 hectares), medium (1–1.5 hectares) and small (0.7–0.5 hectares) *oppida*, and *atalayas* and hamlets (less than 0.25 hectares); in this last group, the first were fortified with a tower in places where access was difficult and visibility good, while the second were enclosures situated on small elevations in the lowlands.

Parallel with this, a chronology for analysis was sought which would conform to the one put forward for Puntal dels Llops and Castellet de Bernabé (Iberian IV–V), although in some later work the beginning of the model was pushed back to Iberian III (Bonet and Mata, 1981) at the end of the fifth century BC. From the analysis it can be seen that the first categories corresponding to *oppida* show just one 'city' in the Edeta–Liria territory, four medium-sized *oppida* and eight small ones. The first two scales are located in the valley; those corresponding to group IV (small *oppida*) on the contrary, like the *atalayas*, take in any part of the territory, while the hamlets, with a few exceptions, occupy the most low-lying points.

Among the conclusions to be drawn, we would point out:

1　The existence of a pyramid structure, if the number of elements is quantified in groups, which will always be smaller as we go down the scale.

2　In differentiating the *atalayas* from the hamlets, checks were made on the basis of visibility, noting that the average visual distance of other settlements from the *atalayas* is 12.27 kilometres while in the hamlets it is 3 kilometres; *atalayas* also have defensive structures like towers.

3　The *atalayas* constitute a lattice of visual networks, which generate three control routes with respect to Liria and, at the same time, with one small exception, cover all the good land in the area.

4　The chronological assessment shows up a tendency to move from the high, fortified point to the plain. It emerges that the majority of the *oppida* and *atalaya* categories disappeared in the transition to Iberian V, leaving only

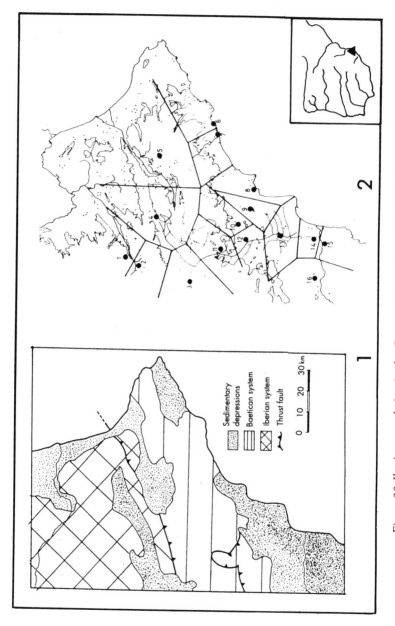

Figure 33 Iberian population in the Contestanian territory (from Domínguez, 1984)

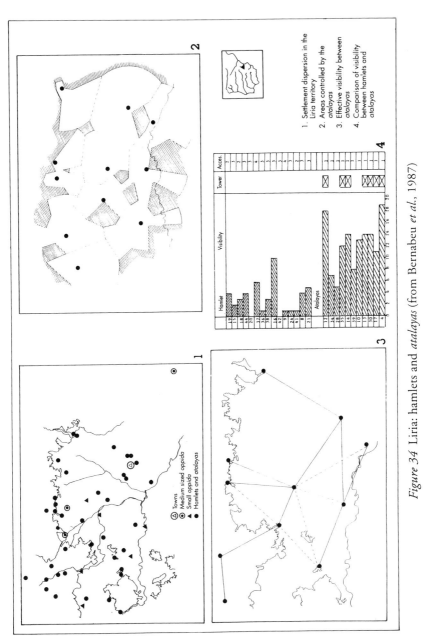

Figure 34 Liria: hamlets and *atalayas* (from Bernabeu *et al.*, 1987)

two medium-sized *oppida*, one small one and one *atalaya*. All the settlements in Iberian IV show fortifications, except for two hamlets severely affected by erosion.

5 More recently, a direct relationship has been established between the *atalaya*, as a centre of refuge, and a hamlet, which would take refuge in the *atalaya* at times of crisis. This is envisaged in the case of Tres Pics-Castellet de Bernabé or in the existence of a second enclosure with no structures at Puntal dels Llops (Bonet and Mata, 1981).

The model enables us to observe how the valley was controlled by a 'city' using a system of points of fundamentally strategic value. In this territory a certain tendency occurs, in the phases discussed, to leave the *oppidum* for small settlements or hamlets and other *oppida* of a secondary character.

The valleys of the rivers Palantia and Mijares, towards the north, again show a physical pattern similar to the above, although on a smaller scale. The same could be said about the settlement (Oliver et al., 1984) of barely one hectare, like Puig de la Misericòrdia or Puig de la Nau de Benicarló. In this case, a significant distribution of towers in the Mijares basin itself should be added, marking a line that separated the north and south of Castellón. This highlights the role of Arse (Sagunto) to the south of Castellón.

As documented in the example in the Valencia area, during the second half of the second century BC castellated sites would be abandoned and the lower zones would be occupied. This must have demanded a great deal of preparatory work, if we bear in mind the existence of marshes (those at Almenara are preserved to this day); solid proof of this is the sparse presence of settlements before the Roman phase in these theoretically very fertile flatlands.

An expansive model for the lower Ebro

The mouth of the Ebro in its lower reaches allows us to extend this type of analysis somewhat further north in a place shut off towards the west by the Celtiberian occupation (so constituting a cultural and political border zone), in a position easily reached from Valencia or Catalonia, mainly across the actual course of the Ebro, which opens up an important basin on the Mediterranean coast. The studies have focused on the tributaries on the left bank of the river and its final stretch, that is to say, the Regallo, Guadelope, Matarranya and Algar, with the advantage over other regions that the area was the subject of intensive study in the first decades of this century, thanks to the work of Bosch Gimpera, Cabré, Vardabiu, Thouvenot and Paris; and with the consequent disadvantage of the excavation techniques that were used on

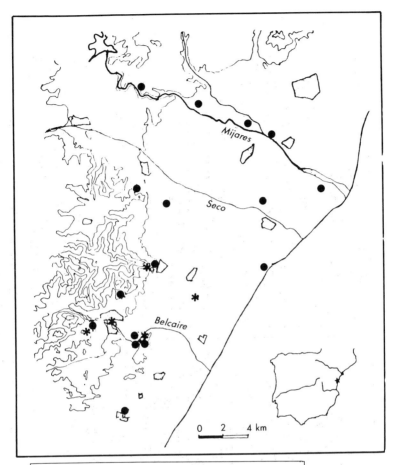

● Final Bronze Age, Early Iron Age and Iberian sites
✱ Roman sites with late-Iberian materials

Figure 35 Iberian population in Castellón (from Oliver *et al.*, 1984)

settlements with such a strong tradition in the Iberian world as San Antonio de Calaceite, Taratrato and Azaila.

The endorheic zone to the east of the Guadalope and along the courses of that river and the Regallo shows the consequences of a major transformation due to a reduction in the rainfall and very probably deforestation, so that it presents a very arid picture, which contrasts with the population pattern documented in the area. The paleoenvironmental reconstruction carried out,

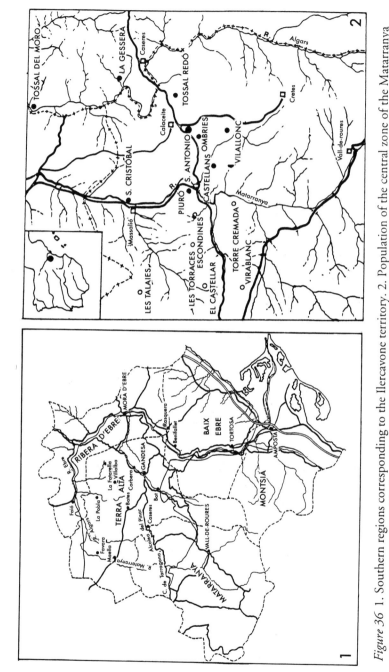

Figure 36 1. Southern regions corresponding to the Ilercavone territory. 2. Population of the central zone of the Matarranya region with the sites of pre-Iberian and Iberian villages (from E. Sanmartí, 1987)

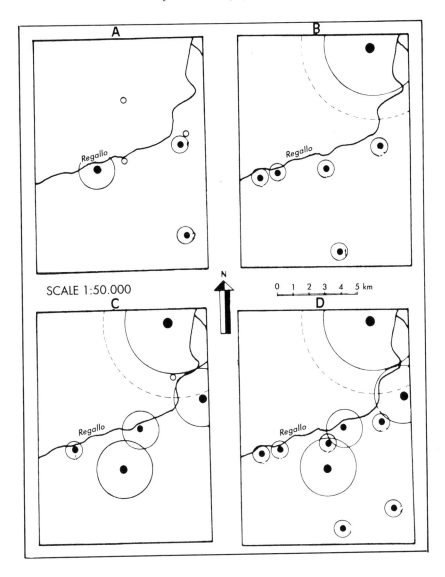

Figure 37 Iberian population in El Regallo. A. Villages with predominantly handmade pottery. B. Villages with predominantly Iberian pottery. C. Villages with Iberian and Roman pottery. D. Middle valley of the Regallo in the second half of the fourth and first half of the third century BC (from Benavente, 1984)

more on hypotheses than concrete data (Benavente, 1984), suggests that the zone offered rather better climatic conditions formerly than now, with a landscape of lakes and pinewoods.

The model for the zone was elaborated by E. Sanmartí. In the sixth century BC, the area showed a series of points with small settlements, which, in the Matarranya–Algar region (Sanmartí, 1987) fluctuated in size between the 0.018 hectares of La Gessera and the 0.6 hectares of San Antonio de Calaceite, with no order that would imply a complex hierarchical model or dependency between settlements. However, from the fifth century BC on, a new system of fortification can be observed with rectangular, dry-linked blocks and a tendency for the size of the settlements to increase (0.8 hectares for San Antonio), as well as the creation of a series of defensive satellites, among which we must include a group of sixth century BC settlements reconverted to this function (Piuró or San Cristobal among others), and others developing preferentially on the west bank of the Matarranya, like Les Escodines or Torre Cremada (up to a total of six). Small settlements are known, too, like Ombries or Vilallong, which, near San Antonio, fulfilled the basic functions of a settlement devoted to agriculture. In the opinion of Burillo (1987), the situation was very different, because San Antonio was much more reduced in size (0.35 hectares maximum) while San Cristobal could have been twice the size shown in Bosch's plan (0.22 hectares). In any case, this means that none of the settlements stands out in the context of the territory studied, but might form part of a larger territorial unit, which could relate to Gandesa.

To the west, in the middle Regallo basin, the same population model held good for the classic period of Iberian culture, with a dual system of classification, taking account of the structure of the place selected – hills of high altitude like La Caraza; low but well-defended hills like el Taratrato and settlements on the plain like El Regallo I – and of size – less than 0.5 hectares, which includes the group on the plain and the second type, while the first includes those between 0.5 and 1.5 hectares, like El Castellar and La Cerezuela, or bigger ones that might be as much as 3 hectares, like La Caraza, or, towards the Guadalope basin, Alcañiz el Viejo, el Paleo; or others of the second order in the size scale, like Tiro de Cañón (Benavente, 1984).

As a whole, in relation to other models studied, the reduced size of the settlements is surprising (Sanmartí gives San Antonio the category of capital although it does not even extend to one hectare), while Benavente categorises this level at a size between 1.5 and 3 hectares. Distances are considerably reduced too in respect of other models (1.6 kilometres for the distance to the nearest neighbour at El Regallo; the nearest sites to San Antonio fluctuate between 3.5 and 6.5 kilometres distance).

The coastal model

The picture on the coast running north from the mouth of the Ebro is very different; on the one hand, because the proximity of the sea favours a different economic model; on the other, because the researchers who made the analysis did so with a theoretical approach based on Henshall's conceptual agricultural models (1967), which set peasant agriculture against plantation agriculture, the latter being understood as typical of the Roman *villa* system and the former characteristic of the Iberian economy, because it is not market oriented and, with its traditional techniques and heavy dependence on the domestic group, it puts great importance on producing for consumption. The zone chosen for assessing the model was the one lying between the rivers Gaià and Llobregat, more specifically, the area between Calafell and Sitges. The type of settlement documented consists of small nuclei, of never more than 0.1 hectares with distances of 500–1,000 metres between them, always in places close to the coastline and on small hillocks at the edge of the cultivated zones with no possibilities of defence (in the eastern zone only, they may occupy higher points). To this assemblage should be added the settlement of Adarró, occupying a central position in the zone close to the sea, and, of different dimensions, a type represented by Alorda Park, of some 0.3 hectares, on a small hillock and also near the coast but away from the area with greater agricultural potential.

Kolb and Brunner's model was used to articulate these three types of settlement; it starts from a hierarchised system of a circular structure which takes account of the law of commercial gravitation and the proportional inferential distance; that is to say, the attraction of a place decreases as the distance increases and varies in direct ratio to its size. Consequently, the small nuclei constitute the base of the model for peasant agriculture, as is demonstrated by the storage pits found in the fourth-century phase at Arguilera and Alorda Park or the second-order nuclei which form centres attracting excess peasant production, distribution of manufactured products and religious observance. This model was maintained, according to the authors, basically until the end of the second century BC, when interaction would have occurred between the peasant economy and that of plantations, specifically through crop specialisation and previous deforestation work and even the draining of the marshes in the western part of the zone, and at the same time through self-sufficiency; hence it is defined as *villa* and not exclusively plantation agriculture (Miret *et al.*, 1988).

In the case quoted on the Costa de Garraf, its mountain isolation is, of course, accounted for by the presence of the Serralada Littoral Catalana, which

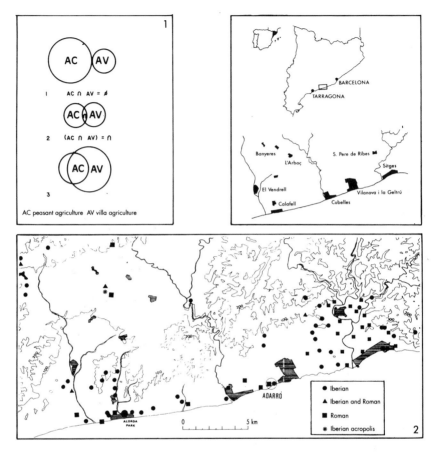

Figure 38 Iberian and Roman population in the coastal plain of Catalonia between the rivers Gaià and Llobregat. 1. Theoretical model for the evoluation from peasant to villa agriculture. 2. Distributions of the settlements (from Miret *et al.*, 1988)

Figure 39 (opposite) Territory of the Layetani. 1. Population during the sixth century BC. 2. Fifth century BC. 3. Fourth century BC. 4. Third century BC. 5. Second century (200–150 BC). 6. Second century (150–100 BC). 7. First century BC. 8. Frequency of population from the sixth to the first century BC (from Barberà and Dupré, 1984)

132

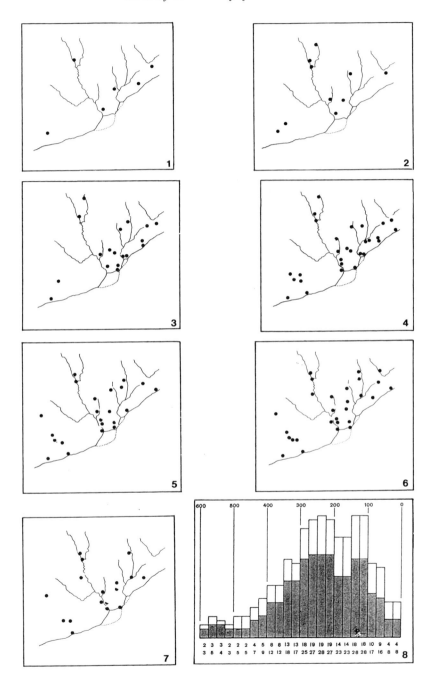

133

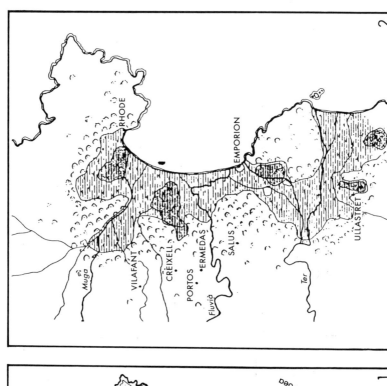

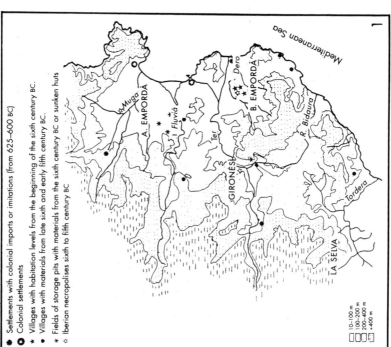

Figure 40 1. Iberian population in the Ampurdán (from Martín, 1987). 2. Reconstruction of the Bay of Emporion
(from Ruiz de Arbulo, 1984)

could act as a genuine defensive barrier; however, that cannot be the only reason, since a similar physical environment can be seen in the coastal region of Castellón province, and fortifications are present there. On the other hand, in Alorda Park (Sanmartí and Santacana, 1991) a fortification is documented that lasted until the third quarter of the fifth century BC at a time preceding the reinforcement of a series of Iberian fortifications in the Catalan area, like Ullastret and Burriac.

Towards the north-east, geographically speaking, various areas are outlined which, in spite of their own special features, show a mixed model of the Edeta–Liria type:

1 Between the lower Llobregat and the river Tordera a coastal model is outlined with a longitudinal distribution and a large centre located at Burriac; at its period of greatest expansion (second century BC) it covered as much as 10 hectares. The model brings together *oppida* like Turó d'en Bosca, Penya del Moro or Montbarbat, always fortified, *atalayas* like Puig Castellet, agrarian settlements, like Turó dels Tres Pins, and fields of storage pits. This arrangement is maintained during the second half of the fourth century BC and reaches its maximum level of territorial defence at the end of the third century, coinciding with the Second Punic War (Zamora *et al.*, 1991). However, from the second century on there is a tendency to nuclearisation, endorsed by the growth of Burriac and the disappearance of *atalayas* and rural settlements (García *et al.*, 1991).

2 The upper Llobregat also shows a mixed system, with the three types of settlement, although distributed in the different valleys which occasionally, depending on their size, might accommodate up to two villages – this is the case at Costa de la Vila and Cogullo in Pla de Bages (Sánchez, 1991). In any case, as far as size is concerned, the norms are still very restricted, Cogullo being the biggest at 0.5 hectares. In the interior of Catalonia, Plana de Vic, south of the middle reaches of the river Ter (Ausetanian territory in theory) is particularly significant, again featuring a mixed model, although with an important centre of 9 hectares at Turó de Montegròs, which, moreover, is the point farthest from the river. In general, as in the coastal zone, the process of fortifying and organising the space took place between the end of the fifth and the beginning of the fourth century BC and it suffered a severe crisis at the end of the third century (Molist and Rovira, 1991).

3 As we follow this description of the settlement models, we come to the Ampurdán, in the north-east of the region under discussion, which continues to display the model we have described. Here Ullastret

135

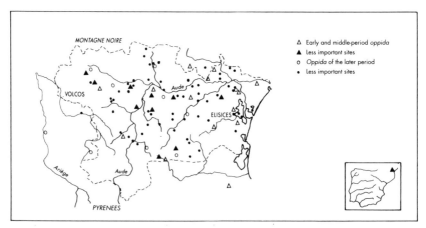

Figure 41 Principal settlements of the second Iron Age in the Aude *département* and the upper Ariège (by the authors based on Rancoule, 1976)

(5.2 hectares) holds a privileged position, the only settlement fortified before the fourth century. Probably, the model would consist of a group of second order settlements like Sant Julià de Ramis (0.7 hectares) showing terraced settlements, of a type found in the Languedoc–Iberian area of the Narbonne zone (Martín, 1987). The Ampurdán zone, as was documented on the coast of the lower Penedés, also has a system of storage pits organised in the most low-lying areas. This system was found too in the area of the trading posts of Roses and Ampurias, as is confirmed by sites like Sana or Siurana, among others, or along the course of the river Fluvià; but consideration must be given to the fact that this zone not only presented an extensive area of marshes near the coast, which remained until quite recently (Ruiz de Arbulo, 1984), but the influence of the Greek trading posts, from the coast to the interior, defining their *chora*, must have had a massive effect on the countryside (Ruiz de Arbulo, 1984). The same could be said of the Languedoc zone, where we know of the existence of settlements on the plain and various scales of habitation sites like Pech Maho (0.5 hectares), Mailhac (5.2 hectares) and even a group of bigger ones like Ruscino (10 hectares) in Roussillon (Almagro Gorbea, 1988), La Haza in Hérault or Montlanes (20 hectares) in Narbonne (Solier, 1983).

Models of the peripheral areas

In this rapid run through the pattern of Iberian population it remains for us, lastly, to give an overall view of the zones in the interior, basically the basin of the Guadiana. Generally speaking, although we are dealing with population models that developed from the fourth century on and little is known of the preceding phases, documented only by sequences like Pedro Muñoz, the population model produces a linear pattern stretching along the *vegas* of the main rivers and the routes leading to the mining regions or along the main drovers' tracks. Indeed, a quick look at the existing maps (López Rozas, 1987; Rodríguez Díaz, 1989) shows one of the greatest concentrations around the river Zújar which is the most direct route to the mines of Almadén, just as the route along the Jabalón, with such interesting settlements as Oreto or Cerro de las Cabezas, opens the way to the passes of the Sierra Morena, which lead to the mining region of Cástulo.

The population structure, too, shows a pattern reminiscent of the one that was already becoming frequent in the models discussed. Alonso has drawn up a scale for Estremadura, in which he points out:

1 A level of large towns (more than 4–5 hectares) like Hornachuelos de Ribera del Fresno, Los Poyatos, Medellín or Castillo de Azuaga.
2 A level of lesser townships of between 1 and 3 hectares, like los Castillejos de Fuente Cantos or Sierra Martela de Segura Lén.
3 Settlements on the plain that are clearly agricultural.
4 Fortifications, small settlements reinforced by fortification and enclosures/towers with characteristics similar to those found in Cordoba and Jaén (Ortiz and Rodríguez, 1985).

López Rozas uses similar terms for his analysis of the middle Guadiana–Zigüela–Jabalón in which he speaks of large *oppida*, like Cerro de las Cabezas, Oreto or Alarcos, medium-sized ones, like Pedro Muñoz, as well as small fortified units, like Motillas de los Palacios and Cañas, between 0.2 and 0.9 hectares in size. These small units are the ones favoured in the final centuries of the millennium, with the denser occupation of the *vega* by small settlements of an agrarian character in the plain and on a few strategic mounds already occupied in the Bronze Age phase. They would have to be defined as towers, or as having the same function as towers, although these structures are not recorded as having the features mentioned in the Estremadura region (López Rozas, 1987).

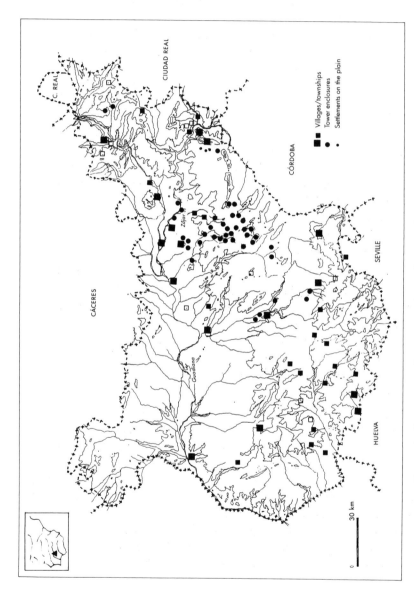

Figure 42 Iberian population in Badajoz (from Rodríguez Díaz, 1989)

Villages/townships
Tower enclosures
Settlements on the plain

CIUDAD REAL

C. REAL

CÓRDOBA

SEVILLE

CÁCERES

HUELVA

Zújar

Guadiana

30 km

Overall assessment

From the different models that have been defined in the whole Iberian area, some with a more sophisticated analysis than others, a series of conclusions must be drawn.

1. There can be no doubt about the markedly agricultural character of the Iberian economy, not only because of the low incidence of goats, already noted previously and only documented as clearly dominant in Puntal dels Llops or Castellones de Ceal, but because the distribution of the settlements in general always takes account of the agricultural potential of the soil and even in places specialising in fishing, like Alorda Park, we observe a compensatory presence of small agrarian settlements.

From this first option, the structure of the basic models must be assessed and for this we shall distinguish:

a) A longitudinal model associated with the structure of the axis of a river (Guadalquivir, Genil) or of small valleys within it (Guadalhortuna in Granada province, south of Alcoy, upper Llobregat, etc.) and which around the mouth is adapted to the special features of the natural environment, so that if a delta is formed, the siting of the settlements takes on a triangular shape (Segura, Turia). The attraction of quaternary sediments, grey-silty soils, richly fertile and with an abundance of water is obvious. In a way a large delta (Ebro, Segura or Turia) might generate a more or less reticular variable.

b) A second alternative consists of the reticular model which, in open territory hardly takes account of the river courses because it relates to an extensive dryland agrarian system. This type can be seen at present in the farmlands of Jaén and Cordoba but might also be present in the Alcores of Seville and in the Guadalquivir valley in general.

2. If two or three models can be deduced from the previous paragraph (if we add the variable of the big river mouths) the arrangement by settlement type is very different. On the coasts of Garraf and the lower Penedés we observe two levels of habitation site associated with settlements in the plain, which are small in size but have absolutely no trace of defences or fortifications; by contrast, in the Camp del Turia, in the analysis of the Edeta–Liria territory, the model creates a new level of settlement of a markedly strategic character; this type and the villages show strong fortification structures which have come to define the mixed model, characteristic of Valencia and Catalonia.

In another area, like the upper Guadalquivir, the settlements are reduced during the fourth century to a single model, the village, with two size variables.

They are well fortified, although generally with no great possibilities for visual control of the territory.

These different processes, generated by the longitudinal/triangular model can also be followed in the reticular model, only at different moments in history. In the Campiña de Jaén and in the sixth century BC, we would place a model of *oppida*–tower–rural settlements, while in the fifth to fourth centuries it would be arranged by *oppida* only.

So we see:

a) A model articulating various village/township levels (with respect to size) and small settlements of a clearly rural function.

b) A second model repeating this pattern, although the townships have been fortified and a system of towers created to couple their defence with that of the small settlements.

c) A model founded exclusively on the villages/townships that are well fortified.

d) A model coupling well-fortified settlements/villages and towers.

So this time the models are not a response to exclusively economic adaptations but a clear factor of functionality and territorial defence intervenes. It would be simplifying things to believe that this effect was produced by external pressure, because, although that could certainly explain certain concentrations of settlements in an expansive area, as appears to be the case of the sixth century towers in the Campiña de Jaén, or the possible Celtic pressure in the north-east (Zamora *et al.*, 1991), the appearance of the small forts, *atalayas* or towers might also be the effect of the actual internal conflicts of a society and consequently be interpreted as arising from a particular set of incompatibilities.

Secondly, the existence or not of small settlements in the plain implies different systems of land tenure at the heart of the two models: the small, possibly family units which indicate a mode of land tenure by physical presence on the ground, and the single settlement which obliges the production units to operate through a settlement on a higher level. This reading must be analysed from the concept of property since, although in the first case a system of family property appears well defined, in the second, while not excluding it, the role of those controlling power in the settlement takes primacy.

3. A third notion takes shape if we introduce the concept of time, since it seems clear, to quote one example, that the appearance of fortification in the primary settlements is an indication of Iberianisation in seventh century BC Andalusia; this would ultimately be imposed throughout the territory from

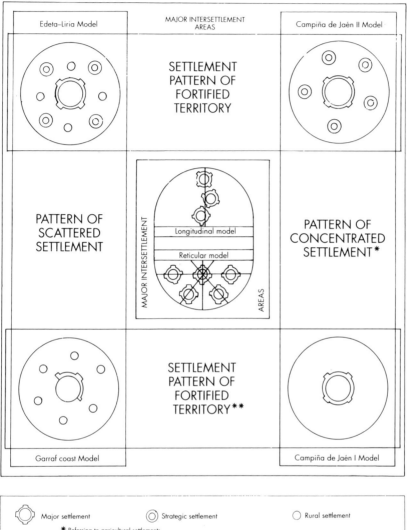

Figure 43 Theoretical models of Iberian population (by the authors)

the fifth–fourth centuries BC on. Consequently, the historical processes leading to the known models mark out a series of lines that we can pick up:

a) A process that starts with a system of medium-sized settlements, sometimes fortified, to give way in a second phase to the small agrarian units

coupled with the ancient settlements (the example already mentioned of Garraf/lower Penedés) now without fortifications.

b) A second process seems to start with one settlement already fortified and other small undefended ones. This generates either the model of village–small settlement–*atalaya* by adding the tower, or else the strategic settlement type (this could be the case in the Edeta–Liria territory, the territory at the mouth of the Llobregat, in examples like Burriac or Ullastret in the Ampurdán), occasionally, as in the case of Burriac, mentioned above, going so far as to foster a nuclearised model.

c) A third process would start from a system of settlements initially without fortifications and later fortified, generating a threefold system (*oppida, atalayas* and rural settlements in the plain) to end up returning to the first period, that is to say, only large fortified settlements (we know them on the upper Guadalquivir, in the Campiña de Jaén and possibly at other points in the valley of that river like Los Alcores de Sevilla). The crisis of this model occasionally generated a return to the model with towers (Campiña de Jaén).

The Roman presence did not impinge on these different processes in exactly the same way. Indeed, whereas from the middle of the second century BC in Catalonia we can see the introduction of *villa* agriculture coexisting with the indigenous model, until it leads to its disappearance in a gradual system, which, for all we know, may have been more rapid on the coast of Garraf/lower Penedés than on the Llobregat, on the upper Guadalquivir we see the indigenous model continuing until well into first century BC, as demonstrated by references in Caesar's *Bellum Hispanorum;* in fact, *villa* agriculture is not documented until the first century AD, although a few medium-sized unfortified settlements are indeed recorded which could be linked to isolated and exceptional processes, an effect of punitive operations after the Second Punic War.

A final thought refers to the line already noted in cases like Puntal dels Llops, which, from its functionality, generated a partial reading of the economic system. From a different angle but with the same result, Alorda Park's specialisation in fishing could be analysed and also what we know from historical sources about flax at Saitabi or esparto on the lower Segura. Of course, these references must have something to tell us about things like mining too; in this respect, it is worth remembering Blanco's references to Cerro Salomón in Rio Tinto, where every house seemed to be converted into a production unit.

— 4 —

The production process in the settlement

By way of introduction

Defining units of production and/or consumption and the work processes generated in them constitutes one of the basic objectives of archaeological work. In order to analyse them, archaeology starts with the artefact–context relationship (technology in the framework of the economic structure). The artefact, appropriately contextualised, carries with it the possibility of analysing the technological fact of production and, building on that, of revealing the social relationships in the situations analysed by archaeological methodology. The context, therefore, makes it possible to read the individual or collective behaviour of the social group and its relationship to the means of work. Technology, as we have observed before, when set in the framework of the economic structure, converts the artefact into a historically determined product.

In an article published in 1986 (Ruiz Rodríguez et al., 1986) we concluded that for the artefact to be defined as a product, it had to be articulated into the spatial units that were its context. In the matrix that was arrived at, three factors of work had to be established (artefact; spatial structure, whether a building or not; and spaces of activity) and also four levels of relationship with the spaces of activity: two relating to the lesser units (places and areas of activity) and two to the greater units (settlement and politico-economic territory).

The artefact-product in its socio-economic context establishes a series of relationships that are defined in a spatial area which cannot be confined to one fundamental and exclusive unit, as Chang (1967) indicates in relation to the settlement; instead it comprises a wide range, from those places of activity where simple and individual processes are carried out to others that have their place in the politico-economic territory (relations between settlements and even between states). All these spaces offer us different levels of information about the economic structure in relation to the work processes defined in the places and areas of activity. In every case, the identification of the lesser units that provide a historical context for the artefact constitutes the first step for archaeological analysis, since any practice in production relationships involves the deposition of a series of elements (means of work, objects, products and waste material), whose presence on the excavation site allows the process to be reconstructed in reverse, and so we can define space for production or for the expenditure of energy in pursuit of an activity. Something similar occurs on the levels of reinvestment (consumption) or of social reproduction, and with exchange relationships, although these are very difficult to define spatially.

In this regard, the spatial representation of these processes has to be established in a broad gradation according to their complexity. This would range from defining the processes of work or consumption devoted to a single activity (places of activity) to that of wider relationships carried on conjointly (areas of activity), and still others, established in the larger units. The most elementary, performed in places and areas of activity, require the introduction of a series of fine details that will be of great interest in subsequent analysis.

1 The level of places and areas of production is coupled with the concept and classification of the different work processes. The aim, as observed when defining area, will be to determine the units of production.
2 In order to define places and areas of consumption, it will be essential to delineate the units of subsistence consumption, since, by enlarging them, it is possible to isolate areas of public consumption and to distinguish functionally those focusing on politico-ideological reproduction or on reproducing the workforce.
3 As to the areas of exchange, we have already indicated the difficulty of locating them. None the less, it will be possible to analyse areas of exchange between intersettlement or interstate units of subsistence consumption.
4 Associated with the three levels, a series of places will have to be defined, that are coupled together and whose function lies in their capacity to store items in order to preserve, consume or discard them.

We should also be aware that the matrix scheme described has a complex reading in archaeology. Altogether, it is the coupling of places and areas, and of areas and their articulation with buildings (structures of places, areas, subareas, etc.) that defines for us the framework of technical relationships, that is to say, the technological assessment of the society–nature relationship which, in conjunction with the inventory and classification of artefacts, delineates the framework of technological analysis. Articulation of the three levels opens up analysis of the social relationships of production, which can be read first and foremost in the framework of the settlement and, in general, in a study of the larger units.

Constructed units

Spatial definition of the places and areas of production is not always possible in archaeology, except when we encounter artificial structures and in other cases where, without a structural location, the circumstances of the find allow activities to be recognised (a workshop for knapping flints does not have to leave any traces other than those derived from the fact of production itself, like waste splinters, nodules and an occasional finished product). In fact, some economic activities, like the practice of agriculture, can be analysed from the tools used, the remains of the product or of other related activities which imply new work processes and so new places or areas of production/consumption (milling activities, for example), but it will be difficult to determine the specific place of its location in space (the field where it is produced) except in general terms and always only approximately.

So, in the spatial analysis of production, it will be on artificial structures that we shall linger. And, of course, one of the most usual structures in archaeological analysis is the one that indicates human habitation: the house, as a microcosm that reflects fundamental aspects of social realities and, at the same time, a space for production and consumption with which a variety of places of production may or may not be coupled.

As regards constructed spaces, in the different Iberian phases we find the quadrangular module almost exclusively, although, as we shall see, with different levels of constructional and structural complexity. This is particularly evident as regards dwellings but can be generalised to other structures that acquire a special complexity from their functional characteristics. This quadrangular character is, in turn, the consequence of a significant development of the productive forces, which are connected with a great variety and simultaneity of activities. In this context (the dwelling house and the constructed space in general), the quadrangular shape allows greater exploitation of the space inside because it is easier to partition the useful space. In addition, this structure, in its relationship to other spaces of a similar shape, facilitates greater urban development at less cost and a more complete exploitation of the space inhabited by a community. By contrast, with the circular structure, internal partitioning is hardly possible, except at the cost of great waste of space or in the case of large areas; it fits elementary economic models, because the level of development of the productive forces is low and the range of

145

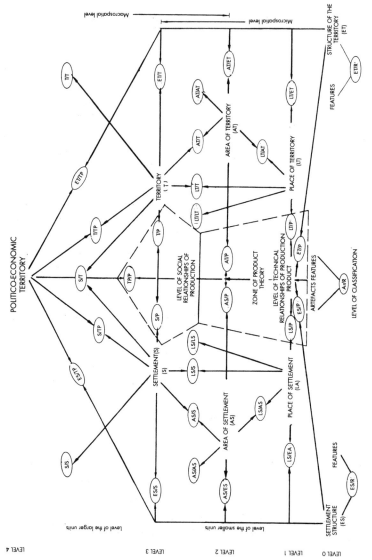

Figure 44 Concept of the product in archaeology (from Ruiz Rodríguez et al., 1986)

(a)

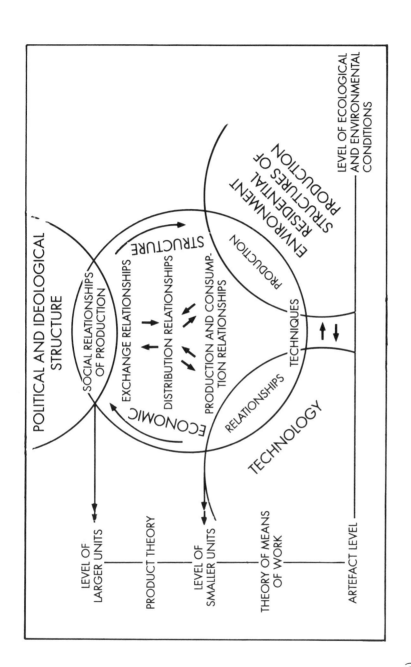

POLITICAL AND IDEOLOGICAL
STRUCTURE

SOCIAL RELATIONSHIPS
OF PRODUCTION

STRUCTURE

EXCHANGE RELATIONSHIPS

DISTRIBUTION RELATIONSHIPS

PRODUCTION AND CONSUMP-
TION RELATIONSHIPS

ECONOMIC

PRODUCTION

ENVIRONMENT
RESIDENTIAL
STRUCTURES OF
PRODUCTION

LEVEL OF ECOLOGICAL
AND ENVIRONMENTAL
CONDITIONS

TECHNIQUES

RELATIONSHIPS

TECHNOLOGY

LEVEL OF
LARGER UNITS

PRODUCT THEORY

LEVEL OF
SMALLER UNITS

THEORY OF MEANS
OF WORK

ARTEFACT LEVEL

(b)

activities is elementary and homogeneous, so there is scarcely any division of labour (Ruiz Zapatero *et al.*, 1986).

It should, of course, be pointed out that the quadrangular structure of itself, leaving aside its partitioning, need not necessarily involve a concept of space different from that implied by the circular pattern, but it is on its relationships with other aspects of construction and with its own internal dynamic that its different conceptualisation rests. Two different examples, the villages of San Bartolomé de Almonto and Cerro Salomón de Río Tinto, both in Huelva, exemplify this question. The village of San Bartolomé shows a horizontal stratigraphic sequence stretching from the first confirmed manifestations of Final Bronze I, pre-Phoenician, between the end of the ninth and the middle of the eighth century BC, to a phase that would comprise the whole of the seventh century, moving on to the beginning of the sixth (Fernández Jurado, 1986). Throughout its development, the village had very few external contacts and metallurgy for the processing of precious metals remained its virtually exclusive activity. The metal was of the 'gossan' type, formed by pyrites deposits emerging as a result of exposure to the atmosphere and subsequent leaching; this leads to enrichment in precious materials. Through all its phases the village is characterised by nuclear dispersion; the huts had excavated floors, no constructed platform and a very flimsy covering of vegetable matter supported on fairly weak posts, according to the excavation reports. These indicate that the settlement must have been occupied for brief but continuous periods. There is no proof of other economic activities going on apart from those derived from the metallurgical process and the purely domestic business of storage for consumption.

The Cerro Salamón site, in the phases that can be related to the previous example, fits a model of habitat specialising in the working of silver extracted from a mineral, 'jarosite', formed like 'gossan' by surface oxidation of a pyrite and porphyritic ore, in contact with which the precious metal was deposited. Its habitat structure was made up of quadrangular dwellings, rising from a stone platform of two or three dry strings of large, coarse stones, with no foundations or faced walls (Blanco *et al.*, 1969). They cannot have been very high and the covering must have been of light materials. The floors were initially of beaten earth but later consisted of slate flags. Within these confines, 'arranged in no apparent order', the metallurgical process of smelting the metal was carried out, so that the 'dwellings' were genuine places of production in which, apart from the extraction process, the first phase of metalworking was completed.

We do not think that the differences between the two sites correspond to different economic strategies and, in fact, in the analyses great similarities were found as far as the technical processes of production are concerned. The differences must be explained by the more permanent character of Cerro Salomón, which entailed a necessary, if elementary, urbanisation.

All this belongs in a clearly delineated horizon, the Tartessian, with a precise location, and it contrasts with what was happening at the same time and in the same area with other, non-specialised settlements. If we turn now to the structure of the Iberian habitat, we are aware throughout its development of the exclusive practice of the quadrangular space, but now with different levels of structural complexity. Only in the case of a few production or storage places, as perhaps storage pits or certain pottery kilns, is the circular type substantiated, but even in these cases, when they are not found out of doors, the structure containing them normally keeps to the quadrangular pattern.

On the level of building technique we find great homogeneity. From Estremadura to Languedoc, the similarities in this respect are striking, with stone, earth, lime and gypsum (the last two only as part of the plaster) forming the basic materials of the walls. Gypsum, beaten earth or stone constitute the raw materials of the flooring, often simultaneously in the same unit. As for the roofs, in addition to mud, the commonest elements are reeds and wood, although we must point out that, in certain regions, this is a deduction rather than an archaeologically verified fact.

If on the level of building materials and even of building techniques (rare appearance of foundations, stone footings and mud-brick walls covered with gypsum or lime) the similarities are great, the same does not hold good for the organisation and arrangement of the internal space. Of course, we are not talking exclusively about houses or dwelling structures but about all the constructed spaces that articulate productive, reproductive and storage activities, etc. These differences are as much a response to functional problems inside the settlements themselves as to their actual typology, varying more in detail between the different Iberian areas, just as differences are also notable in relation to the chronological variable.

Andalusia

Knowledge of the minor buildings is very limited as a result of the bias of the archaeological information, owing to the scarcity of extensive excavations in Iberian settlements, especially in the earliest levels. Thus, at Puente Tablas for the sixth century BC, although we know fundamental aspects of the urban pattern from the layout of various street structures in this horizon (Puente Tablas IV), the design of which would not be modified in the subsequent phases, knowledge of the dwellings is deficient because of the later structures superimposed on them. We have only partial knowledge of the quadrangular character of the buildings and of some aspects of the building technique (walls on platforms with no foundations, made of limestone, mud-brick elevations, generally plastered, beaten earth floors with cobbles and pottery fragments). In a few of the spaces excavated, presumably dwellings, the inner face of the fortification serves as the rear wall. In Cerro de la Coronilla de Cazalilla, its phase IV structures (sixth century BC) acquire special features derived from its particular strategic function. Despite the limited excavation, the quadrangular character inside it is confirmed as well as a building technique similar to that described at Puente Tablas. Inside some of the structures, variations in level were noticed, remedied by means of a transverse step. In the excavation it was reported that some of the production and storage places were located in structures backing on to the inner face of the fortification that defined the edge of the settlement. The type of material stored suggested that it was produced elsewhere, which would indicate, given the military-strategic character of the settlement, that this store was destined for consumption. No significant or complementary agricultural activities are reported for this sector. Only the appearance of a large but indeterminate number of weights of identical make might indicate textile activity, which would have taken place close to the store.

The limited information regarding the sixth century BC phases has been extended by a recently excavated site, situated like the previous ones in the present-day province of Jaén, but in a different setting, the *vega* of the Guadalquivir. The excavation was a matter of urgency because of the danger that the settlement in the Campiña (Marmolejo) would disappear as a result of earth removal; it was small in size, barely 700–800 square metres overall and this advanced our knowledge of a type of settlement operating a complex productive activity (Molinos et al., 1988).

The settlement, barely 200 metres from the Guadalquivir, with no fortification structures or even reinforcement of the external walls, covers various phases unfolding in a short space of time (middle of the seventh to early sixth century BC) revealing a rapid development of building techniques and of the general structure of the habitat. In the final phase, the Iberian, the only one for which we know the layout, we observe how the whole thing, in reality a single edifice, constitutes a heterogeneous unit of spaces not apparently articulated into the whole. The line of the walls does not fit a reticular system, so that many of the dwellings are genuine irregular parallelipipeds; this is more evident in the outer dwellings, the last to be built. This fact suggests a system of building in which the units are raised in response to specific sets of circumstances. Something similar occurs with the floors in the different dwellings, which were subject to continual general refurbishments (in the final phase in some of these rooms up to three successive levels of flooring were found). Generally speaking, the settlement fits an agricultural model; this is obvious from the spatial setting (very fertile soils) and the technology (an abundance of stone objects – axes, adzes, hammers, etc.). It should be pointed out in this connection that the absence of metal tools is not interpreted as reflecting the level of technology in the settlement, but rather as an indication that it was abandoned in circumstances in which an undoubtedly important possession could be deliberately retrieved. Proof of the presence of metal lies in the appearance of copper slag, which is concentrated in one of the dwellings (but it cannot be firmly defined as a place of metallurgical activity). However, together with agriculture (and elementary metal working) other activities took place in the settlement; in some cases with no spatial definition (various spindles and loom weights were located) and in others marking complex places and areas of production (for example, a whole area is devoted to pottery activity which, in the final phase, included places with some sort of outbuildings linked to that production, and other structures, the function of which is unknown).

During the following phases, information about the structure of the habitat is more plentiful, especially regarding those traditionally considered as belonging to the full Iberian horizon. The first evidence, which becomes general throughout the area, is that all forms of habitat are confined within the limits of the *oppidum*-type settlement on the upper Guadalquivir. So we do not come across spatial units of the Cazalilla or Marmolejo type with special features, since they are now contained within the perimeter walls of the *oppidum*. On the other hand, the trend towards a more urban character had a considerable effect on the structure of the smaller units, which now follow a more reticular plan as they adapt to urban space. By contrast, on the level of building technique, no substantial changes are observed compared with the previous phase, because of the limited nature of the materials used.

In Puente Tablas we are able to follow some aspects of the spatial organisation of the habitat structure. So, whereas during the last years of the sixth and the first half of the fifth century BC a housing pattern is documented with longitudinal partitioning into three consecutive rooms, during the following phase, at the end of the fifth and in the fourth century, in addition to this type of partitioning, other more complicated systems are documented, associated with an increase in the division of labour in the habitat. The simplest pattern is the result of converting the first two compartments of the previous phase into a single one of considerable size (5 × 7 metres) with a central pillar, the positioning of which could indicate the partial covering of the room at the entrance down one side, along which runs a continuous line of benches; the

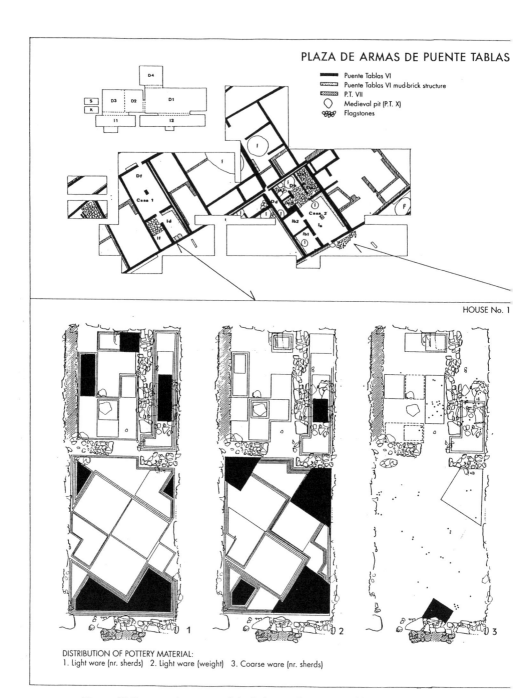

Figure 45 Structural aspects of the habitat of Puente Tablas in phases VI–VII
(from Ruiz Rodríguez and Molinos, 1989)

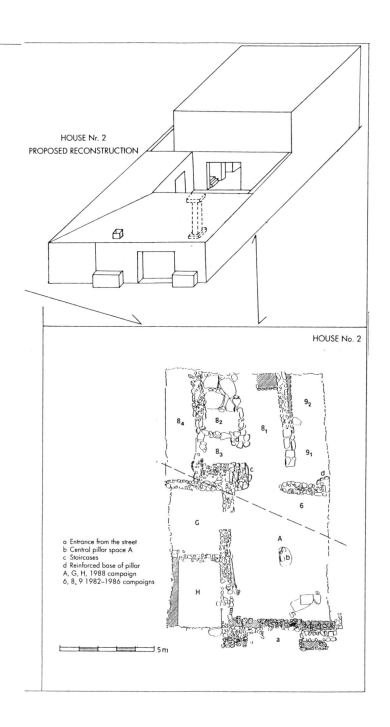

HOUSE Nr. 2
PROPOSED RECONSTRUCTION

HOUSE No. 2

8_4 8_2 8_1 9_2

8_3 9_1

c

d

6

G

A

b

H

a

a Entrance from the street
b Central pillar space A
c Staircases
d Reinforced base of pillar
A, G, H, 1988 campaign
6, 8, 9 1982–1986 campaigns

5 m

153

third (which is bounded by a wall shared with another line of habitat structures backing on to it) is divided lengthwise into two or three rooms, which, in turn, may or may not have been partitioned transversely. The structure, which is entered from the street, has a beaten earth floor, sometimes with a covering of plaster, while at least a few of the rooms at the back may have a floor of limestone flags carefully fitted together. In the structures excavated, one of the flag-paved rooms always has an unpaved area, the purpose of which is unknown, but which must be connected with some perishable structure, possibly of wood. At times the model becomes extraordinarily complicated, as in house no. 2 (7 × 14 metres, see Figure 45), in which, parallel to and along the length of the principal module, a second wing is added with access from the semi-covered patio and transverse partitioning. In the first module and at the entrance to the back part, there is a staircase exploiting the space of a possible small inner courtyard, which must have served as a rubbish dump; the stairs would have given access to a second floor lying above the partitioned sections of the first module. In the absence of the results of analyses currently being carried out, the function of these different spaces has not been determined, although places for storage are reported (at least one part of the patio must have served that purpose), as well as places of production for consumption, identified in space 8–4 (milling activity) and, next to the entrance door of the house, a hearth and close by places of consumption (Ruiz Rodríguez and Molinos, 1989).

In Tejada la Vieja (Fernández Jurado, 1987b), even though it is not possible to generalize given the state of the excavation (the final phase belongs to the first half of the fourth century BC) the structure of the habitation units may have followed a more disorganised model as to their disposition. The investigator reports the existence of an open internal space or vestibule around which are separate rooms with access across thresholds made of very large slabs of slate.

In general, unlike Puente Tablas, while the houses at Tejada also sometimes have a central pillar when the dwelling is big, more use is made of slate slabs than in the Campiña de Jaén, no doubt because they are more plentiful in that zone. This seems to be true even of some of the roofs, judging by the large amounts found on the floors in some of the dwellings.

Fernández Jurado has divided the structures in the area so far excavated into two groups, and if on the one hand, he has identified the dwellings, he also reports the existence of a few storehouses: the abundance of amphorae would support this view, as would a more rational internal arrangement and a better finish to the building (wider walls, roofs of slate slabs and larger size).

For a later phase, corresponding to the second century BC, recent work in

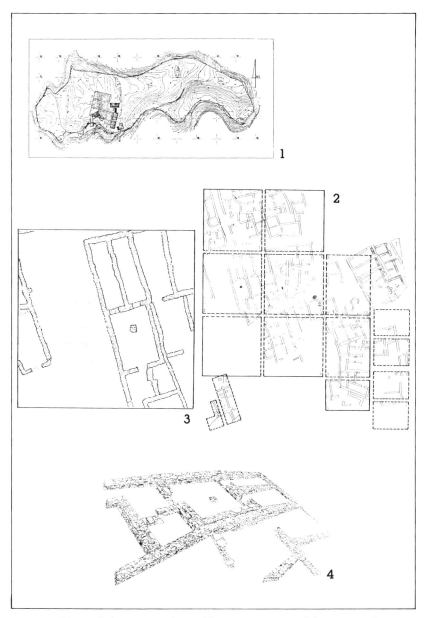

Figure 46 Tejada la Vieja. 1. General layout. 2. Layout of the excavated area. 3–4. Plan and view of an 'unusual building' (from Fernández Jurado, 1987b)

the *oppidum* of Cerro de la Cruz in Almedinilla (Cordoba) allows us to put forward a few suggestions (Vaquerizo *et al.*, 1991).

The excellent state of preservation of the archaeological site, as a consequence of its destruction by fire, makes observation leading to an almost perfect analysis of the levels of deposition possible. The two zones excavated, which have been the subject of a preliminary analysis, have revealed a series of buildings which cannot, for the moment, be separated into complete house units. Nevertheless, in the central and northern sector the following have been documented:

1 open spaces of a public nature (terraced streets, rubbish dumps, etc.);
2 spaces used for production, in which the existence of a quern together with a loom have been observed (buildings AB and O). In some cases, like building O, a cistern has been recorded next to the quern.
3 storage spaces, as in the case of building P, next to O, with an important assemblage of amphorae, or in space Ñ, which is thought possibly to have been a store for loom weights.

In the opinion of the investigators, the absence of consumption activities suggests it might have been an artisan area; however, the references to productive activities do not indicate that work here was very specialised; for that we shall have to await the development of the dig and the delineation of whole areas.

Secondly, the prospect of spatial specialisation has been raised, to show an advance compared with the earlier stages, in which buildings with multifunctional activities are more frequent. The question has still to be decided.

The La Mancha region

Knowledge of built structures is very limited here. Only excavations such as that at El Amarejo (Bonete, Albacete) (Broncano and Blánquez, 1985) tell us something about a few aspects relating to the distribution and characteristics of the places of habitation. The excavations have located a series of compartments, all of them rectangular and well planned, consisting of mud-brick walls on stone footings and making use of the rock base either as part of the walls or as floors. The roofing of these buildings, which the authors think were dwelling units, was made of plant material, except in one case, compartment no. 4 (see Figure 47), which was covered with a lime and earth plaster supported on branches. The dwellings are arranged consecutively in terraces that follow the profile of the hill and one or more roads must have existed

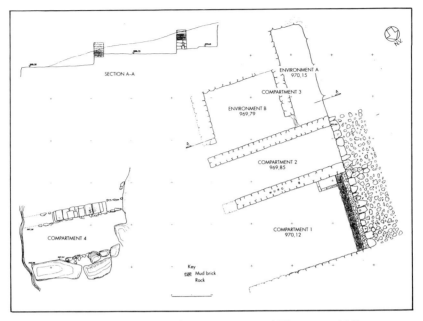

Figure 47 El Amarejo (from Broncano and Blánquez, 1985)

linking the high plateau at the top with the plain that stretches away at the foot of the hill.

The limited area excavated at present prevents identification of functional aspects. Only in compartment no. 4 has a functional role been identified, associated with pottery production (storage), and it is possible that this structure belongs to a more extended production area. There is also, in compartment no. 3, the presence of at least two cart wheels, which, after analysis and reconstruction, are described as consisting of an iron rim, quadrangular in section, that would have been joined by means of nails to a solid, circular, wooden surface. This type of wheel, which is commonly associated with the transport of merchandise (its massive character is suitable for carrying heavy loads) must have been connected with exchange activities. Its proximity to compartment no. 4, just a few metres away, might indicate a relationship between the two, although, with our present knowledge, this could be no more than a working hypothesis.

157

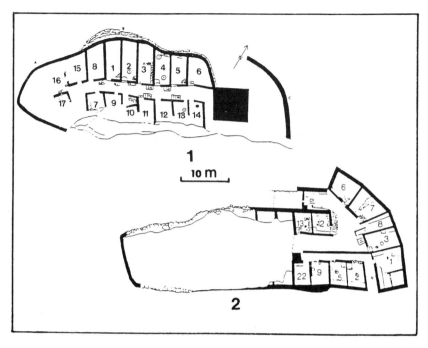

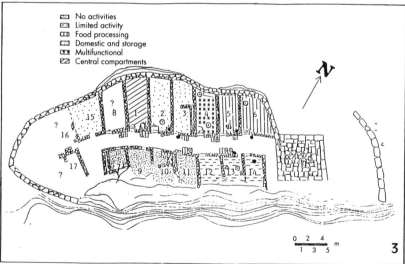

Figure 48 1. Plan of the settlement at Puntal dels Llops (Olocau). 2. Plan of the settlement at Castellet de Bernabé (Liria). 3. Functional distribution of the compartments at Puntal dels Llops (from Bernabeu *et al.*, 1986)

Valencia

Typical of the realities of habitat archaeology in Valencia is the variety of the settlements and their built features and also the difficulty of defining many of them stratigraphically. For the analysis that follows we shall work with a few of the most significant, either because of their complexity (La Bastida de les Alcuses), or because of the definition of the internal spaces (Puntal dels Llops), or of certain special aspects (Castellet de Bernabé or Los Villares de Caudete). It should also be pointed out that the studies carried out around these settlements have received very unequal treatment as far as spatial analysis of their structures is concerned.

The village of Puntal dels Llops (Olocau, Valencia) is a settlement on an elongated plan and small in size (60 × 15 metres maximum). Its structure is very basic, generically, with two features defining the space: the tower situated on the highest point of the hilltop and a street running right across the settlement towards the tower with individual dwellings arranged on both sides. Their definition, which in aspects of the building technique is reminiscent of those described in the Andalusian region, suggests a type of single cell dwelling incapable of being grouped into larger units (except the settlement itself). There is no communication between the buildings except across the street and they show no internal partitioning (except numbers 3 and 10, see Figure 48). The researchers (Bernabeu et al., 1986) classified them into a total of six groups on the basis of a factorial analysis which studied the association of the features in each compartment:

1 Non-active compartments.
2 Compartments with limited activity.
3 Compartments for processing food.
4 Compartments for domestic and storage activities.
5 Compartments of a multifunctional character.
6 Central compartments.

Leaving aside the first group, for which we have hardly any information, in the rest, one or more economic activities are defined, which in some cases are identified with clearly defined places of production. Thus the association between kitchen, domestic and table wares is significant only in compartments 2 and 3, while compartment 4 comes into the group of those classified as multifunctional: in them there is, on the one hand, a concentration of metal and domestic equipment, 'which must be interpreted as a repository', and, on the other, two querns are reported, which seem to indicate food-processing activities. Compartment number 1 is exceptional, since a great many activities

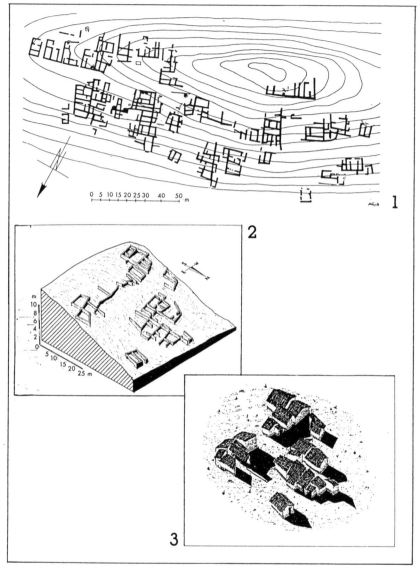

Figure 49 La Bastida. 1. Layout. 2–3. Partial reconstruction
(from Llobregat, 1972)

are concentrated there, including two that are unique in the site: 'a series of weights, sufficiently indicative in themselves' were located there and 'an association of weights and spindles which could be interpreted as the result of certain textile activity' (Bernabeu et al., 1986). Here too a few elements appear that give it a special relevance in the whole. In general, the settlement seems to be arranged in two blocks separated by the central street, with compartments of nil or limited activity on one side and the area of greater activity on the other.

This articulation of spaces and places of activity leads these authors to conclude that:

> The notion that Puntal dels Llops might be not a village but a structurally and functionally uniform settlement proves an attractive and coherent hypothesis, both because of the spatial distribution of the areas of activity on the site and from the notion that we are dealing with an *atalaya*, a place for keeping watch over and controlling the territory; this hypothesis had been put forward previously from a consideration of strictly macrospatial criteria.

We find a different concept of settlement and of its internal structures in La Bastida de les Alcuses, also in Valencia, with a violent end which facilitates a microspatial study. The extent of the excavations, with more than 200 compartmental units excavated, provides plenty of information about the urban layout and the structure of the lesser units of the habitat. The compartments are grouped into dwellings or larger units, which in turn form clusters separated by unevenly and irregularly aligned streets, in contrast to the Puente Tablas model. The typology of the larger compartment units is not uniform, giving the impression of a structure that follows no predetermined pattern. In any case, the delineation of the larger units raises numerous problems that the researchers attribute to the absence of gaps in the platforms of the different living spaces. Llobregat, for one, in his study of Contestania (1972), and Santos Velasco, in an analysis of the housing and the uneven distribution of wealth in La Bastida (Santos Velasco, 1986a), have made some attempts to bring the different rooms/outbuildings together into larger units, following different patterns and achieving results that are also different, which leaves the question still open. Anyway, as far as the definition of the different places and areas of activity is concerned, on the basis of Santos Velasco's work and our own observations, a few approximations to defining the spatial units can be made, bearing in mind that the distribution of the materials in their spatial location creates correlations that allow compartments destined for storage, domestic production and consumption to be distinguished. Thus in compartments f, m, n, o, p and q, reported as

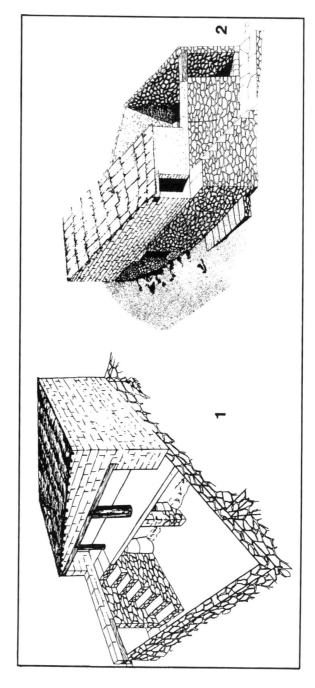

Figure 50 Iberian house at Puig de Bencarló. 1. From the south-west. 2. From the north-west (from Gusi and Olaria, 1984)

dwellings, a specialised use of space in order to define places and areas of activity is detected.

Analysis of the spatial distribution within the dwellings in the settlement of Los Villares de Caudete entails more difficulties, although here, in the full Iberian phase (stratum 2), definition of the larger units presents no problem, since we can see that dwelling structures of differing typology are coeval. In this case house no. 1 stands out, composed of two modules of similar structure, with an entrance space and a rear wing partitioned into smaller units, reminiscent of house no. 2 at Puente Tablas. The same pattern is repeated at Castellet de Bernabé, although in this case access to the dwelling is at the side; this seems to have been imposed by the actual urban structure and the alignment of the streets.

Catalonia–Aragon

The region of Catalonia provides a great deal of information concerning the structure and distribution of the habitat inside the settlements. Excavations have been numerous and extensive and have given rise to studies on different levels, from defining places of habitat of the house type to identifying larger units, which involve problems of urban layout. During the sixth century BC the appearance of the first square houses is noted, a fact which seems to occur towards the middle of the century, at Illa d'en Reixac, for example, during phase II, or in the houses cut into the rock at Puig de Sant Andreu. At Moleta del Remei in Tarragona province, in its first occupation phase from the end of the seventh to the middle of the sixth century BC, the dwelling area is characterised by circular huts of 3 metres diameter with their base cut out of the rock, in a historical setting that is clearly pre-Iberian (Gracia *et al.*, 1988). Firm information about the distribution and articulation of the spaces and places of habitation is only partially available, starting from the fifth century BC, partially, and chiefly during the fourth century and at later periods. The case of the Alorda Park site in Calafell (lower Penedés) (Sanmartí and Santacana, 1987b) provides information about the evolution of a small settlement with special functional characteristics from the beginning of the fifth century BC. Throughout this evolution and up to the final period of occupation, around the end of the second century BC, the permanence of some aspects of the original layout can be observed, together with modifications that not only affect the structure of the habitation units but hint at important changes in the functioning of some of them. This is the case with space A, which in the fifth century seemed to function as a place for cultural activity and would subsequently be converted to domestic use. Defining the places of activity becomes extremely complicated, especially in the third century BC. The dimensions of the different structures and their articulation, as well as other information from the archaeological record, led the researchers to conclude that the primary sector must have been of very little importance in this settlement, at least as far as agriculture is concerned; they deduced this from the actual typology of the habitat which they came to designate as a block-house with little or no storage capacity. As for the unit consisting of rooms G and F, it seems they were strictly homes, with a dormitory/living room (G) and another linked to production and storage for consumption (appearance of two rotary querns). A few of the dwellings do seem to indicate specialised production, as in E2, which is definitely linked with a worker in lime. All in all, the most notable activity deduced for the settlement is connected with collecting shellfish by means of rakes with nets attached to them, 'which implies a certain specialisation', and, possibly, fishing in the open sea, deduced from the location of scales from very large blue fish, as well as a few tools that might be related to this activity. Mention is also made, although with no spatial reference, to finding loom weights and spindles, as well as iron and lead slag, which would seem to indicate a certain industrial activity. In the same district of Calafell, less than 3 kilometres from Alorda Park, the site at Arguilera must have been a small 'back-up' nucleus devoted to agricultural exploitation of the surrounding plains. The discovery of a series of storage pits dug into the clay (the two located have a capacity of 9,050 and 10,014 litres respectively), in an ideal environment for grain preservation, demonstrates an agrarian economy based on cereals with a production clearly in excess of domestic needs (very much so if we bear in mind that there may have been many more identical storage pits); given the size of the site, these could have been connected with storage for exchange within a range that is difficult to determine accurately (Sanmartí *et al.*, 1984).

Of much greater structural, functional and productive complexity is the previously mentioned settlement of Moleta del Remei. Its layout corresponds to a model that implies evolution from what Maluquer called 'villages divided into two districts, separated by a central street' and 'assumes a stage prior to the adoption of systems inspired by Hippodamian plans' (Maluquer et al., 1986). In general, the layout of Moleta in its second phase, and carrying on through the third, is dominated by the plan of a fortification that is an extraordinarily complex construction. Inside it, a series of interlinked streets mark out districts consisting of habitation structures and other constructions considered unusual. The buildings of the fourth century BC are generally trapezoidal structures backing on to the inner line of the fortification. Access to the habitation units is by steps down from the level of street no. 2 and there is

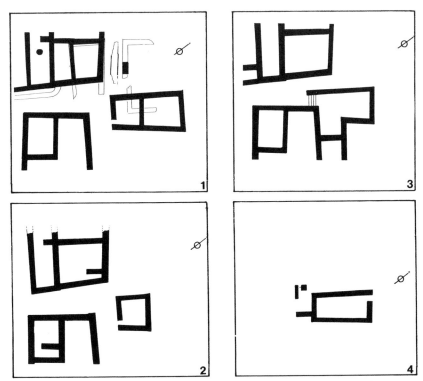

Figure 51 Alorda Park. 1. Middle of fifth century (in white), end of fifth and start of fourth (in black). 2. End of fourth century. 3. Middle of third century. 4. End of second century (from Sanmartí and Santacana, 1987a)

evidence of the existence of a second floor, at least in dwellings 1 and 12. The covering would have been a single slant up against the town wall and sloping towards the street. During the phase corresponding to the transition from the IIIrd to the IInd century BC, the living spaces underwent slight remodelling, such as transverse or longitudinal partitioning of structures from the previous phase, but without modifying the general organisation of the habitat. The majority of the units had a hearth occupying a central position during the periods of the fourth century BC, but later, after the partitioning, the hearths were placed back to back and were of a more elementary character. In general, the dwellings/habitation units show few productive enterprises, if we except those of a domestic nature, and then not in all the structures excavated (querns appear in only three of them, if no. 14 is excluded, which has a special importance).

In the settlement, three assemblages stand out as exceptional buildings. Odd building no. 1 shows 'a rectangular shape, 4 × 5 metres and is set on a podium of flat rectangular slabs, perfectly worked so as to leave a surface of uniform appearance' (Gracia *et al.*, 1988). The functionality of the building is connected with structure 14, situated facing its west side in street no. 2. This habitation is described as a communal place for food preparation, in view of the presence of twin hearths of considerable dimensions and an oven marked out with mud bricks; there is also a storage area and an assemblage of four boat-shaped querns. 'The economic and communal character of H. 14 suggests that Odd Structure 1 may have functioned as a store for sacks of grain, the surviving rectangular and parallel walls being supports for a floor raised on wooden staging which would serve to isolate it from damp' (Gracia *et al.*, 1988). So we could be in the presence of a series of productive areas of obvious importance (the other two fit a similar model), devoted to processing grain for subsequent trading. The scope of the model might indicate that the village specialised in those tasks and this could be endorsed by the absence of other productive spaces and the limited nature of the domestic sphere.

La Penya del Moro de Sant Just Desvern is situated on a hill dominating the estuary of the river Llobregat (Barberà and Sanmartí, 1982). The topographic characteristics of the terrain ensure that the village is built on a terraced pattern following the curve of the contour and this determines the structure of the habitation spaces. The same characteristics of the terrain influence the building technique of the houses; these are cut into the rock, which forms the rear wall and supports the flooring. The dwellings are square or rectangular in shape and vary in size, with a living area that fluctuates between 15 and 25 square metres. The features marking the end of the occupation of the site at the very end of the fourth century BC, when it was abandoned with the removal of everything that might be usable, make it difficult to determine the functionality of the different structures, with the exception of a few places defined as storage. All this fits in with the domestic and limited nature of the parts excavated.

As to the functionalities of the smaller places within the habitat area, which, as we have seen in the previous examples, are difficult to define, a site excavated in Lérida (abandoned in special circumstances, since fire put an end to the life of the place in the late third or early second century BC) enables a reconstruction of this aspect to be made: namely the house in the settlement of Mas Boscà (Junyent and Baldellou, 1972).

The dwelling, which is rectangular, partly hewn out of the granite rock, is divided crosswise into two rooms giving a total space of 45 square metres. The rear structure is partitioned in turn into two small rooms, one of which constitutes a genuine storeroom where twenty-two Iberian flat-mouthed amphorae and a few other vessels came to light. In the space parallel to it a quern was found, twenty loom weights, spindles and some bits of pot. In the sector communicating with the outside, table ware predominated, together with a great variety of utensils, mainly containers, and an accumulation of numerous loom weights on a line opening into the inner compartments, ninety-six of them carefully piled up. In the entrance room, a storage pit with a capacity of 4,500 litres was found, cut into the rock, and in the entrance to the dwelling what appeared to be a hearth was detected.

All in all, the structure of the dwelling, its partitioning and the distribution and variety of the materials mean that we can speak of a complex but limited area of domestic and productive activity – varied insofar as it reflects the multitude of activities identified (storage, textiles, production for consumption, etc.) and limited as regards the scope of production, which, aside from the storage space, is confined to family and domestic use. On the other hand, the extent of the storage space does seem to exceed that limit; and this, combined with the richness of some of the materials and the abundance of imports, might suggest the surplus nature of the economy of the putative family unit residing there.

If the examples so far mentioned in the region of Catalonia refer to population entities that developed productive activity in a variety of economic sectors, the site of Puig Castellet (Lloret de Mar, La Selva, Gerona), with a very short time span (250/240 and 220/210 BC) (Pons *et al.*, 1981), has special features, being a fortified enclosure with an obvious strategic function, but with a life inside 'that allowed a whole series of domestic and labouring activities to develop, comparable to those of a village'. Definition of the space in the enclosure led the researchers to identify four spatial levels:

1 House or living space, although it might share other work functions.
2 Working space, intended exclusively for work functions, either for processing or storing.
3 Space for communal use.
4 Complementary space.

In general, both in the building technique and in the distribution of space within very reduced limits, remarkable planning work is in evidence, starting with the construction of the walled enclosure and later with the structures that divide up the interior. In the construction dynamic of the settlement, three phases are reported 'without solving the continuity'; given the limited period of activity, they appear to reflect only a building sequence and so do not relate

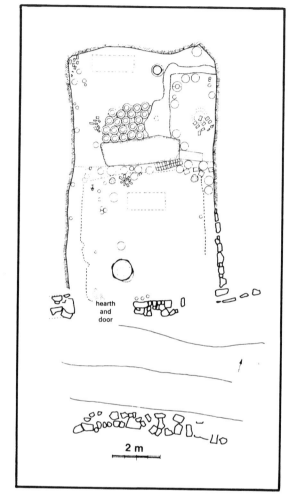

Figure 52 Iberian house at Mas Boscà (from Junyent and Baldellou, 1972)

to different moments in history. The different spaces are defined as follows (see Figure 53):

1 Houses: domestic activities: hearth, domestic utensils; work activities: querns and items to do with weaving. Spaces 0, 3, 6–6 bis, 1, 7 and 9–10 would fit this definition.
2 Work spaces: processing and storage activities. Spaces 2 and 8 would fit into this group.

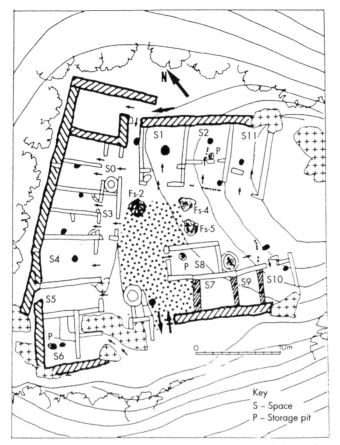

Figure 53 Puig Castellet: Spatial–functional definition of the enclosure
(from Llorens i Rams *et al.*, 1986)

3 Spaces for communal use with presumably collective activity (space 4).
4 Complementary spaces: refers only to no. 5 with a drainage function.

The characteristics of the settlement and the definition of buildings and space are in some ways reminiscent of what was noted in Puntal dels Llops in Valencia, inasmuch as the settlement is characterised by integral planning, such that all the productive activity within it is for the sole purpose of sustaining an established community functioning on strategic lines. The absence of agricultural implements, or any others connected with activities outside the purely domestic, could support the suggestions of the authors of the report on Puig Castellet.

169

The Puntal dels Llops pattern, a settlement with a central street with living spaces along either side, and a tower dominating the whole, seems to be documented in Aragon too. In general, villages with a central street abound and perhaps El Taratrato de Alcañiz, excavated in the 1920s by Bardaviu and Paris, may be one of the most interesting, in view of the recent revision by Burillo. This is a settlement adapted to the dimensions of the hill it is built on, surrounded by a wall that serves as the rear wall of the buildings inside it, just as at Puntal. These units, varying in extent, with exceptions, between 40 and 45 square metres, are all rectangular structures and usually exhibit inner partitioning which defines various models; it is not possible to speak of typological evolution in them, since the settlement has a very restricted time span (fourth century BC) and suffered no breaks in its short existence (Burillo, 1982).

Defining the work processes

Definition of the habitat units brings us to a consideration of the Iberian dwelling, the house, as an important sphere of a residential-domestic but also a productive nature. The house, articulated into wider spheres and into the settlement in particular, gives us an idea of the spatial level of the economic structure, with the location of different areas and places where the work processes are to be found. This conclusion brings us to a consideration of the family as a fundamental productive unit, but to the existence of other units as well, that transcend that sphere; this might be the case in a few settlements specialising in economic or strategic functions in a dual relationship, coordinating domestic economy and a particular specialisation of the settlement that transcends the family.

From what has been written in the preceding pages and from a reading of the sources, it can be deduced that work processes in the Iberian world varied greatly with differing levels of complexity. Those relating to complementary work are particularly important, because they show clearly the existence of a developed division of labour and, more importantly, genuine specialists apparently dedicated to an exclusive field, at least in certain economic sectors. This complexity in the systems of production shatters and largely supersedes the techno-sexual division of work, which, if not completely superseded, is relegated to a secondary plane, the dominant one being that relating to a class structure in a broad sense.

Unfortunately, the dynamic of the excavations in Iberian settlements has made hardly any advance in identifying the productive spaces, except in very general terms. At present, although from analysis of the artefacts we know of the existence of numerous work processes, the same is not true of spatial definition of the boundaries that could delineate likely areas and places of production.

So in spite of the relatively well-attested series of activities inferred from analysis of the artefacts, knowledge of the technical processes of production is very limited, being restricted in practice to certain 'industrial' processes, while the economic activities that are crucial in the Iberian world, particularly those of agriculture, can only be dealt with indirectly in relation to the complementary processes devolving from them. In the following pages we shall pay particular attention to three of the industrial processes of special relevance in Iberian archaeology.

Pottery

In Iberian societies, the manufacture of pottery was a process of capital importance, both in itself and for its connection with other economic sectors and practices, for which it provided a basic means of work (storage, transport, consumption, etc.). It can be said that in general Iberian pottery was a product reflecting a highly sophisticated technology, was largely wheel made and showed very wide techno-functional and typological variety, as has been made plain in previous chapters. Its manufacture was the result of a complex process of production which shows up well in the archaeological record. Indeed, if the making of pottery shaped by hand can be limited to a domestic space with minimal specialisation, the use of the wheel demands a specialisation that can only be achieved after a long process of apprenticeship and a dedication which, at the most sophisticated levels, has to be more or less exclusive. This is particularly so in the case of certain vessels, especially the medium to large sizes and the closed forms. By contrast, manufacture of certain open forms (bowls) is achievable after a minimal apprenticeship; not so, of course, the standardisation normally seen in the production of these receptacles.

The process of pottery production is the combined result of various concurrent work processes:

1 *Obtaining the clay:* contrary to what may be supposed, locating suitable clays not only reqires a knowledge of the medium, but is a highly specialised skill. On its qualities depend most of the related processes. After extraction, the clay has to undergo a mechanical transformation process, involving at least one phase of trituration and another of cleansing by means of decantation.

2 *Turning:* this is a highly specialised phase in which the peculiar features of

171

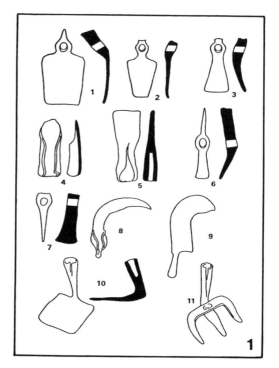

Figure 54 1. Iberian agricultural implements in the País Valenciano. 2. Agricultural scene on a vase from Alcorisa (Teruel)

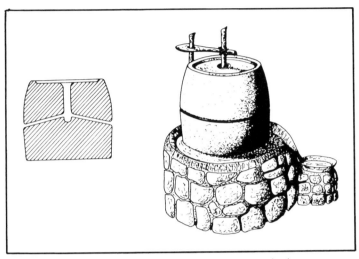

Figure 55 Iberian olive press (reconstruction)

the raw material have to be balanced against all the formal characteristics of the vessel that is the object of the process. Manipulation of the clay and of the turned article before firing is perhaps the most complex phase of the whole process.

3 *Firing:* demands an empirical mastery of fire, since the absence of measuring instruments means that experience alone can judge the state of the kiln, the vessels and the conditions inside: this is when some of the fundamental characteristics of the vessel (oxidation, reduction) are determined.

4 *Decoration:* this phase, which is optional, may take place before firing, after it or may even require a second specific firing. The character of the decoration also influences the technique employed. Whether it is done on the wheel (bands) or by mechanical instruments (compasses), it demands equally high specialisation.

The places and areas of pottery production that have been confirmed in the Iberian world are not particularly numerous, but they allow a few parameters of the processes followed to be established. However, some of the phases indicated have produced hardly any information, because analyses – chemical ones in particular – concerning the origin of the clays or the pigments used in making the paints or glazes are non-existent or poor. A similar state of affairs prevails when defining the mechanical apparatus (wheel); this is due, of course, to the characteristics of the materials it would have been made of (basically,

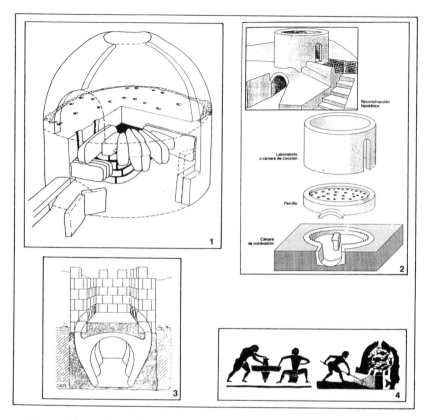

Figure 56 1. Iberian kiln at Pajar de Artillo (Seville) (from Luzón, 1973).
2. Kiln at Alcalá del Júcar (Albacete) (from Coll Conesa, 1987). 3. Pottery kiln
from Fontscaldes (from García y Bellido, 1952). 4. Depiction on Attic pottery
of the manufacturing processes using the wheel and firing.

wood). By contrast, identifying where the firing took place, the kilns, is a very
easy matter, and, despite the absence of a formal typology for them, a clear
evolution can be observed, in which an increase in complexity is noted that can
be related to an ever-more standardised and specialised work process; the kiln
excavated in Pajar de Artillo, dated to the second century BC (Luzón, 1973)
can serve as an example. This kiln is circular in shape, with a single upward
draught and consists of a furnace, from which a central pillar rises to support
the grating of the firing chamber, covered with a dome of which barely 20 cm
in height has been preserved; it has a clear antecedent in the one excavated at
Alcalá del Júcar, Albacete, defined by its investigator as 'a structure on a

174

circular plan with a vertical draught and double chamber, a lower or furnace chamber and a higher or firing chamber (laboratory), separated by a central pillar that is rectangular in section' (Coll Conesa, 1987). The kiln, which is dated to the third or early second century and was presumably intended for the production of large vessels (amphorae or urns), undoubtedly, given its complexity, required the presence of 'highly specialised craftsmen'. A very different case, given the elementary nature of the installations and its chronology, (late seventh and early sixth century), but very important for identifying the area of production, is the one recently excavated in the *campiña* of Marmolejo. The complex is marked by various places of different structure and functionality, which, at the very end of the occupation of the settlement, seem to have been functioning simultaneously:

1   A circular structure with a small limestone base with a central axis dividing it into two symmetrical and identical spaces is interpreted as the platform for a Mediterranean-type kiln with a mud-brick vault and single up-draught. The furnace lies opposite the central axis of the chamber. The height of the homogeneous stone platform is 50 cm. The space inside the firing chamber is not known as we do not know how thick the vaulting was, but it could not in any case have been more than 500 cubic cm.

2   A circular platform of small stones, well bonded. At one side are two large flagstones, which may indicate access to a furnace/firing chamber. The location, next to the presumed access, of a heap of wheel-thrown grey-ware dishes, with a high shoulder, all of them half fired, suggests that this is a primitive kiln, possibly without differentiation of the two chambers. Next to this structure, large quantities of ash were found, possibly the result of cleaning it.

3   A circular structure made of small cobbles. The accumulation of clay on it leads to its being interpreted as a possible place for storing and/or kneading clay.

4   Two rectangular structures, 60 × 70 cm, lying next to the previous ones; their function is unknown.

5   An assemblage of four parallel, longitudinal structures formed by low, mud-brick walls with stone footings. The space separating these walls is never more than 30 cm and the floors of the spaces formed are always different; all this led the investigators to consider them to be supports for manipulating the pots at different stages of the production process, once they had been on the wheel (Molinos et al., 1988).

From its chronology and given the characteristics of the settlement (in reality a single built structure apparently for specialised agricultural use), the

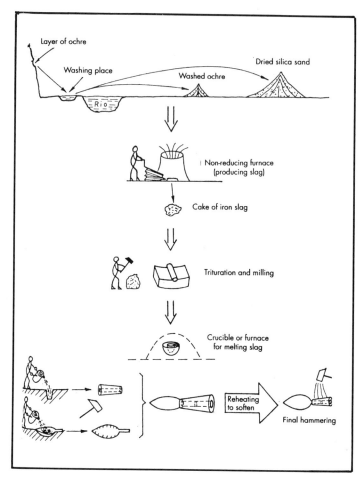

Figure 57 Manufacturing process of an iron lancepoint
(from Madroñero and Ágreda, 1988).

assemblage in the *campiña* is surprising for the complexity of the area devoted to producing pottery, rather than for the complexity of the different installations, which, individually, are no more than structures for a production that is not intended for more than domestic use. However, the assemblage could indicate the existence of a wider circuit of distribution for the manufactured product, in relation to other small settlements with similar characteristics in the immediate surroundings.

The production process in the settlement

Metallurgy

In general, not much is known at present about the minero-metallurgical process. Indeed, more work has been done on earlier phases in the Bronze Age and concerning copper and bronze metallurgy and ores of precious minerals, particularly silver. As in other sectors, it is analysis of artefacts, for the most part, that has provided information, and even there the results are generally slight because of the paucity of analyses to complement the purely typological.

As happens in pottery production, metallurgy requires a series of tasks to be developed concurrently, starting with the extraction of the mineral, continuing with the processing of the metal and ending with the making of the manufactured product. As in pottery too, the whole process demands at least a certain level of specialisation, which, in some cases, means inevitably the existence of artisans devoted entirely to the work, especially when it comes to making some of the manufactured articles found in Iberian archaeology.

Identification of the provenance of the mineral, the places of mining operations, is possible even when knowledge is somewhat limited; but beyond that, it would require systematic, specific prospections and verification by chemical and metalographic analyses of the relationship between the mineral and the manufactured products. In this respect, it should be noted that these products can be moved over large areas and, obviously, this makes the reconstruction of the metallurgical process quite difficult.

Only in exceptional cases do we know the relationship between the processes of extraction and those of the subsequent treatment and processing of the metal. This can be seen at Rio Tinto, in a pre-Iberian setting, where it has been possible to reconstruct the metallurgical process from the extraction of the mineral by opening up low galleries with a few working tools, consisting mainly of picks and stone hammers, to the work of transforming it in order to obtain silver. This last operation was performed in the domestic sphere, which might be an indication that it was the family structure, embedded in a wider and specialised context, that constituted the economic unit of production. Something like this took place in San Bartolomé de Almonte (Ruiz Mata and Fernández Jurado, 1986), although here the seasonal character of the settlement could imply work that was more coordinated and so more remote from the domestic sphere.

In both cases it was cupellation that seemed to form the basic technique for processing the precious metal and this technique was carried out by artisans using procedures that imply a considerable loss of yield in relation to the metal content of the mineral. This artisan type of production with regard to certain metals may have lasted throughout the Iberian phases, at least in some parts, seeing that the location of some of the means of production and of residues in many of the sites are typically very scattered. Only in a few cases do areas appear to be identified where the presence of slag or other items might indicate that they existed inside the settlements, as Fernández Jurado points out in the case of Tejada; there a possible metallurgical area is reported, on the basis of the association of a few items like slag or crucibles in the space between the inhabited nucleus and the inner face of the fortification.

Anyway, the paucity of studies addressing the minero-metallurgical problem in relation to the Iberian phases, and particularly to iron working, is surprising. As an example, even if only partial, Madroñero and Agreda's (1988) study at Estacar de Robarinas in Cástulo deserves attention, because, in fact, as the authors point out, the relative abundance of that metal in the Iberian horizons contrasts with the apparent scarcity of metal-bearing deposits that are economic in modern terms, at least in some areas. However, as they report, outcrops of red ochre abound and, when subjected to a process of washing and later scorification, this mineral would yield a supply of iron, within reasonable limits, to a settlement the size of the one in Cástulo. Indeed, Iberian remains are frequently found associated with seams of ochre; this is often the case on the upper Guadalquivir and in zones where there are outcrops of land described geologically as Trias-Keuper. Generally speaking, the process for extracting iron from ochre would require two firings: one for scorification and the other, later, to extract the iron from the product of the first.

After these operations, but certainly with no interval, the molten metal would be transferred to smelting moulds from which the manufactured product would emerge. The whole process cannot be performed without a rigorous empirical knowledge; it demands a particularly high level of specialisation in the production of a few things such as agricultural implements, weapons or items for transport – in this case a combined and concurrent metallurgical and carpentry operation – especially if we bear in mind that it is means of work that are being produced and their use in any activity implies wear and tear, so it must be underpinned by maintenance work, which would be difficult to perform in an exclusively domestic sphere. A particularly good illustration is provided by items of equipment connected with transport and, more especially, the cart, both the military version and the one for transporting merchandise. For Iberian carts, apart from their appearance in a host of paintings and sculptures, we have an archaeological dossier enabling us to appreciate their structural complexity and sophisticated construction. We are referring to the occasional presence of remains of metal mountings for the wheels and axles of these vehicles throughout the Iberian region from

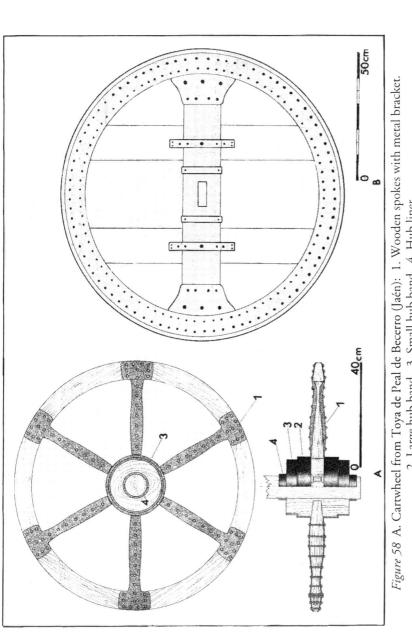

Figure 58 A. Cartwheel from Toya de Peal de Becerro (Jaén): 1. Wooden spokes with metal bracket.
2. Large hub band. 3. Small hub band. 4. Hub liner.
B. Cartwheel for carrying merchandise from Casares de la Cañada de los Ojos (Guadalaviar, Teruel)
(from Fernández Miranda and Olmos, 1986)

Catalonia to Estremadura; they can be roughly classified into wheels for military vehicles and wheels for vehicles to carry merchandise. The first group, well represented by the wheels from Toya, is perhaps the more complex because their construction requires the casting of a host of pieces (outer covers for spokes and sometimes for the rims, large and small hub bands, hub liner, nails, rivets, etc.). Assembling all these together, and with the rest of the wooden structure and further metal components is work that requires great precision. This type of wheel turns up with a very similar typological pattern in many settlements (Mirador de Rolando, Baza, Galera, San Miguel de Sorba, etc.) and with a chronological range that, although problematic in a few cases, given the situation of the find, covers basically the fifth and the first half of the fourth century BC (Fernández Miranda and Olmos, 1986).

The other model, the wheel for transporting merchandise, is sparsely documented and the construction suggests less cost and preparation. The model is represented by the wheel from Montjuïc, with a metal rim which would be nailed on to a solid wooden disk, reinforced at the axle by two brackets, likewise nailed to the disk (Fernández Miranda and Olmos, 1986). Those from Amarejo (Albacete) are of the same type and, as already indicated, the researchers associate them with a storage structure and so with the transport of merchandise (Broncano and Blánquez, 1985).

Textile industry

References in the sources and archaeological documentation tell us of the importance of this sector of production. The former serve to indicate the variety of the raw materials, of both plant and animal origin, used in the spinning and subsequent manufacture of fabrics; they also tell us how specialised it became in some settlements (Saitabí). From these references it is possible to deduce that esparto, wool and flax were the most usual raw materials. Particularly noteworthy is the abundance of references to flax in places like the environs of Ampurias (Domínguez, 1986); this might be explained by its being more valuable, although, coincidentally, it is the fabric most frequently found in archaeological excavations (Castro Curel, 1983). References to cotton are, by contrast, very rare (Ruano Ruiz, 1989).

On the other hand, in archaeological excavations it is not unusual to find a series of items commonly associated with the structure of a loom. Verification of the specific processes that might be inferred from this is still uncertain, save for the domestic nature of at least part of the production, as evidenced by the abundance of these bits of looms found in Iberian houses. Moreover, we should point out that the quality of some of the made-up articles, evidence of

180

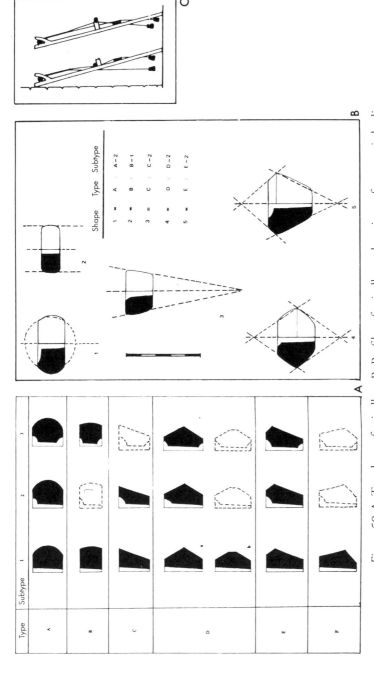

Figure 59 A. Typology of spindles. B. Profiles of spindles and sections of geometric bodies. C. Diagram of the position of the weights on a vertical loom (from Castro Curel, 1986)

which is seen in a host of figurative representations, and their presumed size, as in the case of some veils and cloaks shown in them, might be linked with a more industrialised type of production, but we have no archaeological evidence for that.

About the structure of the looms we have very little specific information, although some concentrations of weights associated with internal walls, as in the house excavated by Junyent and Baldellou at Mas Boscà, or the instance at Almedinilla, Cordoba, to quote just a few, might indicate a type of upright loom, leaning against the walls 'in such a way that the warp threads, stretched from a higher crosspiece, hang vertically' (Castro Curel, 1986).

For the processes after weaving (dyeing industry, processes involved in making clothes), we rely on the testimony of the sources and on the styles of clothing deduced from the figurative representations (Bandera, 1977–8).

— 5 —

Iberian society

Aristocracy and peasants

Economic or territorial models, the presence of rich materials produced in other societies, analyses recently carried out of the necropolises (Almagro Gorbea, 1982b and 1983a; Santos Velasco, 1989), all point to a marked social differentiation, giving rise on the social plane to groups of very different levels of wealth or power. The question has also been followed through the written historical sources, with well-known works such as that of Rodríguez Adrados (1948) on the *fides* or that of Caro Baroja (1971). In this way a panorama has taken shape, a contradictory one incidentally, defining chiefdoms (Domínguez, 1984) or kings (Caro Baroja, 1971; Almagro Gorbea *et al.*, 1990), presenting us with opposing images of the same society (Alvar, 1990).

Moreover, the theoretical approach that laid the foundations of these interpretations usually started from an indirect view of the society that was to be the subject of analysis: on the one hand, because the historical sources, drawn from Roman or Greek informants, have generated readings, sometimes very varied in time; on the other, because they transferred to Iberian society subjective positions and concepts that were typical of the society they came from. In general, it is because, on the archaeological plane, the reading of the dominant classes of Iberian society had started with the effect of colonisation (Phoenician or Greek at first; Roman or Carthaginian later), with the presence of the colonists' products in that society (thereby consolidating a single angle from which to represent the process of group differentiation at its heart, on the basis of an exogenous effect characterised by the interests of the coloniser) and, on the same level, with the system of exchange. In short, it is strictly an effect of the economicist conception of Ricardo, who, in our particular case, made his interpretation in diffusionist terms, thereby continuing mechanically to confuse the strictly indigenous process with the objectives of colonisation:

sometimes in emulation of it, in the better examples, at others with that lamentable assumption of indigenous infantilism compared with the maturity of the coloniser.

As Marx (1904) wrote in his *Contribution to a Critique of Political Economy*, production, consumption, distribution and exchange are parts of the same productive process, since production on its own would lack reality if it could not count on those other aspects (consumption, distribution and exchange), which, in the last resort, are what gives it its specific historical character.

The alleged opposition between the Rowlands/Frankenstein and the Bintliff models concerning the origins of social hierarchies (Andouce and Buchsenschutz, 1989) is meaningless when the first pair emphasises that they are produced by controlling the circuits of exchange and distribution, while for the second power rests on possession or control of agricultural land.

Indeed, a third model would be needed, showing how these two theoretically opposed positions should be considered in conjunction, since if the argument tends exclusively towards the Rowlands/Frankenstein model, it will be unaware ultimately of the bases on which the difference between a chief, who has grown rich, and a king are founded; and, as in the case of the Iberians, it will end up presenting, from the same data, one model of monarchy and another of a clan that has evolved conically, initiating a debate of the formalism–substantivism type.

However, in both models, the key to what we are proposing so as to follow the process of differentiation in Iberian society, by establishing the factor, mentioned elsewhere in the text, that stamped the fundamental nature of social relationships in the world of the Iberians, is the land and, therefore, its appropriation. But land in relation to the individual, as Marx emphasised, has a dual articulation. In the first place, because the objective conditions of work, which imply land appropriation, are not the effect of work itself but are interpreted as typical of nature, so the relationship of the individual to the land is a natural condition of production. Secondly, because the process, set out in these terms, never takes place directly but is impeded by defining the individual within a group; the social group the individual belongs to is in turn an effect of the specific form of the ownership of the objective conditions of work.

Having outlined these theoretical terms of reference, we are obliged by the process of understanding the Iberian world to spell out the actual terms in which the relationship of the individual to the land takes place and the extra-economic elements that lead production back towards a restricted group in society and not to the community as a whole. Consequently, one of the keys to this process consists in evaluating the real nature of these different defined groups.

Iberian society

Later, the systems of product distribution make the connection to the coloniser possible, starting from the framework of the restricted receiving group. But this is not a secondary relationship; hence the value of the Rowlands/Frankenstein model, since this articulation is productive in itself; that is to say, it forms part of the process of production inasmuch as it defines what is most attractive for the exchange circuits and consequently this is reflected in the actual system of land appropriation.

Hierarchies in the settlements

If we look at it on a functional level, Iberian society defines a fourfold population system in the territory, as we have been able to assess it so far. In three of the systems, the presence of fortifications becomes a fundamental element; so in them the *oppidum* is the key element to the system and is hierarchically at the top.

Consequently the role of the *oppidum* is central to the population system and it is there that the framework of social conflicts and the spatial representation of the different groups can best be defined, since the functional nature of the *atalaya*, defined in terms of consumption and strategic value, and of the agricultural trading post, representing a more or less extended family unit, generally militate against precision of analysis in settlements of lesser status or very well-defined functionality.

Palaces or temples

Sadly, no extensive excavations have so far been done in the highest levels of the hierarchy, of the size of the *oppidum*, so examples such as Carmona, Cástulo or Elche will for the future have to illustrate more clearly the differences we are claiming to establish through spatial distribution within the settlement. Nevertheless, nowadays, we can count on information about a few spaces that are clearly differentiated from those occupied by basic economic units. Usually, these spaces have been given the name of temples or public buildings, by a process of transposition of Mediterranean models, although without the theoretical analysis necessary for making such a radical assertion.

The first level of analysis of these buildings indicates the need to determine whether they are sited outside or inside the settlement and consequently the fortifications that delineate the inhabited and defended space. At the end of the seventh century BC, that is, at a time before consolidation of the Iberian model, we know of a structure in the settlement of Muela near Cástulo displaying a clearly extra-economic function (Blázquez and Valiente, 1981). It is a complex of which an irregular-shaped patio has been excavated, to the east

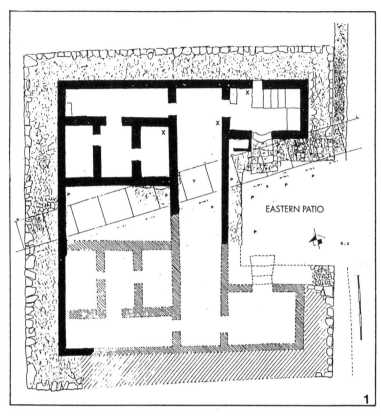

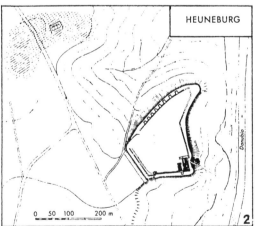

Figure 60 1. Palace sanctuary at Cancho Roano (Zalamea de la Serena, Badajoz) (from Maluquer de Motes, 1983). 2. Heuneburg: the Talhau house lies 500 metres from the fortification (from Andouce and Buchsenschutz, 1989)

186

of which lie two rooms; the first occupies almost the whole of the front of the patio and adjoins the other room as an independent construction with walls backing on to each other. Its sophisticated construction, with a magnificent mosaic of pebbles in a chequered design of black and white squares surrounded by a border with a decorative theme of running waves and possibly scrolls and rosettes, as well as its situation on the bank of the river Guadalimar, have suggested that the structure be interpreted as a cult enclosure for the practice of feasting rites, remains of which were recovered later in a 'consecration pit'. To arrive at this conclusion, parallels were followed in the rural sanctuaries of Cyprus and Crete, serving small peasant or artisan communities (especially metal workers). The investigators stress two further aspects: firstly, the markedly indigenous character of the material production documented here, combined with certain building techniques acquired from relations with the semitic colonist; secondly, the presence of items (graphite pottery) which might suggest a *mesetan* presence, as well as certain cult elements (sacrifice, represented by the 'consecration pit').

Towards the west, in Estremadura, with a later chronology, Maluquer has excavated the so-called 'palace-sanctuary' of Cancho Roano in Zalamea de la Serena (Maluquer de Motes, 1981 and 1983). This is a building on a square plan standing on an external stone terrace with a cyclopean wall. The structure is laid out around an open central patio with a continuous bench, the wall elevation being covered with slabs of slate. From the north and to one side, a staircase gives access to a large room giving on to the terrace by means of a second staircase in one place, while to the west it opens on to an extended nave running the length of the edifice. This is arranged in three spaces, the most northerly of which is a rectangular nave giving access to a second tripartite nave. To the south, another nave gives access to a bipartite space, while in the centre is a closed space (an *adytum*), in the central part of which a large pilaster supports the roof, and above the pilaster was a main altar. Lastly, to the south of the patio, a staircase leads up to a storeroom with an abundance of wine amphorae.

In Maluquer's opinion, the sanctuary was dedicated to a female deity of the Ataecina group, although he does not rule out its having been, at the same time, the palace residence of some kinglet, who adapted the eastern tradition, converting it into the house of a divinity within a gentilic ruling group, managed and ordered by an economic and politico/religious chief (Maluquer de Motes, 1981).

Inside, a cart with four horses was in fact discovered and among their trappings, a representation of *Potnia* is documented. The settlement, with important finds of gold and silver jewellery, dates from the beginning of the

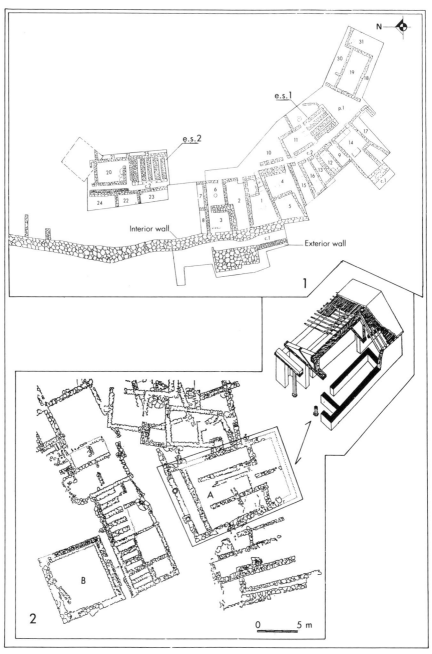

Figure 61 1. Moleta del Remei (Alcanar, Montsià): location of unusual
structures 1 and 2 (from Pallarés *et al.*, 1986). 2. Illeta dels Banyets
(El Campello, Alicante): general plan indicating 'temples' A and B; top,
attempted reconstruction of temple A (from Llobregat, 1985)

188

sixth century BC, until it fell into ruin at the end of the fifth or beginning of the fourth century and was definitively abandoned around 370 BC.

A necropolis is documented in its environs and, yet again, a river, the Ciganche, which flows on the east.

The third example of this type of supposedly cult building we have selected are the so-called temples of Illeta dels Banyets de Campello in Alicante (Llobregat, 1985). The first one, lying to the east, is a rectangular building with a portico with two octagonal columns and a great door giving access to three chambers; at the back appear the remains of two more chambers. In the interior, only partially excavated in the recent digs, amphorae are recorded and the rear fragment of a man's head in stone. Facing it on the other side of the street, a rectangular building has been defined, divided into four naves while at the back ten small spaces can be distinguished, which, from the remains of amphorae and receptacles, are interpreted as the temple storehouse. To the west of the storehouse and separated by another narrow street, is a second cult building on a square ground plan, with the door to the south; in the centre rise two stone and mud-brick platforms, into one of which a slab had been thrust which could be interpreted as a stele. Later, the building was silted up as far as the base of the walls and the place was reconstructed on a new base with the internal elements rearranged. On the eastern platform stood the tambour of a Doric-type column, while in the west stood another tambour and between the two a slab of sandstone backing on to another stone sticking up to the north. Lastly, a second platform had been formed in the east. Next to the first column was located an oriental-type perfume altar of the type known as 'horned'.

For dating, we rely on the presence of black-glazed Attic ware and a few items such as a perfume burner in the form of a female head, which might be of later date. The significant thing about the assemblage is that it is documented inside a settlement, just like the so-called 'temples' at Ullastret, one of which shows two columns *in antis* in the portico, located in an open space, where storage pits of a communal kind are also recorded. Similar in structure, that is to say with two columns in the entrance, dated to the first half of the fourth century BC and abandoned in the following phase, is the building, also defined as a temple, at Molí d'Espígol de Tornabous (Maluquer de Motes, 1986a). The unusual building at Alcores de Porcuna, dating from the end of the second and the first half of the first century BC, displays similar characteristics, with two columns, also at the entrance, and close to other unusual edifices in what appears to be a square (Arteaga and Blech, 1988). In Alorda Park, too, a building has been documented dated between the end of the fifth century and the fourth century BC, which does not seem to be a domestic structure, since, inside it, an area of ritual offerings deposited on the

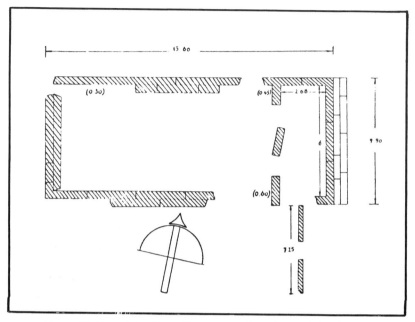

Figure 62 Plan of the Ibero-Roman temple at Cerro de los Santos
(from García y Bellido, 1952)

floor and a hearth were recorded. The place was transformed functionally
from the third century BC on (Sanmartí and Santacana, 1987b). Very similar
characteristics to the example at Campello are seen in two buildings located in
the central zone of the settlement at Moleta del Remei, one of which we have
described in the previous chapter. The building has been dated to the end of
the fifth century BC. The investigators relate this structure to the room situated
on the other side of the street, interpreted as a communal zone for processing
food because of the existence of two hearths and an oven as well as storage
space and four querns. The building is interpreted as a store for sacks of grain,
which would have been placed on flooring resting on the four walls. Added to
this is the find of bone needles, bronze punches and retouched antlers, whose
function, as interpreted, would be to tie and sew up the sacks. The second
building lies to the north of this one and also reveals in the centre five walls of
the same type but arranged in the opposite way in relation to the patio (Gracia
et al., 1988).

Taken as a whole and in spite of the spatial complexity of the few finds, the
assemblage of unusual buildings shows us a first Andalusian/Estremaduran
group lying outside the settlement, as at Cancho Roano, and a second group

190

(Campello, Ullastret, Tornabous and Alorda Park) situated chronologically between the end of the fifth and the middle of the fourth century BC and located inside the *oppidum.*

In general, all the authors agree in suggesting a religious character for these buildings because of the ritual items documented in most of them and the existence of some unusual features of construction already mentioned. Specifically, the assigning of spaces for storage (some inside, as at Cancho Roano, and others outside the building itself, as at Campello) is a fact of great significance, as is the consumption of food inside, which Blázquez explains at La Muela on the basis of the increase in the 'feasting ritual' (Blázquez and Valiente, 1981).

So the presence of temples contrasts with the absence of houses belonging to the most important individuals in the settlement, who, however, as we shall see, are very much there, on the other hand, in the necropolises. This fact obliges us to reflect on the indisputable ritual functionality of some of these buildings and on the possible coupling of the dominant social group with the religious horizon, in the way Maluquer envisaged at Cancho Roano or more recently Almagro Gorbea, commenting on the same site (Almagro Gorbea *et al.*, 1990).

In their analysis, the authors stress:

1 The existence of a private area in the north-western zone, used for feasting.
2 An area of storehouses to the south-west where the implements and reserves of food would have been kept.
3 A zone, the central patio, with some kind of sacred function, as a place for worshipping the dynastic deities or as a throneroom.
4 The upper storey, function unknown, which may have provided further storage or dwelling areas.
5 Two towers sited in the projecting parts of the building.

Apart from an attitude of mind that prevents the private area (women's quarters) from being associated with the feasting area (men's quarters) as the place where the aristocrat met his peers, and which would reinforce the notion of transposing the private (domestic) area to the second floor, Almagro Gorbea's interpretation may constitute a qualitative leap in the investigation of the indigenous aristocracy.

The case is reminiscent of the mesapic settlement at Cavallino in Apulia, where a very large house is documented, characterised by stone items decorated in the Greek taste; in Torelli's interpretation (Gross and Torelli, 1988) it was a princely residence, suitable for a *basileus* of the place. The building is dated to the second half of the sixth century, as in the case of Braida, near Serra de Vaglio in Lucania, where, incidentally, there is no fortified enclosure in its environs. As Torelli points out, in this aristocratic world of southern Italy it is difficult to establish a clear distinction between the categories of the sacred and the private, not to mention the political. A case on the same lines is, as at Heuneburg (Würtemberg) during the end of the Hallstatt period, the house at Talhau, which must have been the family residence of a prince and is sited some 500 metres from the fortification (Andouce and Buchsenschutz, 1989).

Again, the role these princely residences played in the settlements of Italian proto-history has been well analysed by Torelli, using examples like the relationship between the palace at Murlo, not far from Siena, and the one at Acquarosa, near Viterbo, both in Etruria. The first (second half of the seventh century BC and refurbished in 580) reveals a complex on a remote hillock above the surrounding countryside, which constitutes a classic model for the gentilic aristocracy; it is built round a patio with the areas characteristic of big gentilic manifestations (feasting, sacrifices, etc.) and terracotta images of processions of ancestors, implying their sacralisation. The palace at Acquarosa, built fifty years later, during the decline of the gentilic system, is an integral part of an inhabited settlement; the size is reduced, although it still has the feasting area and the pit for the ashes of the sacrifices, but the significant thing is that, facing the building, there now arises a small temple and this limits the religious capacity of the gentilic group, now established on a hero-cult, while the space sacred to the gods is structured outside and no longer controlled by the aristocrat (Gross and Torelli, 1988).

Apparently, the complexes at La Muela and Cancho Roano seem to fit the gentilic model of the Murlo type, although the analysis will require more fine tuning to take account of other finds that may emerge in future.

The fifth to fourth century BC models, however, cannot be considered as parallels to the Acquarosa phase. Firstly, because, as we shall see, no process similar to the one identified in Etruria has taken place, although characteristics do appear like those observed in southern Italy, where the local aristocracies collapsed causing the destruction of residences like Braida (Lucania) and giving rise to the development of seigniorial houses; this can be seen in the five studied in Lavallo, in Daunia. In these, on the principle of some kind of isonomy, aristocratic residences were created with similar plans and identified structurally by a large patio preceded by a portico decorated with an imposing acroter depicting the 'lord of the horses'. All this from the middle of the fifth to the beginning of the fourth century and without involving the appearance of temples or collective spaces like the agora (Gross and Torelli, 1988).

In short, and failing a microspatial analysis of these unusual buildings, the possibility of their being gentilic residences must be considered before assessing them as temples. Account must also be taken of the fact that their

192

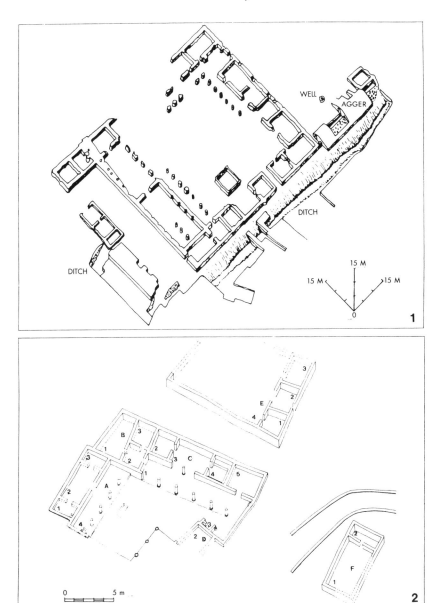

Figure 63 1. *Anaktoron* at Murlo. 2. *Anaktoron* at Acquarosa (west); to the east, a large house; to the south, a probable temple (from Gross and Torelli, 1988)

destruction at the end of the fourth century implies in some cases (Alorda Park or Tornabous) their use as simple houses. It is difficult to imagine such a thing for a former sacred space but, nevertheless, it is acceptable when the gentilic group has dissolved or been replaced by another.

Looked at from another perspective, the transition from the highly complex and isolated models of the seventh and sixth centuries, clearly belonging to a Tartessian environment or its periphery, or to others like that at Campello, is indicative of a process of transformation in the aristocracy which we shall have to continue analysing in other historical and archaeological horizons, but which gives grounds for thinking in terms of a tendency to the diversification of large gentilic units, although it must not be forgotten that the comparison is being made between the south-west area of our cultural sphere and the north and east of it, where no antecedents are known by which to check either case.

The oppida

The question revolving round the difficulty of coupling religious and political functions in one and the same space (assuming that we are not dealing here with rural sanctuaries) raises the problem of the appearance of towns. In fact, this, combined with the absence for the time being of public-political spaces like the agora (we except the meeting place in the square at Astapa when it was under pressure from the Roman army, although not even in this case should it be assumed that the space chosen for depositing weapons and creating a huge pyre was a public space in the sense we intend) means we cannot speak of urban models in the style of those identified in the Mediterranean world (Greek and Roman).

So if, in order to define towns among the Iberians, we adopt evolutionist or functionalist positions, such as population size and monumental religious centres (Kluckohn, in Morris, 1984) or think exclusively in terms of demographic tables (Davis, 1967), or the number of non-agrarian sectors present in the structure (the Iberian *oppida*), or at least of those holding a central position in the territory, such cases can be classified as towns. Our position with regard to this type of concept is not specified in gradual scales of size or the number of services, as we have just stated, but rather in the impact this spatial structure has on a social formation. Thus the fortified Iberian *oppidum*, with a system dictated by the plan of the basic axes of the blocks or houses, with aristocratic residences, where political, religious and probably economic power were fused together, can be a town, provided that the town is redefined in the terms put forward by Castell (1974); that is to say, as the projection of society in space and always understood as the concrete expression of a social formation, which, in its articulation into the countryside, marks out a political territory that is either public (the Greek or Roman town) or private, as in our case. From this point of view, the town has its starting point at the very moment when the social differences leading to classes and the appearance of a definite state structure are generated, and always arises from different models, the opposite extremes being the *polis* of the citizens of classical Greece and the palace-city of the Mesopotamian and Egyptian world.

From that point of view, the scenarios generated by the settlement models described in previous pages, that is to say, the model that should be described as '*oppidum*–trading post–tower' or the one based exclusively on the *oppida*, were, insofar as they fitted into structures of the type reported in their space, aristocratic towns which could, as they developed, attain astonishing levels of services, although they would never reach the point, as in Rome, where their inhabitants came to be citizens with the political right to define their own living space.

The *oppidum*, shut off from the countryside yet dependent on it and thus delineated in its urban and aristocratic residential space, became not only the graveyard of the kinship system – as we might say, paraphrasing Engels – but also the definition of aristocratic power.

With marked differences, particularly in chronology, being later, and of course of disproportionate size, compared with the Iberian *oppida*, this is the view advanced by Collis (1989) concerning the Celtic *oppida* , when he affirmed that they were basically expressions of the power of the aristocracy but, at the same time, generated within them a system of services which, at certain moments, could have given rise to genuinely distinct districts or *barrios*; spatially, these would foster guild-type class attitudes similar to the feudal models in the periods immediately preceding the development of the late medieval towns. Perhaps this may explain the frequent practice of describing the *oppida* as proto-towns; but it is done from an evolutionist standpoint that confers such a status on the Greek city and, consequently, values only those elements in the *oppidum* that could lead to that model.

The problem, and here we end this proposition, must be linked with the relationship between this system of structures and its economic territory; this may already have been defined in other terms by Marx (1964) when he said that 'modern history consists of the urbanisation of the countryside and not, as with the ancients, in the ruralisation of the town'. Indeed, the way the Iberian economic model was supported by agrarian production rendered the *oppidum*–countryside relationship indissoluble. But for all that, it cannot be entirely dissociated from classical society either, since, although as the preceding quotation from Marx says, it is a 'history of towns', its foundations

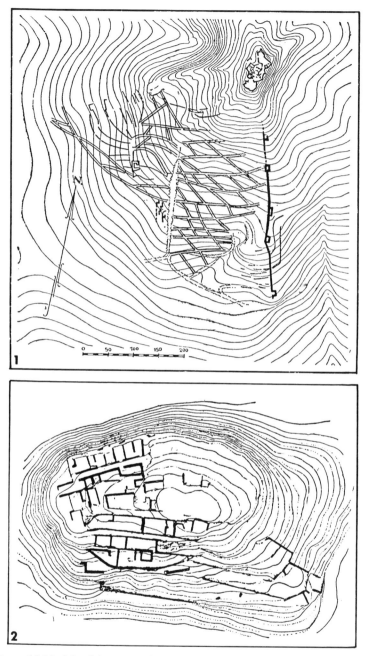

Figure 64 Models of the internal layout of the *oppidum* (from Arribas, 1965).
1. Burriac: gridiron model (from Serra Ráfols in Maluquer, 1952).
2. Puig Castellar: conical model (from Bosch Gimpera, 1932)

196

continued to be ownership of land. In any case, we have still a long way to go in understanding the Iberian countryside and the impact on it of the *oppidum* in terms of size of holdings, and getting them functioning, or of specific appropriation. However, the move we seem to see of the aristocratic house from outside to inside the mighty fortifications, and especially the presence of these fortifications in a setting closely coupled economically with the country-side, where its genuine basic interests lay, suggests that a rapid process was under way for defining new economic sectors of an urban type. At the same time, the internal pressure of aristocratic power on the system of social relationships is seen to be stronger. Lastly, the conflicts between aristocracies for possession of the land, which was controlled symbolically by the *oppidum*, were continuous and entailed a high degree of instability. We shall now follow that process, analysed in the actual structure of the *oppidum*.

In his work on the Iberians Arribas (1965) had already pointed to various models of internal layout, such as the 'grid', located on the terraces of a hill and following the contours (examples at Sant Julià de Ramis, Castell de Fosca de Palamós or Ullastret or Puig d'Alcoi). A second 'cone-type' model, sur-rounded by a wall and with a very regular chequerboard plan, would be found at sites like Puig Castellar de Santa Coloma de Gramenet. Lastly, he quotes a third model, in the Aragonese region with a central street; most characteristic of this model is Azaila, with tortuous streets linking up on a predetermined plan with the main road axis.

A second classification on the basis of the fortifications was proposed by Maluquer de Motes for Catalonia (1982) and taken up recently by Sanmartí and Santacana (1991):

1 Settlements on platforms. Situated on cone-shaped mounds with extensive visibility and, typically, a perimeter wall enclosing the platform on all sides to form a circular or elliptical plan in the majority of cases. The houses were arranged against the inner face of the fortifications, leaving the space in the centre empty or else occupied by other constructions. Vilaró is an example of the first type, and La Moleta del Remei or Puig Castellar de Santa Coloma de Gramenet of the second. In many instances, because of their small size (the ones that have been studied in Catalonia do not exceed half a hectare) they usually had strategic functions and, in a few, there was a possibility of urban development.

2 Settlements with a barricade or on a peninsula. These were well-defended settlements, situated on a geomorphological structure in the form of a 'peninsula' joined to the rest of the landscape by an isthmus that had been fortified, although occasionally a less substantial perimeter wall is recorded.

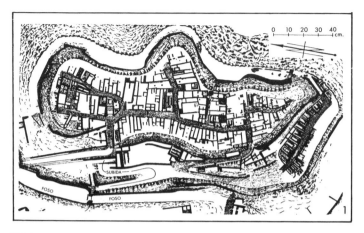

Figure 65 Models of the internal layout of the *oppidum* in Aragon.
1. Azaila. 2. San Antonio de Calaceite (by the authors)

The model is recorded at places like Castellet de Banyoles, Tivissa, in Alorda Park, Olèrdola, Cogullo or el Turó de Montgròs, in el Brull. They may have extended to a considerable size, as in the last example, which covered 9 hectares. The fortifications were more massive than in the previous example, with a more sophisticated technique and they had towers facing the isthmus.

3 Settlements on hillsides. Even though in some cases they may have started from a platform model, they were less rigidly planned and could spread across the hillside, thus getting larger with signs of urban development. This is the case at Burriac (10 hectares) or Ullastret (11 hectares) although it may also be documented in small nuclei. Because they were geomorphologically weak, the fortifications were more complicated, with a great many towers.

A model has likewise been worked out to assess the evolution of the Iberian settlements in Catalonia (Maluquer et al., 1986), starting from two concepts:

1 The existence of distinct districts, or *barrios*, which is described and rests on the exclusive articulation of party walls and on the separation of the groups of houses by public spaces. In reality, and expressed in these terms, the concept should be based more on functional aspects than on items of the type mentioned. The recent excavation at El Oral, in the province of Alicante (Abad, 1986) with a chronology of the late sixth and early fifth centuries BC, shows an arrangement round a fortified platform with two strong square towers marking the point of easiest access to the township. Inside, and we want to draw attention to this, backing on to the inner wall of the fortification, was a row of houses, some of them intended as metallurgical workshops, which might point to the idea of a specialised area, or *barrio*, such as Collis (1989) reported as feasible in the structure of the *oppidum*. Towards the centre of the platform and on the other side of the street, a block of houses has been excavated, which opens on to other side streets, and inside it, a large oven in one of the corners.

2 The pattern of development suggested for Catalonia is organised, according to Maluquer de Motes, on the basis of two models. The first would comprise a single *barrio* as at Les Escodines Baixes, in the Matarranya, offering two variables, depending on whether a fortification existed providing a rear wall for the group of houses, or whether it was the walls of the houses that formed a sinuous line. Put another way, the variability would be established depending on whether the wall at the back had been built before or after the houses and remembering that frequently there were no rear walls, the houses abutting directly on to the rock, as at La Ferradura.

199

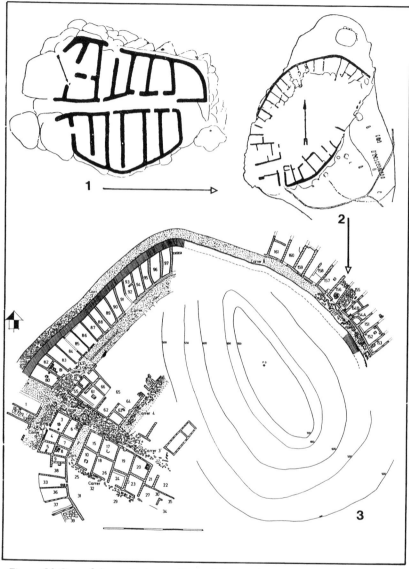

Figure 66 One of the evolutionary lines of Iberian habitation sites in Catalonia (from Maluquer de Motes, 1986a).
1. La Gessera (Teruel). 2. Vilaró (Olius). 3. Tornabous (Molí d'Espígol)

The second model, in two *barrios* separated by a street, is represented by La Gessera. As in the previous instance, the model tends to become complicated with the passage of time; this is the case at Margalef, in Torregrossa, which eventually developed two streets with others crossing at intervals; or at Molí d'Espígol de Tornabous, where the *barrios* faced each other, backing on to the fortifications and left a large central space in which the more unusual buildings of a later phase are beginning to be reported. The same may have happened at la Moleta del Remei, although in this case it might be possible to establish yet another level of development with the appearance of a row of houses outside the fortifications, leaving a new street between this row and the town wall. In other instances, a lower terrace was occupied, when the township was on a hilltop and the population found itself forced to overflow down the slope (Mas Boscà, Sant Julià de Ramis).

These developments are undoubtedly thought-provoking but the example is valid only in Catalonia, as the complex system at El Oral de Alicante in an earlier phase, or the one at Puente Tablas, demonstrates; the latter appears to foreshadow a sytem of parallel streets from as early as the fifth century BC and what appears to be a continuation of the earlier phase is observable in the small area so far excavated: two parallel streets, separated by a distance of 28 metres, delineate a space that is cut parallel to the streets by a much-rectified dividing wall, with successive additions on either side, separating two blocks of houses at different heights, which open on to another street with similar bases of 14 metres and very varied widths (Ruiz Rodríguez and Molinos, 1989).

Regarding the structure of services in the *oppida*, we know nothing at present about most of the resources used, although paving is documented in a few townships from the end of the fifth century BC. These resources vary from one case to another; thus there are records of a slope from the sides of the street towards the centre, of the entrance to the houses being reinforced by a small flagstone immediately in front of the door (as appears to be the case in some Andalusian villages), or of genuine underground drainage systems in Tornabous or in Tivissa, in the late fifth or early fourth centuries.

Since we have touched on the theme of Iberian fortifications on various occasions, let us introduce it by stating that they are another of the elements delineating settlements, although, as we have seen, they have not been the subject of in-depth analysis. It has already been stated somewhere that they are documented in Andalusia with chronologies that coincide with the appearance of the first wheel-thrown pottery and, for the moment, at two locations very distant from each other, Tejada la Vieja and Puente Tablas, with certain fairly similar characteristics and a chronology that should be set between the end of the eighth and the early seventh centuries BC.

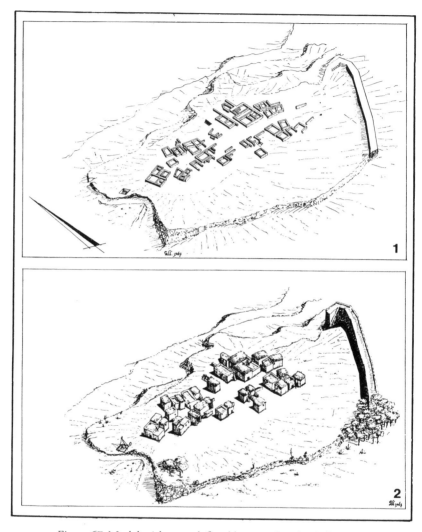

Figure 67 Model without a defined layout: Covalta (Albaida).
1. Isometric view. 2. Proposed reconstruction (from Llobregat, 1972)

In the earliest phase at Puente Tablas (Ruiz Rodríguez and Molinos, 1986), the fortifications ran round three sides of the extensive plateau, leaving undeveloped the open zone above the river, where the actual limestone base of the hill rises abruptly, making it completely inaccessible at that point. It having been decided to build on a rather sloping terrain, the site has been levelled by steep terracing and by arranging the facing walls in sections adapted to the terrace system, sometimes with large stones at the base. In front of the wall of the fortification, rows of large stones have been set up at intervals to contain any possible slippage of the land base on which the system has been constructed. At times, however, it was built directly on to the rock. At Tejada, on top of the vertical panel a 'pie de Amigo' (support) appears; under this supporting base, in a few zones only, a roadbed of small stones is found, levelling the terrain before setting up the support, together with large stone blocks adapting the fortification to the hillside. In neither of these examples is a foundation trench documented. At Puente Tablas, the outer face rises as a big vertical wall with another one parallel and a filling of earth and stones in between. This face is built with medium-sized pieces held in place, dry, by wedges of small stones and earth. However, this wall is not visible on the outside because over it a new vertical wall has been constructed. Every so often, square bastions-buttresses occur, built with the same technique as the facing; lastly, the whole external surface of the wall was plastered with gypsum. On the outside, remains of mud bricks have been noted; these must have been set on top of the stone wall, which, in the earliest phase, was very variable in width, with intervening passages, although in later phases (sixth century BC) it was remodelled on a broader base, above which would have risen the mud-brick facing in the same building technique. At Tejada, (Fernández Jurado, 1987b), a very similar technique can be seen, with two walls, in-filled with stones and earth, on top of which rested huge rectangular and circular buttresses with the same technique of heaping up stone.

In the fifth to fourth centuries BC, the system of construction shows certain variations, as documented in the revetment of a few buttresses, already using the very crude 'rope and brand' technique and larger stones, but in general keeping the same facing wall documented in the first phase. At the end of the third century BC, the system was completely modified when a wall was built using the *spicatum* technique and a base of larger, flat stones, which occasionally rested on the old fortifications and at other times were laid on sediment deposited over the old work. In this phase, the buttresses are much smaller and square and arranged at intervals all along the wall. Finally, one of the entrance gateways to the settlement has been documented with two turrets of the same type as the buttress-bastions, tending to create a funnel narrowing from the inside towards the outside. We know nothing of the internal details of this structure, which has been only partially excavated.

In the fortifications at El Oral, a large outer facing wall of unworked stone in a style that might be called cyclopean has been documented, although we can speak only of the first courses because they are the only ones preserved; the

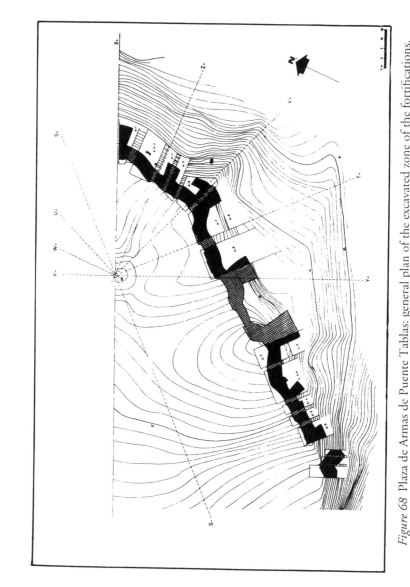

Figure 68 Plaza de Armas de Puente Tablas: general plan of the excavated zone of the fortifications, indicating the system of coordinates (by the authors)

Figure 69 View of the *oppidum* at Puente Tablas

inner facing is of small, dressed stones with an in-fill of stones and earth. The fortification is set on the rock or on a levelled bed of stone and mud brick. In the north-east corner, and it must be supposed in the one opposite too, a square bastion is recorded with an in-fill of stone and earth (Abad, 1986). The same technique is known in other instances, with or without bastions, and is also seen in towers and *atalayas*, like Cazalilla, with a single bastion-buttress on its weakest side.

A second model of fortification construction, looking exclusively at technique, is the one documented in the magnificent curtain wall at Ullastret, characterised by towers that are normally circular, although there is an occasional square one, certainly of much later date; by contrast, the northern sector of the wall presents no bastion of any kind. The facing wall shows four sectors, set slightly back, returning to the 'zip fastener' or 'rack' construction already documented elsewhere, as at Pic de l'Aguila or Sagunto. It is topped in the north by a large tower with wings which close in a pyramid shape. The gate separating it from the next section is encased in one of the circular towers, whereas the one to the south forms a strongly recessed elbow with a circular tower, which was later enclosed in a polygonal tower. According to Maluquer (Maluquer et al., 1986), the towers show spiral staircases on the inside; these were later blocked up and other straight ones were built against the outside of the tower. As to the facings of the curtain wall, they are very elegant on the outer face with elbowed ashlars. The Ullastret model, with a strong Greek influence, explained by its proximity to Ampurias, is undoubtedly the earliest example of those showing Greek influence, like Sagunto or Tarragona.

Coinciding with this more sophisticated technique might be the work on certain square enclosures in the Cordoba and Jaén regions; an instance is El Higuerón de Nueva Carteya (Fortea and Bernier, 1970) with rows of large blocks joined without mortar, isodomic bonding and trapezoidal-shaped squared blocks and recessing of the sharp-cornered ashlars.

A third model which is corroborated daily in parts of Castellnou and Tarragona is defined in settlements like Coll de Moro de Gandesa (Rafel Fontanals and Blasco, 1991). In this case we have an enclosure with an impressive ellipsoidal tower situated in the zone of easiest access, which at the same time is the highest point of the geomorphological structure. The tower, with axes of 14 and 18 metres, is preserved to a maximum height of 8.65 metres and its walls are very wide (4 metres at the base) with an external bank and a filling of stones and earth between the two faces. In the rear part of the tower, a defensive line with bastions and a curved front have been discovered, which leaves the big tower and the defensive ditch outside the occupied

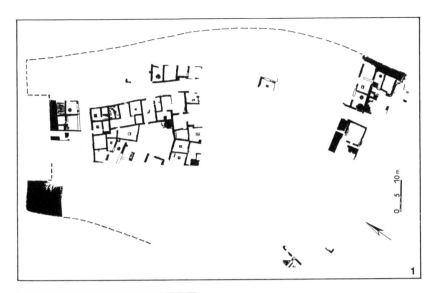

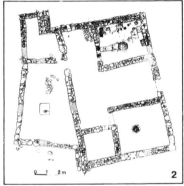

Figure 70 El Oral. 1. General plan. 2. Layout of one of the dwellings
(from Abad, 1986)

enclosure. This model had already been confirmed in this area in well-known settlements like the Torre de Foios but now the inventory has been significantly extended in Castellnou with a large number of sites (Gusi *et al.*, 1991).

A particularly significant example is the one at Castellar de Meca (Ayora, Valencia) where the approach has been recut out of the rock with an incline of 31 per cent, a depth of over 4 metres and width of 1.93–2.15 metres over a distance of 110 metres (Broncano, 1986). Two vertical lines of holes would be cut in the walls to hold untrimmed wooden logs. Altogether, as Broncano

207

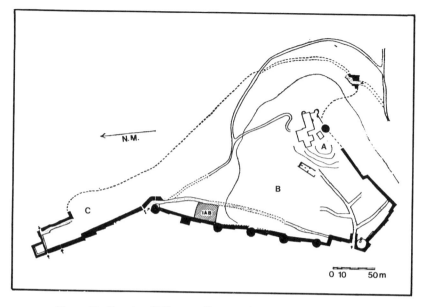

Figure 71 Sketch of Ullastret (from Maluquer de Motes, 1986a)

points out, to execute work of this type would have meant solving engineering problems, not only because of the energy required to carry it out, but also because of problems of height and the steep slope of the site or of sytems for removing water.

The dual reference to layout and fortification in the *oppidum* is yet another new element to be borne in mind when determining the capacity of the dominant classes to respond by organising the building of their settlements; and so is the factor expressed in the organisation of the territory by the appearance of tower-enclosures or *atalayas*. Sadly, we have no analysis that could quantify work like the Castellar de Meca project or the fortifications at Tejada or Ullastret or even new layout plans like those produced at Puente Tablas. However, the mere description of the work should suffice to throw the objective we are claiming into relief.

Altogether, the typological versions so far produced enable us to make a few points:

1 The difficulty of working out a paradigmatic typology for the whole Iberian area can be seen.
2 For typological treatment, it is normal to work towards the interior of a settlement and very occasionally variables concerning the settlement's

Figure 72 View of the fortifications at Ullastret

surroundings are considered. This is combined with an exclusively descriptive evaluation of the variables, which hinders their verification even when, in many cases they could be quantified.

3 In spite of the difficulty arising from the absence of extensive excavations, when it comes to a socio-economic reading of the settlements, aspects relating to the spatial arrangement of the internal structures have to be incorporated and also the labour costs for the major works on the infrastructure. The difference in the labour hours involved in the building of Castellar de Meca should be looked at in comparison with the small fortifications at Puntal dels Llops or Puig Castellet. On the other hand, as far as the spatial arrangement of the unusual structures is concerned, it is as well to remember the concentration of granaries or possible princely residences at sites like Tornabous or Moleta del Remei, or the eccentricity of Ullastret, Campello or Puente Tablas, where recently an edifice very much bigger than the others, with a colonnaded portico has been documented at one end, and raised above the rest. Indeed, incorporation of the aristocrat into the settlement makes various different models possible, ranging from introducing him directly into the urban structure, as in the cases mentioned, to a partial link which could be the model for the acropolis that is outlined in cases like the Coll del Moro.

Hierarchies in death

In recent decades, the excavation of necropolises has been approached in the context of a theoretico-methodological debate similar to the one that has been taking place in other spheres of archaeology. Lately, works have been published in Spain re-examining the process followed in the debate, from Gordon Childe's first approaches to its definition as a theoretical problem in the works of Binford (Ruiz Zapatero and Chapa, 1988; Lull and Picazo, 1990).

Binford's scheme starts from a classic functionalist model. Indeed, as Lull and Picazo point out, even though the complexity of the societies is recognised, the relationships between the different economic, social and ideological spheres are not established nor is there any appraisal of the social relationships of production. Consequently, the social complexity is reduced to a mechanical effect between the status of the deceased's social position and the social rank of the group performing the ritual.

Perhaps it has been this latent reductionism in the rigid neopositivist laws that has fostered a dual critical position, represented by a return to positivist positions, chiefly when faced with the difficulty and simplicity, in many cases, of articulating the world of the living with that of the dead, either by means of a mirror model (Piggott, 1973) or by a willingness to enter the field of symbols as the dominant factor (Hodder, 1982). A third way, represented by D'Agostino (1987), would start by recognising the overriding importance of ideology and the consequent impossibility of effecting direct transpositions between the two worlds unless the historical process is taken into consideration.

In line with this latter current, but taking for granted the implications of the debate over these years, we must appreciate that the process unleashed in Iberian society by the death of one of its members generated various fields of analysis:

1 Concerning Lull and Picazo's proposition, the cost of the social work invested must be determined, though not solely in terms of Tainter's (1978) concept of energy, but placing the work in the socio-economic set-up that makes the outcome achieve that category.
2 Regarding the prospect enunciated by Bottini, D'Agostino, Peroni and Bietti Sestieri, and exemplified by the advances of Italian archaeology in this field, a scheme for reading the ideologies operating in Iberian society and expressed in the burial ritual must be evaluated, although the difficulty of doing so is patently obvious, owing to the problem of working in a field where verification is difficult. However, reading the ideological horizon can indeed make it possible to adjust it to the social model defined on the basis of the existing system of social relationships, provided it is accepted that the reading between the society of the living and that of the dead cannot be made in terms of a mechanical reflex.

From the excavation of the group of big Tartessian tumuli in Lower Andalusia we know that these gigantic structures existed and were obviously visible from a great distance. We have detailed knowledge of the one at Setefilla, because inside it was a central burial in a rectangular stone chamber designed for inhumation, while the assemblage of tombs around it was for cremations. The central burial, moreover, was accompanied by pieces of gold, silver, amber and bronze. According to Aubet, the model of burial followed a few very simple guidelines, similar to the funerary system on the coast, monopolised by the Phoenician culture. We have a process typical of an indigenous society that has grown rapidly rich, thanks to its control of wealth (Aubet, 1975). In tomb 17 at la Joya, another inhumation, a small bronze brasier was discovered, with lotus flowers on the ends of the handle and palmettas in the brace in which the handle is fitted; also a bronze mirror with an ivory handle, a bronze *thymaterion* with ornaments of lotus flowers and a pear-shaped bronze jug with a double handle ending at the top in the form of a serpent's head and at the bottom in a palmetta. To the north of the chamber the metal structure of a war chariot was discovered, with two wheels, which Garrido and Orta (1978) describe as each having four spokes, and two feline heads decorating it. Close by lay two bag amphorae and numerous handmade bowls; lastly, the existence of an ivory chest is reported with four figurines of the same material, bronze brackets and nails, silver hinges, a pair of horse bits, a silver object, two curved knives, two bronze mountings and a trapezoidal shovel with a handle.

The richness of this Tartessian tomb, dated by the researchers to between the seventh and sixth centuries BC, poses a problem of chronology, since the contexts were dated from a C14 sample from layer IX at Setefilla. The assemblages reveal an orientalising world more typical of the seventh than the sixth century BC, hence the still striking presence of handmade pottery. But aside from this chronological disparity, which today contrasts with the sequences from Torre de Doña Blanca or from Huelva itself, the interesting thing to note is the great concentration of wealth in a few tombs, compared with the poverty of the rest, and the apparent polarity of inhumation/cremation, matching the concentration of wealth/poverty of the grave goods. In the first case, because, as the communal tombs at Setefilla show, the grave goods consist mostly of a burial urn for the ashes of the dead, plates and bowls, handmade like the urn, and the few bits of metal characteristic of the deceased's apparel (double-springed fibulae, belt buckles, bracelets) and the occasional curved knife or piece of iron that is difficult to interpret and might, in any case, be described as a horse bit. This would represent the most complex of the group inasmuch as the standard tomb usually contained simply the urn, a dish of some kind and an item of clothing. Furthermore, this tendency to impoverishment in the communal grave goods can also be seen in the necropolis at Cerrillo Blanco on the middle to upper course of the Guadalquivir and near Porcuna; of twenty-four tombs there, fifteen had no grave goods at all; four had only belt buckles or beads (in one) and five had goods of which the only things worth mentioning were the odd knife, the odd bone point and a comb (Torrecillas González, 1985). However, it is interesting to note that all the tombs in the assemblage at Cerrillo Blanco are inhumations, whereas it so happens that a tomb excavated at La Guardia, with handmade bowls that have burnished reticular decoration and are datable somewhat earlier, is in fact a cremation. For the moment, there is no direct interpretation relating one type of ritual to the other, as happens in other parts of Europe, except in specific cases like Setefilla, where a clear contrast between the two rites and their grave goods can be seen because of their spatial arrangement.

In addition, the system of tumular burial in Setefilla, showing the contrast between rich grave goods, associated with a chambered tomb and inhumation, and the rest with impoverished grave goods, cremation and rock-cut graves, indicates a marked contrast between the individual buried in the first instance and the rest. Now, if in Setefilla or La Joya, as we have seen, and in the terms set out by Lull and Picazo, the social effort required for the principal burial had been vastly superior to the rest, in terms of both quality and quantity and on the level of the container and the content, at Cerrillo Blanco, on the other hand, the main tomb, a double burial, apparently in a circular chamber with a central pillar, had no grave goods to distinguish it from the rest. Consequently, the effect produced by comparing these two examples, from different points along the Guadalquivir, reveals a definite hierarchisation in the system of building and in the model of the container. This hierarchisation was more formal towards the west, where not only the container but also the content and even the burial ritual were differentiated. However, the picture presented by both models starts from the same principle of social relationships, which tends to define hierarchisation between one or several individuals and the rest, while in the structure of the tumulus a social unit is involved that in life was certainly defined on the basis of a system of relationships about which we still know little.

So what marks the difference between one model and the other is not just the more formal description of Setefilla or La Joya, that is to say, of groups more clearly defined as Tartessian, nor even the wealthier distribution circuits of orientalising products, which undoubtedly reached the upper Guadalquivir in smaller numbers, but it is essentially the internal process consolidating an elite in Lower Andalusia (remember the great treasures of Aliseda or Carambolo), which, with new items like the chariot, seems to break the old patriarchal patterns of the extended family, patterns which still seem to be represented at Cerrillo Blanco.

However, the process spread rapidly to the upper Guadalquivir. The chambered tomb at La Bobadilla and particularly the better-known one at Cástulo proclaim the fact. The former (robbed in antiquity) is a chamber with a platform where the remains must have been deposited. The grave goods, attributed to a woman, consisted of an *aryballos* in vitreous paste of an Egyptian type from Naukratis or Rhodes, two small vessels made of blue vitreous paste (one pear-shaped with an *oenochoe* rim with two handles, and the other of the type known as *anforiskos*), fragments of a Greek *skiphos* and of an *oenochoe*, three pottery *aryballos* in the shape of a pomegranate, two bowls and, in gold, a group of pendants in the form of pairs of tendrils and a ring. The rest of the necropolis, although dated by Maluquer to the same phase

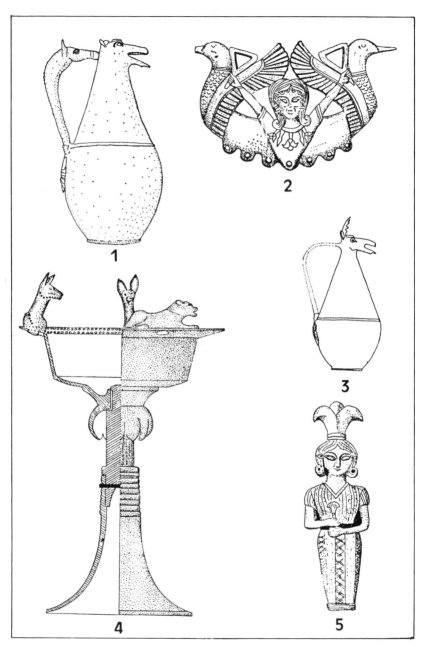

Figure 73 1. Ritual ewer found in Niebla. 2. Astarté appliqué with lotus flowers and ducks, found in Seville. 3. Ritual juglet found in Mérida. 4. Perfume burner from Cástulo. 5. Astarté statuette from Cástulo (from Blázquez, 1975b)

214

(Maluquer *et al.*, 1981), displays features suggesting that the tombs should be ascribed to a later stage.

The tomb at Cástulo (Blanco, 1962b), near Cortijo del Estacar de Robarinas, even though it has not been systematically excavated, has yielded rich grave goods that are worthy of note. The assemblage, cremations, consists of two urns, which have flared necks and profuse decoration in bands on the body, while, on the neck, one of them has a floral border painted in red on a white ground. In addition, there is a grey-ware bowl with a very pronounced lip and two vessels of coarse ware, also grey. Outstanding items in precious metals are a silver patera and a gold ring. Among the weapons, always iron, are three lance points, ferrules, a sword with a button and antennae with iron and bronze nails, as well as a knife. Lastly, we would draw attention to three bronze female statuettes with Hathor coiffures, topped with an iris composed of two thick petals and a central bud, and carrying a flower, perhaps of papyrus, in hands folded on their chests. They surely formed the ends of a receptacle. The assemblage has been dated to a time late in the sixth or early in the fifth century BC, although it could be attributed to the earlier sixth century BC.

The third example, also dated to the late sixth or early fifth century deserves special treatment, because it is situated in a stratigraphic sequence and is of outstanding interest as a monument in an area remote from that of the two tombs on the upper Guadalquivir. This is the tomb at Pozo Moro (Almagro Gorbea, 1982a and 1983b), in Chinchilla, Albacete. The monument was built directly on to the natural clay and humus soil; the structure was prepared with a layer of adobe on top of another of heat-resistant clay, and in the centre was placed a *bustum*. The grave goods, only part of which has been preserved, consisted of an Attic *kylix* by the painter of Pithos, a bronze *oenochoe*, probably Greek with a handle in the form of a naked youth between lions, and a *lekythos* with a scene of satyrs, and coins of the Athens 581 class. The whole assemblage is dated to around 500 BC. Lastly, the monument presents a tower-like arrangement on a terraced base, a continuous frieze, lions in the corners, mouldings and the ogee at the top. The reliefs on the frieze represent on one face a warrior wearing a short tunic, a helmet with a crest, a round shield and a lance. On another of the faces a two-headed deity is depicted enthroned, supporting in one hand a bowl with a small figure inside it, while with the other it grasps a dead wild boar, which is lying on a table of offerings. In front of it stands another monstrous creature with a forked tongue, who is offering another bowl. To the right, a third monster with a horse's head, is holding a knife in one hand and in the other a small bowl with another small figure lying on another table of offerings (Almagro Gorbea, 1982a). Other scenes show a female head holding a lotus flower in its mouth and a deity advancing through dragon smoke, carrying a tree with branches ending in lotus buds, where small figures are nailing up a gallows, which they are grasping in both hands, or a sexual scene or a wingless goddess close to a tree, or a two-headed wild boar face to face with snake-footed monsters, etc.

The comparison of these three tombs, dated to around the same period, late in the sixth century enables us to draw certain immediate conclusions, such as the spread of the process observed in Lower Andalusia to the upper Guadalquivir and the Albacete region, but furthermore it allows us to observe certain factors:

1. From the point of view of construction, Pozo Moro is undoubtedly exemplary. From it, Almagro has defined a binary scale for burials, which have their starting point in the sixth century and may have continued until Romanisation. For the first, defined in Pozo Moro, the terminology 'monumental, tower-like burials' has been used; their typical distribution is peculiar to the south-east and Lower Andalusia, with isolated examples appearing at strategic points like Pozo Moro or Alcoy, or grouped in necropolises like Osuna or La Alcudia de Elche. The second scale, identified as of lower rank, are 'burials with monumental stele-pillars', which are finished with animal figures (bulls, lions, sphinxes, etc.), extending from Sagunto to Lower Andalusia and continuing until the fourth century and possibly even up to the Roman period. The most significant examples reconstructed by Almagro Gorbea are those at Monforte del Cid, Coy and Los Nietos (the latter in Murcia, the former two in Alicante). These models form a contrast with chambers of the type documented at La Bobadilla, which, from the construction of the container, suggest a lower scale, owing either to the absence of sculptures or to some other difference, concerning their spatial location. So we can point to three different scales of burial as far as the construction of the tomb goes, always related to social levels, which at least had access to imported products at an early period.

2. As to the grave goods, leaving aside those of Pozo Moro, because it was robbed, in the two known examples the presence of gold/silver is recorded (although the number of pieces is not very great, nor their importance as raw material); imported products were also present, orientalising in the case of Cástulo, the result of Greek trade at Pozo Moro, and likewise possibly the *aryballos* from Naukratis or Rhodes discovered at La Bobadilla. These imported goods, moreover, enable us to evaluate a fact present in the *oenochoe–kylix* (pitcher–goblet) association, linked with the consumption of wine (Olmos, 1979 and 1984) in the rite of libation, as has already been documented in a few items of the previous phase, like the bronze jugs recorded at La Joya and associated with small brasiers. Secondly, and also documented

216

Figure 74 Some complex models of tombs. 1. Tower-like monument from Pozo Moro (Albacete). 2–4. Stele pillars (2. Corral de Saus, Mogente, Valencia; 3. Monforte del Cid, Alicante; 4. Los Nietos). 5–6. Mythological reliefs from Pozo Moro (from Almagro Gorbea, 1983b). 7. Chambered tomb at Baza (Granada) (from Presedo, 1982)

by Olmos, the *lekythos* is associated with the perfume ritual, likewise corroborated in the faience *aryballos* from La Bobadilla. In the opinion of Olmos, these two items (wine for the symposium/perfume ritual) are what defines Hellenisation, being much in evidence in Huelva from the end of the seventh century and very clearly in Ampurias and in the rest of the Iberian settlements from the sixth century BC, although directly related to a prominent social group identified by its aristocratic status; and even in the choice of certain themes like the wild-beast trainer depicted on the altar at Pozo Moro, this group tends to display signs of hero cults.

The presence of the weapon assemblage in the tomb at Cástulo, comprising the antenna sword–lance–dagger association, demonstrates the second level of information from grave goods. The association reported (where the absence of the sabre and the presence of the sword with antennae should be stressed) contrasts with the communal tombs of Setefilla or Frigiliana (Arribas and Wilking, 1969), where only curved knives are found, which need not in fact be considered as weapons; and, looking further afield, with the necropolises of Lower Aragon, such as Ferradura or Mas Mussols (Maluquer de Motes, 1984).

Weaponry can be taken as another defining element of the dominant social group in the sixth century BC and must be understood as such, although, as will be pointed out later, these references cannot be extrapolated to periods beginning in Iberian II. The sculptural assemblage at Porcuna, discovered in the phase following the seventh century necropolis at Cerrillo Blanco and dated to the fifth century (González Navarrete, 1987) consists of 1,288 catalogued pieces, all smashed and buried in a sacred place. The assemblage reveals a complex with countless battle scenes, with static figures, etc. The whole enables us to observe and define the image of the warrior and his weapons, witness the head wearing a helmet with a plumed ridge and spirals on both sides; or other depictions like the warrior with a horse, or others, outstanding among them the antenna sword, the *frontón* dagger, the curved knife, the *caetra*, sets of *phlalerae* with pectoral and larger pouldrons. Altogether, a weaponry associated with cavalry and representative of a social elite that found its main form of expression in a taste for things Greek, returning to such scenes as fighting with griffins, duels between animals or the *Pothnia Theron*, all connected with the cult of the hero, much in evidence in the rites already cited involving wine and perfumes.

Now, acceptance of these elements of Greek tradition at the end of the sixth or in the first half of the fifth century in no way demonstrates either that the Iberian social elite was embarking on a process similar to that of the Greek *polis* or that it seized on certain 'rare' products, which it accepted without

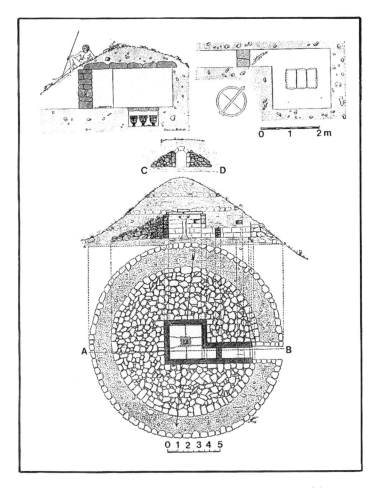

Figure 75 Burial chamber at Tutugi (Galera, Granada)
(from Cabré and Motos, 1920–1)

understanding their role in the society that produced them, as if they were of a
'primitive-infantile' mentality that saw in these things only the foreign factor,
monopoly of which would bestow social distinction. The Iberian elite, with a
long tradition going back to the Tartessian phase, adopted these rites of the
hero cult structurally, as Olmos has demonstrated (Olmos, 1984), but they
adopted them rather from the actual historical process followed by an aristocratic group and – why not? – by their clients and kin, who found in Hellenic

taste, as earlier in certain orientalising practices, a way of reproducing the system of social relations defined within their own society.

The transition to Iberian III, which we can already identify from pottery production, marks the moment about which most is known in the Iberian necropolises of the south-east and Upper Andalusia. As Almagro Gorbea reported, the phase coincides with the appearance and consolidation of new types of burial, like the princely tumulus or the burial chamber. The first, well represented in Albacete (Hoya Gonzalo, Hoya Santa Ana, Los Villares, Pozo Moro) (Blánquez, 1990) and Murcia (Cabecico del Tesoro or Cigarralejo) but reaching as far as Valencia (Corral de Saus), has been designated type C by Almagro Gorbea (types A and B correspond to the tower-like burials and those with monumental stele-pillars) and typically take the form of great tumular paved areas, square in shape and probably terraced. With dimensions in excess of 16 square metres, they were positioned over the cremation site. On the other hand, the preferred area for the chamber is towards the south of the province of Jaén and in Granada, and it may be a continuation of the model documented at La Bobadilla in the previous phase.

For the first of these groups, tomb 200 at El Cigarralejo (Cuadrado, 1987a) may serve as an example; it is defined as a cobbled tumulus with a square ground plan measuring 6.7 metres along the sides and with a second dais, measuring 2.5 × 2.2, preserved in the tumulus. The place of burial was located in the extreme south-east of the cobbled area, with two niches: an irregular one of 1.7 × 1.2 metres and another of 1.4 × 0.9 metres; the urn was placed in the first and the grave goods deposited in the second. In Cuadrado's opinion, it is a case of a double burial, of a man and a woman, evidenced by the assemblage of items: masculine (three lances, a javelin, sabre, shield and items from horses and chariots) and feminine (small wooden spoons, bone hairpins, a bronze needle, glassy paste beads from a necklace, bone beads, an alabaster jar, spindles, etc.). In addition to these there are a chair, items of silver, bronze, bone, textile, seeds, etc. Amongst the pottery, as well as the Iberian urn and other items of indigenous production, an abundance of black-glazed Attic ware is documented (five pateras, three *kantharos* and seven *kotyle*) and red-figured ware (two *kylix*). The assemblage is dated between 425 and 375 BC.

The second burial model, of an aristocratic type, the chamber and the large cyst, appears well documented in the necropolises of Galera and Baza (Presedo, 1982). In tombs 155 and 176 at Baza, the dominant model of the region can be assessed. Tomb 155, enclosing inside its walls the seated sculpture of the Lady of Baza, was a kind of shaft with sides measuring 2.6 metres and a depth of 1.8 metres; at the bottom and right round it a low mud-brick wall is recorded, some 15 centimetres high and very damaged. Furthermore, in the four corners, a system of chimneys going down to the bottom of the tomb was excavated. In the north wall the sculpture containing the ashes of the person cremated was placed. In the corners the four amphorae were deposited, while the rest of the grave goods were found scattered on the floor of the chamber, notably remains of weaponry in the centre. Equally interesting is tomb 176, with a shaft structure similar to the previous one, measuring 3.3 × 2.4 metres, with a second shaft, 2.38 × 2.30 metres, dug into the floor of the first, allowing the construction of a stage (or bench) 0.2 metres high and varying in width from 0.18–0.70 metres. Inside were again four amphorae, deposited in each corner of the base. As for the rest of the grave goods, in no apparent order, the use of bell craters with red figures as cinerary urns was observed (five have been located of which at least two fulfilled that function); also found were six black-glazed paterae, two *skyphos* and one *kylix*; weapons recorded include sabres, *soliferra*, lance points, remains of a shield and of a chariot wheel.

The chamber at Toya, not far from Baza and just into the province of Jaén is particularly interesting. A study of it (Cabré, 1925) shows a rectangular plan, made up of five compartments in three naves. The entrance gate, which distinguishes it from the Baza model, creates a shaft of light of 1.74 × 0.64 metres. The central nave is the only one with no internal subdivision and measures 4.55 metres × 1.40 at the rear and × 1.26 at the entrance; a continuous bench can be seen running from the very back as far as the doors to the side aisles. At the back, 60 centimetres from the bench a niche has been made with a slab at the base projecting like a ledge with moulding. The roof consists of large flagstones laid from one side to the other at a height of 2.10 metres. The doors to the side naves have the final blocks of the jambs cut in a curve to form a false pointed arch broken by the lintel. The two side naves are each divided into two; in the rear compartment, each has a niche similar to the one documented in the central part but in the one on the right another niche has been made in the west wall and a ledge that runs under the two niches and projects further, supported in the middle by a foot rising from the ground, attached to the wall and cut away to miss the lower ledge or bench.

As for the grave goods, little is known apart from the existence of a bell crater in the west nave, removed by Cabré, close to a coffin, fragments of others, craters, remains of sabres and lance points, as well as a helmet with a button on top and a chariot wheel (Cabré, 1925; Fernández Miranda and Olmos, 1986). The indigenous pottery studied later by Pereira (1979) provided no concrete data because of its chronological spread, the result of

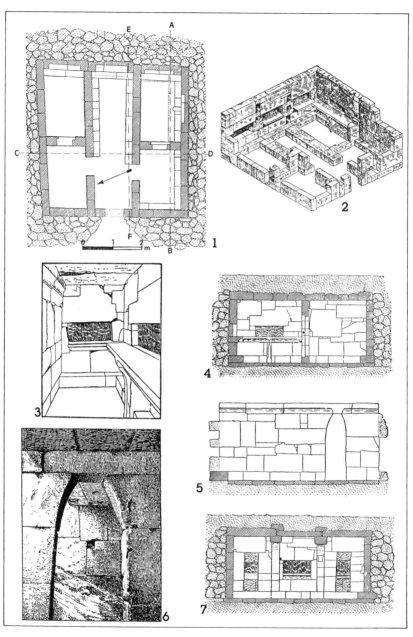

Figure 76 Burial chamber at Toya (Peal de Becerro, Jaén). 1. Plan,
2. Axonometric view. 3. Right side chamber. 4. Section A–B. 5. Section E–F.
6. Detail of the entrance door to the side room. 7. Section C–D
(from Cabré, 1925)

222

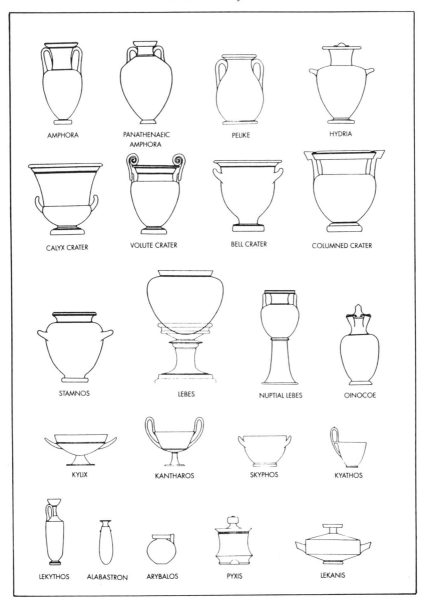

Figure 77 Principal forms of Greek vases (by the authors)

unsystematic activity not only inside the chamber but probably in the entire necropolis.

In general terms, these burials of prominent social groups reveal significant differences from the earlier, orientalising phase of the sixth century BC. Indeed, with respect to the actual construction, we are undoubtedly again faced with identifying richer grave goods with constructions more costly in man hours, since these are features of both the chambered tomb and the cobbled tumulus, in comparison with the remaining types. The transition, then, from a first level to a second scale, that is to say, the big difference between the tower burials of the Pozo Moro type, or the monumental stele-pillars, and the succeeding range of burials in the matter of construction now shows an intermediary phase, attested by the so-called 'tumular' burials (Almagro Gorbea's type D); these continue the scale of the princely tumular burials, but smaller in size (the sides do not usually exceed 2 metres), with all that implies of reduced work costs, while the chambers with stone foundations, mud-brick walls, unpartitioned and small in size, or the moderate-sized cysts (sides of about a metre and a half), like tombs 43 and 130 at Baza, occupy the second level in the area of the large, rich, 'Bastetanian' chambers. This is documented at Cástulo, Puente del Obispo and La Guardia among others.

At the same time, the grave goods reveal important changes relative to the earlier phase. For one thing, in the weaponry, sabre–*soliferrum*–lance–*caetra*–helmet assemblages begin to become important, and to these must be added, in some instances, the chariot. Recently, the suggestion has been made (Fernández Miranda and Olmos, 1986) that, rather than having a role associated with the weapon assemblage as a quality differential, the latter might play a part in the context of the 'heroising and transitional' tendency so widespread in the Mediterranean in the fourth century BC. In our opinion, the two factors should be coupled together, since the quality status of the chariot and its association with the horse is not just a Hellenic heroising programme in the full sense, but the conversion of a civic ritual, now assigned to reproducing an aristocracy, which, as we have seen, was to become the dominant social group in the indigenous society. From that point of view, there may be a considerable difference between the chariot in tomb 17 at La Joya and those at Toya, Baza, Mirador de Rolando, among others (which in their turn are different from the remains of the massive wheel for transport at El Amarejo or Montjuïc), since the first are associated not with weapons but with the ritual that couples a bronze ewer with a brasier, while the second belong in a society that has given the 'warrior' factor a position of privilege. On the other hand, from the middle of the fifth century BC, weapons became generalised not only in the 'princely tumular' and chambered tombs but also in the simpler ones, and this, combined with constructional factors already highlighted, implies a certain isonomic tendency, observable in other levels of the grave goods. So the retrieval and display of isolated items, like the chariot, in the furnishings of a grave, become qualitatively a basis for differentiating social groups that are endeavouring to perpetuate themselves through their death ritual.

We could use the same example in connection with imported pottery, since the crater (whether columned or bell shaped) seems to be the only piece that is qualitatively different in its distribution from a product that may be present in forms like the *kylix* in even the poorest tombs. Indeed, the crater, associated with the coffin, develops as the key element in the richest grave furnishings in an area coinciding with the chambered tombs and chariots, because this association goes beyond the differentiation of a social group to define an ethnic group and a cultural dynamic (Almagro Gorbea, 1982b). Olmos, studying paintings on craters, stresses that very factor of 'heroisation' and demonstrates it in an excellent study of a tomb at Galera, where an individual owning horses had been buried and where the funeral libation of a winged demon, the Greek Nike, is depicted on his arrival in the great beyond, but it is at the same time a classic model of the wine ritual coupled with the rite of the symposium (Olmos, 1982). Other zones, however, do not replicate this association and will lean more to coupling the *kantharos* and the patera, or the *lekane* and the *pyxis*, as in the area round Ampurias.

In all these respects, we cannot exclude the possibility that the late sixth and fifth century BC types of aristocratic tomb may have disappeared during this period. It is true that the reference to a tower-like monument in Osuna (Almagro Gorbea, 1983a), probably later, shows them to have been present in subsequent periods; however, it is our opinion that there may have been a hiatus in the building of these monuments (at least the tower-like ones), coinciding with the middle of the fifth century and the fourth century BC, clearly associated with the crisis in certain states, and with progress towards a more organised and complex society, but one whose power was more fragmented.

Signs of isonomy in aristocratic power in the world of the dead in the fourth century BC

Analysis of the burial assemblages in the classic Iberian necropolises has posed great difficulties for the researcher, even when in some cases a considerable number of tombs have been excavated (El Cigarralejo, Cabecico del Tesoro,

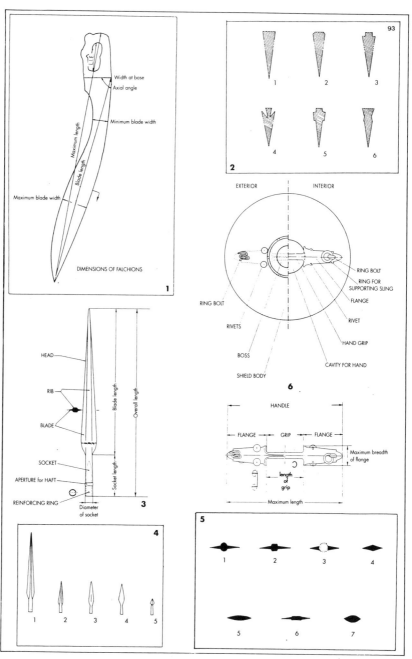

Figure 78 Some types of Iberian weapon. 1. Diagram of the Iberian sabre.
2. Sections of sabres. 3. Diagram of a lance. 4. Lance types from Cabecico del
Tesoro. 5. Sections of lances. 6. Diagram of the elements of a shield
(from Quesada, 1986–7)

226

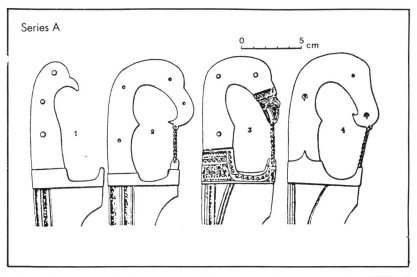

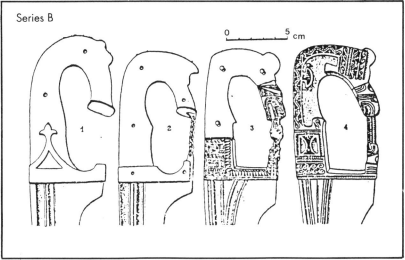

Figure 79 Types of sabre hilt (from Cabré, 1934)

Baza, among the most outstanding), because at no time can a clear articulation be detected, as happens in other societies. The reality is that, seemingly, the Iberian necropolis distributes weapons or objects indiscriminately with no apparent ritual rhythm. An interpretation in a negative sense and taking account of the time factor provides the first version of the analysis.

If we consider the presence of weapons in the sixth or early fifth century BC necropolises like Mas Mussols (Maluquer de Motes, 1984), we become aware of the associative structure the weapon has in these groups of burials, since it is found only in proportions of less than 15 per cent and in the presence of lancepoints or *soliferra*, the sword being either non-existent, or present in small numbers, less than 15 per cent again, in cases like Solivella in Castellón, or El Molar in Alicante (where, moreover, there is a possibility that burials of later phases may be interspersed). The situation is reminiscent of tumulus A at Setefilla, where not a single tomb with weapons exists, if we except the curved knives that we have not reckoned as such. It is surprising to observe how, coinciding with the transition to Iberian III, the presence of weapons increases in relation to the number of tombs, fluctuating between 25 per cent at La Alcudia and 48 per cent at Castellones de Ceal by way of 39 per cent at El Cigarralejo and 32 per cent at Cástulo. This distribution, which implies a ratio of almost 4 to 1 in instances with a lesser and 2 to 1 with a larger presence, extends over an area that would be occupied by the present-day provinces of Alicante, Albacete, Murcia, Granada and Jaén. We must point out, none the less, that in the west of this area the ratio seems to change, although this might be due to the smaller number of tombs excavated. Thus, at La Guardia, we find weapons in only 6.66 per cent and in a ratio of 15 to 1 while at La Bobadilla, with an appreciably earlier date, according to the authors, weapons are found in only 5 per cent at a ratio of 19 to 1. The only case evaluated by centuries was Cabecico del Tesoro in Murcia (Quesada, 1989), but it is extremely interesting because in the second century BC 37.8 per cent of the tombs were recorded with weapons, in the third century 29.7 per cent and in the fourth 32.4 per cent, demonstrating that after the arrival of the Carthaginians and Romans there was no substantial change in the appearance of the burial ritual, at least not at first. This increase in tombs with weapons may be given a different interpretation if we look at their associations. Thus in the zone under discussion, various studies (Quesada, 1986–7 and 1989; Santos Velasco, 1989) agree in stressing the existence of a type–assemblage, consisting of sword–long weapon, which, however, is not present in every case. Indeed, in the necropolises at Baza, Castellones and El Cigarralejo it dominates with over 50 per cent, although towards the north of this group the ratios drop to somewhere between 20 and 30 per cent. Lastly, Cástulo is not included in this assessment as it does not reach 10per cent and there the long weapon is being identified, sometimes accompanied by a knife, as the dominant item (over 80 per cent of the burials with weapons). Quesada, in his weapon analysis, has detailed the relation of the lance, as a weapon that is not thrown, to the *soliferrum/pilum* that is, and he found an association between the two items in

228

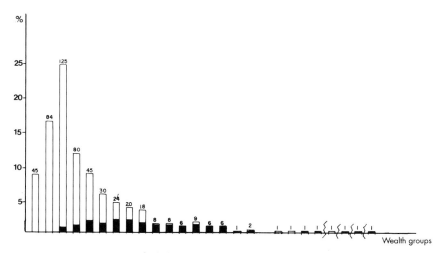

Figure 80 Division of all the burials at Cabecico into wealth groups. The numbers above the columns indicate the total number of tombs in each group. The dark areas represent the tombs with weapons. The value of the intervals is three points (from Quesada, 1986–7)

this necropolis of 33 per cent, while by contrast no association exists between thrown weapons. On the other hand, he has pointed out that although the long weapon–sword association is the most frequent, a single piece (be it sword or lance) may be dominant over the weapon in association (37.6 per cent of the tombs at Cabecico del Tesoro). Maybe this distinction conceals a principle of social differentiation as a function of other parameters like age, as is shown in Gubbio's tables in Umbria.

Whether with the lance or the sword as the dominant factor or with the sabre–lance combination, and without paying particular attention to the type of tomb, that is to say, without forcing any association in its distribution with the more complex constructions, the spread of this item in the necropolis leads us to conclude that the value of the work invested in the average type of grave goods has appreciated. This rise in the standard of funerals of the deceased means we must acknowledge a general increase in the wealth of the community but not an even distribution, as Santos Velasco shows in his work, observing the sudden gulf produced on a quantitative plane between tombs 200 and 277 at El Cigarralejo and the rest; this is certainly less clear-cut at Cabecico del Tesoro and tends, too, to decrease with the passage of time. Similarly, the spread of weaponry comes to be related to the more generalised role of the warrior in Iberian society, or, put another way, to the image the Iberians have of their relationships in society, which are now governed

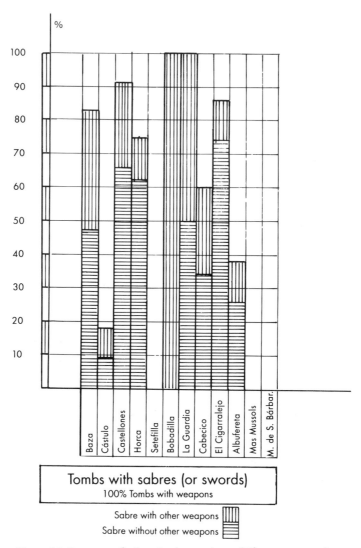

Tombs with sabres (or swords)
100% Tombs with weapons

Sabre with other weapons
Sabre without other weapons

Figure 81 Presence of sabres in the tombs at different necropolises (by the authors)

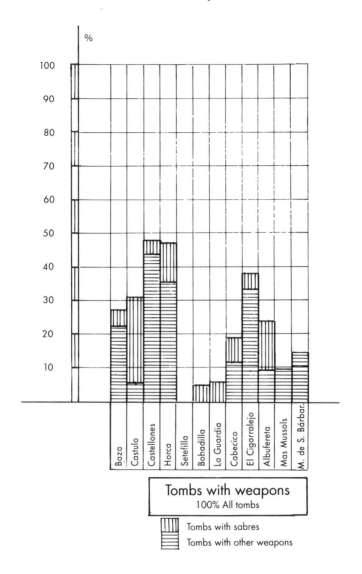

Tombs with weapons
100% All tombs

Tombs with sabres
Tombs with other weapons

231

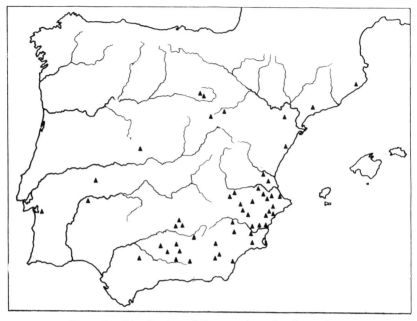

Figure 82 Distribution of Iberian sabres (by the authors)

definitively by their association with weapons. Indeed, as Quesada demonstrates, evaluation of articles tomb by tomb furnishes proof that the mean wealth (assigning a numerical value for each type of article) is greater in tombs with weapons than in the rest (7.3 per cent and 16.9 per cent in a system without weighting or 4 per cent and 7.68 per cent of all tombs with weighting). Quesada also underlines the fact that all levels of tombs have weapons, but while they occur only in a restricted number of poor tombs, they are by contrast, always present, in the wealthy ones (Quesada, 1989).

All this leads us to be more than ever convinced that the system of dependence between aristocrat and warrior was now the basic factor defining their relationship. The exceptional nature of Cástulo, where, on the other hand, there is no record of a chambered tomb of the Toya or Baza type, nor of coffins, seems to suggest an equal development but in relation to other cultural traditions, expressed in the lance rather than the sword. In any case, the sword would play a more selective role in its distribution. The apparent reduction in tombs with weapons in the western Jaén region might likewise be indicative of a different historical process, reflecting a more organised society.

A second element of special interest is provided by the imports of black-glazed and red-figured Attic wares. In his study of El Cigarralejo, Santos Velasco (1989) emphasises the qualitative leap occurring between the two princely tombs, with twelve and fifteen pieces respectively, and the subsequent group in which only 3 per cent of the burials have four or five pieces. Altogether, 32 per cent of the total yield black-glazed or red-figured wares (the most frequent being a piece found in 22 per cent of the tombs). It is significant that this proportion is maintained in similar terms in the rest of the necropolises in the area, declining towards Alicante or Baza (11.8 per cent and 13.3 per cent respectively) and rising towards Cástulo (40 per cent at Los Patos, 46 per cent at El Estacar and 36 per cent at Castellones). The most significant example is Baños de la Muela, where, of the seventeen tombs excavated, all yielded Greek pottery; at the other extreme is La Guardia, with only 3.3 per cent of the total. Cástulo again appears to be an exceptional area, putting a greater quantity of Attic pottery imports into circulation and distributing them more widely, compared with La Guardia or Puente del Obispo, where they are considerably restricted. This is not to imply that the explanation lies in the remote location of these last two sites, a notion contradicted by the abundance of such imports in the excavations at Puente Tablas or in the surveys of the Campiña area. But no doubt the reproduction of the ritual is marked by some very different rhythms, already noticeable in the weapon distribution.

Moving on, it is interesting to look at the distribution of gold and silver products; at El Cigarralejo, only six tombs yield any, seven in La Albufereta, one in Baza, two in La Guardia. Of course, these items are much more restricted than either of the other two. The distribution in terms of the character of the tombs, shows how gold is documented in princely tumular cobbled tombs (tombs 200 and 277 at El Cigarralejo); whereas silver is recorded in tombs of no significant structure from the point of view of construction. In a study of the distribution of this product in the necropolises of Jaén (Ruiz Rodríguez, 1978) a similar state of affairs is noted at La Guardia and Cástulo (contrary to what happened in the case of Greek pottery imports); jewellery is documented only in tombs of some importance, although in no case is the presence of these products obligatory in the better-built tombs, as can be seen from their absence from tomb 155 at Baza.

So, the identification of weaponry associated with imported products does not indicate a dominant class but reflects certain relationships that appear to extend to the whole of the society, that experiences them in the different roles assigned by the system of social relationships. At times by quantity (like the abundance of imported objects in the princely tombs at El Cigarralejo), at others by quality (like the significance of the chariot or the crater or, on another level, of gold), one social group stands out above another, without necessarily having to be a group that is smaller in number. This fact is reflected in the difference existing between the princely cobbled tumular tombs already highlighted and those simply called cobbled tumular tombs, appreciably smaller in size. In the whole assemblage in which gold is seen to circulate, and in some instances at El Cigarralejo, like tombs 217 and 301, even without the presence of gold, an association is revealed between cobbled tumular tombs, imitations of craters and above all horse bits, and this obliges us to speak of the role of the warrior-horseman as opposed to those fighting men who either formed the infantry or did not carry the material remains of their status over into the ritual. It is interesting to note that a similar relationship is found at Cabecico (Quesada, 1989), where only one tomb yielded a chariot and eight had horse trappings; in Baza the ratio is two with a chariot and seven with horse trappings. The possibility exists that this second group, which some authors have identified with a class of *équites* or knights (Santos Velasco, 1989), is not associated exclusively with a secondary, but fairly expensively constructed, type of tomb; but, although its existence has not at present been defined in all its complexity, it is undoubtedly a limited group within the broad confines of the tombs studied. Recently, a faunal analysis carried out on bones from Estacar de Robarinas in Cástulo (Molero, 1988) showed a clear predominance of remains of horse and dog, species which, although not absent from the settlements, are nevertheless there in very small quantities. Their presence in tombs of very differing quality tells of greater complexity in the ritual (chiefly in the case of the horse) of the process followed, but we do not know whether this is common to all the necropolises or specific to Cástulo, the exceptional nature of which, from what has been studied so far, seems beyond all doubt. Nor should it be forgotten that, alongside these tombs with horse trappings, other assemblages are documented with furnishings of four or five Attic pieces, which, in the opinion of Santos Velasco, should be interpreted as people who were buried with great ostentation as testimony to a newly affluent social sector, independently of their membership of the class of knights. In this respect it is significant that, of the ten tombs that make up this group, eight are of the cobbled tumular type and one is as much as 5 metres wide, so bordering on the princely model. It must be borne in mind that craters, as in tomb 47, silver, as in 244, and in some cases complete sets of weapons are associated at the same time with these tombs.

Recently, an attempt has been made to present a picture based on the group buried in the Baza necropolis, of which 178 tombs from a relatively short period of time between 410 and 350 BC will have been excavated (Ruiz Rodríguez *et al.*, 1992).

Two interpretations of the spatial distribution of the tombs can be extrapolated from the analysis, depending on the container and its content:

1 Concentric reading: the first nucleus consists of two tombs (155 and 176) which are shaft graves and the largest in size; one contained the Lady of Baza, thirteen ceramic vessels and eleven urns. The other held eight indigenous vessels, fourteen Attic imports, including craters, and nine weapons, as well as the remains of a chariot and a bronze brasier. As to the cremated remains, tomb 155 has been interpreted as that of a woman, while 176 has more than one burial (Reverte Coma, 1986). In our opinion, the tomb with the chariot (176) is the key to the system of spatial distribution, while that of the Lady of Baza belongs to a slightly earlier date. So, taking tomb 176 as the key to the system and starting with a radius of 10 metres from it, a series of burials in large cysts is documented, in most cases 1.5 metres wide (including numbers 43 and 130), with numerous imports (six or seven pieces) and associating valuable weapons like the sabre, the *soliferrum* or the shield. The presence of craters among the imports gives these tombs pride of place, as does that of the bronze brasier (but as yet there is no chariot). If the radius is extended to 16 metres we again encounter a circle of cysts the same size as before, sometimes with as many as ten imported vessels (tomb 131) or gold objects (tomb 27), but with no weapons, crater or brasier. Up to this second circle, which seems to define the area of the greatest concentration of tombs and superpositions, we have a range that includes most of the tombs with horse trappings or with *kylix*, although the style and structure of the tomb is in no way outstanding.
2 Radial reading: if we consider the typology of the urns, we see that, along the radii starting from the key tomb and passing through the first circle of graves, a predominant type of urn (*kalathos*, red-glazed ware, etc.) is placed around it.

From this dual interpretation we have concluded:

1 That, with a few exceptions in time (tomb 155 and the stratigraphically lower group) and space (to the east, a second group seems to show up around tomb 142, which is also very big), the group of tombs at Baza constitutes the burial space of an aristocrat and his followers, in which the chief tomb, as at Galera, is set at one end of the area from where the distribution of the group is arranged in concentric semicircles and along radii.
2 The principal tomb typifies the aristocratic burial, marked by the greater

size of the structure and the crater–brasier–chariot association in the grave goods. A second level is seen in the cysts of the first circle, which continue to associate crater and brasier although the size of the grave is reduced and the chariot disappears. Finally, a third level, difficult to define because of the absence of weapons, closes the circle of the aristocratic burial space.

3 The fourth group consists of tombs located inside the 16-metre circle, containing either horse bits or imported pieces, like red-figured *kylix*. The fifth is made up of tombs set outside the circle and although in some cases they may contain a weapon or a black-glazed import, on average they are appreciably smaller than the fourth group. A final group is likewise set outside the outer circle but does not follow the line of the radii. This group has no imports and only exceptionally a weapon.

The interpretation of the first two levels is undoubtedly the basic structure of the aristocratic group. In their grave goods we see the crater–*kylix*–brasier association which gives archaeological expression to the existence of the symposium and libation, personal practices in the classical cities, but here expressing a ritual practice of cohesion by the aristocratic group. This factor, which to some extent affects the lowest levels in the scale of burials (presence of *kylix*, imitations of craters), forms a contrast to the still existing consequences of the distancing rituals of the orientalising stage (greater size of the aristocrat's tomb, presence of the chariot, concentric arrangement reminiscent of the old tumular model, etc.).

To sum up, we are seeing for the first time how an aristocratic client group could be organised, although still with serious gaps when it comes to interpreting certain aspects of the information obtained.

These references to different social sectors cannot, unfortunately, be linked to the anthropological analyses of the occupants of the tombs, for lack of specific studies; it is only the work carried out on the human remains from the Pozo Moro necropolis (Reverte Coma, 1985) that enables us to raise some very interesting questions. It is significant that, from a total of forty-three individuals, only 9.3 per cent are aged over fifty; this implies a high mortality since 23.2 per cent are children who died at under four years of age and the highest percentage mortality, 37.2 per cent, lies between thirty and forty years of age. But it is even more significant that, of the four individuals over fifty, two were buried in the monument that is only too well known and one in a princely tumulus; this undoubtedly favours the view that the dominant social class had better living conditions than the rest of the population. It is interesting, too, to confirm that although, as a whole, males outnumber females, we see that death occurs earlier in women than in men, who more often survive until fifty, whereas in more than 50 per cent of cases the women die between the ages of thirty and forty. The same factors are observed in the recent analysis carried out at Los Villares (Blánquez, 1990), to quote just one report. If the average life expectancy was 34.4 years for Pozo Moro, for Los Villares it was 38.14.

Apart from the reports mentioned, Reverte Coma has found the combined cremation of a woman and child on several occasions, a function of some acute infectious illness or even of some unconfirmed form of euthanasia; he has also observed, among other disease factors, a tendency to suffer from arthrosis of the joints.

Reverte Coma's investigation, using criminological techniques, confirms, among other factors:

1 That the temperature reached during cremation must have been between 850 and 950 °C; these maxima were attained, according to the author, by burning woods like *Quercus ilex.*
2 The bodies were burnt on the ground or in hollows dug into it and were placed in the supine position.

In his systematisation of Iberian rituals, Rafel Fontanals (1985) distinguished between primary and secondary incinerations. The latter, as the case cited from Pozo Moro shows, involved the place of cremation's being located away from the place of burial, while burials of the primary type have the cremation taking place on the site of the tomb, with the slight modification that the remains are laid to one side and the rest of the grave contents are deposited beside the ashes.

In general, no connections between these two types of burial can be seen as far as questions of a social, spatial or temporal nature are concerned, except in the necropolis of Gil de Olid in Puente del Obispo (Ruiz Rodríguez et al., 1984), where it was possible to define one stage that could be situated in the fifth century with the primary ritual, and another from the end of the fifth to the middle of the fourth centuries BC with the secondary ritual. Nevertheless, the sample is not big enough to produce a law that can be generalised, although at El Cigarralejo, Cuadrado's recent publication points out that the characteristic burial model is the secondary one; it developed at the same time as this ritual occurred at Puente del Obispo. From the spatial angle, Rafel states that the primary model is not documented to the north of the Corral de Saus in Valencia but from that point on, necropolises become considerably fewer. Cuadrado makes another reference to the ritual, which might be expressed as a chronological factor. He points to the existence of a destructive ritual that consisted in depositing a considerable part of the grave goods during cremation; against this, from the third century BC on, a conservative ritual takes over, depositing grave goods after the cremation has taken place, so there is no destruction. So once again we seem to be dealing with the tip of the iceberg of a proposition still barely enunciated; it does not seem, therefore, that it is a matter of differences representing separate elements of the social structure.

Natives and colonisers

As Coarelli points out, the colonising (Greek) culture as such is an abstraction; it does not exist, nor does the native world, so long as these questions have not been defined dialectically: 'what elements of the colonising culture entered the native world? why? when? and in which geographic region?, and above all, in relation to which social strata?' (Coarelli, 1972).

In the first place it must be shown that if the aristocrats identified themselves with the indigenous area, they did so no doubt in response to the existence of a peasantry which, in its relationship of dependency on them, depicted the prevailing system of socio-economic order. For this reason, it was not the colonisers alone who defined the aristocracy, although they did tend to determine its nature and character; above all, they had the final say in the process of their interrelationship with the indigenous social group, by generating a second system of incompatibilities which would have to be defined in terms of centre and periphery.

In the second place, the limits within which the encounter between the two worlds took place (centre = coloniser/periphery = native) did not fit in with the conditions favoured by historicism, whereby coloniser and native represent two peoples on different levels, or scales, of civilisation and culture, or economic development. It is obvious, and the written and archaeological sources never fail to confirm it, that this contact occurred as a function of the interests of different social groups on either side; thus not all the natives maintained the same level of dealings with the colonisers, and in their turn not all the colonisers related to the natives in the same social conditions. Positivism, with its strict limits on knowledge, historicism, transcending the internal contradictions of a society in its outlook, and lastly diffusionism, have generated a theoretical plan of colonisation that touches only on normative and culturalising aspects, returning, in the best instances, to the traditions of Polányi, which express the contact between the two sectors exclusively in terms of the rules of reciprocity or redistribution.

In the third place, the terms defining the context of the encounter are not culturalist, as we have tried to make clear, but neither are they the mechanical effect of certain mercantile and, in the last resort, economic models. And they are not so because the existence of optimising strategies is not the exclusive prerogative of capitalist societies, since, as Godelier states (1981, p. 49), 'each economic and social system lays down a specific way of using cultural assets', and also because it is not possible to transpose the strict laws of the market economy and the quest for profits as the result of investment to the past, when work had not yet been converted into just another commodity.

Consequently, the framework of the native–coloniser relationships cannot be realised today from the classic diffusionist plane, because the relationship generated by this contact is not of a cultural nature, nor a civilising project, nor one for the exclusive circulation of products and/or commodities. The case must be set out in the following terms:

1 In the internal logic of the nature of indigenous social relationships and, within them, in the setting of the conflict between the dominated and the dominant social sectors, fragments of classes or subgroups, and in the development deriving from the historical process studied.

2 In the logic of the centre–periphery incompatibility, insofar as it occurs in a setting of confrontation of opposites in space, because it is a matter of different social formations; and in the framework of the circulation of particular products which, in turn, stand in a direct relationship to their work processes and to the nature of the exchange relationships derived from coupling them with the factor just mentioned.

Colonies and emporia

Recently, Aubet's work ([1987] 1993) on the character of Phoenician colonisation has questioned the old theory which saw in this operation only the expression of a process of commercial expansion. The reality of the Phoenician colonies in the south of the Peninsula, in Aubet's opinion, is that, apart from Gadir, which arose with the clear aim of controlling Tartessian resources, the assemblage of colonies in the eastern region of the south coast of Andalusia was more a territorial strategy aimed at control of the agricultural territory from scattered units of exploitation. Consequently, Toscanos, Morro de Mezquetilla and Almuñecar make up a genuine system of colonies with authentic *chora* run by a merchant oligarchy (which must not be excluded) and landowners. The most obvious models of this type occurred between 720 and 700 BC, when this group of settlements attained its most spectacular growth, coinciding stratigraphically with the construction of the most significant buildings at Toscanos and with the fortification of the so-called 'trading post'

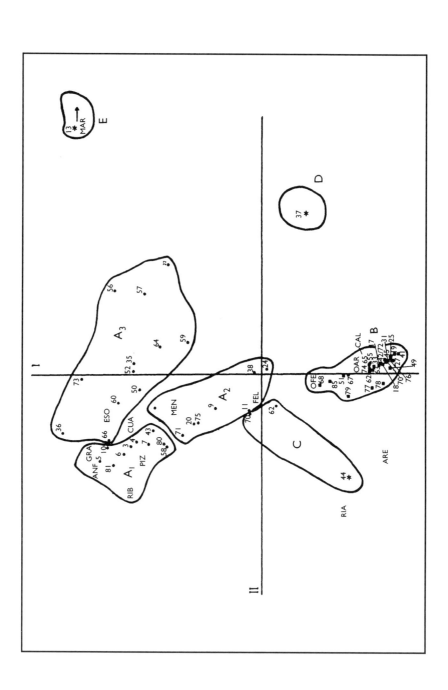

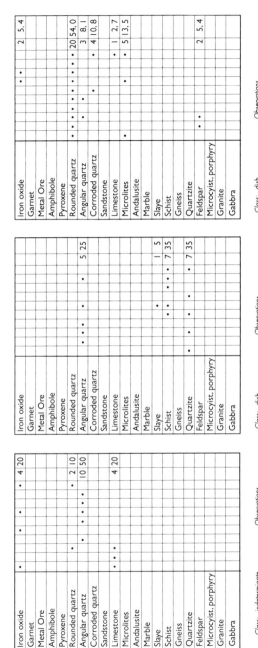

Table 1

Class: indeterminate — Observations
Typological group: E
Type of paste: homogeneous
Degreaser: very fine
Provenance: Sector 1A surface
Catalogue Nr.:
Bibliographic location: unpublished

Mineral	n	%
Iron oxide	4	20
Rounded quartz	2	10
Corroded quartz	10	50
Limestone	4	20

Table 2

Class: dish — Observations
Typological group: D
Type of paste: with nucleus
Degreaser: medium
Provenance: surface
Catalogue Nr.:
Bibliographic location: unpublished

Mineral	n	%
Angular quartz	5	25
Slaye	1	5
Schist	7	35
Quartzite	7	35

Table 3

Class: dish — Observations
Typological group: B
Type of paste: homogeneous
Degreaser: medium/fine
Provenance: Sector VII, strata 1c–1d, 1980–81
Catalogue Nr.: VII-5164
Bibliographic location: GONZÁLEZ, 1983, Fig. 14

Mineral	n	%
Iron oxide	2	5,4
Rounded quartz	20	54,0
Angular quartz	3	8,1
Corroded quartz	4	10,8
Limestone	1	2,7
Microlites	5	13,5
Feldspar	2	5,4

Figure 83 Defining various pottery groups (all, except group B, are imported). Tables showing mineral composition, description and provenance of a few samples (from González Prats and Pina, 1983)

– the motivation for this was to mark out a territory that it wished to control and defend.

Opposing Aubet's reading, Arteaga (1987) has put forward the case for the Phoenician presence on the coast on the basis that the colonies were always commercial and were organised and planned in advance in accordance with three categories of settlement: the first, represented by examples like Lixus, Gades, Malaka, Sexi or Abdera, would define the model of capital status for each 'colonial circuit'. From these 'capitals' secondary nuclei and satellites arose forming the structure of the model; however, it was the main centre, as with Gadir, that appropriated the most valuable agricultural lands in order to meet from them the basic necessities of subsistence.

Obviously, the two positions described go way beyond the idea of a strictly commercial settlement model with no links to the territory, one that for years characterised the image of the Phoenician coloniser on the Iberian peninsula. Indeed, we must point out, firstly, the importance in both arguments of the part played by the territory and the coloniser's control of it, opening up the prospect of a farming sector that is clearly fundamental in the concept of colonisation. Secondly, in both positions, a determining factor appears to be the existence of a process (a colonising model) starting from mercantile beginnings and giving way to articulation with the land, although some would say because of a strategic change in the model, which at the end of the eighth century BC, came to constitute an escape route for a peasant population. In any case, in spite of these differences, we are faced with a model of Phoenician colonisation as an ever more complex process – an enigma that cannot be solved in these pages but can indeed be evaluated in terms of one of the problems deriving from it: what was the relationship with the native?

Torelli (1977) has stressed the difference between the emporium model and the classical one of the Greek colonies of Magna Grecia, because the distinction between the settlement for trade and those for territorial acquisition does not just lie in what is implied at the organisational heart of the colonising structure; it also defines a different system of interaction with the native. Indeed, referring to the colonial system, Torelli states:

> When the Greek presence did not imply the immediate expulsion or subjection of indigenous groups and merely opposed such groups, [the ideological inter-ference] was certainly not just very much diminished, it was non-existent, as is normal in relations between subordinate and dominant groups and classes.
>
> (Torelli, 1977, p. 49)

Unlike this example, the emporium model shows an immediate effect on the indigenous groups in terms of a strengthening of relationships and an increase in the level of the ideological or economic impact of the coloniser on them. We should remember in this connection, what seems to be the very beginning of the occupation of Ampurias (Emporion) after its foundation, when it appears to be defined toponymically and archaeologically as a classic port for the redistribution of manufactured goods and not as a colony for settlers (Ruiz de Arbulo, 1984).

Apparently, and for reasons that we cannot for the moment unravel, Ampurias may, with a reasonable time lag *vis-à-vis* the Phoenician model, have shown a similar type of response, since if, at its foundation, between 600 and 575 BC (Sanmartí *et al.*, 1978), always according to the references in the sources, it was apparently a commercial emporium, the transition to the fifth century implied its conversion to an *apokia*, in a process similar to that of places like Agatha, also on the Golfe du Lion, where a *chora* in the style of a colony for settlers has been defined. Although it has not been possible to demonstrate this transformation at present, the existence of fields of storage pits throughout the area of the Gulf of Rosas, which are not necessarily associated with the Iberian *oppida*, might signal this tendency. In any case, the process is fairly late there and has no direct association with the Phoenician model; it may possibly be the normal effect of a settlement that has grown rich over the years and generates a *chora* in the broad sense around it.

Colonists confronting colonists

To all this must be added a new element for analysis stimulated by the encounter between colonisers, the most concrete evidence for which can be seen in the abundance of Phoenician material collected all along the Valencian–Catalan coast and similarly in the Phocean material at Huelva coupled, of course, with the references in the historiographic sources concerning Argantonios and his offer of lands to the Phoceans.

The first of the Phoenician examples in Valencia–Catalonia shows appreciable differences in two zones as dissimilar as the lower Segura/lower Vinalopó, in the Alicante–Murcia region, and the lower Ebro between Castellón and Tarragona, since in the first zone, González Prats (1985) has no doubt that it forms part of the same policy that was being applied generally in Andalusia. However, the presence of Phoenician products in Catalonia and in the zone specifically mentioned is very different in character, since, although it even entails the existence of a centre distributing Phoenician amphorae in Aldovesta (Benifallet) (Mascort *et al.*, 1988), it shows us a type of settlement similar to the one at Villasmundo in eastern Sicily or at L'Incoronele, near Metaponto. That is to say, native settlements affected by an expansive trading model, which in our case, at the end of the seventh century BC, was unfolding in a Phoenician setting, owing, according to some authors, to the search for direct routes to the great tin centres, possibly because of the actual crisis of relations with Tartessos and the closing of certain Atlantic routes.

In fact, the recent finds at Huelva, to which we have referred on several occasions, show that it was roughly that same date of 630 BC that saw the start of good relations between the Tartessians and the Phoceans (Cabrera Bonet, 1986; Fernández Jurado, 1986).

We have no precise knowledge of the processes that brought the Phoceans to the lower Guadalquivir and the Phoenicians to the immediate environs of Marseilles and Ampurias, but we do have proof of the end of the affair, as the changes that took place in the middle of the sixth century BC show, coinciding with such important landmarks as the fall of Tyre; although a recovery may have taken place there later, the moment of crisis in the western Phoenician circle is defined chronologically by the battle of Alalia, around 540 BC, and the Tartessian crisis. These last two events, as we have stated, coincided with the withdrawal of the two groups of colonisers, so that the Phoenicians abruptly stopped sending materials to the north, causing the abandonment of a few indigenous settlements in Catalonia and to the north of Valencia (we are thinking of Vinarraguell and, in general, a good number of the places studied stratigraphically on the lower Ebro), and restricted their sphere of activity to the advanced 'orientalising' world of the course of the Vinalopó. In the same way, the Tartessian crisis seems to constitute the turning point for Phocean activity; they no longer sent their basic products to Huelva and restricted their primary sphere to Catalonia and, later, from that point southwards to a boundary that is difficult to determine today, but which, judging by the classic late-Ampuritanian products, (like the famous small pitchers) reached, at its high point, a line from Murcia to Albacete (El Amarejo–El Cigarralejo) (Aranegui, 1969).

In any case, the conflicts between colonisers were not settled with the definition of spheres of influence. We are reminded how, on successive occasions later, references were made to treaties, alien to the indigenous world, that attempted to establish firmly the influence of the territories of the litigant groups (later, Romans and Punic–Carthaginians). Undoubtedly, the treaty of 348 BC between Rome, representing the Greek interests, and Carthage is one of the toughest in this historical need to define areas. Relating directly to the one signed in 509, the treaty of 348 states among other things, according to Polybius, that 'beyond Kalon Akroterion and Mastia of Tarsis, the Romans may not take captives, or trade, or found cities'. These same terms were repeated in the treaties of 306 and 279, close to the time when the family of the Barcidae arrived in the south of the peninsula.

Iberian society

What is certain is that after the treaty of 509, the peninsula appears to have been organised in accordance with the strategic-economic designs of Carthage; Herodoros of Heraclea shows us a defining effect of this relationship when he states, between 435 and 420, that the Libio-Phoenicians are *Carthaginian colonists*. In reality, as Aubet ([1987] 1993) states, the second half of the sixth century BC represents the replacement of a world of merchants by another of armies and political treaties.

Colonisers and aristocrats

A detailed analysis of the distribution of Phoenician products during the seventh century demonstrates the existence of various distinct circuits as far as the quality of the products traded is concerned. Thus we see how the ivories, to quote one item, are documented over a wide area, reaching well inland; however, we see their frequency diminishing more or less in step with the distance from the coast and the same occurs with other goods like Phoenician red-glazed wares, so that regions like Puente Tablas and other settlements on the upper Guadalquivir yield only imitations of these products, possibly coming from the lower Guadalquivir, whereas Aguayo records their abundance in Acinipo.

The commercial influence of the merchant/coloniser on the indigenous world operated on at least two levels, depending on the receiving group. On the one hand, receivers of exceptional goods are identified, so we must assume a ruling social class directing the system of contacts; on the other, for the most frequent or common products, the receiving group was widened till it covered the whole community. In the first case, not only was this behaviour restricted to the ruling class which could embark on processes of identification with the coloniser, but from that postion it could act as an intermediary between the enterprise of the latter and its own community; that is to say, it could control the second circuit. So this dual operation by the rulers must be understood not in terms of culture and civilising beneficence, but as projecting a model that reinforced and consolidated their own position at the forefront of the community. This model, which can be recognised through products like the ivories, already mentioned, bronzes representing figures like Hattor, scarabs, etc. (Aubet, 1986), and can be followed later, and with other protagonists in the distribution of Greek craters with their scenes of heroisation studied by Olmos (1984), shows how rapidly an understanding was reached between these socially prominent sectors and the coloniser, and in reality it is on this level that the success of the enterprise was founded.

The second level of circulation of goods undoubtedly affected the community as a whole and, indeed, was associated with a broad cultural impact that led to the internal transformation of the society. This second level, however, was not a programme in an opportunistic sense, but an outcome of the indigenous colonising model itself and of its interaction with the previous level, although it could become standardised as can be seen in the massive productions of Cástulo goblets, San Valentín *kantharos*, or Pintor de Viena 116 *kylix*, to which the great mass of the population appear to have had access without much problem. But the circuit of the coloniser took good care to keep one item apart, in this case the crater, which further reinforced the aim of strengthening the dominant group.

Returning to the process mentioned in differentiating between the models of emporia and colonies, the rapid effects produced and observed in the indigenous community on the level of the settlements, highlight the impact the new cultural tradition had on the autochthonous model. Indeed, this was soon detected from the positivist analysis, when it confirmed the change from the round hut to the rectangular and partitioned house or verified the rapid assimilation of new techniques like that of iron or the potter's wheel, which, as we have said, is not merely a question of cultural influence. The mercantile factor present at the start of the Phoenician model would account for the rapid contact established between the indigenous world as a whole and the coloniser. Cases like Acinipo or Pinos Puente, in different parts of Andalusia, demonstrate this; and the process would be repeated too a few years later in the Indketan environs of Emporion: in this respect, the work on the stratigraphic sequence at Illa d'en Reixac is worth remembering.

But this first effect of cultural change was based on a first system of contacts that approached the most powerful social sectors of the community, whose social power was reinforced precisely because of their control and domination of those circuits organised by the coloniser.

Consequently, it was the circulation of goods for the privileged groups that paved the way for the cultural change which would never have been brought about by the coloniser, had it not fitted into the internal dynamics of the indigenous system, where the aristocracy now saw itself underpinned by a model that appeared to it to be common to many points in the Mediterranean, and in which many expedients had been successfully tested. The native aristocracy, economically and ideologically reinforced by the first model of contact with the coloniser, set about managing the process of change going on in the indigenous world and that can be seen in specific examples like the building of fortifications at places as far apart as Puente Tablas in Jaén or Tejada in Huelva; and in the common process that modified the habitat model within the settlements, it brought about a genuinely planned change at their very heart, clearly as a result of its power. The second circuit, then, was not an ethnic circuit, as might have been supposed from a first reading, but a circuit for the distribution of goods that were directed at the aristocracy as well, in order, with its consent, to be passed on to wider social groups who thus experienced the cultural and economic change that would consolidate the position of the dominant indigenous groups. Things became complicated and at the same time clearer later on, when the aristocracy achieved their social definition as a group, as we have defined it on the basis of a certain isonomy, coinciding with greater affluence in the social base of the dependants or slaves. This second period enables us to observe how, while the first circuit continued to keep certain imported goods as the prerogative of a dominant social class (the crater, for example), the second had increased the quantity and quality of the products, bringing a wider social group to share in this process and so allowing the model to go on functioning as a means of sustaining the aristocratic system.

This tendency towards contact with the native by strengthening the aristocracy, which was foreshadowed at the beginning of the Phoenician and Phocean model and was a constant factor in the later stages, contrasts with possible changes that would take place in the world of the coloniser. Indeed, consideration must be given first of all to the internal processes relating to the conversion of emporia into colonies with their own territory, because we believe the process could not have led to the creation of a barrier against the indigenous world, such as was conceivable for the first colonial foundations of Magna Grecia. So the development of a possible *chora* at Emporion coincided theoretically with the clearest signs of Hellenisation in the territory of the Indiketes (an example might be the city walls at Ullastret). Secondly, since it was carried out and managed by indigenous aristocratic groups, the process followed its own dynamic and in turn generated new tensions between the centre and the periphery at the heart of the indigenous world (Tartessians–Mastienians) and made the gestation of new circuits for goods possible, indigenous ones this time, which reproduced the framework of the relationship between the coloniser and the native aristocracy, but this time it was between central and peripheral aristocracies.

— 6 —

Ethnic groups, states . . . socio-economic formations

Written historical sources between the sixth and fourth centuries BC

A first approach to the written historical sources provides information about the area corresponding to Tartessos and its periphery and also its links with the axis defined by the river Guadalquivir from source to mouth. Thus, and from the earliest written sources connected with the Massiliot Periplus, collected by Rufus Festus Avienus in his *Ora Maritima*, we know that the river kept the west apart from a people, the 'Iberian', while to the east lay the Tartessians and Cilbiceni. Also, towards the interior, Avienus mentions the Etmanei, Ileates and Cempsi and, to the east of Tartessos, the Libiophoenicians on the coast and the Mastieni with their capital at Mastia, traditionally located at Cartagena (see Bosch Gimpera, Almagro, Schulten, etc.). The latter are linked with Tharsis (the treaty of 348 BC mentions 'Mastia of Tharsis'), an indication of its dependence on Tartessos. If to all this we add the pressure exerted, according to Almagro Basch's interpretation of the text, by Tartessos on the island of Cartaré, controlled by the Cempsi, we find indications of the group's expansionist capacity and its stable role within its sphere of influence. Later, references in Hecateus of Miletus and Herodoros of Heraclea would again touch on the preponderant role of Tartessos in the south of the Iberian Peninsula, returning to some of the peoples mentioned, as happens in the first of the two authors, who cites, with a chronology of the late sixth century BC, the presence of Tartessians and Mastieni, recounting in a simplified form the Massiliot Periplus, already alluded to, although a few other names are added, like that of the Elbestii to the west of Tartessos and at a point that must coincide with Huelva, according to Bosch Gimpera's interpretation (1932). The mention in the second of the two above-mentioned authors is more complicated, on the one hand, because it deals with a century later, since his information is dated around 435–420 BC, when the historical landscape had changed considerably; on the

Figure 84 Iberian 'peoples' according to references in the written historical
sources of the sixth and fifth centuries BC (by the authors)

other, because he introduces a new bone of contention by giving a hierarchy
in his references to groups:

> this Iberian people dwelling on the coast of the straits is given various names,
> being a single people with different tribes. First, those living in the most
> westerly part are called Cinetes (after which, going northwards we find the
> Gletes), then the Tartessians, then the Elbisini, then the Mastieni, then the
> Celcii and then you come to the straits.

This approach contradicts another quotation from the same author which
clearly separates the two groups: 'Beside the Sardinian sea live firstly the
Libiophoenicians, Carthaginian colonists, then, it is said, come the Tartessians
and beside them the Iberians.'

The archaeology of the Iberians

In the above passages we see new names like the Gletes or *kelkianoi*, who, while they can be related in one instance with other peoples of the Periplus (Gletes = Ileates), in another serve to introduce the problem of the Celts into the south. The texts of Herodoros, as a whole, create great confusion, being very inconsistent, but apart from this, or other old controversies like the famous one concerning the whereabouts of the Iberians, the reading of Herodoros' texts introduces the ethnic problem by distinguishing between a people and a tribe and making the Tartessians and Mastieni share a common root, which, in one case, finds expression under the name of the Iberians and in the other (remembering the second text) under that of the Tartessians.

Beyond Mastia, towards the province of Alicante, the situation referred to in the sources is also complicated. The *Ora Maritima*, referring to this zone, says: 'Here, in other times was the boundary of Tartessos. Here was the city of Herma. The tribe of the Gymnetes was settled in these parts up to the course of the river Sicano which flows close to them' (Avienus, 449–98). The reading of this text has produced different interpretations, according to the historicist debate and the position of each author, but it is obvious that in Avienus' text the edge of the Tartessian sphere of influence is unequivocal and that the Mastieni are included in this group, as are the Gymnetes, unless we understand Avienus' reference as excluding the Gymnetes–Tartessian relationship. One way or another, what is certain is that the references to the following group are again arranged on a different axis, that of the Iberians–Beribraces this time:

> And in front the Iberians extended their domains to the Pyrenean mountains
> . . . Beyond that, where the land withdraws far from the sea, extends a region of
> wooded hills. There the Beribraces, a wild and fierce tribe, roamed among
> herds of many head of cattle . . . they led a very hard life like wild animals.
> (Avienus, 449–98)

Hecateus of Miletus is even more specific, stating that these Iberians were represented in a series of tribes, among which he mentions the Esdetes, Ilaraugates and Mysgetes. In the ancient texts, other groups are mentioned, like the Sicani, near the river of the same name, who were later linked with Succo and identified with the Júcar.

The most complicated case of those mentioned is that of the Mysgetes, who had established themselves between the Garraf Massif to the south and the strip bounded by the rivers Orb and Hérault to the north (Padró and Sanmartí, 1992). Later, the zone absorbed a broad assemblage of groups, among whom were found Layetani, Ausetani, Indiketes, Sordones and Elisices; some of them (Indiketes, Sordones and Elisices) had already been men-

250

tioned in Avienus, although in his text the boundaries between Iberians and Ligurians do not agree with those given later in Hecateus, who does not include the Elisices, a Ligurian people, among the Mysgetes. What stands out, however from all this is that Avienus' text describes all these groups in fairly harsh terms, very similar to those used for the Beribraces: 'A people of fierce hunters living in crude shelters.' He speaks in the same way about groups further inland, like the Ceretes or Ausoceretes, although at that time they were already considered to be tribes of the Iberians.

Leaving aside the attempt to determine the definitive location of each group, a very difficult matter to pinpoint from the scant sources available and on which much work has already been done by writers such as Schulten, Bosch, Almagro and García y Bellido, we plan a two-pronged approach to this topic: on one side, assessing those aspects that might form a genuine conceptualisation of what is contained in the available information; on the other, analysing this level in the temporal projection imposed by the second block of information, referring to the final centuries of the millennium and the need to relate it to the historical archaeological sources already mentioned. Let us take the first question.

From a reading of both Avienus and the rest of the authors, a hierarchisation in the terminology used for the zones is undoubtedly foreshadowed. Thus we know that for both Avienus and Hecateus, there existed a first rank stretching from the Júcar to the Rhône and given the name Iberian as opposed to Ligurian. Meanwhile in the south, although there seems to be a greater mosaic of peoples, the Tartessians are presented as the defining group of that rank, in line with the references to the boundary apparently constituted by the Gymnetes. The same reading can be seen in Hecateus, who has no hesitation in defining as Iberian the three groups of the present-day Franco–Catalan–Valencian coastline, while in the south he shows us the Tartessian–Mastienian polarisation. From a reading of this block an immediate series of conclusions could be drawn:

1 The existence of large population units at the end of the sixth century BC, such as Iberians, Tartessians, Beribraces or Ligurians.
2 The existence of a second rank of units, frequently defined by the sources as tribes and linked to a lower rank in the population.
3 A third conclusion, likewise of special interest, enables us to state that the categories used in the first assessment do not appear to correspond to the same concept since, although the term Iberians could represent an ethnic unit embracing other sub-units, yet the case of Tartessos is presented as a political unit in a phase of expansion, as demonstrated by the conflict with

the Cempsi on the island of Cartaré or the apparent domination over the land of Mastia.

Bosch Gimpera already signalled this particular difficulty about the area controlled by this latter group when he said that either the Mastieni were the tribe of Mastia which dominated a conglomerate of townships that were federated at one time with the Tartessians (therefore they were a political consequence that lasted until the fall of Tartessos, at which time the different subjugated tribes would have recovered their individuality), or else the name of Mastieni was given to a conglomerate of townships on a scale higher than the second, similar to that represented by the case of the Iberians in the Periplus, which disappeared all of a sudden leaving partial tribes to surface (Bosch Gimpera, 1932).

In both interpretations, Bosch Gimpera's assessment introduces a component that is never present for the other zone and of which the author is unaware: Mastieni are simply the result of a political decision that grouped tribes together and came to have a state unit, like that of Tartessos, over it. This political factor is something that will no doubt be corroborated by the historical archaeological sources when they show the long politico-cultural tradition of the Andalusian–Murcian–Alicanten settlements, which, from the end of the eighth century BC, were breaking with the old traditions of the Final Bronze Age and defining a more structured population system, more in harmony with a social division of labour, adapted to the interests of an aristocracy that was beginning to dominate. These political factors did not come singly and in practice they produced a cultural homogeneity that was able to merge successfully into what has come to be called orientalising or early Iberian, and which, in accordance with the sources, and recalling the work of Arteaga or González Prats, grouped together the area that Avienus collected under the term Gymnetes, who were now described as Iberians by the Periplus.

So did Tartessos really come to hold sway over the whole of the territory thus defined? Apparently not in the political terms of a project of expansion by conquest, which may have been present in its immediate hinterland but not necessarily at points as remote as the provinces of Jaén, Granada and Murcia and in the Mastienian territory in general. In our opinion, the impact of Tartessian expansionist policy was felt in an obvious form at the end of the seventh century BC, when a colonising policy is defined archaeologically for the first time. Indications of this could be the reference to a territorial occupation documented in the *vega* of the Guadalquivir and the *campiña* of Cordoba, and identified by a significant development of small rural settlements that sprang up without any particular defence and under the shelter of some large settlement; this is the case at Marmolejo in Jaén in relation to Los Villares de Andújar or the settlements documented around other *oppida* like Torreparedones or Porcuna. As a political experiment, then, this model soon found itself in crisis, as can be seen from the disppearance of these settlements, which arose at the end of the seventh and disappeared before reaching the end of the sixth century BC, coinciding with the political decline of Tartessos.

But what is more important and puts an end to this expansionist development is the rapid reaction observed in the indigenous population of the *campiña* (Etmanei? Mastieni?). They promptly strengthened the boundary between the *vega* and the *campiña* by building a frontier line bristling with towers, already mentioned in cases like Cazalilla, which ultimately came to mark the limits of their own political territory. In this way, the Tartessian periphery became effective as a political entity through the existence of a centre like Tartessos (Ruiz Rodríguez and Molinos, 1990).

The process becomes more interesting if we introduce the development of the fifth century BC, and with it the post-Tartessian stage, since we notice with surprise, remembering the text of Herodoros of Heraclea, that not only does mention of Tartessians and Mastieni continue, but now they are presented in the guise of 'tribes of the Iberian people'. The text shows us the extent to which the Tartessians and their periphery (Mastieni mainly, but there were others) were defining their ethnic role when the political directives were leading to a marked fragmentation, which might even make us think in terms of aristocratic groups attached to an *oppidum*. The gap left by Tartessos in its building of an ethnic unit that would assimilate the centre and its periphery would soon be filled, as Herodoros shows, by an ethno-geographic reading consistent with extending an exclusively cultural concept based on the Periplus and Hecateus.

In fact, the problem emerges more clearly in the case of the Mysgetes, defined by Padró and Sanmartí, because of their Greek etymological root, on the basis of the idea of a mixture of Iberian population and early Iron Age groups, with people from southern Gaul. It is obvious that an indigenous ethnic group would never have given itself such a name and that the concept of a mixture could only be in the mind of the outsider observing them. If this, which deals with the lowest level on the scale, shows the weakness of the ethnic case, it will be much more difficult to talk of an Iberian race from the Rhône to the Júcar, at least in the terms in which we were conceptualising the problem at its historical limits; this implies, in our opinion, that rather than defining an historical race, the Periplus and Hecateus were determining cultural traits within a geographic framework.

Indeed, the views of Pereira, Arteaga, Almagro Gorbea and González Prats all agree in noting how similar products are recorded over large areas and define a material culture that, in the sixth century BC, as we have hinted, has to be called orientalising, or early Iberian, or late Tartessian. The fact is that products such as the slender-necked vessels with duck-head-type rims, lugged urns, variants of the 'thistle' vase shape or, in other materials, curved knives or ring fibulae are recorded in an area covering all the Iberians of the Massiliot Periplus and the area corresponding to Tartessos with its periphery. The conclusion we can draw for the moment could be set out in the following terms:

1   It is necessary to keep the distinction between state and ethnic group because confusing them has often given rise to error, especially in archaeological research, by constructing a cultural spectrum in which it is frequently claimed that a geopolitical plan can be detected. Certainly, barring slight, barely detectable, cultural differences, some states may assimilate various cultures within them and, more frequently, a single cultural block may contain various state structures. From this angle, the only references to state structures in the sources quoted appear to be confined to Tartessos: the conquest of Cartaré, its influence on Mastia and, inevitably, other texts used here, such as the mentions of Gárgoris and Habidis or Argantonios and the Phoceans.

2   The Tartessian political project tended to be expressed culturally in the building of an ethnic group that may also have found expression in Avienus' reference, situating the Tartessian border towards the province of Alicante; this agrees with the contribution of archaeology, as the materials recorded at Penya Negra de Crevillente or Saladares de Orihuela show. We shall never know if the building of this ethnic unit, which is expressed, as Bate and Torelli point out, through ethnic awareness and not just through its external cultural features, came to fruition because of the political collapse of Tartessos, which all through the fifth century BC left an ethnic vacuum that was mistakenly covered up from outside (from the Greek historian and geographer), mitigating the weakness of the ethnic concept in a cultural-geographic scenario like the Iberian. Nevertheless, all in all, the fifth century began, at least on the cultural plane, to penetrate deep into traits that, for example, show the Mastienian in contrast to the Tartessian. So we confirm that the Mastienian area, with its burials in chambers and coffins, was idențfied and differentiated from the Tartessian (Almagro Gorbea, 1982b). This is borne out by certain productions like the imitations of columned and bell craters in indigenous pottery or by the burial ritual itself, which is not documented on the lower Guadalquivir (Escacena, 1987a).

3 Obviously, the situation to the north of the Vinalopó is very different, in spite of the cultural overlaps noted by the archaeologists and recorded in writing by authors like Herodoros. It is undoubtedly distinct, because so is the ethnic substrate and the political structure supporting it but, further-more, we do not at present know, except for a few questions of a cultural nature, what the Urnfield substrate documented in Catalonia–Valencia was like, nor the political form in which these groups found expression, nor how the first ones interacted with the Phoenician world and ultimately that of the Greek coloniser. It is possible that, like the Mastieni, Tartessians, Elbisini, Etmanei, etc., they were the product of ancient races (Esdetes, Ilaraugates), or even of new ones that were beginning to grow stronger at the end of the sixth century, when the Phoenicians had already withdrawn, abandoning that area; and it may have been the Greeks who now seized the opportunity to make contact with the older peoples.

4 The Franco–Catalan Mysgetes are certainly interesting, as we have stated, because gathered under that name, if Avienus' accounts are reliable, were the Indiketes, Ausetani and Sordones, that is to say, those peoples who would be the Iberian groups in the sources after the third century BC, although they are presented with a name for savagery, which has no bearing on their subsequent cultural structure.

So the case of the Mysgetes is yet another cultural reading that could lead to an ethnic reality, although, apparently, not by the end of the sixth century. From this point of view, the location of Ampurias might distort their situation, but not so that of the Esdetes and Ilaraugates; they eventu-ally formed the classic Edetanian and Ilercavonan ethnic groups, and others connected with them like the Sedetani or Ilergetes, as we shall see later.

5 In conclusion, and still as a working hypothesis, the process defining the fifth century seems to tend towards cultural homogenisation and the formation of different ethnic groups with regard to political development. But, for precisely that reason, the process of change that each of these ethnic units would follow would be different, depending on its own specific history. In this way, while the Tartessian collapse seems in reality to have precipitated a fragmentation of the old ethnic groups, once the project of the great Tartessian race was lost, the original ethnic groups in other regions would eventually be consolidating their position and getting organised (as in the Esdetes–Edetani or Ilaraugates–Ilercavones relationships). Finally, we have a special case: the Mysgetes, for whom first the weight of the colonies (Marseilles, Rodhe and Emporion) and then the establishment of the *chora* would bring about the collapse of their ethnic development and

an apparent return to the old ethnic forms, although culturally transformed and in a political framework defined by the coloniser and the indigenous aristocracies.

New ethnic groups in the third century (sanctuaries, languages and other problems)

The southern Iberians

The scene had been appreciably modified at the conclusion of the second Punic war. The references in Livy, Polybius and Apianus and the later ones in Strabo, Pliny and Ptolemy, while disagreeing among themselves, sketch out a very different geopolitical map, although the process can be followed in some of its fundamental modifications. Indeed, no one doubts, to quote one example, that the references to Turdetanians stand in a direct relationship to the old Tartessian groups, but now lacking the vigour and political power attributed to them in another age.

This continuity, endorsed by the quotation from Strabo concerning the Turdetanians, when he says that they had 'writings' of ancient memory, poems and laws in verse (Strabo, III-16), or in the references to Argantonios as an ancient king of that people (III-2-14), is an indication of the extent to which, with a change of name, Tartessos had maintained its ethnic values through time, although restricted to its old core area of the lower course of the Guadalquivir; for not even the Turdulans, located, according to Strabo, to the north of the Turdetanians (and according to other authors surrounding the ancient territory: Ptolemy), were of the same ethnic group, in the opinion of Polybius. Towards the east, the Mastienian group appears to be identified with the Bastetani. Untermann (1984) supports this idea on the basis of the difficulty in transcribing the Iberian *m* and *b* (Mastieni–Bastieni). They inhabited a stretch of territory that took in the coastal fringe and also an extensive zone in the interior, occupying part of the provinces of Jaén, Granada, Almería, Albacete and Murcia. To the north of these peoples and to the north-east of the Turdetanians and Turdulans, an Oretanian group was established, for whom Strabo highlights two main centres in Oria and Cástulo and to whom Ptolemy ascribes as many as fourteen settlements. The Oretani do not appear to correspond to any of the old ethnic groups of the sixth century, although sites like Cástulo and Puente del Obispo have yielded archaeological sequences that reveal their existence from early times. This inclines us to include them in a group of small units that may have existed before (Gletes, Etmanei, Cilbiceni, etc.) and are not now documented, or a

Figure 85 Iberian 'peoples' according to references in the written historical sources of the third century BC (by the authors)

group of new political formations that arose in the processes started in the fifth and fourth centuries BC. The location of Herodoros' Celts appears to be more of a problem; they continue to be documented in Ptolemy in a nucleus not so very far from the Serranía de Ronda, evidence for which is the siting of Acinipo in Ronda la Vieja or the case of a few Mentessani whom Pliny mentions and places between Oretani and Bastetani, or the highly controversial Deitani of the Murcia region.

Altogether, the written texts highlight three large nuclei. The first two, Turdetanian–Turdulan and Bastetanian–Bastulan, correspond on the whole to the Tartessians–Mastieni of the previous phase. The third is clearly defined in the Oretani and the mentions of petty kings, like Orisson and Culchas,

257

Figure 86 Bronze ex-votos from Collado de los Jardines (Santa Elena, Jaén)

controlling a certain number of *oppida;* and even cases of settlements that could constitute a state model in themselves. Everything leads us to think that around this date (third century BC) we are again encountering the rebuilding of new ethnic groups, which, however, and in spite of their initial vigour, would see their development cut short through the conquest of their territory by Rome. On the other hand, the appearance of new ethnic groups or group names assimilated to *oppida* (Oretani to Oreta, Bastetani to Basti or Mentessani to Mentessa) reinforces the idea of a reality generated or reinforced politically throughout the third century BC, but failing to reach its logical culmination due to successive interruptions: first, by the Barcas in the name of Carthage and then by the Scipios in the name of Rome. So the idea must be envisaged that the Bastetani or Oretani, for example, would eventually have controlled the rest of the territories in the trend towards the second ethnic pattern that was foreshadowed. Remember Pliny's mention of an important group of settlements which he included in Bastetania, a classic territory of the Turdulans or Turdetanians; or Strabo's of the Bastetani who were living in Turdetania. The case of the Oretani should be interpreted in the same way;

258

their connection with La Mancha, on the grounds of the siting of the capital, seems to be correct, as is their irruption into the Guadalquivir valley in order to control the rich mining centres of Cástulo.

It is interesting to stress that this ethno-political pattern coincides with the revival throughout the third century BC of sanctuaries and religious precincts like Cerro de los Santos in Albacete, among the Bastetani, or the Cueva de la Lobera in Castellar and the Santuario del Collado de los Jardines among the Oretani; or lastly, El Cigarralejo in Murcia whose chronology suggests that it originated in the fourth century and was destroyed at the end of the third century BC.

The case of Castellar, has recently been studied by Nicolini, Zafra and Ruiz Rodríguez (1987), although it has been known from ancient times for the vast number of decontextualised ex-votos (Nicolini, 1969; Prados, 1988), as has the sanctuary of Despeñaperros (Collado de los Jardines). It consists of a natural shelter, which must have been running with water in its day. There are no traces of human intervention to be seen, unless it be a system of steps and ramps cut into the rock and lined with large stones to mark the access to the interior. From the second terrace, immediately in front of the cave, occupation of the hillside began and ran from the cave down to the plain. The structures are not very sophisitcated as to construction and have no discernible internal partitions. Furthermore, in front of these structures and between them run the streets, ill-defined but paved and, in those giving access to the cave, with steps. The model is simple and seems to fit some predetermined plan.

The sanctuary poses interesting problems, such as its origin, which, in Nicolini's opinion (1969), based on the style of some of the ex-votos, goes back to the end of the seventh century BC; there is documentary evidence for others from the fifth to fourth centuries as well as a later group coinciding with the period of expansion. However, the efforts, first of the pillagers and later of unsystematic and extensive excavations have emptied the upper terrace, which is the only one that might confirm that hypothesis; similarly the stratigraphic sequences obtained, all from the second terrace, record a stage corresponding to the third century exclusively and in many ways at the end of the fourth century, as in other cases already mentioned.

Apart from the problem of chronology it poses, we can be certain that the siting of the settlement is special because of its isolation on one of the ridges that rise from the river Guadalquivir towards the Sierra Morena (which will remain in the frame as a central nucleus in Oretania), coinciding with the mining area. It is difficult to get away from the theory that the sanctuary of Castellar was an early religious centre revived in the third century BC to become a rural-ethnic sanctuary of the Oretanian group. This example could

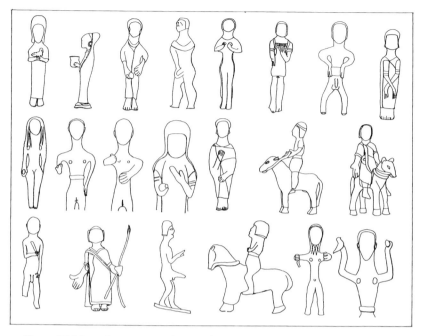

Figure 87 Most characteristic forms of ex-voto figures (from Nicolini, 1969)

equally well be extended to others that have been mentioned. The resurgence of these sanctuaries or, if this approach is not accepted, their development at these periods, could be the result of the ethnic pattern that defined a series of groups, who achieved their territorial political reality in the third century BC and planned a comparable expansion towards their own periphery. It would be very interesting to make an analysis of these sanctuaries right across the area where they operated, like the one for the Valencian caves studied by Gil Mascarell (1985).

On the linguistic plane, the dichotomy noted between the area of the greater Tartessian tradition and the Bastetanian–Oretanian area can also be detected if we turn to the investigation undertaken by Untermann, and the distribution map of the records of Tartessian and southern Iberian writing. It shows a frontier zone in the most westerly area, that is to say, Cordoba, where the finds of southern Iberian writing are superimposed on a series of toponyms connected with the traditionally Tartessian area, like those beginning with *ob-* and *ip-* and those ending in *-uba (oba)* and *-ippo (-ipo)*, which extend as far as the most easterly part of the Cordoba–Obulco area. So this area seems to be a

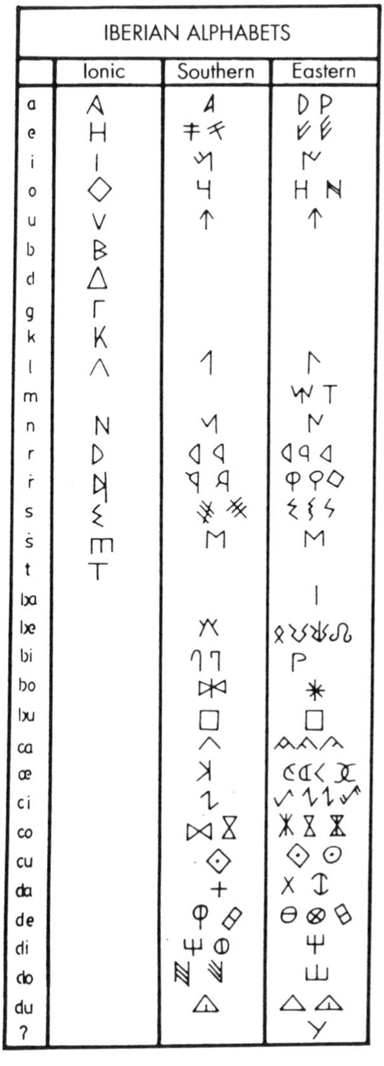

IBERIAN ALPHABETS		
Ionic	Southern	Eastern
a		
e		
i		
o		
u		
b		
d		
g		
k		
l		
m		
n		
r		
ŕ		
s		
ś		
t		
ba		
be		
bi		
bo		
bu		
ca		
ce		
ci		
co		
cu		
da		
de		
di		
do		
du		
?		

Figure 88 Iberian alphabets (from Fletcher, 1983)

zone where the two great regions overlap, just as the most easterly zone of the Portuguese Algarve is identified with Lower Andalusia in the samples of writing and in the occasional toponym (*-oba*). Similarly, the zone is distinguished by the *ili-, iler-, ilu-* forms, so much in evidence in the whole Iberian area (Ilerda in Catalonia, Ilercavones in the Castellón area, Iliturgi on the upper Guadalquivir), and the toponym with *-brice* develops covering a good part of the remaining peninsular area and, of course, the basin of the river Guadiana and southern Portugal in general (Untermann, 1984).

It is important to clarify the role played by writing in the Iberian world as a cultural factor and an ethnic component of the utmost interest. Basically, the authors have evaluated this question in different terms:

1 For De Hoz, the origin of writing in the Iberian peninsula must be followed in the graffiti of the burnished reticular wares, dated prior to the seventh century BC and documented likewise in Crevillente, although at a late date (beginning of the sixth century BC). According to this author, it occurred as a result of the changes that took place at the end of the Final Bronze Age in the eastern Mediterranean; these led to the presence of scribes in the Iberian peninsula, who, uprooted from their palace world, found their way into the zone. Writing arose as a local adaptation of the orientalising horizon, at least from the seventh century BC, under the stimulus of colonisers in the complex framework of Tartessos (De Hoz, 1969 and 1979).

2 Untermann (1975–80), for his part, interprets it as a combination of Phoenician and Greek writing, which improved on the former by incorporating vowels to the consonants. The date of this event must have been in the region of 500 BC in the south-east of the peninsula, although its parallel invention in the south-west cannot be ruled out.

Both authors agree in placing writing at an early phase, always preceding the development of the Iberian culture. Consequently, the birth of this socio-cultural world is coupled with a system of writing, which, with its links to early Iberian, gives some idea of the complexity of the socio-economic structure being analysed. On the other hand, the distinction established by Untermann between Tartessian and southern Iberian writing, less precise than that set out by De Hoz, amply explains the two big ethnic groups already studied (Tartessian and Mastienian). To this must be added the remarks of De Hoz about the gap in post-Tartessian writing in the Guadalquivir valley, filled only belatedly by the inscriptions on coins in Obulco or Cástulo. The evidence could imply the collapse of the old state units observed at the end of the Tartessian period, but not that of the ethnic traditions, which persisted into a later period because there was nothing to replace them.

The area of present-day Valencia is of special interest in this field, since we have already noticed a sharp break there between the Vinalopó area and the Turia region. So writing is yet another of the very interesting pointers, since it is the Júcar that marks the division between the so-called 'southern Iberian'

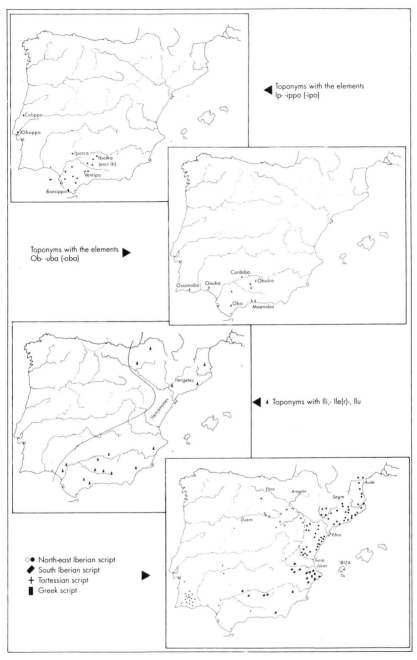

Figure 89 Distribution maps for toponyms and scripts
(from Untermann, 1984)

263

writing and the Levantine or north-eastern writing, as Untermann likes to call it. The fact is that, with the exception of *Abengibre* to the north of that river, all the finds of southern Iberian writing, including the lead from La Bastida de Mogente and the inscription from the Serreta de Alcoy, lie to the south of the river, where, moreover, a greater concentration of these finds has come to light. The area thus designated is the one that Llobregat would define as Contestania, which has traditionally been linked to the province of Alicante. Moreover, this Contestanian area is the nucleus marking the northern limit of the sculptures and, of course, has its richest centre around La Alcudia de Elche, the site of Ilici, its theoretical capital; it would become known as one of the most important production centres for decorated pottery of the Elche–Archena type.

In fact, this example appears to contradict Llobregat's interpretation when it comes to determining the south-western limit. Indeed, while this author places the southern boundary of Contestania on the northern bank of the river Segura, the texts of Ptolemy (III, 6, 61) and Pliny (III, 19, 20), by contrast, even include New Carthage itself (modern Cartagena and, in another age, the putative Mastia) in the zone. All this without verifying Deitania, mentioned in Pliny (III, 19) as between Bastetania and Contestania; its presence in the territory has not so far been confirmed.

The Contestanian world, and in this we agree with Llobregat, forms an environment with a clear cultural identity (Elche–Archena pottery, abundant written information and well-defined sculpture workshops) but, at the same time it is a world with strong hints of a frontier region, as witness the incursion from the north of grey-ware productions, such as the small Ampuritanian pitchers (Aranegui, 1969) or the sharing of red-burnished (we recall Cuadrado's classification) or stamped wares with other parts of Andalusia and La Mancha; and, on another level, the spread of the sanctuaries already known in the area of Jaén and Albacete (Oretanian–Bastetanian). These are documented at a series of sites like the Santuario de la Luz, Verdolai, Monteagudo, Coy in Lorca, La Encarnación in Caravaca or El Cigarralejo in Mula; the latter is of special interest because of the repeated finds of terracotta figures of horses. In other cases, the bronze ex-votos exist alongside others made of clay and stone (Lillo, 1981). In Alicante, the Serreta de Alcoy is a centre of the same type, which received a series of terracotta ex-votos as offerings and, in line with those documented in Santuario del Castillo de Guardamar (Abad, 1987), very different from the sanctuary caves documented by Gil Mascarell more to the north, which do not represent a natural sanctuary model, as we have already stated, if only from the absence of ex-votos like those documented in this area.

The Iberians of the north

The direct relationship that seems to exist between Avienus' Esdetes–Ilarau-gates, and the Edetani–Ilercavones of Ptolemy and other ancient authors, has already been pointed out; if to these we add the Ilergetes and the controversial Sedetani (described by Fatás (1963) and indirectly by other authors like Uroz, who, by identifying them with the Edetani, excludes points like Caesar Augusta (Saragossa), contrary to opinions like that of Ptolemy himself), we shall have assessed one of the assemblages most representative of the Iberian world between the Ebro Valley and that of the Júcar.

We have a more or less accurate idea of the location of the Edetani from the investigations of the SIP (Servicio de Investigaciones Prehistóricas) (with the excavations at San Miguel de Liria, Puntal dels Llops and Sagunto, among other settlements), from recent studies of settlement patterns (Bernabeu et al., 1987) and from compilations like that made by Uroz (1983). The area conforming to Edetania is not only located around the triangle formed by Edeta (San Miguel de Liria), Arse (Sagunto) and Saitabi (Játiva), but is identified from a well-defined cultural element like the pottery production of the Liria group and also from significant absences like sculpture or ex-votos in the sanctuaries. Its borders are clearly defined, apparently between the river Júcar to the south and the Mijares to the north; it is shut off in the west by the foothills of the Subbaetic range (Uroz, 1983).

The linking of the group to the old Esdetan race must be connected, moreover, with the existence of a toponym like Edeta and also with allusions to personages like the petty king Edecón; this cannot fail to reinforce the unitary role of the area, which seems to give a glimpse of a continuous historical line, ethnically speaking, from the first to the second group of known facts.

The same is true, even if the information is more limited in this case, of the Ilercavone group, whose linking with the Ilaraugetes is known, although in this case the identification of the latter with the Ilergetes as well, from the siting of Ilerda, should not be ruled out. The hard fact of its existence is recorded in Pliny (III, 4, 21) and Ptolemy (II, 6, 16), who mentions Dertosa as one of its centres; both situate it to the north of the Edetani and always around the river Ebro.

Beltrán (1976) has already stressed break up of the two coastal groups (Edetani and Ilercavones) towards the interior into Sedetani, with their centre at Caesar Augusta, and Ilergetes, around Ilerda and Athanagre in the basin of the Cinca–Segre rivers along their middle and lower courses. In line with an undeniable impact from the lower Ebro, not necessarily by its people, some authors explain a definite move towards Iberianisation of the region (Junyent, 1979; Sanmartí, 1984 and 1987; Burillo, 1989), although there can be no doubt about the weight of earlier traditions. The most sophisticated analysis of this approach is that of Sanmartí concerning the expansion that took place from the Matarranya, starting at the end of the fifth century BC from a settlement model with a central tower on an absidal plan; this is seen as a siege-resistant model, exemplified at the Coll del Moro de Gandesa; the same feature was present in Tossa del Moro de Pinyeres and in Terra Alta and again in San Antonio de Calaceite in the Matarranya. Starting from this point, according to the author, a genuine defensive line was planned, separating this group from the territory of the Sedetani, marking the boundary of Ilercavone territory and distinguishing it, among other things, by the abundance of painted pottery and the absence of storage pits, compared with the Iberian areas of Old Catalonia. None the less, the Ilergetan area features special items (like the strong tradition of handmade pottery, the marked Ampuritanian influence and the interesting world of the red-glazed wares, which are explained by questions of a historical nature, documented in the case of the Ilergetan kinglet Indíbil and his presence in Cartago Nova during the second Punic War). These distinguish it from the Ilercavones on one side and the old Mysgetan nucleus on the other.

Burillo, opposing this theory, does not dismiss the existence of other alternative routes connecting Upper Andalusia and Aragon across the *Meseta* and the *Sierra*, using transhumance routes that still exist, or routes from the south-east involving the Valencian–Albacetan area, where good proof of this is the extension of the sanctuary caves documented in the Edetanian area to the upper Mijares zone. From Livy (XXVIII, 24) we know that in the third century the situation among the groups in that zone was not stable and that the Ilergetes relied on a coalition with the Lacetani – situated further east – against the Suesetani and Sedetani.

To the north (Padro and Sanmartí, 1992), towards the Garraf massif, the Cosetani appear to shut off the the world of the Iberian tradition of the lower Ebro, although, as happened in areas with a strong frontier tradition, they were already beginning to use the system of storage pits, the expression of a model that was not just economic but cultural as well; and the same thing would take place towards Ampurdán. So this example reveals its own symptomatology based on the population model reported on the Adarró–Alorda Park axis. The absence of this group from references in Ptolemy is significant; he includes them among the Layetani, so highlighting the transitional role already mentioned.

The social pattern that took shape in that area, strongly influenced by the

Greek world, because of the active presence of the centres at Ampurias and Rosas, consisted of a series of groups among which we should mention, on the coast and moving from south to north, the Layetani, Indiketes, Sordones and Elisices; while towards the interior, on a first line and on the course of the river Llobregat and its tributary, the Cardener, the Lacetani were located, in direct contact with the Layetani, and in the valley of the Ter (around the Plana de Vic and Osona) the Ausetani, in contact with the Indiketes.

In general, it is worth emphasising the special significance of certain cultural elements that were a prime cause of its cultural malfunction. So, in fact, the presence and dominance of grey ware should be considered; it largely made up for the decline in painted ware, while even handmade pottery was in evidence; furthermore, in the Indiketan world there was the pottery decorated with white paint, mentioned above (Martin, 1987), or the existence of grey wares with stamped decoration, typical of the Lacetanian area. Indeed, to this decline in importance of the traditional Iberian painted decoration, we should add its absence from the area of the Ausetani and Lacetani, which does not rule out their Iberian character, revealed by the language.

A significant element is the one that led to the assumption that storage in pits was a cultural factor; it was already confirmed in the Cosetanian world but now became frequent among the Layetani, Lacetani and Indiketans.

Notwithstanding these common features, the case of the Indiketes seems to be particularly significant in this assemblage of peoples; they have recently been identified strictly with the ambit of Ampurias, and their capital, Indika, has been identified with Emporion (Padró and Sanmartí, 1992), just as the storage pits were interpreted as supply centres for the Greek colony (Ruiz de Arbulo, 1984; Martín, 1987). This would indicate a special significance for the whole *chora* (the Indiketes) and the appearance of a belt of peoples (Layetani, Lacetani, Sordones, Ausetani and Elisices) having direct links with them.

Further inland, the Ceretani define a limited Iberian culture attested by their language but not yet by their pottery production, in which handmade wares with incised decoration predominate. We shall have to wait for Bell Beaker B wares to get the first wheel-turned products (Campmajó and Padró, 1976).

In general terms, these two large groups, that is to say, the one revolving round Emporion and the one a bit further south, represented by the groups from Edetani to Ilergetes, correspond to the area of expansion of north eastern or Levantine Iberian writing, characterised by a greater Greek influence. Texts worth mentioning include those on lead, like the one from Orleyl, found in a red-figured Attic crater dated to the middle of the fourth century and also those found at Ampurias and Ullastret, and pottery graffiti such as that on the vase with the inscriptions from Liria, associated with figures of various horsemen.

─── 7 ───

Models of servitude for analysing the history of the Iberians

From the orientalising princes to the kinglets

The splendid assemblage of sculptures at Porcuna, dated to the first half of the fifth century BC (Chapa, 1990), shows us the figure of a soldier with his horse, equipped with all the accoutrements typical of his most characteristic activity: war. In various scenes isolated from the assemblage, a man is confronting a griffin, fighting with another warrior, revealed as a hunter; in other words, he is defined in the different styles that reflect the aristocracy.

In the same context of the find, attention is drawn to the features of a complicated process of territorial definition, which, in broad outline, and as we have stated, can be summed up as follows:

1 Towards the end of the seventh century the area of the *vega* of the Guadalquivir between Mengíbar and Montoro was occupied by small rural enclaves, for example, in the Campiña de Marmolejo (Molinos *et al.*, 1988). Alongside these and throughout the *campiña* and *vega*, large forti-fied nuclei existed from the beginning of the seventh or end of the eighth century BC.

2 It must have been in the first decades of the sixth century that a system of small forts began to be built, which, like the one at Cazalilla (Ruiz Rodríguez et al., 1983) drew a line isolating the world of the *campiña*, where hardly any small-scale rural enclaves are recorded, from the world of the *vega*, which could have been coupled with *oppida* like Los Villares de Andújar.

3 The reaction was immediate and we can see how, before Cazalilla reached the following phase (Cazalilla IVb), that is, from the middle to the end of the sixth century BC, the inhabitants of the rural enclaves abandoned them and withdrew, presumably, to the nearest *oppida*. Some time later the defensive and frontier towers were dismantled.

269

Figure 90 Sculptured group from the Porcuna assemblage.

In fact, the process that started at the end of the eighth century in the wake of the involvement of Tartessos with the Phoenician colonies, had, in the course of time not just produced a new style of house or a siege-resistant complex in the treatment of the settlements, but had generated an aristocratic group which found in these models its form of political, economic and cultural expression. This development was accomplished at a late stage in the sixth century, perhaps when, within a sphere subject to the tutelage of Tartessos, a few groups of aristocrats achieved a certain level of power and came into conflict with the political centre of the territorial area. The fact is that the process that defined the world of the upper Guadalquivir was not without clashes, tensions and conflicts, as shown by the appearance of the said frontier or, in a still more obvious form, by the known destruction of the Porcuna sculptures.

In this last case two facts emerge that are worth emphasising in the context being analysed (Negueruela, 1990). In the first place, the scenes depicted, in spite of revealing a Hellenising stylistic technique, have none the less an iconology not depicted by the Greeks except in the minor arts or, more especially, among peoples bordering on Greece. In the second place, the depiction of the warriors, which Negueruela considers a different group from the rest, shows an iconography very different from single combat or general conflict, in that the two warring bands confront each other on an equal footing; in fact, in the scenes from Porcuna, the vanquished warriors show obvious signs of having been taken by surprise (sheathed swords, no helmets, no cnemids on their knees, no pauldrons, no armour), while the group of victorious warriors is fully equipped. In short, it is not apparently a ritual battle that is being shown but a historical fact, the result of surprise and possibly an internal fight, since we see that both the victors and the vanquished wear the same military panoply and have similar features.

It may be that some day we shall come to understand exactly what happened to suggest this system of peripheral conflicts and tensions but, meanwhile, let us at least consider that, in this seventh century BC, territories governed by an aristocracy had been carved out, and that those Mastieni or Etmanei mentioned in the sources would already at these dates have been creating a reflection of the concept of aristocratic power that must have been more clearly defined in the Tartessian world. This is what Caro Baroja meant when he stated in 1971 that the organisation of the Tartessian state was more like certain Mediterranean states with legendary, mythical kings as legislators in their early stages (Habis) and with historical but idealised rulers (Argantonios) later on, rather than like the early Greek *polis.*

It would be rash to posit features of an Asian–oriental type in the Tartessian political model, with complex bureaucratic systems and monumental buildings, that have yet to be located. Archaeology has not confirmed this, but we need not be rigid in our evaluation of the state models and we do have to consider that, in the framework of the Tartessian political mindset, the concept of community was very much present and that it was there that the aristocracy had to find its chief support and, at the same time, its opposition. The articulation of community and aristocracy maintained and indeed fostered factors like kinship through ancestor worship, but it also opened the way to future conflict between the community, socially segmented and structured in kinship units, and an aristocracy that tended more and more to

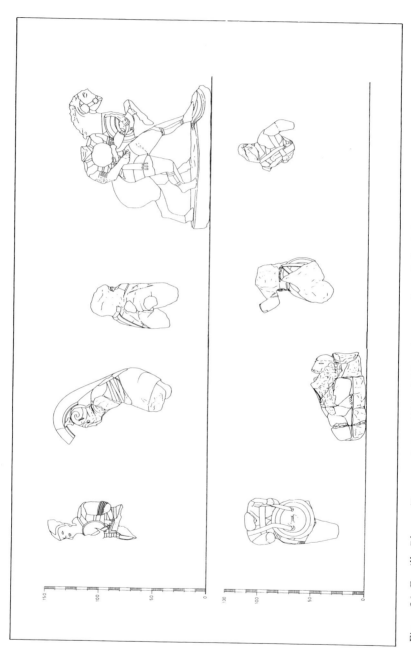

Figure 91 Cerrillo Blanco (Porcuna, Jaén). (Above) Victorious warriors; (below) the vanquished (from Negueruela, 1990)

encourage the breakdown of social equality within a transitional scenario in which the existing political structure itself could come to be inimical to it. Without explaining himself in these terms, Polybius (VI, 7,8) underlined it when, speaking of political revolutions, he stated that when kings overstep the mark, royalty ends up being replaced by the aristocracy.

In practice, the transition we observe in the population models of upper Andalusia in the course of the fifth century BC, the concentration in the *oppidum* (an expression of aristocratic power like the feudal lord's castle) should be understood only as the gradual replacement of the old orientalising princes like Argantonios. This process would lead to the dominance of an aristocracy opposed to the old communal and ethnic concepts and championing a social model of servitude, such as finds less harsh expression in the Iberian institution of the *fides* and, more radically, in the *devotio* (Ramos Locertales, 1924; Rodríguez Adrados, 1948).

The greater flexibility produced in the territory of the Campiña de Jaén as the size of the *oppida* rose or fell and the small settlements, whether strategic or rural, completely disappeared, does not imply mere demographic readjustments, as processual archaeology would have it, but a profound change in the concept of property, which ceased now to pass through the filter of the community and followed a system that would lead to the undisputed property of a class of gentilic client aristocracy, whose power was exercised by the aristocrat on duty. This fragmentation process which at one point we had defined as the '*oppida* model', created an *oppidum*–aristocrat–*gens* matrix which eventually downgraded certain supposedly civilising features, like sculpture; and this is confirmed because, in the opinion of some researchers, in the middle of the fifth century BC, a considerable drop in the number of finds that could be ascribed to this zone was experienced, and even significant iconographic changes, as is demonstrated by the presence of the representations of Damas. Indeed, the upper Guadalquivir is one of the poorest regions as far as this type of find is concerned in the 'full' Iberian phases.

In the same way and on a more archaeological plane, the disappearance of the frontier towers would be explained, since from the middle of the fifth century BC the *oppidum* was the real frontier of each social unit; it would also explain the destruction of sculptures like those at Porcuna, which were the embodiment of the old, orientalising political conception that was feeling the impact of a logical readjustment between aristocracies defining their areas of power. The apparent isonomy recorded in the mass access to exotic products in the region must also be explained on these lines. They must now, of course, have been much more widely in demand and have acted as a cohesive factor in the gentilic client group, but that is no reason to conceal that this more

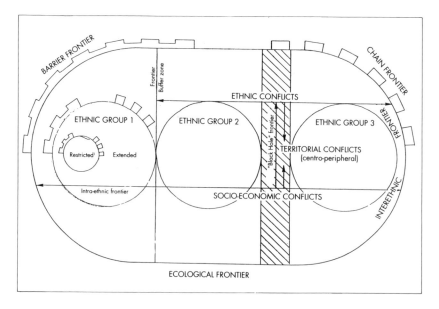

Figure 92 Theoretical matrix of the frontier
(from Ruiz Rodríguez and Molinos, 1989)

'democratic' circulation in practice meant different circuits for products, some more restricted, like that of precious metals or certain pottery items such as the crater, as opposed to others like weapons or items of Attic ware such as the *kylix*, which indeed could not fail to make society more hierarchical.

Torelli (1988b) has made an extraordinary synthesis of what he imagines to have been the model of client servitude, first between the Etruscans and Rome and then in the populations of southern Italy:

> At the same time, the growth of more prosperous family units, in terms of possessing better lands and of a greater available work force, finally destroyed the old equality (in terms of reciprocal projects and social status) among the members of the community and transformed the *gens* into an original form of aristocratic dominance . . . thus the old kinship institution of the *gens* came to be a new productive reality and one of power.
>
> (Torelli, 1988b, p. 243)

In specific terms, the gentilic aristocratic group can be defined thus:

1 A modification of the *gens* concept (ancient cult of the family ancestors),

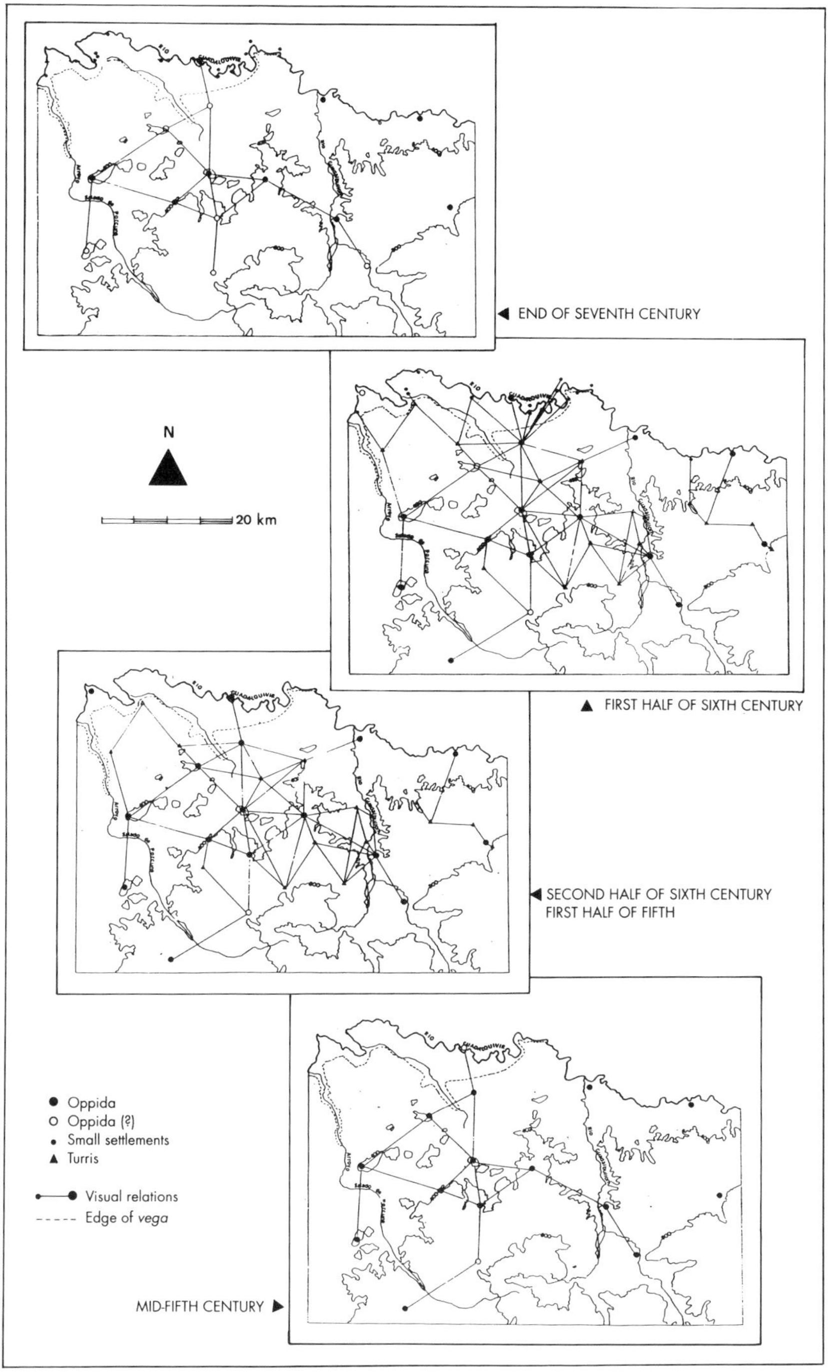

END OF SEVENTH CENTURY
N
20 km
FIRST HALF OF SIXTH CENTURY
SECOND HALF OF SIXTH CENTURY
FIRST HALF OF FIFTH
Oppida
Oppida (?)
Small settlements
Turris
Visual relations
Edge of *vega*
MID-FIFTH CENTURY

Figure 93 Various stages of a frontier in the Campiña de Jaén area (from Ruiz Rodríguez and Molinos, 1989)

which now continued and acquired the form of servitude towards a personnage (the aristocrat) on the basis of the old institution, but constructing a model of non-consanguinity, in which the serf was acknowledged in the worship of his lord's forebears and not his own. In this way the growth of the aristocratic *gens* was assured and with it the power of one sector of society over another.

2 This fact had its origin in the weakest point of the communal system: the family which, because of its autonomy, was the only institution capable of generating inequality; but it became inevitable when one family unit, that of the future aristocrat, imposed itself on the whole village (*vicus*) community or even the *pagus*, the common fountainhead, as Torelli calls it, imposing its own forebears over those of the rest of the families, in other words, assuming the power of the law, which is what organised the military under the old communal pattern.

3 The new system of gentilic servitude led to new methods of institutional articulation among the groups. This is reflected in the appearance of pacts based on the mutual trust of aristocrats who guarantee protection and assistance, and dependants who promise obedience; all this was sanctioned in the *fides*, 'a reciprocal guarantee that eventually regulated the entire scenario of social relationships as well' (Torelli, 1988b, p. 243).

4 The princely model (the foremost gentilic-client aristocracies) by its partial control of the system (the family, the law, and in exceptional cases, the *pagus*) was soon at cross-purposes with the superior unit, the ethnic community of the territory, which henceforth became the target for control. The variants to this situation could be seen, as time passed in two, not necessarily opposed models: either the dissolution of the ethnic community (nuclear servitude) or its appropriation or replacement by another (territorial servitude).

(a) Gentilic nuclear servitude.

This implies absorption on the part of an aristocratic *gens* of scattered family units or even of other consanguineous communities based on enforced amalgamation. This has been confirmed among the Iberians, in the models of *oppida* already described, in which the aristocratic group identified with the *oppidum* brought about the absorption of the scattered habitat, that is, of the different consanguineous and extended families that must surely have been represented in places like the small rural settlements on the *vega*. But the model is there too in the disappearance of villages in the eastern zone of Jaén or the present-day province of Granada, and possibly, on the township level, in the abandonment of a few settlements on the lower Guadalquivir in the sixth century BC.

(b) Gentilic territorial servitude.
This model differs from the enforced amalgamation of the previous example because the system does not bring about nuclearization, but it does impose forms of communal dependence (on the losers), evidence of which is the development of a pyramid structure in the *gens*. Hence the non-slave character of the model that aroused so much interest in authors such as Vigil (1973) or Mangas (1977) and in ourselves (Molinos *et al.*, 1986) after reading the decree of Emilius Paulus:

> L. Emilius, son of L., emperor, decreed that the serfs of Hasta who lived in the Torre Lascutana, should be free and he ordered that they should own and retain the district and town that they then possessed as long as the Senate and people of Rome should desire. Issued in the encampment twelve days before the calends of February.
>
> (C. IL, 11.5041, p. 201)

From this theoretically alternative, although not necessarily contradictory dynamic, the *oppida* model (gentilic nuclearised servitude) was eventually imposed in the setting of the upper Guadalquivir, as can be appreciated from important work such as the analysis of the size of the settlements and their catchment area from one phase to another, that is to say, from the princely phase of the sixth century to the nuclearised model of the *oppidum* in the middle of the fifth century BC.

To carry out this analysis, we set up a prior working hypothesis (Ruiz Rodríguez, 1990). If a territory opted for the nuclearised model and not for territorial servitude, it would have to create around it a catchment area capable of making the *gens* self-sufficient and generating the surplus necessary to reproduce the system. If, on the other hand, the system was territorial servitude, the dominant settlement would not have the problem of relying on a catchment area, whether large or small, because the surplus, in the form of tribute, would come to it from the other *oppida*. Furthermore, it would tend to attract the rest of the settlements to the economic effects, generating a belt of dependent settlements in its immediate environs. So this analysis too takes note of the historical process followed in the zone, comparing the cartographies of different centuries.

Further to this hypothesis and from an evaluation of the land favoured by an economic model like the one in this zone, interested for preference in good-quality land for dry farming, we made an assessment for the fourth

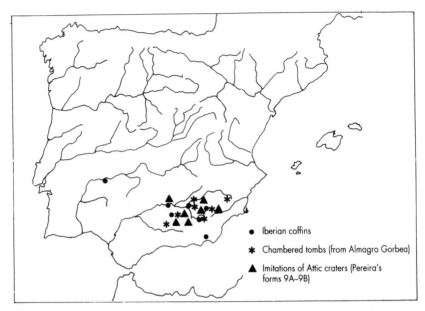

● Iberian coffins

✳ Chambered tombs (from Almagro Gorbea)

▲ Imitations of Attic craters (Pereira's forms 9A–9B)

Figure 94 Association of cultural elements in Bastetania (by the authors)

century BC of the *oppida* by size, on a geometric scale, and we put a value on the soils 2, 3 and 4 kilometres around each *oppidum*, determining the mean production potential and setting up a model for scoring per unit of size. From this system, it was concluded that the settlement of Porcuna, allegedly one of the big centres in the seventh century BC and on through the fifth and fourth centuries, established a vast area around it, assuming the old scattered population. The *oppidum* of Cerro de Villagordo, also very big (18 hectares) and shut in by its neighbours, forced the latter to shrink appreciably in size in the course of the fifth century (the *oppidum* of Atalayuelas went from 6 to 2.5 hectares) so as to increase its catchment area.

Consequently, each *oppidum*, theoretically equal with the land surrounding it, from the point of view of agricultural potential, tended to increase the distance to its nearest neighbours in a ratio directly proportional to its size.

This factor produced a latent conflict in the model because of the tendency of each aristocrat to expand within the framework of the process, leading inevitably to a confrontation with neighbouring aristocracies in their programme of consolidation of power and in their quest for wealth and especially for land. So it may well be that, faced with the signs of crisis that appear in the model in the middle of the fourth century BC (which we shall attempt to evaluate later), a move was accomplished towards political regrouping and so

278

towards gentilic territorial servitude, opening up a pattern of domination by a few aristocrats over others, and consequently widening the territory.

Conversely, this process is seen in a different form on the ethno-cultural level since the ethnic vacuum produced by the model of the *oppida* meant that ethnic features had persisted from the earlier period, giving a glimpse of a broader cultural unit – remember the work of Almagro Gorbea on the elements of the material culture of the Bastetanian world in the fourth century BC, or Pereira's pottery studies on the two main areas (Tartessian/Mastienian, Lower and Upper Andalusia) between the fifth and fourth centuries BC. When territorial servitude was put into practice, leading to an enlargement of the political and economic territory of a social formation, it opened up the process towards a reduction – surprisingly – of the old ethnic territory, in contrast to the broad ethno-cultural scales of previous phases, so as to make room for the appearance of new examples like the Oretani and Mentesani, etc.

To conclude, gentilic territorial servitude did not imply a change in the nature of the social relationships of production from the aristocratic model, but an adaptation to the development of the transitional process that began with a segmentary society and led to an aristocratic society.

In the third to second centuries BC, which is when we can see this movement towards the forming of new state units most clearly, relics of past ages could still be seen, as in the case of Luxinius, who in 197 BC was king of two 'cities', Carmo and Bardo, and who allied himself with Culchas, a minor king of seventeen *oppida* who had previously reigned over twenty-eight in the geographic area of Bastetania (for, although it is not shown, it is included in Hispania Ulterior and is to be found halfway between Cástulo and Cartago Nova on a road coming in south of Jaén and north of Granada, opened after Scipio took Cartagena). The same process can be seen in the region of Cadiz and in the predominance of Hasta Regia over its surroundings and likewise in the dependence of Torre Lascutana.

To the north, the model gives rise to certain difficulties of analysis, although, if we consider the end of the process we shall see some similarities.

Indeed, Uroz (1983) picks up a text of Zonaras (9.3.8.) referring to Edetania: 'The Scipios marched against Sagunto's tributary townships, the causes of the war and of the ruin of that city, destroyed their population, put the inhabitants to death and, arriving at Sagunto, returned it to its former citizens.' He adds, following Livy (XXVIII, 39): 'From then on, the Saguntinos received tribute from the lands of the enemy city.' This example shows that the model of gentilic territorial servitude was in force during the Second Punic War. But two further pieces of information must be added, which we have acquired on various occasions, this time from archaeology: on the one hand, the territorial strengthening of areas like Edetania using fortfied *atalayas* like Puntal dels Llops and, on the other hand, the definition of cultural features, now confined to specific zones, like the red-glazed wares in the Liria or Elche–Archena style which broadly define the Ilergetans, the Edetanians or the Contestanians.

This state of affairs is particularly interesting if we bear in mind that it originates in those zones from which most of the information on the subject of the *fides* has been obtained. Rodríguez Adrados wanted to see, in what Livy tells us about the populations of the river Ebro, that a union of peoples was being formed around the Ilergetes when the Romans arrived in the Peninsula (Rodríguez Adrados, 1948), and that only the Sedetani and the Suesetani resisted this pressure, since the Lacetani appear repeatedly alongside the Ilergetes, and the Ausetani seem to play a similar role. Indeed, at the very beginning of the Second Punic War and in succeeding stages, Scipio confirms that, while the coastal peoples (Indiketes and Cosetani) looked favourably on the arrival of the Romans, the kinglets Amusico of the Ausetani, Andobales of the Lacetani and Indíbil and Mandonio of the Ilergetes opposed it, appearing, especially the last two characters, as the firmest allies of the Carthaginians. Just as the Ilergetes appear to have been the coordinating force of possible coalitions around the Ebro, so Edecón, king of Edetania, appears in pro-Carthaginian guise and, at a given moment, faced with the pressure exerted by Hasdrubal to make him hand over hostages in the person of his wife and daughter, decided, like Indíbil, to embrace the Roman cause; and we are told that after his decision, the remaining townships of the region followed his example (Polybius, 10, 34). Lastly, it seems we can affirm that the process reported in Andalusia was stronger here, since we are given the spectacle of a community united in action with the figure of its king or kinglet and, more frequently here than in the south, we see the crucial association of group with group and even at times with the name of the kinglet (Edeta–Edetani–Edecón, Ilerda–Ilergetes, Ausa–Ausetani, etc.).

In recent years, various authors have disseminated the idea that, in practice, a model of chiefdom would become general among the Iberians (Domínguez, 1984; López Domech, 1986–7), if by that we mean the conditions typical of that model in terms of its non-hereditary nature and the absence of any repressive apparatus, in other words, as power exercised through control of the redistribution of wealth. The reality is that the reasons adduced to define chiefdom among the Contestani (social hierarchy and population density) are not adequate to distinguish chiefdom from aristocracy or kingship, since they take no account of the background against which it had been set up. Moreover, the complex scale created, following the Hallstatt models in central

Figure 95 The Tivissa patera (from Blázquez, 1955–6)

Europe (with a supreme chief, vassals, subchiefs, lesser chiefs and minor chiefs), is difficult to follow among the Iberians, as its defenders freely admit, for lack of archaeological data to corroborate it.

A second alternative has been championed recently, from a very different position, for the Ilergetes (Junyent, 1979). Outstanding among their characteristics is their urban development with public services, 'exceptional buildings of a public, civic or religious nature', stable power, control of the territory based on the hierarchisation of settlements, and division of labour with a specialised workforce. Lastly, a set of values which, in the opinion of the author, is suggestive of a '*civitas*, an organised state that had ceased to be a tribe or a *populus*, stages that precede the formation of a city' (Junyent, 1979, p. 104). In short, the Ilergetan model looks almost like a *polis* system as outlined in other recent works (Jacob, 1985).

But, faced with a model of this type, reality does not explain the coupling of a *polis*-type model with an emerging aristocracy, a civic model with a system that sees even war as *bellum privado*, as we are reminded by the Fabian *gens* with its attack on the city of Veio in 477 (Torelli, 1988b).

In short, the model supplied by the sources, which can be followed in the Ilergetes or the Edetani, still remains, at least in the third century BC, an example of an aristocratic state, which, however, differs from the examples analysed in the south in its consolidation of the ethnic group, always associated with its aristocrat-king, owing perhaps to a difference in its earlier history.

Moreover, the process also has its foundations in the *fides*, and possibly in a more religious form such as the *devotio*, by which the client-serf even offered his life to his lord in the case of the latter's death. The question can be followed in an extraordinary form in the role played by Indíbil during the Second Punic War and in the maintenance of a client relationship with Hasdrubal until, not trusting the pact established, the latter demanded hostages. Some time later, it was Scipio who won over the Ilergetan by restoring his family to him without asking anything in return; this precipitated a second client pact, a second *fides* between the Iberian and the Roman. In the end, after Indíbil's rebellion in which he spread false news of the death of the lord Scipio and obtained his pardon, the Iberian kinglets agreed to a *devotio* with the Roman general.

It is undoubtedly here that the model that comes to our notice at the end of the third century BC has its foundations. But if this can be evaluated, the same does not hold good for earlier phases for which we have very little information, since a progression along the same lines as in the southern zone, that is, of an *oppida* model with nuclearised aristocracies, does not seem to be so clearly delineated in the earlier archaeological analyses. In short, we do not know what process was followed in these areas between the groupings in the river basins studied by Ruiz Zapatero and Fernández (1984) and the phase of the aristocracies established in the role of *reguli*, although we should rule out any likelihood that the process passed off in the same terms as in the south.

From this point of view, the process is more reminiscent of those occurring in areas further removed from the Tartessian heartland in the south, like the Oretani, who apparently managed it in better conditions than the various Bastetanian or Turdetanian groups, on whose former territories they succeeded in putting pressure. The clearest example is that of Cástulo and, basically, of Toya. As for the sources, they mention a linking up of these groups, dominated, according to Ptolemy, by Cástulo and Toya, with the south mesetan sphere, and especially the strong connections that were established from then on in particular products like the stamped or red-glazed wares, breaking with the Bastetanian forms, that had been picked up in Toya in the previous phase (Pereira, 1979). The same might be said of the inclusion of Mastia and Contestania.

This second model, which, as we see, had its best representatives among the Ilergetes, the Edetani or the Oretani, seems much more lineal in the strengthening of the aristocracy without apparently including a princely phase. So, because of the process selected, this hypothesis, which needs to be adequately verified, involves major variations from the other line cited, since where it took place, and this is a theoretical problem, no conflict occurred between a community organised on a kinship system and an orientalising aristocracy that tried to impose a non-consanguineous mode of functioning; or perhaps it was the communities of the *pagus* themselves who moved directly to the conversion of their chiefdoms into aristocracies. Hence, perhaps, the persistence of the old ethnic units; the unity and confidence of the behaviour of Indíbil, Edecón or Orissón himself in Oretania when they achieved kingship, assuming the role by identifying their power with the community, although without the strong political and economic backing noted in the Guadalquivir valley.

The crisis in the fourth century BC and the beginnings of external conflict

We have already noted elsewhere that, at the end of the fourth century, substantial modifications took place in the general framework of the Iberian world. It was Tarradell (1961) who first attempted to explain what a massive destruction of places like La Bastida, Puig d'Alcoi, Covalta, Cabezo Lucero, Lloma de Galvis or Corral de Saus, all in the Alicante–Valencia region of Contestania, and a few settlements in Murcia, like Cabecico del Tesoro, might have had to do with the Roman–Carthaginian treaty of 348 BC, which, as we gather from Polybius, said: 'On these conditions there was amity between the Romans and the allies of the Romans, and the Carthaginians, Turians, Uticenses and their allies. Beyond Kalon Akroterion and Mastia of Tarsis the Romans shall not be allowed to take prisoners, nor to trade nor found cities.' The consequent readjustment of borders resulting from the treaty may have hastened such a situation. The fact is that, although the consequences and later studies have modified the ending of a few settlements, it seems clear that some places, like Cabezo Lucero, were abandoned and even destroyed at the end of the fourth century BC (Aranegui et al., 1983), which might lend force to Taradell's first reading.

However, the effects of modifications at the end of the fourth century become more apparent in areas further away from the site of the readjustment: Tejada la Vieja in Huelva (Fernández Jurado, 1987b), Puente Tablas in Jaén (Ruiz Rodríguez and Molinos, 1985). To these must likewise be added the accounts among the Eleusices of a few changes in the date quoted (Mayhac, Cayla III) (Solier, 1976–8), or the new forms of settlement that are recorded from then on, like the *atalayas* (Puntal dels Llops in Valencia, Puig Castellet in Barcelona, or Castillarejo in Cordoba).

When we are considering the case of Puente Tablas we realise that we may be dealing with a local problem, owing to the exhaustion of the economic model emanating from the aristocracy of the *oppida*. The fact that this state of affairs spread to different parts of the Iberian area, and that we confirm something similar in the last years of the third and the start of the second centuries BC, this time as a consequence of the Second Punic War and the first interference from Rome, should not rule out specific reasons and local conflicts, nor yet readjustments on a wider scale. Indeed, the opportunity to take a broad view of the case in the Guadalquivir valley coincides with the sudden cutting off of imports of Greek material, which will not be documented again in the area. In our opinion, Tarradell's analysis and the implications of a readjustment of the areas of economic influence in the Mediterranean must be coupled with the elements of crisis that become apparent in the archaeological data and which, coupled with the sudden break in access to foreign products, could have fostered and accelerated some of the internal processes we have mentioned. Alongside this, the Carthaginian factor comes very much to the fore at this time, even though we need not necessarily see Punic sailors physically travelling up the Guadalquivir. Carthage had, in fact, designed a system of commercial networks that, starting from the economic axis of Ebussus (Ibiza)–Gades (Cadiz) with an intermediate point at Cartagena, which would become more effective later after the founding of Cartago Nova, can be sensed all through the research into Wreck of El Sec (Arribas et al., 1987). Indeed, we are already aware in the fifth century BC of the increasingly active presence of the military-commercial power in the Mediterranean, moving products from all over the place – amphorae from Samos, 30 per cent of the total production of amphorae there, from Sicily, from Corinth (Will a2), red-figured vases and Attic black-glazed ware, outstanding among them the Pinto de Viena *kylix* 116, bronzes from Etruria, hopper mills, common wares more typical of Carthage or Sicily than Greece – and acting as a centre of redistribution, with secondary points like Ibiza. The island, which forms part of this axis, experienced a boom in coastal settlements (Colonia de Sant Jordi, La Guardia, etc.) and more sophisticated town planning and, ultimately, the complete colonisation of its territories (Tarra-

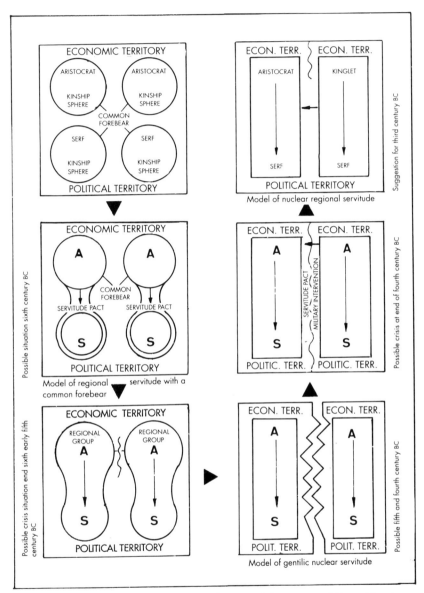

Figure 96 Proposal for a theoretical definition of the process followed by the Iberian aristocracy in the Campiña de Jaén (by the authors)

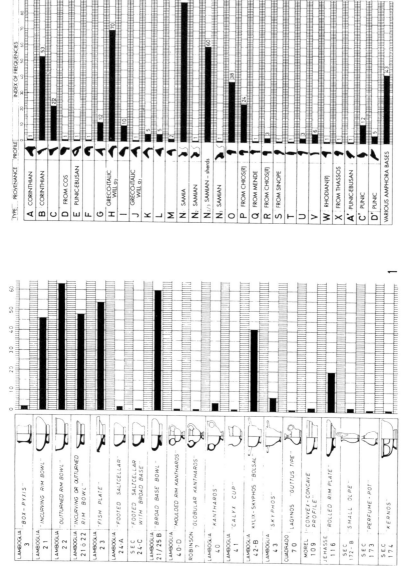

Figure 97 El Sec. 1. Index of frequencies of black-glazed Attic wares. 2. Index of frequencies of amphora material in the ship at El Sec (from Arribas *et al.*, 1987)

dell, 1975) from the fifth century on. For its part, El Sec points to a route leading towards the Spanish Levant and the Guadalquivir valley, quite separate from the others that led to the north and brought Punic (Ibizan) amphorae to Emporion and the whole north-eastern area of the Peninsula (Solier reports it for the Narbonne zone and these productions are documented generally throughout the Indiketan area, in Ullastret and other settlements).

The crisis in the fourth century can be looked at from many different points of view, with regard to the internal problems of the different indigenous communities, always with reference to conflicts between aristocrats; yet it had one factor linking the different episodes to the problem of Carthaginian trade, when the breakdown of the routes and networks that covered the Balearics–Levant–Andalusia axis with Greek products began to be felt; from then on, although Punic products continued to reach the old area of the Phocean colonies, the axis was cut off from the framework defining the economic status of the fifth to fourth centuries. In fact, the items of black-glazed ware documented in the south would be exceptional. Suffice it to say that one of the few documentations of these Ampuritanian products was recorded in El Amarejo de Albacete (Broncano and Blánquez, 1985).

Among the events occurring subsequent to these years, we must add the behaviour of the Barcas, who, from 237 BC, made their presence felt in the Peninsula as conquerors rather than in the role previously assumed by the Carthaginians. Their active presence became clear definitively in actions like the founding of Akra-Leukre and especially of Cartago Nova; and also, after the difficulties at the beginning which led to the death of Hamilcar at the hands of Orissón, in the successive marriages of Hasdrubal and Hannibal with Oretanian princesses, placing them through kinship at the pinnacle of the aristocratic political model in the zone and so able to control the rich mining output of Cástulo and its surroundings. However, the history of the Iberians was not yet the same as that of the Carthaginians, their conquerors, but reflected a war situation (the Second Punic War), which would end in the confrontation between Carthaginians and Romans and, above all, would turn the Iberian territory into a battlefield.

Rome and the Iberians: from territorial subservience to the classic city oligarchy

The sentence: 'The Gaditanians submitted to Rome' (Livy, 28–37) signalled the end of the conflict between Rome and Carthage. Research has fixed the beginning of Romanisation from that moment, as a shift towards social and ethnic uniformity, a cultural phenomenon that led unswervingly to civilisa-

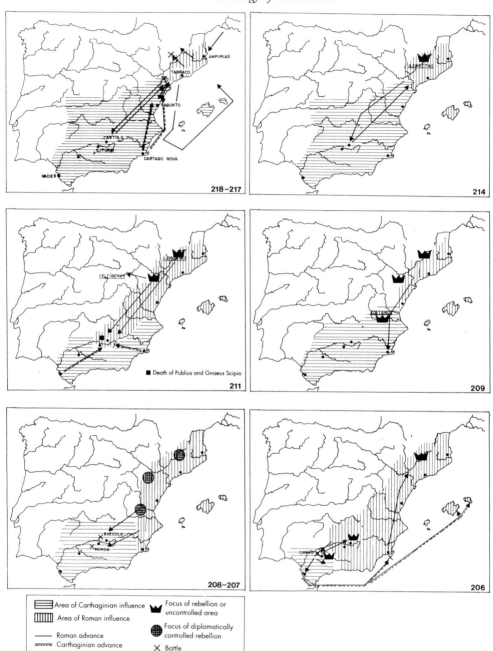

Figure 98 The Second Punic War (218–206 BC) (by the authors)

tion. The process itself has taken old platitudes for granted when interpreting the encounter between natives and conquerors, as if the greater or lesser degree of development, or concepts like wealth or pacifism, were more helpful in their cultural adaptation to Rome. Specifically (Ruiz Rodríguez *et al.*, 1992), one of the elements that has aroused most interest is the development of the town, insofar as it can be considered a catalyst for the transformations that were leading to an agrarian economy based on slavery, in a scenario of increasing regional specialisation and promotion of market exchange.

The problem is much more complex because there are definite signs of urbanisation, making it possible to speak of towns. The orthogonal layout, certain common elements of an urban rank or the actual arrangement of the internal space with the fortifications show that the indigenous settlements had adopted these elements previously (Bendala et al., 1988; Ruiz Rodríguez, 1988). The town is an empty space if the social relationships that define its inhabitants are not taken into consideration, and in this case it must not be forgotten that, at the beginning of the second century BC, an aristocracy existed with different interlinked models of performance and development. It was this aristocracy that met Rome on the battlefield of the Second Punic War, as the behaviour of successive Roman generals has shown in their dealings with the Ilergetan Indíbil, with Edecón or the leading personnage of Cástulo, Cerdubeles, with whom a *foedus* was signed (before entering the settlement and after the fall of Iliturgi in 208 BC).

In 197 BC, in the future Bética (Further Spain), the first reactions of the aristocracy against Rome began. Culchas, who in 208 was pro-Roman, now appeared in the party of the rebellion (Livy, 32, 21, 6). In the year 195 it was the Turdetanians who rose up, certainly 'the least warlike of all the Iberians' (Livy, 34, 17). In the year 192, L. Flaminius came into conflict with the Oretani (Livy, 35, 22). A few years earlier, in 205 and in the northern zone, it was Indíbil stirring up the Ausetani and other neighbours (Livy, 28, 1, 19). The references to conflicts in the sources are indicative of these facts, but at the same time they show a tendency to lay more stress on the conflicts of the Iberians in the south than on those in the north. In other words, if at the beginning there was a common politico-economic plan on the part of Rome, this would provoke a much more negative effect in the *oppida* model than in the model we know in the northern zone. In more recent research, archaeology has returned to this very question when dealing with one of the most effective indicators of the Roman economy: the *villa*. We shall look at two different analyses of territorial organisation as a function of this type of rural settlement or, more significantly, of the process leading to the urbanisation of the countryside and consequently to a new concept of the town.

We can follow the first in the territory of the Cosetani, between the rivers Llobregat and Gaía, which has been dealt with in the Iberian period. An analysis was made in this zone comparing the two agricultural models studied by Henshall (Miret, Sanmartí and Santacana, 1988): peasant agriculture as opposed to that of the plantation.

In the first place, and this holds good for the ancient territory of the Layetani (Prevosti, 1981; Biasot et al., 1984), we see a common date at the end of the second century BC for the appearance of the villa economy, which, according to the researchers, shows the plantation economy in greater historical detail.

Secondly, all the investigators recognise that not all the rural-type settlements of the Roman period that have been studied fit into the conceptual framework of the villa, which Prevosti has described in general terms on the basis of the presence of stone walls or footings and, occasionally, paving with *opus signinum*, brick or mosaic, but which is expressed more broadly in the concept of self-sufficiency and the commercial outlook of the settlement.

Lastly, these authors (Miret *et al.*, 1988) state the case from a perspective immersed in systems theory: a principal system of agriculture and two different subsystems; one is a peasant economy represented by the Iberian settlements, and the other subsystem is *villa* agriculture, represented by a new concept in the treatment of the countryside. The two subsystems are complementary because the second (that of the *villa*) needs an essential period of investment for working on new productive areas (zones that have to be drained) and investment in planning new crops. During this stage (late third to early first centuries BC) and until the system would be capable of surviving, the villas had more need of the rural agricultural settlements than of bigger settlements. Indeed, from the reports we can see that Alorda Park, an average-sized settlement, disappeared at the end of the second century BC, when the small settlements still showed no sign of doing so. To the east, Adarró, the biggest centre in the zone, was transformed into a *villa*, at a time when a series of small settlements were springing up which would eventually occupy the flat land, at an average distance of 900 metres apart and replacing the old pattern of small Iberian nuclei on the hillsides.

So, until the system succeeded in establishing itself somewhere where a model of agricultural surplus could be organised, the scattered Iberian model would adapt to the new economic model, starting by dismantling the very dense settlement pattern that was incompatible with the new reality and operating a dual system of small rural settlements coupled with *villae*; in the opinion of the researchers in this territory, this system would tend increasingly to be swallowed up in a dominant *villa* model.

This situation was modified somewhat further to the north, in the zone of the Layetani, because, even if the process in the countryside followed similar lines, the Iberian upland settlements, by contrast, with a few exceptions that disappeared in the middle of the second century BC (Puig Castellar de Santa Coloma de Gramenet or Castell Ruf de Martorelles), persisted until the middle of the first century BC, and in a few cases till the Augustan period (Turó de Can Olivé in Cerdanyola, Turó de Mas Boscà in Badalona or Burriac de Cabrera among others) (Miret *et al.*, 1988).

In short, the authors of the investigation set the village model against that of the villa, insofar as they believed that a perfect balance existed, at least in the early days, between the villas and the small rural settlements. This was because of the compensatory nature of the latter, but was not the case with the village model because of an element of competition on the level of commercial functions or services. So the founding of Roman towns (Baétulo in the year 100 BC, Barcino in the Augustan period, Iluro) was the only way to bring about the collapse of the indigenous settlements of the first and second order and the subsequent biological depopulation.

In the area dominated by the nuclear model of the *oppida*, the situation was very different because for the greater part of the process, the indigenous system seems to have remained in force (Choclán and Castro, 1986–7; Ruiz Rodríguez *et al.*, 1992), and in any case there was a steady tendency to depopulation of the large *oppida* units which became very tangible after the Second Punic War; but, we must assume this to have been a result of the attitude of their ruling group. Thus we see the definitive abandonment of places like Puente Tablas and, apparently, of other settlements, like Villagordo and Torrejón, all in the same area. In these cases it might be a matter of an immediate reaction after the conflict, in a zone that may not have been particularly favourable to Roman interests. On one side, then, Puente Tablas was razed and, on the other, a few unfortified settlements began to spring up in the plain (Ruiz Rodríguez *et al.*, 1992), which we take to be a political effect of the dispersal of the gentilic aristocracy; they formed themselves into large villages and certainly not into villas, only very exceptionally present. Alongside this, a dual tendency is noted: in the countryside from the second century BC and almost from its very beginning, the colonisation of new zones occurred, like the course of the river San Juan in the south, with settlements like Cabeza Baja de Encina Hermosa in Castillo de Locubín or Almedinilla (Montilla et al., 1989), on the principle of the *oppida* model, that is, without rural settlements in the plain. Another example is that of the Guadalquivir *vega* itself, fortified at this time with settlements like Sevilleja.

Elsewhere, in the classic *oppida*, new events of interest were taking place,

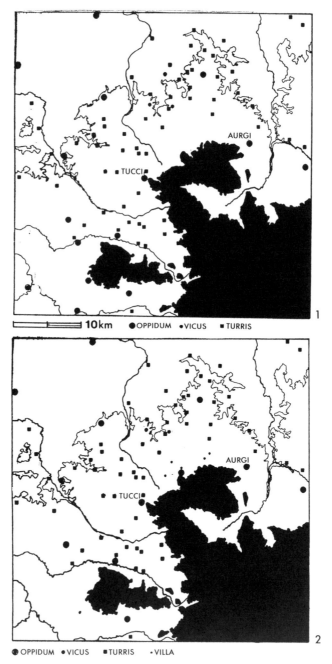

Figure 99 Romanisation in the Campiña de Jaén in the area of the Aurgi-Tucci.
1. Situation during the second century BC. 2. Situation in the Augustan period.

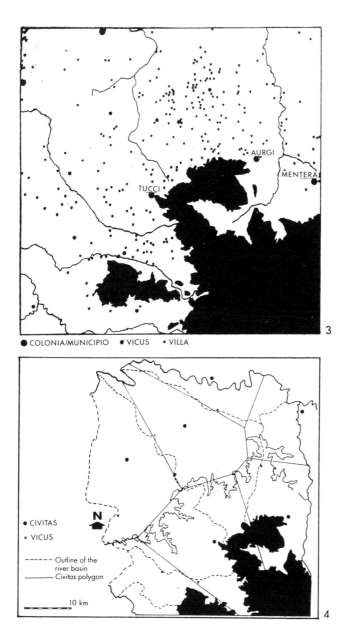

3. Situation in the Flavian period. 4. *Civitas* and *Vicus* during the Flavian
period to the south of the Guadalquivir
(from Ruiz Rodríguez, Castro and Choclán, 1992)

293

such as the appearance of temple sanctuaries in the outlying parts of the fortification, coinciding with the decline in importance of the ethnic sanctuaries of the Castellar or Despeñaperros type. This was the case at Torreparedones (Cordoba), dated to the end of the second century BC (Morena, 1989) with an assemblage of stone ex-votos, one with a Latin inscription, an indication of the ideological onslaught to which the aristocrat was beginning to be subjected as the classic Roman town was being formed; but, focusing as they do on a point outside the *oppidum*, they also indicate the ability of the traditional aristocrat to resist the model of a civic oligarchy.

The process in general implies in a very direct way the existence of a pact between the local aristocracy and Rome. This can be seen more clearly if we analyse the case of rural occupation, since it is noticeable that the breakdown of the *oppida* model only took place from the founding of the Augustan colony of Gemella Tucci, situated, significantly, on top, or in the territory, of an *oppidum*, Tucci, which had demonstrated its continued adherence to the Pompeyan faction. Indeed, it is from this time on that the first signs of indigenous participation in the Roman trading circuits are seen, displacing in a few years the production of the local potters and giving entry as early as the Tiberian–Claudian period (Sotomayor *et al.*, 1979) to the first centre producing 'Terra Sigillata Hispanica' at Los Villares de Andújar. In fact, coinciding with this, we see the extension of something that was distinct from simple taxation. For this, it was Vespasian's decree on the granting of Latin law (Pliny, *Historia Natural*, 3, 30) that created and defined more clearly the legal framework necessary for breaking up the traditional alliance between the local aristocracy and Rome, because the political situation made way for new social groups, which, now as citizens, broadened the social base in support of the Flavians and at the same time transformed the economic tax model with more personal forms of taxation. It was this process that opened the way to a genuine occupation of the countryside by the town, although starting from small rural settlements with a peasant economy, supported by *vici* and towns organised on the basis of the historical process defined in the centuries immediately before (Ruiz Rodríguez *et al.*, 1992; Choclán and Castro, 1986–7).

We could follow this process in other areas with different results. For example, the Valencian zone of the former Edetania, where, coinciding with the last century of the millennium, new ways of peopling the hillsides and the plain are noted with no fortifications (Bernabeu *et al.*, 1987). Alongside this, perhaps supported by the small indigenous rural settlements, it may be that, at the end of the second century BC, the first rural colonisation of a Roman character would take place, coinciding with the founding of Valentia (Abad,

1985; Ribera, 1982), and producing a process similar to the one beginning to take shape in the Catalan area and generally wherever a scattered Iberian habitat model was dominant.

In any case, the presence of Rome in the Iberian area again reveals a complicated scenario of incompatibilitiess, between natives and conquerors, and between the natives themselves; this would have to be the subject of another book, which would reflect the first death of the aristocracy.

Cartographic appendix

SETTLEMENTS		LOCATIONS
Acinipo	27	II-E-2
Adarró	173	IV-K-7
Agde	199	IV-L-10
Aguilar	41	II-3-3
Agullana	193	IV-L-9
Alarcos	93	II-F-4
Albares, Los	79	II-H-4
Albufereta, La	118	III-I-4
Alcañiz el Viejo	161	IV-I-7
Alcudia, La	104	III-I-4
Aldovesta	149	IV-J-6
Alhonoz	40	II-E-3
Almadén	94	II-E-4
Almedinilla	52	III-F-3
Almuñécar	32	II-F-2
Alorda Park	170	IV-K-7
Alozos, Los	37	II-F-2
Altos de Benimaquia	121	III-I-4
Amarejo, El	109	III-I-4
Andújar	61	III-F-3
Aragonesa, La	45	II-F-3
Archena	76	II-H-3
Arguilera	171	IV-K-7
Arse	133	III-I-5
Atalayuelas	57	II-F-3
Ategua	42	II-E-3
Azaila	166	IV-I-7

Badalona	174	IV-K-7
Baetulo (see Badalona)		
Bastida, La	111	III-I-4
Baza	69	II-G-III
Bobadilla, La	49	II-F-3
Bolbax	80	II-H-4
Burriac	178	IV-K-7
Cabecico del Tesoro	74	II-H-3
Cabecico del Tío Pío (see Archena)		
Cabeza Baja de Encina Hermosa	54	II-F-3
Cabezo Lucero	101	III-I-3
Cadiz	1	I-D-1
Caleta, La	142	III-K-4
Campello	119	III-I-4
Campiña de Marmolejo	47	II-F-3
Can Oliva	176	IV-K-7
Cancho Roano	21	I-D-4
Carambolo, El	8	I-D-3
Caraza, La	168	IV-I-7
Carencia, La	128	III-I-5
Carmona	12	I-D-3
Cartagena	97	III-I-3
Cartago Nova (see Cartagena)		
Casillas, Las	53	II-F-3
Castañuelo, El	16	I-D-3
Castell de fosca	183	IV-L-I
Castellans, Els	159	IV-J-7
Castellar	88	II-G-4
Castellar, El	167	IV-I-7
Castellar de Meca	85	II-H-4
Castellet de Banyoles	151	IV-J-7
Castellet de Bernabé	130	III-I-5
Castellones de Ceal	68	II-G-3
Castillejos de Fuente Cantos	18	I-D-4
Castillo de Azuaga	20	I-D-4
Castillo de Doña Blanca (see Torre de Doña Blanca)		
Cástulo	65	II-F-3
Cazalilla	59	II-F-3

Galera	70	II-G-3
Gandesa (see Coll del Moro)		
Gessera, La	155	IV-J-7
Gil de Olid	62	II-F-7
Giribaile	66	II-F-3
Granada	39	II-F-2
Guadalhorce (see Cerro del Villar)		
Guardamar	100	III-I-3
Guardia, La	55	II-F-3
Higuerón, El	50	II-F-3
Hornachuelos de Ribera del Fresno	19	I-D-4
Huelva	7	I-C-2
Huerta Tujena	5	I-C-2
Ibros	64	II-F-3
Ilerda	188	IV-J-8
Iluro	179	IV-L-8
Illa d'en Reixac	184	IV-L-8
Itálica	9	I-D-3
Játiva	124	III-I-5
Luz, La	73	II-H-3
Llano de la Consolación	83	II-H-4
Lloma de Galvis	112	III-I-4
Macalón, El	87	II-G-4
Mailhac	197	IV-L-9
Malaga	29	II-E-2
Margalef	187	IV-J-8
Martela	17	I-C-3
Martos	56	II-F-3
Mas Boscà	177	IV-K-7
Mas Mussols	150	IV-J-7
Mataró (see Iluro)		
Medellín	22	I-D-4
Mesas de Asta	3	I-D-2
Mesas de Gandul	13	I-D-2
Mirador de Rolando	35	II-F-2

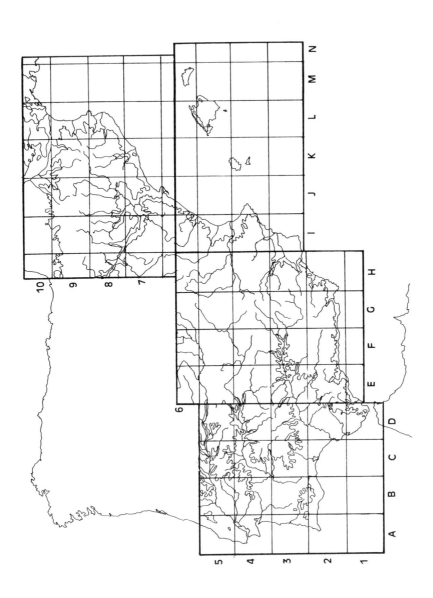

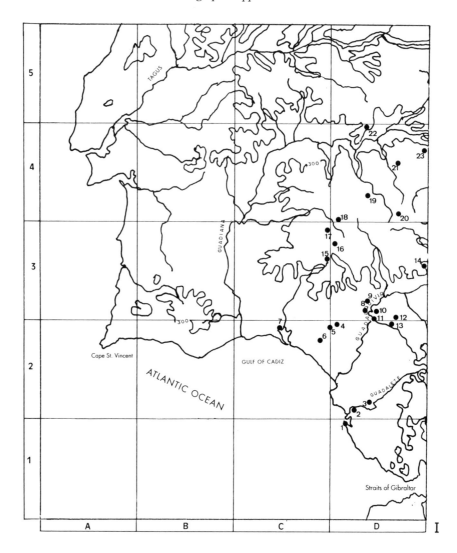

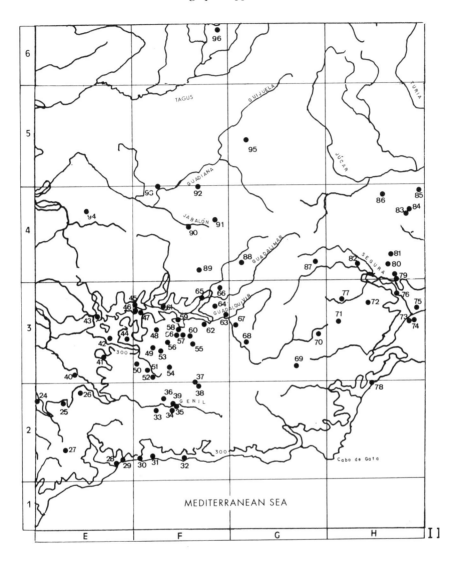

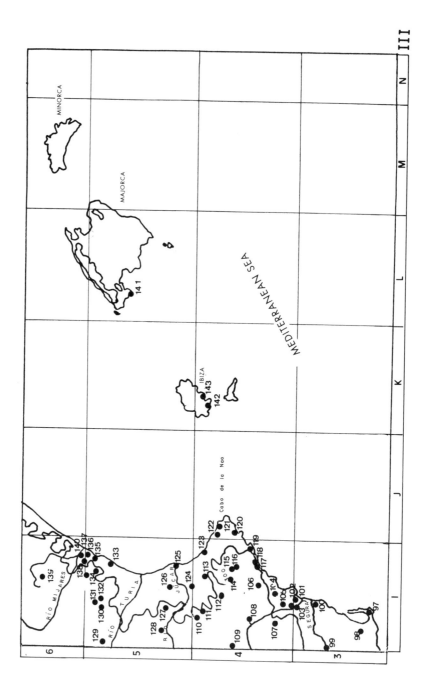

III

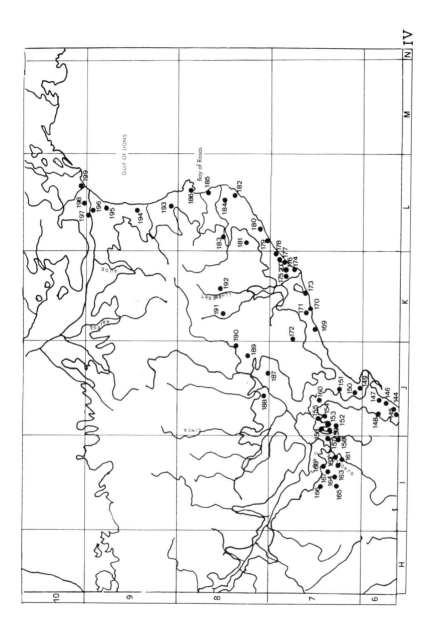

Bibliography

Abad, L. (1985), 'Arqueología romana del País Valenciano. Panorama y perspectivas', in *Arqueología del País Valenciano. Panorama y perspectivas (Lucentum)*, Alicante.

(1986), 'El Oral', in *Arqueología en Alicante: 1976–1986*, Alicante.

(1987), 'El poblamiento ibérico en la provincia de Alicante', in *I Jornadas arqueológicas sobre el mundo ibérico* (1985), Jaén.

(1989), 'Las culturas ibéricas del área suroriental de la Península', in *Paleoetnología de la Península Ibérica*, Madrid.

Aguayo, P., M. Carrilero and G. Martínez (1986), 'Excavaciones en el yacimiento pre y protohistórico de Acinipo (Ronda, Málaga)', *Anuario Arqueológico de Andalucía*, 1, Seville.

Aguayo, P., M. Carrilero, M. Pino de la Torre and C. Flores (1985), 'El yacimiento pre y protohistórico de Acinipo (Ronda, Málaga). Campaña de 1985', *Anuario Arqueológico de Andalucía*, Seville.

Aguayo, P. and V. Salvatierra (1987), 'El poblamiento ibérico en las altiplanicies granadinas', in *I Jornadas arqueológicas sobre el mundo ibérico* (1985), Jaén.

Albertini, E. (1906–7), 'Fouilles d'Elche', *Bulletin Hispanique*, 8–9, Paris.

Almagro Basch, M. (1947), 'Dos cortes estratigráficos con cerámica ibérica en Ampurias', in *III Congreso de Arqueología del Sudeste*, Murcia.

(1948), 'Sobre el origen y cronología de la cerámica ibérica', in *IV Congreso de Arqueología del Sudeste*, Elche.

(1949), 'Cerámica griega gris de los siglos VI–V en Ampurias', RSL, 15, Bordighera.

(1950), 'El estado actual de la clasificación de la cerámica ibérica', in *VI Congreso de Arqueología del Sudeste*, Alcoy.

(1952), 'La España de las invasiones célticas', in *Historia de España*, (ed.) R. Menéndez Pidal, t. I, vol. II, Madrid.

(1953), *Las Necrópolis de Ampurias*, vol. I, Barcelona.

Almagro Gorbea, M. (1977), *El Bronce Final y el período orientalizante en Extremadura*, Biblioteca Prehistórica Hispana, vol. XIV, Madrid.

(1976–8), 'La iberización de las zonas orientales de la Meseta', in *Simposi internacional orígens del món ibèric, Ampurias*, 38–40, Barcelona.

Bibliography

(1982a), 'Pozo Moro y el influjo fenicio en el período orientalizante de la Península Ibérica', *Revista di Studi Fenici*, 10, Rome.

(1982b), 'Tumbas de cámara y cajas funerarias ibéricas. Su interpretación sociocultural y su delimitación del área cultural', in *Homenaje a Conchita Fernández Chicarro*, Madrid.

(1983a), 'Arquitectura y sociedad en la cultura ibérica', in *Architecture et société*, Collection de l'École Française de Rome, vol. LXVI, Rome.

(1983b), 'Pozo Moro. El monumento orientalizante, su contexto sociocultural y sus paralelos en la arquitectura funeraria ibérica', *Madrider Mitteilungen*, 24, Mainz.

(1988), 'El área superficial de las poblaciones ibéricas', in *Asentamientos ibéricos ante la romanización*, Madrid.

Almagro Gorbea, M., A. Domínguez de la Concha and F. López-Ambite (1990), 'Cancho Roano. Un palacio orientalizante en la Península Ibérica', *Madrider Mitteilungen*, 31, Mainz.

Alvar, J. (1990), 'La jefatura como instrumento de análisis para el historiador: *basileia* griega y *regulos* ibéricos', in *Espacio y organización social*, Madrid.

Amin, S. (1974), *Sobre el desarrollo desigual de las formaciones sociales*, Barcelona.

Amores, F. de (1982), *Carta arqueológica de los Alcores. Sevilla*, Seville.

Amores F. de and I. R. Temiño (1984), 'La implantación durante el Bronce Final y el período orientalizante en el término de Carmona', *Arqueología Espacial*, 4, Teruel.

Anton Bertet, G. (1973), *Análisis por difracción de rayos X de cerámicas ibéricas valencianas*, Valencia.

Aranegui, C. (1969), 'Cerámica gris de los poblados ibéricos valencianos', *Papeles del Laboratorio de Arqueología Valenciana*, 6, Valencia.

(1975), 'La cerámica gris monocroma. Puntualizaciones sobre su estudio', *Papeles del Laboratorio de Arqueología Valenciana*, 11, Valencia.

(1985), 'El Hierro Antiguo valenciano. Las transformaciones del medio indígena, entre los siglos VIII y V a. de C.', in *Arqueología del País Valenciano. Panorama y perspectivas (Lucentum)*, Alicante.

(1988), 'Algunas construcciones preaugústeas de Sagunto', in *Los asentamientos ibéricos ante la romanización*, Madrid.

Aranegui, C., A. Jodin, E. A. Llobregat, P. Rouillard and J. Uroz (1983), *Fouilles du site ibérique de Cabezo Lucero, Mélanges de la Casa de Velázquez*, vol. XIX, Paris.

Arcelin, C. H. (1978), 'Recherches sur la céramique grise monochrome de Provence', in *Les céramiques de la Grèce de l'Est et leur diffusion en Occident*, Paris/Naples.

Arribas, A. (1965), *Los Iberos*, Barcelona.

(1967), 'La necrópolis bastetana del Mirador de Rolando (Granada)', *Pyrenae*, 3, Barcelona.

Arribas, A. and J. Wilking (1969), 'La necrópolis fenicia del Cortijo de las sombras (Frigiliana, Málaga)', *Pyrenae*, 5, Barcelona.

Arribas, A. and O. Arteaga (1979), *El yacimiento fenicio de la desembocadura del río Guadalhorce (Málaga), Cuadernos de prehistoria de la Universidad de Granada*, Serie Monográfica, vol. 2, Granada.

Bibliography

Arribas, A., G. Trías, D. Cerda and J. Hoz (1987), *El Barco de El Sec (Galvia, Mallorca)*, Palma de Mallorca.

Arteaga, O. (1987), 'Perspectivas espacio-temporales de la colonización fenicia occidental. Ensayo de aproximación', in *I Jornadas arqueológicas sobre el mundo ibérico* (1985), Jaén.

Arteaga, O. and M. Blech (1988), 'La romanización en la zona de Porcuna y Mengíbar (Jaén)', in *Los asentamientos ibéricos ante la romanización*, Madrid.

Arteaga, O. and M. R. Serna (1975), 'Los Saladares, 71', *Noticiario Arqueológico Hispánico*, 3, Madrid.

Arteaga, O., J. Padró and E. Sanmartí (1986), 'La expansión fenicia por las costas de Cataluña y el Languedoc', in *Los Fenicios en la Península Ibérica*, Sabadell.

Aubet, M. E. (1975), *La Necrópolis de Setefilla en Lora del Río (Sevilla)*, Programa de Investigaciones Protohistóricas de la Universidad de Barcelona.

— (1986), 'La necrópolis de Villaricos en el ámbito del mundo púnico peninsular', in *Homenaje a Luis Siret*, Seville.

— (1987), *Tiro y las colonias fenicias de occidente*, Barcelona.

— (1993), *The Phoenicians and the West: Politics, Colonies and Trade*, Cambridge (Spanish: Barcelona).

Aubet, M. E., M. R. Serna, J. L. Escacena and M. Ruiz Delgado (1983), *La Mesa de Setefilla Lora del Río (Sevilla). Campaña de 1979*, Excavaciones Arqueológicas en España, 122, Madrid.

Audouze, F. and O. Buchsenschutz (1989), *Villes, villages et campagnes de l'Europe celtique*, Paris.

Ballester, I. (1943), 'Sobre una posible clasificación de las cerámicas de San Miguel con escenas humanas', *Archivo Español de Arqueología*, 16, Madrid.

Ballester, I., D. Fletcher, E. Pla, J. Jordá and A. Alcocer (1954), *Corpus Vasorum Antiquorum. Cerámica del Cerro de San Miguel de Liria*, Madrid.

Bandera, M. L. de la (1977–8), 'El atuendo femenino ibérico', *Habis*, 8–9, Seville.

Barba, Elvira (1979), 'Aproximación al estilo florido o rico de la cerámica de Liria', *Archivo Español de Arqueología*, 52, Madrid.

Barberà, J., and E. Sanmartí (1982), *Excavacions al poblat ibèric de la Penya del Moro. Sant Just Desvern (1974, 1975, 1977, 1981)*, Monografías Arqueológicas, vol. I, Barcelona.

Barberá, J. and X. Dupré (1984), 'Els Laietans, assaig de síntesi', *Fonament*, 4, Barcelona.

Bate, L. F. (1982), 'Relación general entre teoría y método', in *Teoría, métodos y técnicas en arqueología*, Mexico.

— (1988), *Cultura, clases y cuestión étnico-nacional*, Mexico.

Belén, M. (1976), 'Estudio y tipología de la cerámica gris de la provincia de Huelva', in *RABM*, vol. LXXIX, 2, Madrid.

Belén, M. and J. Pereira (1985), 'Cerámica a torno con decoración pintada en Andalucía', *Huelva Arqueológica*, 7, Huelva.

Beltrán, M. (1976), *Arqueología e historia de las ciudades antiguas del Cabezo de Alcalá de Azaila (Teruel)*, Monografías Arqueológicas, vol. 19, Saragossa.

Benavente, J. A. (1984), 'El poblamiento ibérico en el Valle Medio del Regallo

(Alcañiz, Teruel)', *Kalathos*, 3–4, Teruel.

Bendala, M. (1982), 'Excavaciones en el Cerro de los Palacios', in *Actas de las primeras jornadas sobre excavaciones arqueológicas en Itálica*, Excavaciones Arqueológicas en España, 121, Madrid.

(1987), 'De la prehistoria a la conquista romana', in *Historia General de España y América*, Madrid.

Bendala, M., C. Fernández, A. Fuentes and L. Abad (1988), 'Aproximación al urbanismo prerromano y a los fenómenos de transición y de potenciación tras la conquista', in *Asentamientos ibéricos ante la romanización*, Madrid.

Bernabeu, J., H. Bonet, P. Guerin and C. Mata (1986), 'Análisis microespacial del poblado ibérico del Puntal dels Llops (Olocau, Valencia)', *Arqueología Espacial*, 9, Teruel.

Bernabeu, J., H. Bonet and A. Mata (1987), 'Hipótesis sobre la organización del territorio edetano en época ibérica: el ejemplo del território de Edeta-Lliria', in *I Jornadas arqueológicas sobre el mundo ibérico* (1985), Jaén.

Bernáldez, E. (1988), 'Estudio faunístico', in *Protohistoria de la ciudad de Sevilla*, Monografías de Arqueología Andaluza.

Bianchi Bandinelli, R. (1982), *Introducción a la arqueología*, Madrid.

Biasot, M., J. Oriel, J. Manel, F. Puig and J. M. Solias (1984), 'El poblamiento de la zona sur de la Layetania litoral en época ibérica y romana', *Arqueología Espacial*, 2, Teruel.

Blanco, A. (1962a), 'El ajuar de una tumba de Cástulo', *Archivo Español de Arqueología*, 36, Madrid.

(1962b), 'El aceite en los albores de la historia de España', *Oretania*, 10, Linares.

(1987), 'Destrucciones antiguas en el mundo ibérico y mediterráneo occidental', in *Homenaje a G. Nieto*, Madrid.

Blanco, A., J. M. Luzón and D. Ruiz Mata (1969), 'Panorama tartésico de Andalucía occidental', in *V Simposium internacional de prehistoria peninsular: Tartessos* (Jerez, 1968), Barcelona.

Blánquez, J. (1988), 'Los enterramientos de estructura tumular en el mundo ibérico', in *Actas del primer congreso peninsular de historia antigua*, Santiago de Compostela.

(1990), *La formación del mundo ibérico en el sureste de la meseta. (Estudio arqueológico de las necrópolis ibéricas de la provincia de Albacete)*, Albacete.

Blázquez, J. M. (1955–6), 'La interpretación de la pátera de Tivissa', *Ampurias*, 17–18, Barcelona.

(1975a), *Diccionario de las religiones prerromanas de Hispania*, Madrid.

(1975b), 'Cástulo I', *Acta Arqueológica Hispánica* no. VIII. Madrid.

Blázquez, J. M., M. P. García Gelabert and F. López Pardo (1985), Cástulo V, Excavaciones Arqueológicas en España, 140, Madrid.

Blázquez, J. M., D. Ruiz Mata, J. Remesal, J. L. Ramírez and K. Clauss (1979), Excavaciones en el Cabezo de San Pedro (Huelva). Campaña de 1967, Excavaciones Arqueológicas en España, 102, Madrid.

Blázquez, J. M. and J. Valiente (1981), Cástulo III, Excavaciones Arqueológicas en España, 117, Madrid.

Bibliography

Boessneck, J. (1966), 'Restos óseos de animales del Cerro de la Virgen (Orce) y Cerro del Real (Galeraz). Granada', *Noticiario Arqueológico Hispánico*, 10, Madrid.

Bonet, H. (1982), 'Nuevas aportaciones a la cronología final del Tossal de San Miguel (Lliria, Valencia)', *Trabajos varios del SIP*, 71, Valencia.

Bonet, H. and C. Mata (1981), 'El poblado ibérico del Puntal dels Llops (El Colmenar), (Olocau, Valencia)', *Trabajos varios del SIP*, 71, Valencia.

Bonsor, G. (1899), 'Les colonies agricoles prerromaines du Valle du Betis', *Revue Archéologique*, 35, Paris.

Bonsor, G. and R. Thouvenot (1928), 'Nécropole ibérique de Setefilla, Lora del Río (Sevilla)', *Bibliothèque de l'École des Hautes Études Hispaniques*, Fasc. XIV, Paris.

Bosch Gimpera, P. (1915), 'El problema de la cerámica ibérica', in *Memorias de la comisión de Investigaciones Paleontológicas y Prehistóricas*, vol. VII, Madrid.

(1932), *Etnología de la Península Ibérica*, Barcelona.

Box, M. and C. Bru (1983), 'Análisis sedimentológico de los estratos arqueológicos de los cortes de 1979 realizados en el sector II de la Penya Negra. Crevillente', in *Estudio arqueológico del poblamiento antiguo en la sierra de Crevillente*, (ed.) A. González Prats, Alicante.

Broncano, S. (1986), *El Castellar de Meca, Ayora (Valencia)*, Excavaciones Arqueológicas en España, 147, Madrid.

Broncano, S. and J. Blánquez (1985), *El Amarejo (Bonete, Albacete)*, Excavaciones Arqueológicas en España, 139, Madrid.

Burillo, F. (1982), 'El urbanismo del poblado ibérico del Taratrato de Alcañiz', *Kalathos*, 2, Teruel.

(1980), *El valle medio del Ebro en época ibérica. Contribución a su estudio en los ríos Huerva y Jiloca medio*, Saragossa.

(1987), 'Introducción al poblamiento ibérico en Aragón', in *I Jornadas arqueológicas sobre el mundo ibérico* (1985), Jaén.

(1989), 'La segunda edad del hierro en Aragón', in *Estado actual de la arqueología en Aragón*, Saragossa.

(1992), 'Sustrato de las etnias prerromanas del valle del Ebro–Pirineos', in *Paleoetnología de la Península Ibérica*, Madrid.

Buxó, R. (1987), 'Adopción de la agricultura en el nordeste de Cataluña', *Revista de Arqueología*, 80, Madrid.

Cabré, J. (1925), 'Arquitectura hispánica. El sepulcro de Toya', *Archivo Español de Arte y Arqueología*, 1, Madrid.

(1944), *Corpus Vasorum Hispanorum. Cerámica de Azaila (Museos arqueológicos de Madrid, Barcelona y Zaragoza)*, Madrid.

(1983–4), 'San Antonio de Calaceite', in *Catálogo monumental de Teruel*, vol. I, *Kalathos*, 3–4, Teruel.

Cabré, J. and J. Motos (1920–1), 'La necrópolis de Tutugi: objetos exóticos o de influencia oriental en las necrópolis turdetanas', *Boletín de la sociedad española de excursionistas*, 28, Madrid.

Cabré, M. E. (1934), 'Dos tipos de falcata hispánica'. *Archivo Español de Arqueología* 30.

Cabrera Bonet, P. (1986), 'Los griegos en Huelva: los materiales griegos', in *Homenaje a Luis Siret*, Seville.

Calvo, J. and J. Cabré (1917), *Excavaciones en la Cueva y Collado de los Jardines, Santa Elena, Jaén*, Junta Superior de Excavaciones Arqueológicas, 8, Madrid.

(1918), *Excavaciones en la Cueva y Collado de los Jardines, Santa Elena, Jaén*, Junta Superior de Excavaciones Arqueológicas, 16, Madrid.

(1919), *Excavaciones en la Cueva y Collado de los Jardines, Santa Elena, Jaén*, Junta Superior de Excavaciones Arqueológicas, 22, Madrid.

Campmajó, P. and J. Padró (1976), 'Els ceretans', in *Els pobles prerromans del Pirineu*, Puigcerdá.

Campos, J. M., M. Vera and M. T. Moreno (1988), *Protohistoria de la ciudad de Sevilla*, Monografías de Arqueología, vol. I, Seville.

Carandini, D. (1984), *Arqueología y cultura material*, Barcelona.

Caro Baroia, J. (1971), *La realeza y los reyes en la España Antigua*, Cuadernos de la Fundación Paster, Estudios sobre la España Antigua, 17, Madrid.

Carrasco, J., M. Pastor and J. A. Pachón (1981), 'Excavaciones en el Cerro de la Mora, Moraleda de Zafayona, Granada, Campaña de 1979', *Noticiario Arqueológico Hispánico*, vol. XII, Madrid.

Castell, M. (1974), *La cuestión urbana*, Madrid.

Castro, P. and P. González (1989), 'El concepto de frontera: implicaciones teóricas del concepto de frontera política', *Arqueología Espacial*, 13, Teruel.

Castro Curel, Z. (1983), 'Notas sobre la problemática del tejido en la península ibérica', *Kalathos*, 3–4, Teruel.

(1986), 'Avances de estudios cuantitativos y cualitativos y localización de pondera en asentamientos peninsulares', *Arqueología Espacial*, 8, Teruel.

Cazurro, A. (1908), 'Fragments de vasos ibèrics d'Ampúries', *Anuari Institut Estudis Catalans*, 2, Barcelona.

Chang, C. (1967), *Rethinking Archaeology*, New York.

Chapa, T. (1985), *La escultura ibérica zoomorfa*, Madrid.

(1986), 'La escultura ibérica: una revisión de sus interpretaciones', *Trabajos de Prehistoria*, 43, Madrid.

(1990), 'La escultura ibérica de Jaén en su contexto mediterráneo', in *Escultura ibérica*, Jaén.

Chaves, F. and M. L. de la Bandera (1984), *Avances sobre el yacimiento arqueológico de Montemolín (Marchena, Sevilla), Papers in Iberian Archeology*, BAR International Series, 193, vol. I, Oxford.

Choclán C. (1984), *Cerámica ibero–romana producida en el alfar del los Villares de Andújar (Campañas de 1981–1982)*, University of Granada.

Choclán C. and M. Castro (1986–7), 'Ciudad y territorio en la Campiña de Jaén. La distribución de los asentamientos mayores durante la época flavia', in *Homenaje a Marcelo Vigil (Studia Historica, 4–5, 1)*, Salamanca.

Clarke, D. L. (1968), *Analytical Archaeology*, London (Spanish translation: *Arqueología analítica*, Barcelona, 1984).

Coarelli, A. (1972), Intervención en el XI Convegno di studi sulla Magna Grecia, Taranto, 1971, Naples.

Colomines, J. and J. Puig (1915–20), 'El forn ibèric de Fontscaldes', *Anuari Institut*

Bibliography

Estudis Catalans, 6, Barcelona.

Coll Conesa, J. (1987), 'El horno ibérico de Alcalá del Júcar, Albacete', *Revista de Arqueología*, 80, Madrid.

Collis, J. (1989), *La edad del hierro en Europa*, Madrid.

Contreras. F. (1984), 'Clasificación y tipología en arqueología: el camino hacia la cuantificación', *Cuadernos de Prehistoria de la Universidad de Granada*, 9, Granada.

Contreras, F., F. Nocete and M. Sánchez (1985), 'Análisis histórico de las comunidades de la edad del bronce de la depresión Linares–Bailén y estribaciones meridionalees de Sierra Morena. Sondeo estratigráfico en el Cerro de la Plaza de Armas de Sevilleja (Espeluy, Jaén)', *Anuario Arqueológico de Andalucía*, 1, Seville

Cruz, M. (1981), *El historicismo. Ciencia social y filosofía*, Barcelona.

Cruz Andreotti, G. (1987), 'Un acercamiento historiográfico al Tartessos de Schulten', *Baética*, 10, Malaga.

Cuadrado, E. (1951), 'Las tumbas ibéricas de empedrado tumular y la celtización del sudeste', in *II Congreso Nacional de Arqueología*, Madrid.

(1957), 'La fíbula anular hispánica y sus problemas', *Zephyrus*, 8, Salamanca.

(1963), 'Precedentes y prototipos de la fíbula anular hispánica', *Trabajos de Prehistoria*, 7, Madrid.

(1969), 'Origen y desarrollo de la cerámica de barniz rojo en el mundo tartésico', in *V Simposium internacional de prehistoria peninsular: Tartessos*, (Jerez, 1968), Barcelona.

(1972), 'Tipología de la cerámica ibérica fina de El Cigarralejo, Mula (Murcia)', *Trabajos de Prehistoria*, 29, Madrid.

(1984), 'Arte ibérico', in *Homenaje a D. Fletcher*, Valencia.

(1987a), *La necrópolis ibérica de El Cigarralejo (Mula, Murcia)*, Madrid.

(1987b), 'Las necrópolis ibéricas del levante español', in *I Jornadas arqueológicas sobre el mundo ibérico*, Jaén.

Cuadrado Insasa, F. (1968), 'Formas nuevas de la ceránica de barniz rojo', in *XI Congreso nacional de arqueología* (Mérida), Saragossa.

Cura Morera, M. (1971), 'Acerca de unas cerámicas grises con decoración estampillada en la Cataluña prerromana', *Pyrenae*, 7, Barcelona.

D'Agostino, B. (1987), *Società dei vivi, comunità dei morti: un rapporto difficile*, *Dialoghi di Archeologia*, vol. I, Rome.

Daniel, G. (1967), *Origins and Growth of Archaeology*, London.

Davis, K. (1967), 'La urbanización de la población humana', in *La ciudad*, Madrid.

Dechelette, J. (1909), 'Essai sur la chronologie préhistorique de la péninsule ibérique', *Revue Archéologique*, Paris.

Domínguez, A. J. (1984), 'La escultura animalística ibérica contestana como exponente del proceso de helenización del territorio', *Arqueología Espacial*, 4, Teruel.

(1986), 'La función económica de la ciudad griega de Emporión', in *VI Colloqui Internacional d'Arqueologia de Puigcerdà* (Protohistòria catalana), Puigcerdà.

Dupré, M. and J. Renault-Miskovsky (1981), 'Estudio polínico', in *Trabajos varios del*

SIP, 71, Valencia.

Enguix, R. (1973), 'Aproximación a la historia de la investigación de la cultura ibérica', in *Papeles del laboratorio de arqueología valenciana*, Valencia.

Escacena, J. L. (1987a), 'El poblamiento ibérico en el bajo Guadalquivir', in *I Jornadas arqueológicas sobre el mundo ibérico* (1985), Jaén.

(1987b), *Cerámicas a torno pintadas andaluzas de la segunda edad del hierro*, doctoral thesis, University of Cadiz.

Esquivel, A. and F. Contreras (1984), 'Una experiencia arqueológica con microordenadores. Análisis de componentes principales y clusterización: distancia euclídea y de mahalanovis', in *Actas del XIV Congreso Nacional de Estadística, Investigación operativa e informática*, Granada.

Esteve, J. (1983), 'La fauna del corte 3: aproximación a la fauna del yacimiento de Setefilla', *Archivo Español de Arqueología*, 122, Madrid.

Fatás, G. (1963), *La Sedetania. Iberización y romanización de las tierras zaragozanas hasta la fundación de Cesaraugusta*, Saragossa.

Fernández, V. (1988), 'El asentamiento ibérico del Cerro de las Nieves (Pedro Muñoz, Ciudad Real)', in *I Congreso de Historia de Castilla–La Mancha*, Ciudad Real.

Fernández Jurado, J. (1984), *La presencia griega en Huelva*, Monografías Arqueológicas, vol. I, Huelva.

(1986), 'Fenicios y griegos en Huelva', in *Homenaje a Luis Siret*, Seville.

(1987a), 'El poblamiento ibérico en Huelva', in *I Jornadas arqueológicas sobre el mundo ibérico* (1985), Jaén.

(1987b), 'Tejada la Vieja: una ciudad protohistórica', *Huelva Arqueológica*, 9, Huelva.

Fernández Miranda, M. and R. Olmos (1986), *Las ruedas de Toya y el origen del carro en la península ibérica*, Madrid.

Fernández Rodríguez, M. (1987), *Alarcos: la cerámica de barniz rojo del cerro de Alarcos*, Ciudad Real.

Figueras Pacheco, F. (1934), *Excavaciones en la Isla de Campello*, Junta Superior de Excavaciones y Antigüedades, 132, Madrid.

Fletcher, D. (1949), 'Defensa del iberismo', *Anales del centro de cultura valenciana*, 23, Valencia.

(1952–3), 'Sobre el origen y cronología de los vasos ibéricos de borde dentado', *Saitabi*, 9, Valencia.

(1964), 'Las urnas de orejetas perforadas', in *VII Congreso Nacional de Arqueología* (Sevilla–Itálica, 1963), Saragossa.

(1975), *La necrópolis de Blivella (Alcalá de Chivert)*, Valencia.

(1983), *Els Íbers*, Col. Descobrim El País Valencià, vol. IV, Valencia.

Fletcher, D., E. Pla, I. Ballester and A. Alcocer (1969), *El poblado ibérico de la Bastida de les Alcuses (Mogente, Valencia)*, anniversary of the foundation of the SIP, Valencia.

Fletcher, D., E. Pla, M. Gil Mascarell and C. Aranegui (1976–8), 'La iberización en el País Valenciano', in *Simposi internacional: els orígens del Món Ibèric, Ampurias*, 38–40, Barcelona.

Fontana, J. (1982), *Historia: análisis del pasado y proyecto social*, Barcelona.

Fortea, J. and J. Bernier (1970), *Recintos y fortificaciones ibéricas en la Bética*, Salamanca.

Fresneda, E., M. O. Rodríguez and E. Jabaloy (1980), 'El yacimiento de la Cuesta de los Chinos, Gabia, Granada', *Cuadernos de Prehistoria de la Universidad de Granada*, 5, Granada.

Garcés, I. and E. Junyent (1988), 'El poblat dels camps d'urnes i ibèrics de Vilars (Arbeca, Les Garrigues)', in *Tribuna d'Arqueologia*, Barcelona.

García J., J. Miró and J. Pujol (1991), 'La porta meridional del poblat ibèric de Burriac (Cabrera de Mar, El Maresme)', in *Fortificacions. La problemàtica de l'ibèric ple (segles IV–III aC)*, Manresa.

García y Bellido, A. (1943), 'Algunos problemas del arte y cronología ibéricos', *Archivo Español de Arqueología*, 16, Madrid.

(1945), *España y los españoles hace 2,000 años según la Geographia de Strabón*, Buenos Aires.

(1947), *La España del siglo I de nuestra era según P. Mela y C. Plinio*, Buenos Aires.

(1952), 'Arte ibérico', in *Historia de España*, (ed.) R. Menéndez Pidal, Madrid.

(1967), *Veinticinco estampas de la España antigua*, Madrid.

García Rincón, J. M. (1987), 'Aproximación al estudio espacial del área de Tejada la Vieja', *Huelva arqueológica*, 9, Huelva.

Garrido, J. and E. M. Orta (1978), *Excavaciones en la necrópolis de la Joya. Huelva II (3.ª, 4.ª y 5.ª campañas)*, Excavaciones Arqueológicas en España, vol. 96, Madrid.

Gil Mascarell, M. (1975), 'Sobre las cuevas ibéricas del País Valenciano. Materiales y problemas', *Papeles del Laboratorio de Arqueología Valenciana*, 11, Valencia.

(1985), 'El final de la Edad del Bronce. Estado actual de la investigación', in *Arqueología del País Valenciano. Panorama y perspectivas (Lucentum)*, Alicante.

Gnoli, G. and J. D. Vernant (1982), *La mort, les morts dans les sociétés anciennes*, Cambridge/Paris.

Godelier, M. (1981), *Instituciones económicas*, Barcelona.

Góngora, M. (1868), *Antigüedades prehistóricas de Andalucía*, Madrid.

González Navarrete, J. (1987), *Escultura ibérica de Cerrillo Blanco*, Jaén.

González Prats, A. (1979a), 'La tipología cerámica del horizonte II de Crevillente', *Papeles del laboratorio de Arqueología Valenciana*, 14, Valencia.

(1979b), 'La tipología cerámica del horizonte II del sector IA de la sierra de Crevillente', *Saguntum*, 14, Valencia.

(1981), 'En torno a la cerámica de cocina del mundo ibérico. Materiales del castillo del río Aspe (Alicante)', *IEA*, 33, Alicante.

(1982), 'La Peña Negra IV', *Noticiario Arqueológico Hispánico*, 13, Madrid.

(1983), 'Estudio arqueológico del poblamiento antiguo de la Sierra de Crevillente (Alicante)', *Lucentum*, appendix 1, Alicante.

(1985), 'Los nuevos asentamientos del final de la edad del bronce. Problemática cultural y cronología', in *Arqueología del País Valenciano. Panorama y perspectivas, (Lucentum)*, Alicante.

(1989), 'El proceso de formación de los pueblos ibéricos en el Levante y Sudeste de la Península Ibérica', in *Paleoetnología de la Península Ibérica*, Madrid.

Bibliography

González Prats, A. and J. A. Pina (1983), 'Análisis de las pastas cerámicas de vasos hechos a torno de la fase orientalizante de Peña Negra (675–550/535 aC)', *Lucentum*, 2, Alicante.

González Román, C. (1984), 'La colonia Iulia Gemella Acci y la evolución de la Bastetania', in *L'encuentro hispano–italiano de Arqueología*, Alicante, Rome.

Gracia, F., G. Munilla and R. Pallarés (1988), *La Moleta del Remei. Alcanar–Montsià. Campañas 1981–1986*, Tarragona.

Gross, P. and M. Torelli (1988), *Storia dell'urbanistica. Il mondo romano*, Laterza, Bari.

Guliaer, V. (1989), *Las primeras ciudades*, Progreso, Moscú.

Gusi, F., M. A. Díaz and A. Oliver (1991), 'Modelos de fortificación ibérica en el País Valenciano', in *Fortificacions. La problemàtica de l'ibèric ple (segles IV–III aC)*, Manresa.

Gusi, F. and C. Olaria (1984), *Arquitectura del mundo ibérico*, Castellón.

Gusi, F. and A. Oliver (1987), 'Poblamiento ibérico en Castellón', in *I Jornadas arqueológicas sobre el mundo Ibérico* (1985), Jaén.

Harris, E. C. (1979), *Principles of Archaeological Stratigraphy*, New York (Spanish translation: *Principios de arqueología estratigráfica*, Barcelona, 1991).

Hagget, P. and R. J. Chorley (1967), *Models in Geography*, London.

Hodder, I. (1982), *Symbols in action. Ethnoarchaeological studies of material culture*, Cambridge.

Hodder, I. and C. Orton (1976), *Spatial Analysis in Archaeology*, Cambridge (Spanish translation: *Análisis espacial en Arqueología*, Barcelona, 1990).

Hoz, J. de (1969), 'Acerca de la historia de la escritura prelatina en Hispania', *Archivo Español de Arqueología*, 42, Madrid.

(1979), 'Escritura e influencia clásica en los pueblos prerromantos de la Península Ibérica', *Archivo Español de Arqueología*, 52, Madrid.

Jabaloy, M. E., V. Salvatierra, J. A. García Granados and A. García del Moral (1983), 'El yacimiento preibérico del Cerro del Centinela', *Cuadernos de Prehistoria de la Universidad de Granada*, 8, Granada.

Jacob, P. (1985), 'Le rôle de la ville dans la formation des peuples ibères', *Mélanges de la Casa Velázquez*, 21, Paris.

Jannoray, J. (1955), *Enserune*, Paris.

Jodin, A. (1966), *Mogador, comptoir phénicien du Maroc Atlantique*, Tangiers.

Jordá Pellicer, F., P. Acosta and M. Almagro Gorbea (1986), *Prehistoria*, Madrid.

Jully, J. J. (1975), 'Koine commerciale et culturelle phenicopunique et ibero–languedocienne en Méditerranée Occidentale a l'âge du fer (Documents de ceramique)', *Archivo Español de Arqueología*, 48, Madrid.

Junyent, E. (1972), 'Los materiales del poblado ibérico de Margalef en Torregrossa (Lérida)', *Pyrenae*, 8, Barcelona.

(1974), 'Acerca de la cerámica de barniz rojo aparecida en el área ilergeta', *Pyrenae*, 10, Barcelona.

(1975), 'Contexto y significado histórico de la cerámica de barniz rojo ilergeta en la iberización del norte del Ebro', in *XIII Congreso Nacional de Arqueología* (Huelva), Saragossa.

(1979), 'Els Ilergetes', *L'Avenç*, 14, Barcelona.

(1987), 'El poblamiento ibérico en el área ilergeta', in *I Jornadas arqueológicas sobre el mundo ibérico* (1985), Jaén.

Junyent, E. and V. Baldellou (1972), 'Estudio de una casa en el poblado de Mas Boscà', *Príncipe de Viana*, 126–7, Pamplona.

Jutglar, A. (1968), *Ideología y clases en la España contemporánea*, Madrid.

Lafuente Vidal, J. (1934), 'Excavaciones en la Albufereta de Alicante', *Memorias de la Junta Superior de Excavaciones Arqueológicas*, 126, Madrid.

Lamboglia, N. (1953), '¿Cerámica ampuritana o cerámica massaliota?', *Rivista di studi Liguri*, 19, Bordighera.

(1954), 'La cerámica ibérica negli strati di Albintimilium nel territorio ligure e tirrenico', *Rivista di studi ligure*, 30, 2, Bordighera.

Lantier, R. (1917), *El santuario ibérico de Castellar de Santisteban*, Madrid.

Lillo, P. (1981), *El poblamiento ibérico en Murcia*, Murcia.

Llorens i Rams, J. M., E. Pons i Brun and A. Toledo i Mur (1986), 'La distribución del espacio en el recinto fortificado ibérico Puig Castellet (Lloret de Mar-La Selva, Girona)', *Arqueología Espacial* 9, pp. 237–256.

Llobregat, E. A. (1972), *Contestania ibérica*, Alicante.

(1985), 'Dos temples ibèrics a l'interior del poblat de l'Illeta dels Bayets', *Fonament*, 5, Barcelona.

López, A., J. Rovira and E. Sanmartí (1982), *Excavaciones en el poblado layetano del Turó del Vent, Llinars del Vallès. Campañas 1980 y 1981*, Monografies Arqueològiques, vol. III, Barcelona.

López, P. (1984), 'Análisis polínico de Castellones de Ceal', *Arqueología Espacial*, 4, Teruel.

López Domech, R. (1986–7), 'Sobre reyes, reyezuelos y caudillos militares en la protohistoria hispana', in *Homenaje a Marcelo Vigil, Studia Historica*, vols. IV–V, 1, Salamanca.

López Palomo, L. A. (1981), 'Alhonoz. Excavaciones de 1973 a 1978', *Noticiario Arqueológico Hispánico*, 11, Madrid.

(1983), 'De la edad del bronce al mundo ibérico en la Campiña del Genil', in *Actas del I Congreso de Historia de Andalucía* (Prehistoria y Arqueología), Cordoba.

López Rozas, J. (1987), 'El poblamiento ibérico en la meseta sur', in *I Jornadas Arqueológicas sobre el mundo ibérico* (1985), Jaén.

Lull, V. and J. Esteve (1986), 'Propuesta metodológica para el estudio de las necrópolis argaricas', in *Homenaje a Luis Siret*, Seville.

Lull, V. and M. Picazo (1989), 'Arqueología de la muerte y estructura espacial', *Archivo Español de Arqueología*, 62, Madrid.

Luzón, J. M. (1973), 'Excavaciones en Itálica: estratigrafía del Pajar de Artillo (Campaña 1970)', *Huelva Arqueológica*, 4, Huelva.

Luzón, J. M. and D. Ruiz Mata (1973), *Las raíces de Córdoba, estratigrafía de la Colina de los Quemados*, Cordoba.

Madroñero, A. and M. N. I. Ágreda (1988), 'Contribución al estudio de la metalurgia de Cástulo', appendix III, in M. P. García-Gelabarl-Pérez and J. M. Blazquez Martinez, *Cástulo Jaen, España I: excavaciones en la necrópolis ibérica del Estacar de Rebarinas*, BAR International Series 425, Oxford.

Maluquer de Motes, J. (1952), 'Los pueblos ibéricos', in *Historia de España*, (ed.) R. Menéndez Pidal, t. I, vol. III, Madrid.

(1968), *Epigrafía prelatina de la península ibérica*, Barcelona.

(1970), *Tartessos*, Barcelona.

(1981), *El santuario protohistórico de Zalamea de la Serena. Badajoz*, Barcelona.

(1982), 'Los núcleos de población prerromana', in *Vivienda y urbanismo en España*, Barcelona.

(1983), *El santuario protohistórico de Zalamea de la Serena. Badajoz*, Barcelona.

(1984), *La necrópolis paleoibérica de 'Mas Mussols', Tortosa (Tarragona)*, Programa Investigaciones Protohistóricas, vol. VII, Barcelona.

(1986a), *Molí d'Espígol. Tornabous. Poblat ibèric*, Generalitat de Catalunya, Barcelona.

(1986b), 'La dualidad comercial fenicia y griega en Occidente', in *Los fenicios en la península ibérica*, Sabadell.

(1987), *La necrópolis paleoibérica de Mianes en Santa Bárbara*, Barcelona.

Maluquer, J., M. Picazo and M. A. del Rincón (1981), *La necrópolis ibérica de la Bobadilla (Jaén)*, Barcelona.

Maluquer, J., E. Huntingford, A. Martín, A. M. Rauret and M. del V. Vila (1986), *Arquitectura i urbanisme ibèrics a Catalunya*, Barcelona.

Mangas, J. (1977), 'Servidumbre Comunitaria en la Bética prerromana', *Memorias de Historia Antigua*, 1, Oviedo.

Maraver y Alfaro, L. (1867), 'Expedición arqueológica a Almedinilla', *Revista de Bellas Artes e histórico–arqueológica*, 3, 71, Madrid.

Martín, J. A. (1987), 'El poblamiento ibérico en el Ampurdán', in *I Jornadas Arqueológicas sobre el mundo ibérico* (1985), Jaén.

Martín de la Cruz, J. D. (1987), *El Llanete de los Moros (Montoro, Córdoba)*, Excavaciones Arqueológicas en España, 151, Madrid.

Martínez Santaolalla, J. (1946), *Esquema paletnológico de la Península Ibérica*, Madrid.

Marx, K. (1904), *Contribution to the Critique of Political Economy*, New York.

(1937), *Capital*, London.

(1964), *Precapitalist Economic Formations*, London.

Mascort, M., J. Sanmartí and J. Santacana (1988), 'L'establiment protohistòric d'Aldovesta (Benifallet. Baix Ebre). Un punt clau del comerç fenici a la Catalunya Meridional', in *Tribuna d'Arqueologia*, Barcelona.

Mata Carriazo, J. de la and J. Raddatz (1960), 'Primicias de un corte estratigráfico en Carmona', *Archivo Hispalense*, 101–4, Seville.

Mata Parreño, C. (1987), Los Villares: origen y evolución de la cultura ibérica, doctoral thesis, Valencia.

Menéndez Pidal, R. (1952–4), *Historia de España*, Madrid.

Mergelina, C. (1926), *El santuario hispano de la sierra de Murcia*, Memorias de la Junta Superior de Excavaciones Arqueológicas, vol. LXXVII, Madrid.

Mesado, N. and O. Arteaga (1979), 'Vinarraguell (Burriana)', *Trabajos varios del SIP*, 46, Valencia.

Miret, M., J. Sanmartí and J. Santacana (1984), 'Distribución espacial de núcleos ibéricos: un ejemplo en el litoral catalán', *Arqueología Espacial*, 4, Teruel.

Bibliography

(1988), 'La evolución y el cambio del modelo de poblamiento ibérico ante la romanización: un ejemplo', in *Los asentamientos ibéricos ante la romanización*, Madrid.

Miró, C. and N. Molist (1982), 'Estudio de la fauna exhumada en el asentamiento de Turó del Vent', *Monografies Arqueològiques*, 3, Barcelona.

Molero, G. (1988), 'Estudio de los restos faunísticos hallados en el Estacar de Robarinas, Cástulo', appendix V, in M. P. García-Gelabarl-Pérez and J. M. Blazquez Martinez, *Cástulo Jaen, España I: excavaciones en la necrópolis ibérica del Estacar de Rebarinas*, BAR International Series 425, Oxford.

Molina González, F. (1978), 'Definición y sistematización del Bronce Tardío y Final en el sureste de la Península Ibérica', *Cuadernos de Prehistoria de la Universidad de Granada*, 3, Granada.

(1983), 'Prehistoria', in *Historia de Granada*, Granada.

Molina González, F., A. Mendoza, O. Arteaga and P. Aguayo (1981), 'Cerro de los infantes (Pinos Puente Provincia de Granada)', *Madrider Mitteilungen*, 22, Mainz.

Molinos, M. (1986), *La Campiña Oriental de Jaén durante las fases ibéricas*, doctoral thesis, University of Granada.

Molinos, M., A. Ruiz and F. Nocete (1986), 'El poblamiento ibérico de la campiña del alto Guadalquivir: proceso de formación y desarrollo de la servidumbre territorial', in *I Congreso de Historia Antigua*, Santiago de Compostela.

Molinos, M., C. Rísquez, J. L. Serrano and B. Coba (1988), 'Excavaciones en la Campiña de Marmolejo', in *Anuario arqueológico de Andalucía*, Seville.

Molist, N. and J. Rovira (1991), 'La fortificació ibèrica del Turó de Montgròs (El Brull, Osona)', in *Fortificacions. La Problemàtica de l'ibèric ple (segles IV–III aC)*, Manresa.

Montilla, S., C. Rísquez, J. L. Serrano and B. Coba (1989), 'Análisis de una frontera durante el horizonte ibérico en la depresión Priego–Alcaudete', *Arqueología Espacial*, 13, Teruel.

Morales, A. (1977), 'Los restos de animales del Castro de Medellín', appendix I in *Bibliotheca Praehistorica Hispana*, vol. XIV, Madrid.

Morales, A. and M. Cabrera (1981), 'Informe sobre los restos faunísticos del poblado de la Muela, Cástulo (Linares, Jaén)', appendix IV to *Excavacionese Arqueológicas en España*, 117, Madrid.

Morena, J. A. (1989), *El santuario ibérico de Torreparedones*, Cordoba.

Morris, A. (1984), *Historia de la forma urbana (desde sus orígenes hasta la Revolución industrial)*, Barcelona.

Muñoz, F. (1986), 'Las monedas del sur de la península ibérica. Consideraciones histórico–financieras', in *I Congreso peninsular de Historia Antigua*, Santiago de Compostela.

Murillo, F., F. Quesada, D. Vaquerizo, J. R. Carrillo and J. A. Morena (1989), 'Aproximación al estudio del poblamiento prehistórico en el sureste de Córdoba: unidades políticas, control del territorio y fronteras', *Arqueología Espacial*, 13, Teruel.

Negueruela, I. (1979–80), 'Sobre la cerámica de engobe rojo en España', *Habis*, 10–11, Seville.

Bibliography

(1990), *Los monumentos escultóricos ibéricos del Cerrillo Blanco de Porcuna (Jaén)*, Madrid.

Nickels, A. (1978), 'Contribution à l'étude de la céramique grise archaique en Languedoc-Roussillon', in *Les céramiques de la Grèce de l'Est et leur diffusion en Occident*, Paris/Naples.

Nicolini, G. (1969), *Les bronzes figures des sanctuaires iberiques*, Paris.

(1982), *La campaña de fouilles de 1981 à Castellar (Jaén)*, Paris.

Nicolini, G., N. Zafra and A. Ruiz Rodríguez (1987), 'Informe de la Campaña de excavación de 1987 en los Altos del Sotillo (Castellar, Jaén)', in *Anuario arqueológico de Andalucía*, Seville.

Nocete, F. (1989), *El espacio de la coerción. La transición al estado en las campiñas del alto Guadalquivir (España). 3000–1500 aC* BAR International Series 492, 1, Oxford.

Nordström, S. (1969), *La céramique peinte de la province de Alicante*, Acta Universitaria Stocholmiensis, vol. I and II, Stockholm.

Oliva, M. (1967), *Ullastret, guía de las excavaciones y museo*, Gerona.

Oliver, A., M. Blasco, A. Freixa and P. Rodríguez (1984), 'El proceso de iberización en la plana litoral del sur de Castellón', *Cuadernos de Prehistoria y Arqueología Castellonense*, 10, Castellón.

Olmos, R. (1979), 'Perspectivas y nuevos enfoques en el estudio de elementos de cultura material (cerámicas y bronces) griegos o estímulo griego hallados en España', *Archivo Español de Arqueología*, 52, Madrid.

(1982), 'Vaso griego y caja funeraria en la Bastetania ibérica', in *Homenaje a Conchita Fernández Chicarro*, Madrid.

(1984), 'La cerámica de importación griega en el mundo ibérico', in *Homenaje a D. Fletcher*, Valencia.

Ortega y Gasset, J. (1921), *España invertebrada*, Madrid.

Ortiz, P. and A. Rodríguez (1985), 'Problemática general en torno a los recintos-torre de la Serena. Badajoz', in *XIX Congreso nacional de arqueología*, Saragossa.

Padró, J. (1987), 'El poblamiento ibérico en el interior de Catalunya', in *I Jornadas arqueológicas sobre el mundo ibérico* (1985), Jaén.

Padró, J. and E. Sanmartí (1992), 'Áreas geográficas de las etnias prerromanas de Cataluña', in *Paleoetnología de la Península Ibérica*, Madrid.

Pallarés, R., F. Gracia and G. Munilla (1986), 'Modelo de reconstrucción del hábitat n.º 1 del poblado ibérico de la Moleta del Remei', *Arqueología Espacial*, 8, Teruel.

Paris, P. (1903–4), *Essai sur l'art et l'industrie de l'Espagne primitive*, vol. I and II, Paris.

Paris, P. and V. Bardaviu (1926), *Fouilles dans la région d'Alcañiz (Province de Teruel): I Le cabezo del Cuervo, II Le Taratrato*, Bibliothèque de l'École des Hautes Études Hispaniques, XI, 1, Paris/Bordeaux.

Paris, P. and A. Engel (1906), 'Une forteresse ibérique à Osuna (Fouilles de 1903)', *NAMSC*, 13, Paris.

Pellicer, M. (1969), 'Las primitivas cerámicas a torno pintadas andaluzas y sus problemas', in *V Simposium internacional de prehistoria peninsular: Tartessos* (Jerez, 1968), Barcelona.

(1978), 'Tipología y cronología de las ánforas prerromanas del Guadalquivir según el Cerro Macareno (Sevilla)', *Habis*, 9, Seville.

Bibliography

(1980), 'Ensayo de periodización y cronología tartésica y turdetana', *Habis*, 10, Seville.

(1982), 'Las cerámicas del mundo fenicio en el bajo Guadalquivir. Evolución y cronología según el Cerro Macareno (Sevilla)', *Madrider Beiträge*, 8, Mainz.

Pellicer, M. and F. de Amores (1985), 'Protohistoria de Carmona. Los Cortes estratigráficos CA-80/A y Ca-80/B', *Noticiario Arqueológico Hispánico*, 22, Madrid.

Pellicer, M., J. L. Escacena and M. Bendala (1983), *El Cerro Macareno*, Excavaciones Arqueológicas en España, 124, Madrid.

Pellicer, M., V. Hurtado and M. L. de la Bandera (1982), 'Corte estratigráfico en la Casa de Venus', in *Actas de las I jornadas arqueológicas en Itálica, excavaciones arqueológicas en España*, 121, Madrid.

Pellicer, M., and W. Schüle (1962), *El Cerro del Real Galera (Granada)*, Excavaciones Arqueológicas en España, 12, Madrid.

(1966), *El Cerro Real. Galera (Granada). El corte estratigráfico IX*, Excavaciones Arqueológicas en España, Madrid.

Perales, M.ª-P., J. V. Picazo and A. Sancho (1983), 'Tiro de Cañón (Alcañiz): los materiales cerámicos I', *Kalathos*, 3–4, Teruel.

Pereira, J. (1979), 'La cerámica ibérica procedente de Toya (Peal de Becerro, Jaén), en el Museo Arqueológico Nacional', *Trabajos de Prehistoria*, 36, Madrid.

(1988), 'La cerámica ibérica de la cuenca del Guadalquivir. I: Propuesta de clasificación', *Trabajos de Prehistoria*, 45, Madrid.

(1989a), 'La cerámica ibérica de la cuenca del Guadalquivir. II: Conclusiones', *Trabajos de Prehistoria*, 46, Madrid.

(1989b), 'Necrópolis ibéricas en la Alta Andalucía. Nuevas perspectivas en su valoración y estudio', in *Tartessos. Arqueología protohistórica del Bajo Guadalquivir*, Sabadell.

Pereira, J. and A. Rodero (1983), 'Aportaciones al problema de las urnas de orejetas perforadas', in *Homenaje al profesor M. Almagro Basch*, vol. III, Madrid.

Pericot, L. (1954), *Cerámica de San Miguel de Liria. Corpus Vasorum Hispanorum*, Madrid.

Piggott, (1973), 'Problems in the interpretation of chambered tombs', in *Megalithic Graves and Ritual III Atlantic Coloquium*, Moesgard.

Pla, E. (1968), 'Instrumentos de trabajo ibéricos en la región valenciana', in *Estudios de economía de la Península Ibérica*, Barcelona.

(1962), Preliminary note on Los Villares (Caudete de las Fuentes, Valencia), in *VII Congreso Nacional de Arqueología*, Saragossa.

(1985), 'La iberización en tierras valencianas', in *Arqueología del País Valenciano. Panorama y perspectivas (Lucentum)*, Alicante.

Pla, E. and C. Aranegui (1981), 'La cerámica ibérica', in *La baja época de la cultura ibérica*, Madrid.

Pons, E. (1986), 'El pas de l'edat del bronze a la del ferro a Catalunya' in *Colloqui Internacional d'Arqueologia de Puigcerdà*, Puigcerdà.

Pons, E., A. Toledo and J. M. Llorens (1981), *El recinte fortificat ibèric de Puig Castellet*, Serie monográfica, vol. III, Girona.

Bibliography

Pottier, E. (1905), 'Le probleme de la céramique ibérique', in *Journal des Savants*, Paris.

Prados, L. (1988), 'Exvotos ibéricos de bronce. Aspectos tipológicos y tecnológicos', *Trabajos de Prehistoria*, 45, Madrid.

Presedo, F. (1982), *La Necrópolis de Baza*, Excavaciones Arqueológicas en España, vol. 119, Madrid.

Prevosti, M. (1981), *Cronologia i poblament a l'àrea rural de Baetulo*, Badalona.

Pujol, A. (1989), *La población prerromana del extremo nordeste peninsular*, 2 vols, Barcelona.

Quesada, F. (1986–7), 'El armamento en la necrópolis ibérica de El Cabecico del Tesoro (Murcia)', *Cuadernos de Prehistoria y Arqueología*, 13–14, Madrid.

    (1989), *Armamento, guerra y sociedad en la necrópolis ibérica de El Cabecico del Tesoro (Murcia, España)*, BAR International Series, 502, (vols. I and II), Oxford.

Quintero, P., *Excavaciones en Cádiz*, Memorias de la Junta Superior de Excavaciones Arqueológicas, 99, Madrid.

Rada y Delgado, J. de D. de la (1875), *Antigüedades del Cerro de los Santos en el témino de Montealegre del Castillo*, Madrid.

Rafel Fontanals, N. (1985), 'El ritual d'enterrament ibèric. Un essaig de reconstrucció', *Fonament*, 5, Barcelona.

Rafel Fontanals, N. and M. Blasco (1991), 'El recinte fortificat del Coll del Moro de Gandesa', in *Fortificacions. La problemàtica de l'ibèric ple (segles IV–III aC)*, Manresa.

Ramos Fernández, J. (1984), 'Historia general del fenómeno ibérico a través de los hallazgos de Ilici (Elche)', in *Homenaje a D. Fletcher*, Valencia.

Ramos Locertales, J. M. (1924), 'La Devotio Ibérica', *AHDE*, 1, Madrid.

Rancoule, G. (1976), 'État de la recherche sur le deuxième âge du fer dans la partie occidential du Bassin de l'Aude', in *II Colloqui internacional d'arqueologia de Puigcerdà*, Puigcerdá.

Remesal Rodríguez, J. (1975), 'Cerámicas orientalizantes andaluzas', *Archivo Español de Arqueología*, 48, Madrid.

Reverte Coma, J. M. (1985), 'La necrópolis ibérica de Pozo Moro. Estudio anatómico, antropológico y paleopatológico', *Trabajos de Preshistoria*, 42, Madrid.

    (1986), 'Informe antropológico y paleopatológico de los restos quemados de la Dama de Baza', *Estudios de iconografías*, II Coloquio, MAN Catálogos y monografías, 10, Madrid.

Ribera, A. (1982), 'Las ánforas prerromanas valencianas (fenicias, ibéricas y púnicas)', *Trabajos varios del SIP*, 72, Valencia.

Rísquez, C. (1992), *Las cerámicas de cocción reductora en el Alto Guadalquivir durante la época ibérica: hacia una tipología contextual*, doctoral thesis, University of Granada.

Rísquez, C., F. Hornos, A. Ruiz and M. Molinos (1991), 'Aplicación del análisis multivariante: una propuesta de tipología contextualizada', *Complutum*, 1, Madrid.

Rodríguez Adrados, F. (1948), 'La Fides Ibérica', *Emérita*, 4, Madrid.

Bibliography

Rodríguez Díaz, A. (1989), 'La segunda edad del hierro en la baja Extremadura. Problemática y perspectiva en torno al poblamiento', *Papeles del Laboratorio de Arqueología Valenciana*, 22, Valencia.

Roos, A. M. (1982), 'Acerca de la antigua cerámica gris a torno de la Península Ibérica', *Ampurias*, 44, Barcelona.

Rouillard, P. (1975), *Les coupes attiques à figures rouges du IV s. en Andalouise*, Mélanges de la Casa de Velázquez, vol. XI, Paris.

Ruano Ruiz, E. (1989), 'Conjunto de pesas de telar del cerro de Pedro Marín (Úbeda la Vieja, Jaén)', *Boletín de la asociación española de amigos de la arqueología*, 26, Madrid.

Rubio Gomis, F. (1986), *La necrópolis ibérica de la Albufereta de Alicante (Valencia, España)*, Academia Cultura Valenciana. Sección de Prehistoria y Arqueología. Serie Monográfica, vol. 11, Valencia.

Ruiz de Arbulo, J. (1984), 'Emporion y Rhode. Dos asentamientos portuarios en el golfo de Roses', *Arqueología Espacial*, 4, Teruel.

Ruiz Mata, D. (1986), 'Aportaciones al análisis de los inicios de la presencia fenicia en Andalucía sudoccidental según las excavaciones del Cabezo de San Pedro (Huelva), San Bartolomé (Almonte, Huelva), Castillo de Doña Blanca (Puerto de Santa María, Cádiz) y el Carambolo (Camas, Sevilla)', in *Homenaje a Luis Siret*, Seville.

(1987), 'La formación de la cultura turdetana en la bahía de Cádiz a través del Castillo de Doña Blanca', in *I Jornadas arqueológicas sobre el mundo ibérico* (1985), Jaén.

Ruiz Mata, D. and J. Fernández Jurado (1986), 'El yacimiento metalúrgico de San Bartolomé de Almonte. Huelva', *Huelva Arqueológica*, 8, Huelva.

Ruiz Rodríguez, A. (1978), 'Los pueblos ibéricos del alto Guadalquivir', *Cuadernos de Prehistoria de la Universidad de Granada*, 3, Granada.

(1988), 'Ciudad y territorio en el poblamiento ibérico del alto Guadalquivir', in *Los asentamientos ibéricos ante la romanización*, Madrid.

(1990), 'Reflexiones sobre algunos conceptos de la arqueología espacial a partir de una experiencia: Iberos en el Alto Guadalquivir', *Arqueología Espacial*, 12, Lisbon/Teruel.

Ruiz Rodríguez, A., M. Castro and C. Choclán (1992), 'Aurgi-Tucci. La formación de la ciudad romana en la campiña alta de Jaén', in *Encuentro Hispano-Italiano de Arqueología*, Elche/Rome.

Ruiz Rodríguez, A. C. Choclán, F. Hornos and T. Cruz (1984), 'La necrópolis Gil de Olid. Puente del Obispo, Baeza', *Cuadernos de Prehistoria de la Universidad de Granada*, 9, Granada.

Ruiz Rodríguez, A. and M. Molinos (1984), 'Elementos para un estudio del patrón de asentamiento en las campiñas del alto Guadalquivir durante el horizonte pleno ibérico (Un caso de sociedad agrícola con estado)', *Arqueología Espacial*, 4, Teruel.

(1985), 'Informe de las Campañas de excavación en el Cerro de la Plaza de Armas de Puente Tablas (Jaén)', *Anuario Arqueológico de Andalucía*, 1, Seville.

(1986), 'Informe de la campaña de excavación en el Cerro de la Plaza de Armas de Puente Tablas (Jaén)', *Anuario Arqueológico de Andalucía*, 2, Seville.

Bibliography

(1989), 'Informe de la Campaña de 1989 en el Cerro de la Plaza de Armas de Puente Tablas: Estudio de los materiales arqueológicos', *Anuario Arqueológico de Andalucía*, Seville.

(1990), 'Informe de la campaña de 1989 (Estudio de Materiales) en el Cerro de la Plaza de Armas de Puente Tablas (Jaén)', *Anuario Arqueológico de Andalucía*, 5, Seville.

Ruiz Rodríguez, A., M. Molinos, J. López, J. Crespo, C. Choclán and F. Hornos (1983), 'El horizonte ibérico antiguo del Cerro de la Coronilla, Cazalilla (Jaén)', *Cuadernos de Prehistoria de la Universidad de Granada*, 8, Granada.

Ruiz Rodríguez, A., M. Molinos, F. Nocete and M. Castro (1986), 'Concepto de Producto en Arqueología', *Arqueología Espacial*, 7, Teruel.

Ruiz Rodríguez, A. and F. Nocete (1981), 'Un modelo sincrónico para el análisis de la producción cerámica ibérica estampillada del alto Guadalquivir', *Cuadernos de Prehistoria de la Universidad de Granada*, 6, Granada.

Ruiz Rodríguez, A., C. Rísquez and F. Hornos (1992), 'Las necrópolis ibéricas en la Alta Andalucía', in *Congreso de arqueología ibérica: las necrópolis*, Madrid.

Ruiz Zapatero, G. (1978), 'Las penetraciones de campos de urnas en el País Valenciano', *Cuadernos de Prehistoria y Arqueología de Castellón*, 5, Castellón.

(1983), *Los campos de urnas del noreste de la península ibérica*, doctoral thesis Complutense University of Madrid.

(1984), 'El comercio protocolonial y los orígenes de la iberización: dos casos de estudio, el bajo Aragón y la Cataluña interior', *Kalathos*, 3, Teruel.

Ruiz Zapatero, G. and T. Chapa (1988), 'La arqueología de la muerte: perspectivas teórico-metodológicas', Madrid.

(1990), 'Necrópolis celtibérica', *II Simposio sobre los Celtíberos*. Institución Fernando el Católico. Zaragoza, pp. 357–372.

Ruiz Zapatero G. and V. Fernández (1984), 'Patrones de asentamiento en el bajo Aragón protohistórico', *Arqueología Espacial*, 4, Teruel.

Ruiz Zapatero, G. and A. Lorrio (1988), 'Elementos e influjos de tradición de "campos de urnas" en la meseta sur–oriental', in *I Congreso de historia de Castilla–La Mancha*, Ciudad Real.

Ruiz Zapatero, G., A. Lorrio and M. Martín (1986), 'Casas redondas y rectangulares de la Edad del Hierro: aproximación a un análisis comparativo del espacio doméstico', *Arqueología Espacial*, 9, Teruel.

Sanahuja, M. E. (1971). 'Instrumental de hierro agrícola e industrial de la época ibero-romana en Cataluña', *Pyrenae*, 7, Barcelona.

Sánchez, E. (1991), 'Distribució del poblament i control del territori a la conca alta del Llobregat en època ibèrica', in *Fortificacions. La problemàtica del l'ibèric ple (segles IV–III aC)*, Manresa.

Sandars, H. (1913), *The Weapons of the Iberians*, Oxford.

Sanmartí, E. (1984), 'Observaciones acerca del poblado ibérico de San Antonio de Calaceite en relación a su funcionalidad rectora en el poblamiento de su área de influencia', *Arqueología Espacial*, 4, Teruel.

(1987), 'La cultura ibérica del sur de Cataluña', in *I Jornadas arqueológicas sobre el mundo ibérico* (1985), Jaén.

Bibliography

Sanmartí, E., J. Padró and O. Arteaga (1978), 'El factor fenici a les costes catalanes i del Golf de Lió. El pobles prerromans del Pirineu', in *II Colloqui Internacional de'Arqueologia de Puigcerdà*, Puigcerdá.

Sanmartí, J. and J. Santacana (1987a), 'El poblat ibèric d'Alorda Park (Calafell, Baix Penedès) i el seu entorn. Anàlisi crítica', in *Tribuna d'Arqueologia*, Barcelona.

(1987b), 'Un recinte ritual al poblat ibèric d'Alorda Park (Calafell)', *Fonament*, 6, Barcelona.

(1991), 'Les fortificacions ibèriques de la Catalunya central i costanera', in *Fortificacions. La problemàtica de l'ibèric ple (segles IV–III aC)*, Manresa.

Sanmartí, J., J. Santacana and R. Serra (1984), *El jaciment ibèric d'Arguilera i el poblament protohistòric a la costa del Penedès*, Barcelona.

Santos Velasco, J. A. (1986a), 'Vivienda y reparto desigual de la riqueza en la Bastida de les Alcuses (Valencia)', *Arqueología Espacial*, 9, Teruel.

(1986b), 'Ensayo de análisis espacial de los materiales de la Bastida de les Alcuses (Valencia)', *Trabajos de Prehistoria*, 43, Madrid.

(1987), *Revisión para un análisis sobre la transición a una forma de estado primitivo en la cuenca media del Segura en época ibérica*, doctoral thesis, Alcalá de Henares.

(1989), 'Análisis social de las necrópolis ibéricas del Cigarralejo y otros contextos funerarios de su entorno', *Archivo Español de Arqueología*, 62, Madrid.

Schaff, A. (1976), *Historia y verdad*, Barcelona.

Schubart, N. (1979), 'Morro de Mezquitilla. Campaña de 1976', *Noticiario Arqueológico Hispánico*, 6.

Schubart, N. and H. G. Niemeyer (1969), 'La factoría paleopúnica de Toscanos', in *V Simposium internacional de prehistoria peninsular: Tartessos* (Jerez, 1968), Barcelona.

Schubart, N., H. G. Niemeyer and M. Pellicer (1969), *Toscanos. La factoría paleopúnica en la desembocadura del Río Vélez. Excavaciones del 1964*, Excavaciones Arqueológicas en España, vol. LXVI, Madrid.

Schulten, A. (1914), *Numantia I: Die keltiberer und ihre kriege mit Rom*, Munich.

(1922), *Avieno: Ora Maritima*, Fontes Hispanias Antiquae, vol. I, Barcelona.

(1924), *Tartessos*, Madrid.

Senent Ibáñez, J. M. (1930), *Excavaciones en la necrópolis del Molar*, Memorias de la Junta Superior de Excavaciones Arqueológicas, 107, Madrid.

Serrano Várez, D. (1987), 'Yacimientos ibéricos y romanos de la Ribera (Valencia, España)', *Academia de Cultura Valenciana, Serie Arqueología*, 12, Valencia.

Shefton, B. B. (1982), *Greeks and Greek Imports in the South of the Iberian Peninsula. The Archeological evidence. Phonizie im Westen*, Cologne.

Siret, L. (1907), 'À propos des poteries pseudo-mycéniennes', *L'Anthropologie*, 18, Paris.

(1906), *Villaricos y Herrerías. Memoria descriptiva e histórica*, Madrid.

Solier, Y. (1976), 'Les *oppida* du Languedoc "ibérique": Aperçu sur l'évolution du groupe narbonnais', in *II Colloqui Internacional d'Arqueologia de Puigcerdà*, Puigcerdà.

(1976–8), 'La culture ibéro–languedocienne aux VI–V siècles', *Ampurias*, 38–40, Barcelona, pp. 211–64.

Bibliography

Sotomayor, M., M. Roca and N. Sotomayor (1979), *Los alfares romanos de Los Villares de Andújar. Campañas de 1974, 1975 and 1977*, Noticiario Arqueológico Hispánico, vol. VI, Madrid.

Sotomayor, N., M. Roca y R. Atienza (1981), 'Los alfares romanos de los Villares de Andújar (Jaén, Campaña de 1978–1979)', *Noticiario Arqueológico Hispánico*, 11, Madrid.

Taffanel, O. and J. (1956), 'Les civilisations prerromaines dans la région de Mailhac (Aude)', in *Études Rousillonaisses*, Rousillon.

—— (1973), 'Necrópole du Grand Bassin a Mailhac (Aude), (Fouilles 1969)', *Bulletin Com. Arch. de Narbonne*, 35, Narbonne.

—— (1976), 'Les civilisations protohistoriques de la région Narbonnaise d'aprés les fouilles de Mailhac (Aude)', in *II Colloqui internacional d'arqueologia de Puigcerdà*, Puigcerdà.

Tainter, J. A. (1978), 'Mortuary practices and the study of prehistoric social systems', in *Advances in Archeological Method and Theory*, New York.

Tarradell, M. (1952), 'Sobre el presente de la Arqueología Púnica', *Zephyrus*, 3, Salamanca.

—— (1959), 'El impacto colonial de los pueblos semitas', in *I Simposium de prehistoria peninsular*, Pamplona.

—— (1961), 'Ensayo de estratigrafía comparada y de estratigrafía de los poblados ibéricos valencianos', *Saitabi*, 11, Valencia.

—— (1968), *Arte ibérico*, Barcelona.

—— (1975), 'Schulten: medio siglo de Historia Antigua de España', *Papeles del Laboratorio de Arqueología Valenciana*, 11, Valencia.

Tarradell, M. and E. Sanmartí (1980), 'L'état actuel des études sur la céramique ibérique', *Annales littéraires de l'Université de Besançon*, 36, Paris.

Torelli, M. (1977), *Greci e indigeni in Magna Grecia: Ideologia religiosa e rapporti di classe*, Studi Storici, vol. IV, Rome.

—— (1988a), 'Le popolazioni dell'Italia antica: societa e forma del potere', in *Storia di Roma*, Rome.

—— (1988b), 'Dalle aristocrazie gentilizie alla nascita della plebe', in *Storia di Roma*, Rome.

Torrecillas González, J. F. (1985), *La necrópolis de época tartésica del Cerrillo Blanco (Porcuna, Jaén)*, Jaén.

Tovar, A. (1960), *Lenguas prerromanas de la Península Ibérica*, Madrid.

—— (1974), *Iberische Landeskunden*, Baden-Baden.

Trías de Arribas, G. (1967), *Cerámicas griegas de la Península Ibérica*, vols. I and II, Valencia.

Tuñón de Lara, M. (1970), *Medio siglo de cultura española*, Madrid.

Untermann, J. (1975–80), *Monumenta Linguarum Hispanicarum*, Wilsbaden.

—— (1984), 'La Lengua Ibérica', in *Varia III. Homenaje a Domingo Fletcher*, Valencia.

Uroz, J. (1983), *La región Edetania en la época ibérica*, Alicante.

Vaquerizo, D., F. Quesada and J. F. Murillo (1991), 'Avance al estudio de los materiales arqueológicos recuperados en el yacimiento ibérico del Cerro de la Cruz (Almedinilla, Córdoba)', *Anales de Arqueología Cordobesa*, 2, Cordoba.

Vigil, M. (1973), 'Edad Antigua', in *Historia de España*, vol. I, Madrid.

Vilar, P. (1974), *Historia marxista, historia en construcción*, Barcelona.

Villacorta, F. (1980), *Burguesía y cultura: los intelectuales españoles en la sociedad liberal (1880–1931)*, Madrid.

Vitta Finzi, C. and E. S. Higgs (1970), 'Prehistoric Economy in the Mount Carmel Area of Palestine. Site Catchment Analysis', *Proceedings of the Prehistoric Society*, 36, Cambridge.

Von den Driesch, A. (1975), 'Sobre los hallazgos de huesos de animales de los Saladares', *Noticiario Arqueológico Hispánico*, 3, Madrid.

Wheeler, R. E. M. (1954), *Archaeology from the Earth*, Oxford.

Zamora, D., J. Guitart and J. García (1991), 'Fortificacions a la Laietània litoral: Burriac (Cabrera de Mar) i el Turó d'en Boscà (Badalona). Cap a un model interpretatiu de l'evolució del poblament ibèric laietà', in *Fortificacions. La problemàtica de l'ibèric ple (segles IV–III aC)*, Manresa.

Index

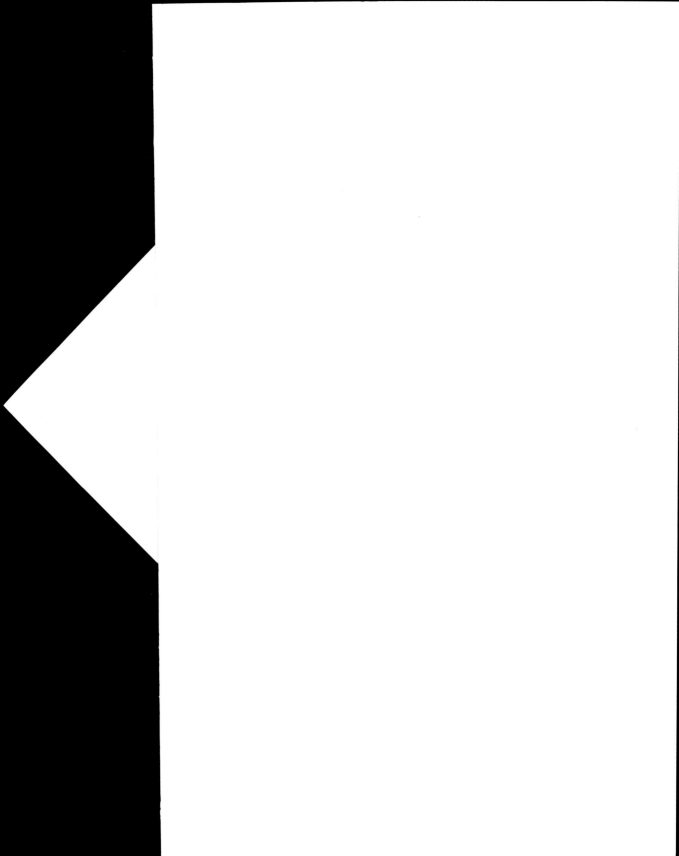

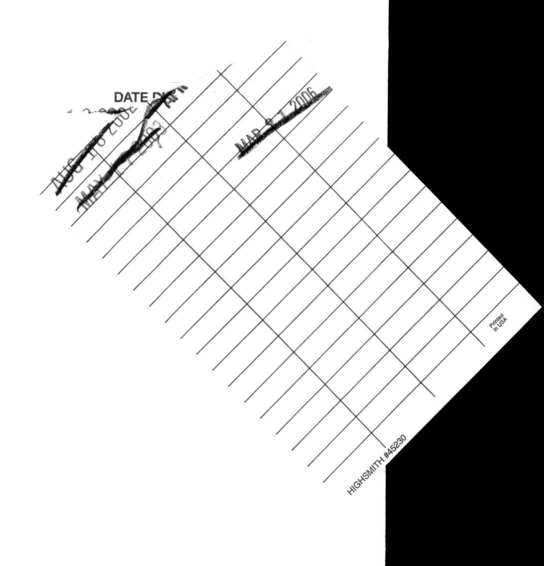